1 & 2 CHRONICLES
A Commentary in the Wesleyan Tradition

*New Beacon Bible Commentary

1&2 CHRONICLES
A Commentary in the Wesleyan Tradition

Mitchel Modine

BEACON HILL PRESS
OF KANSAS CITY

Copyright 2014
by Beacon Hill Press of Kansas City

ISBN 978-0-8341-3217-7

Printed in the United States of America

Cover Design: J.R. Caines
Interior Design: Sharon Page

Unless otherwise indicated all Scripture quotations are from the *Holy Bible, New International Version*® (NIV®). Copyright © 1973, 1978, 1984, 2011 by Biblica, Inc.™ Used by permission. All rights reserved worldwide.

The following version of Scripture is in the public domain:

King James Version (KJV).

The following copyrighted versions of the Bible are used by permission:

The *New American Standard Bible*® (NASB®), © copyright The Lockman Foundation 1960, 1962, 1963, 1968, 1971, 1972, 1973, 1975, 1977, 1995.

Hebrew-English Tanakh (NJPS), © 2000 by The Jewish Publication Society. All rights reserved.

The *New King James Version* (NKJV). Copyright © 1979, 1980, 1982 Thomas Nelson, Inc.

The *New Revised Standard Version* (NRSV) of the Bible, copyright 1989 by the Division of Christian Education of the National Council of the Churches of Christ in the USA. All rights reserved.

Library of Congress Control Number: 2013948797

10 9 8 7 6 5 4 3 2 1

DEDICATION

To Mark, at the beginning of a life of scholarship;
and to Herb, at the end;
from me, in between.

COMMENTARY EDITORS

General Editors

Alex Varughese
    Ph.D., Drew University
    Professor of Biblical Literature
    Mount Vernon Nazarene University
    Mount Vernon, Ohio

Roger Hahn
    Ph.D., Duke University
    Dean of the Faculty
    Professor of New Testament
    Nazarene Theological Seminary
    Kansas City, Missouri

George Lyons
    Ph.D., Emory University
    Professor of New Testament
    Northwest Nazarene University
    Nampa, Idaho

Section Editors

Joseph Coleson
    Ph.D., Brandeis University
    Professor of Old Testament
    Nazarene Theological Seminary
    Kansas City, Missouri

Robert Branson
    Ph.D., Boston University
    Professor of Biblical Literature
        Emeritus
    Olivet Nazarene University
    Bourbonnais, Illinois

Alex Varughese
    Ph.D., Drew University
    Professor of Biblical Literature
    Mount Vernon Nazarene University
    Mount Vernon, Ohio

Jim Edlin
    Ph.D., Southern Baptist Theological
        Seminary
    Professor of Biblical Literature and
        Languages
    Chair, Division of Religion and
        Philosophy
    MidAmerica Nazarene University
    Olathe, Kansas

Kent Brower
    Ph.D., The University of Manchester
    Vice Principal
    Senior Lecturer in Biblical Studies
    Nazarene Theological College
    Manchester, England

George Lyons
    Ph.D., Emory University
    Professor of New Testament
    Northwest Nazarene University
    Nampa, Idaho

CONTENTS

General Editors' Preface	11
Acknowledgments	13
Abbreviations	15
Bibliography	19

INTRODUCTION — 23
    A. The Importance of Chronicles — 23
    B. The Place of Chronicles in the OT — 27
    C. Chronicles and Kings as OT "Synoptics"? — 28
    D. The Relationship Between Chronicles and the Deuteronomistic History — 30
    E. The Relationship Between Chronicles and Ezra-Nehemiah — 33
    F. Who Wrote Chronicles? — 35
    G. Chroniclers' Presentation of Yehud/Judah/Judea — 36
    H. The Importance of the Temple — 37
    I. Theological Issues — 39

COMMENTARY — 41

FIRST CHRONICLES — 43

    I. The History of the World (In Brief) (1 Chr 1:1—9:44) — 43
        A. Adam to the Sons of Israel (1:1—2:2) — 45
        B. The Israelite Tribes (2:3—9:1) — 52
            1. The Tribe of Judah (2:3—4:23) — 53
            2. The Tribe of Simeon (4:24-43) — 61
            3. The Tribe of Reuben (5:1-10) — 62
            4. The Tribe of Gad (5:11-17) — 63
            5. The Israelites on the East Side of the Jordan (5:18-22) — 63
            6. The Half-Tribe of Manasseh (5:23-26) — 64
            7. The Tribe of Levi (6:1-81) — 65
            8. The Tribe of Issachar (7:1-5) — 69
            9. The Tribe of Benjamin (7:6-12) — 69
            10. The Tribe of Naphtali (7:13) — 70
            11. The Tribe of Manasseh (7:14-19) — 70
            12. The Tribe of Ephraim (7:20-29) — 70
            13. The Tribe of Asher (7:30-40) — 71
            14. The Tribe of Benjamin (8:1-40) — 71
            15. Summary (9:1) — 75

    C. The Exile and Aftermath (9:2-34) — 77
    D. The Genealogy of Saul (9:35-44) — 79
II. The History of the United Kingdom
    (1 Chr 10:1—2 Chr 9:31) — 81
    A. Saul (10:1-14) — 82
    B. David (11:1—29:30) — 85
      1. The Beginning of David's Reign (11:1-9) — 87
      2. Identities and Exploits of David's Mighty Men (11:10—12:40) — 89
      3. David's Plans to Build the Temple (13:1—17:27) — 94
        a. Bringing the Ark to Jerusalem (13:1-14) — 95
        b. First Assistance of King Hiram of Tyre (14:1-2) — 97
        c. David's Children in Jerusalem (14:3-7) — 97
        d. The Battle of Baal Perazim (14:8-17) — 98
        e. Moving the Ark in the Proper Way (15:1—16:1) — 101
        f. Appointing Some of the Ministers (16:2-6) — 104
        g. David's Song of Praise (16:7-36) — 104
        h. Leaving the Ministers to Their Work (16:37-43) — 109
        i. You Will Not Build a House (Temple) for Me, but I Will Build a House (Dynasty) for You (17:1-27) — 110
      4. More Events in David's Reign (18:1—21:17) — 112
        a. Defeating Nations, Capturing and Dedicating Spoils (18:1—20:8) — 113
          (1) David's Victory Stela (18:1-17) — 113
          (2) The Ammonite Incident (19:1-5) — 114
          (3) The Defeat of the Aramean/Ammonite Coalition (19:6-19) — 115
          (4) The Defeat of the Ammonites (20:1-3) — 116
          (5) Defeating the Philistines Again (20:4-8) — 116
        b. The Evil Census (21:1-17) — 117
      5. Restarting Temple Construction (21:18—22:19) — 119
        a. Purchase of the Temple Site (21:18-30) — 120
        b. Gathering Materials and Laborers (22:1-4) — 121
        c. The Charge to Solomon (22:5-16) — 122
        d. The Charge to the Workers (22:17-19) — 125
      6. Divisions of Labor for the Temple (23:1—27:34) — 125
        a. Designation of Solomon as Successor (23:1) — 125
        b. Assembly of the Officers, the Priests, and the Levites (23:2-5) — 126
        c. Another Genealogy of the Levites (23:6-24) — 127
        d. A New Assignment for the Levites (23:25-32) — 128
        e. Aaronide Tribal Allotments (24:1-31) — 129
        f. The Musicians (25:1-31) — 130
        g. The Gatekeepers (26:1-19) — 132
        h. Temple Treasurers and Secular Officials (26:20-32) — 133
        i. Army Divisions (27:1-24) — 134
        j. Other Leadership Positions (27:25-31) — 135
        k. Some of David's Courtiers (27:32-34) — 136

7.	Transition from David to Solomon (28:1—29:30)	137
	a. Designation of Solomon as Heir (28:1-7)	137
	b. The Charge to Solomon (28:8-10)	140
	c. David Gives Solomon the Plans (28:11-21)	141
	d. The People Dedicate Themselves (29:1-9)	142
	e. David's Hymn of Praise and Sacrifices (29:10-22)	144
	f. The Death of David (29:23-30)	147

SECOND CHRONICLES — 151

C. Solomon (2 Chr 1:1—9:31) — 151
   1. Solomon Builds the Temple (1:1—4:22) — 152
      a. Description of Solomon's Greatness (1:1-17) — 152
      b. Dialogue with King Hiram (2:1-18) — 155
      c. Description of the Building (3:1-17) — 158
      d. Temple Furnishings (4:1-22) — 160
   2. Dedication of the Temple (5:1—7:22) — 160
      a. Bringing the Ark to the Temple (5:1-14) — 161
      b. Solomon Recites What Yahweh Has Done (6:1-13) — 164
      c. Solomon's Prayer of Dedication (6:14-42) — 166
      d. Solemn Assembly and Sacrifices (7:1-10) — 170
      e. Yahweh Appears to Solomon (7:11-22) — 173
   3. Solomon Secures His Reign (8:1-18) — 175
      a. Fortification of Key Cities (8:1-6) — 176
      b. Foreigners and Israelites Treated Differently (8:7-11) — 176
      c. Solomon Finishes All the Work (8:12-18) — 178
   4. The End of the Reign of Solomon (9:1-31) — 179
      a. The Visit of the Queen of Sheba (9:1-12) — 179
      b. The Wealth of Solomon (9:13-28) — 181
      c. The Death of Solomon (9:29-31) — 183

III. The History of Judah After the Division of the Kingdoms
    (2 Chr 10:1—36:23) — 187
   A. The Reign of Rehoboam (10:1—12:16) — 188
     1. From the Beginning of Rehoboam's Reign to the Division (10:1-19) — 189
       a. Appeal from the Northern Tribes for Leniency (10:1-5) — 189
       b. Rehoboam Seeks Counsel (10:6-11) — 191
       c. Rehoboam's Unwise Answer (10:12-15) — 193
       d. Beginning of Israel's Rebellion (10:16-19) — 194
     2. Rehoboam After the Division (11:1—12:16) — 195
       a. Preparations for War Turned Back (11:1-4) — 196
       b. Rehoboam's Fortifications (11:5-12) — 197
       c. The Priests and Levites Support Rehoboam (11:13-15) — 198
       d. Others from Israelite Tribes Support Rehoboam (11:16-17) — 199
       e. Rehoboam's Wives and Sons (11:18-23) — 199
       f. Attack of Pharaoh Shushak (12:1-12) — 201
       g. The Death of Rehoboam (12:13-16) — 203
   B. The Reign of Abijah (13:1—14:1) — 204

C.	The Reign of Asa (14:2—16:14)	207
	1. Asa's Reform (14:2-7)	208
	2. Victory over Zerah (14:8-15)	209
	3. Asa Is Encouraged by the Prophet Azariah (15:1-19)	210
	4. Dispute with King Baasha of Israel (16:1-6)	211
	5. Asa Is Scolded by the Prophet Hanani (16:7-10)	212
	6. The Death of Asa (16:11-14)	213
D.	The Reign of Jehoshaphat (17:1—21:1)	214
	1. Description of Jehoshaphat's Administration (17:1-19)	215
	2. Alliance with Ahab (18:1—19:3)	218
	3. Jehoshaphat's Reform (19:4-11)	223
	4. War Against the Ammonites and Moabites (20:1-30)	225
	5. Conclusion of Jehoshaphat's Reign: Positive and Negative (20:31—21:1)	228
E.	The Reign of Jehoram (21:2-20)	229
F.	The Reign of Ahaziah (22:1-9)	233
G.	The Reign of Athaliah, Judah's Only Queen Regnant (22:10—23:21)	235
H.	The Reign of Joash (24:1-27)	239
I.	The Reign of Amaziah (25:1-28)	242
J.	The Reign of Uzziah (26:1-23)	244
K.	The Reign of Jotham (27:1-9)	246
L.	The Reign of Ahaz (28:1-27)	247
M.	The Reign of Hezekiah (29:1—32:33)	249
	1. Hezekiah's Reform (29:1-36)	249
	2. Passover Celebration (30:1—31:1)	251
	3. Restoring Temple Personnel (31:2-21)	255
	4. Deliverance from Assyria (32:1-31)	256
	5. The Death of Hezekiah (32:32-33)	259
N.	The Reign of Manasseh (33:1-20)	260
O.	The Reign of Amon (33:21-25)	264
P.	The Reign of Josiah (34:1—35:27)	265
	1. Josiah's Reform (34:1-13)	266
	2. The Book of the Torah (34:14-33)	268
	3. Passover Celebration (35:1-19)	272
	4. The Death of Josiah (35:20-27)	275
Q.	The Reign of Jehoahaz (36:1-4)	276
R.	The Reign of Jehoiakim (36:5-8)	277
S.	The Reign of Jehoiachin (36:9-10)	278
T.	The Reign of Zedekiah (36:11-21)	279
U.	The Ending That Does Not End (36:22-23)	283

GENERAL EDITORS' PREFACE

The purpose of the New Beacon Bible Commentary is to make available to pastors and students in the twenty-first century a biblical commentary that reflects the best scholarship in the Wesleyan theological tradition. The commentary project aims to make this scholarship accessible to a wider audience to assist them in their understanding and proclamation of Scripture as God's Word.

Writers of the volumes in this series not only are scholars within the Wesleyan theological tradition and experts in their field but also have special interest in the books assigned to them. Their task is to communicate clearly the critical consensus and the full range of other credible voices who have commented on the Scriptures. Though scholarship and scholarly contribution to the understanding of the Scriptures are key concerns of this series, it is not intended as an academic dialogue within the scholarly community. Commentators of this series constantly aim to demonstrate in their work the significance of the Bible as the church's book and the contemporary relevance and application of the biblical message. The project's overall goal is to make available to the church and for her service the fruits of the labors of scholars who are committed to their Christian faith.

The *New International Version* (NIV) is the reference version of the Bible used in this series; however, the focus of exegetical study and comments is the biblical text in its original language. When the commentary uses the NIV, it is printed in bold. The text printed in bold italics is the translation of the author. Commentators also refer to other translations where the text may be difficult or ambiguous.

The structure and organization of the commentaries in this series seeks to facilitate the study of the biblical text in a systematic and methodical way. Study of each biblical book begins with an ***Introduction*** section that gives an overview of authorship, date, provenance, audience, occasion, purpose, sociological/cultural issues, textual history, literary features, hermeneutical issues, and theological themes necessary to understand the book. This section also includes a brief outline of the book and a list of general works and standard commentaries.

The commentary section for each biblical book follows the outline of the book presented in the introduction. In some volumes, readers will find section ***overviews*** of large portions of scripture with general comments on their overall literary structure and other literary features. A consistent feature of the commentary is the paragraph-by-paragraph study of biblical texts. This section has three parts: **Behind the Text**, **In the Text**, and **From the Text**.

The goal of the **Behind the Text** section is to provide the reader with all the relevant information necessary to understand the text. This includes specific historical situations reflected in the text, the literary context of the text, sociological and cultural issues, and literary features of the text.

In the Text explores what the text says, following its verse-by-verse structure. This section includes a discussion of grammatical details, word studies, and the connectedness of the text to other biblical books/passages or other parts of the book being studied (the canonical relationship). This section provides transliterations of key words in Hebrew and Greek and their literal meanings. The goal here is to explain what the author would have meant and/or what the audience would have understood as the meaning of the text. This is the largest section of the commentary.

The **From the Text** section examines the text in relation to the following areas: theological significance, intertextuality, the history of interpretation, use of the Old Testament scriptures in the New Testament, interpretation in later church history, actualization, and application.

The commentary provides ***sidebars*** on topics of interest that are important but not necessarily part of an explanation of the biblical text. These topics are informational items and may cover archaeological, historical, literary, cultural, and theological matters that have relevance to the biblical text. Occasionally, longer detailed discussions of special topics are included as ***excurses.***

We offer this series with our hope and prayer that readers will find it a valuable resource for their understanding of God's Word and an indispensable tool for their critical engagement with the biblical texts.

Roger Hahn, Centennial Initiative General Editor
Alex Varughese, General Editor (Old Testament)
George Lyons, General Editor (New Testament)

ACKNOWLEDGMENTS

I am thankful, first, to God for gracefully allowing me opportunity and energy to complete this project. Writing a commentary is difficult, and even more so on a book with which one is little more than casually acquainted. Of course, any OT teacher should be able to work competently with anything in the OT, but nevertheless it has been a delight to stretch beyond the familiar. Experiences such as this never fail to help one improve.

I thank Beacon Hill Press of Kansas City, and particularly my editors Alex Varughese and Jim Edlin, for their patient work with the manuscript. Without their efforts, this commentary would probably exist in a very different, and vastly inferior, form.

I thank my colleagues and students at Asia-Pacific Nazarene Theological Seminary for their support during my five years of teaching. In particular, I acknowledge Mark Torcuator, one of those to whom this book is dedicated. He has been my best student so far, and I am sure he will exceed his teacher before long.

I especially thank my wife, Marnie, who constantly keeps me guessing.

Mitchel Modine

ABBREVIATIONS

With a few exceptions, these abbreviations follow those in *The SBL Handbook of Style* (Alexander 1999).

General

→	see the commentary at
ANE	Ancient Near East/Eastern
ANET	*Ancient Near Eastern Texts Relating to the Old Testament*
B.C.	before Christ
BHS	*Biblia Hebraica Stuttgartensia*
ch(s)	chapter(s)
Dtr	Deuteronomistic History
e.g.	*exempli gratia*, for example
esp.	especially
HB	Hebrew Bible
Heb.	Hebrew
idem	the same
i.e.	*id est*, that is
JPS	Jerusalem Publication Society
lit.	literally
LXX	Septuagint (the Greek OT)
MT	Masoretic Text (of the OT)
n.	note
n.d.	no date
n.p.	no place; no publisher; no page(s)
NT	New Testament
OT	Old Testament
PN	Personal Name
Radak	Rabbi David Kimchi (1160-1235), Jewish medieval biblical interpreter
v(v)	verse(s)

English Versions

KJV	King James Version
NASB	New American Standard Bible
NIV	New International Version (2011)
NJPS	Jewish Publication Society Tanakh: Jewish Bible (Torah, Nevi'im, Kethuvim)
NKJV	New King James Version
NRSV	New Revised Standard Version

Print Conventions for Translations

Bold font	NIV (bold without quotation marks in the text under study; elsewhere in the regular font, with quotation marks and no further identification)
Bold italic font	Author's translation (without quotation marks)

Behind the Text:	Literary or historical background information average readers might not know from reading the biblical text alone
In the Text:	Comments on the biblical text, words, phrases, grammar, and so forth
From the Text:	The use of the text by later interpreters, contemporary relevance, theological and ethical implications of the text, with particular emphasis on Wesleyan concerns

Old Testament

Gen	Genesis	Dan	Daniel	
Exod	Exodus	Hos	Hosea	
Lev	Leviticus	Joel	Joel	
Num	Numbers	Amos	Amos	
Deut	Deuteronomy	Obad	Obadiah	
Josh	Joshua	Jonah	Jonah	
Judg	Judges	Mic	Micah	
Ruth	Ruth	Nah	Nahum	
1—2 Sam	1—2 Samuel	Hab	Habakkuk	
1—2 Kgs	1—2 Kings	Zeph	Zephaniah	
1—2 Chr	1—2 Chronicles	Hag	Haggai	
Ezra	Ezra	Zech	Zechariah	
Neh	Nehemiah	Mal	Malachi	
Esth	Esther			
Job	Job			
Ps/Pss	Psalm/Psalms			
Prov	Proverbs			
Eccl	Ecclesiastes			
Song	Song of Songs/ Song of Solomon			
Isa	Isaiah			
Jer	Jeremiah			
Lam	Lamentations			
Ezek	Ezekiel			

(Note: Chapter and verse numbering in the MT and LXX often differ compared to those in English Bibles. To avoid confusion, all biblical references follow the chapter and verse numbering in English translations, even when the text in the MT and LXX is under discussion.)

New Testament

Matt	Matthew
Mark	Mark
Luke	Luke
John	John
Acts	Acts
Rom	Romans
1—2 Cor	1—2 Corinthians
Gal	Galatians
Eph	Ephesians
Phil	Philippians
Col	Colossians
1—2 Thess	1—2 Thessalonians
1—2 Tim	1—2 Timothy
Titus	Titus
Phlm	Philemon
Heb	Hebrews
Jas	James
1—2 Pet	1—2 Peter
1—2—3 John	1—2—3 John
Jude	Jude
Rev	Revelation

Secondary Sources

BDB	*A Hebrew and English Lexicon of the Old Testament* (see Brown)
JSOTSup	Journal for the Study of the Old Testament: Supplemental Series

Greek Transliteration

Greek	Letter	English
α	alpha	a
β	bēta	b
γ	gamma	g
γ	gamma nasal	n (before γ, κ, ξ, χ)
δ	delta	d
ε	epsilon	e
ζ	zēta	z
η	ēta	ē
θ	thēta	th
ι	iōta	i
κ	kappa	k
λ	lambda	l
μ	mu	m
ν	nu	n
ξ	xi	x
ο	omicron	o
π	pi	p
ρ	rhō	r
ρ	initial *rhō*	rh
σ/ς	sigma	s
τ	tau	t
υ	upsilon	y
υ	upsilon	u (in diphthongs: au, eu, ēu, ou, ui)
φ	phi	ph
χ	chi	ch
ψ	psi	ps
ω	ōmega	ō
‛	rough breathing	h (before initial vowels or diphthongs)

Hebrew Consonant Transliteration

Hebrew/Aramaic	Letter	English
א	alef	ʾ
ב	bet	b
ג	gimel	g
ד	dalet	d
ה	he	h
ו	vav	v or w
ז	zayin	z
ח	khet	h
ט	tet	t
י	yod	y
ך/כ	kaf	k
ל	lamed	l
ם/מ	mem	m
ן/נ	nun	n
ס	samek	s̩
ע	ayin	ʿ
ף/פ	pe	p; f (spirant)
ץ/צ	tsade	ṣ
ק	qof	q
ר	resh	r
שׂ	sin	ś
שׁ	shin	š
ת	tav	t; th (spirant)

BIBLIOGRAPHY

Allaby, Martin. 2013. *Inequality, Corruption, and the Church: Challenges and Opportunities in the Global Church.* Regnum Studies in Global Christianity. Oxford, UK: Regnum Books International.
Allen, Leslie C. 1999. *The First and Second Books of Chronicles.* New Interpreter's Bible, vol. 3. Nashville: Abingdon.
Assmann, Jan. 2007. "Monotheism and Polytheism." Pages 17-31 in *Ancient Religions.* Edited by Sarah Iles Johnston. Cambridge, Mass.: Harvard University Press.
Barker, Philip C. 1890/1985. *Chronicles.* The Pulpit Commentary, vol. VI. Edited by H. D. M. Spence and Joseph S. Exell. London and New York: Funk and Wagnalls. Repr. Peabody, MA: Hendrickson.
Bennett, Robert A. 1996. *Zephaniah.* New Interpreter's Bible, vol. 7. Nashville: Abingdon.
Berquist, Jon L. 1995. *Judaism in Persia's Shadow: A Social and Historical Approach.* Minneapolis: Fortress.
Braun, Roddy. 1986. *1 Chronicles.* Word Biblical Commentary, vol. 14. Waco, Tex.: Word Books.
Bright, John. 1959. *A History of Israel.* First ed. Philadelphia: Westminster.
_____. 1967/1975. *The Authority of the Old Testament.* Nashville: Abingdon. Repr. Grand Rapids: Baker.
Brown, Francis, S. R. Driver, and Charles A. Briggs. 1952. *A Hebrew and English Lexicon of the Old Testament.* Oxford: Clarendon.
Brueggemann, Walter. 1994. "Revelation and Violence: A Study in Contextualization." Pages 285-318 in idem, *A Social Reading of the Old Testament: Prophetic Approaches to Israel's Communal Life.* Edited by Patrick D. Miller. Minneapolis: Fortress.
Brueggemann, Walter, and Hans Walter Wolff. 1982. *The Vitality of Old Testament Traditions.* Second ed. Atlanta: John Knox.
Carroll, Robert P. 1992. "The Myth of the Empty Land." *Semeia* 59:79-93.
Cline, Eric H. 2007. *From Eden to Exile: Unraveling Mysteries of the Bible.* Washington, D.C.: National Geographic Society.
Cohen, Shaye J. D. 2006. *From the Maccabees to the Mishnah.* Second ed. Louisville, Ky.: Westminster/John Knox.
Craigie, Peter C. 1986. *The Old Testament: Its Background, Growth, and Content.* Nashville: Abingdon.
Cunningham, Floyd, ed. 2009. *Our Watchword and Song: The Centennial History of the Church of the Nazarene.* Kansas City: Beacon Hill Press of Kansas City.
Curtis, Edward Lewis. 1910/1976. *The Books of Chronicles: A Critical and Exegetical Commentary.* International Critical Commentary. Edinburgh, Scotland: T&T Clark.
Davies, Philip R., and John Rogerson. 2006. *The Old Testament World.* Second ed. Louisville, Ky.: Westminster/John Knox.
Dever, William G. 1992. "How to Tell a Canaanite from an Israelite." Pages 27-56 in *The Rise of Ancient Israel.* Edited by Hershel Shanks. Washington, D.C.: Biblical Archaeology Society.
Division of Christian Education of the National Council of Churches of Christ. 1957. *The Apocrypha of the Old Testament: Revised Standard Version* (RSV). New York: Thomas Nelson and Sons.
Dunning, H. Ray. 1988. *Grace, Faith, and Holiness: A Wesleyan Systematic Theology.* Kansas City: Beacon Hill Press of Kansas City.
Eco, Umberto. 1983. "Postscript to *The Name of the Rose.*" Pages 502-36 in idem, *The Name of the Rose.* Translated by William Weaver. San Diego: Harcourt, Brace.
Edelman, Diana. 1991. "The Manassite Genealogy in 1 Chronicles 7:14-19: Form and Source." *Catholic Biblical Quarterly* 53:179-201.
Endres, John C., William R. Millar, and John Barclay Burns, ed. 1998. *Chronicles and Its Synoptic Parallels in Samuel, Kings, and Related Biblical Texts.* Collegeville, Minn.: Liturgical Press.
Fee, Gordon D., and Douglas Stuart. 1993. *How to Read the Bible for All Its Worth.* Second ed. Grand Rapids: Zondervan.
Finkelstein, Israel, and Neil Asher Silberman. 2001. *The Bible Unearthed: Archaeology's New Vision of Ancient Israel and the Origin of Its Sacred Texts.* New York: Free Press.

Greengus, Samuel. 2011. *Laws in the Bible and in Early Rabbinic Collections: The Legal Legacy of the Ancient Near East*. Eugene, Ore.: Cascade Books.

Gutiérrez, Gustavo. 1987. *On Job: God-Talk and the Suffering of the Innocent*. Repr. Quezon City, Philippines: Claretian.

Halpern, Baruch. 2001. *David's Secret Demons: Messiah, Murderer, Traitor, King*. Grand Rapids: Eerdmans.

Havea, Jione. 2003. *Elusions of Control: Biblical Law on the Words of Women*. Edited by Danna Nolan Fewell. Semeia Studies 41. Atlanta: Society of Biblical Literature.

Hicks, John Mark. 2001. *1 and 2 Chronicles*. The College Press NIV Commentary. Joplin, Mo.: College Press.

Hill, Andrew E. 2003. *1 and 2 Chronicles*. The NIV Application Commentary. Grand Rapids: Zondervan.

Hobbs, T. R. 1985. *2 Kings*. Word Biblical Commentary, vol. 13. Dallas: Word.

Isser, Stanley. 2003. *The Sword of Goliath: David in Heroic Literature*. Atlanta: Society of Biblical Literature.

Japhet, Sara. 1968. "The Supposed Common Authorship of Chronicles and Ezra-Nehemiah Investigated Anew." *Vetus Testamentum* 18:330-71.

_____. 1993. *I and II Chronicles*. Old Testament Library. Louisville, Ky.: Westminster/John Knox.

Jarick, John. 2007a. *1 Chronicles*. Readings: A New Biblical Commentary. Sheffield, England: Phoenix.

_____. 2007b. *2 Chronicles*. Readings: A New Biblical Commentary. Sheffield, England: Phoenix.

Johnston, Sarah Iles. 2007. "Introduction." Pages vii-xi in *Ancient Religions*. Edited by Sarah Iles Johnston. Cambridge, Mass.: Harvard University Press.

Kelle, Brad E. 2002. "What's in a Name? Neo-Assyrian Designations for the Northern Kingdom and Their Implications for Israelite History and Biblical Interpretation." *Journal of Biblical Literature* 121:4, 639-66.

Keller, Werner. 1965/1980. *The Bible as History*. Second rev. ed. New York: Morrow.

Kimchi, David. 2008. *The Commentary of Rabbi David Kimchi to Chronicles*. Brown Judaic Studies 345. Edited and translated by Yitzhak Berger. Providence, R.I.: Brown University Press.

Kitchen, Kenneth A. 2003. *On the Reliability of the Old Testament*. Grand Rapids: Eerdmans.

Klein, Ralph W. 1999. *1-2 Chronicles*. New Interpreter's Bible, vol. 3. Nashville: Abingdon.

Laffey, Alice L. 1998a. "1 and 2 Chronicles." Pages 117-22 in *Women's Bible Commentary*. Expanded ed. Edited by Carol H. Newsom and Sharon H. Ringe. Louisville, Ky.: Westminster/John Knox.

_____. 1998b. *An Introduction to the Old Testament: A Feminist Perspective*. Philadelphia: Fortress.

Lincoln, Abraham. 1862/2001. "To Horace Greeley." *Collected Works of Abraham Lincoln*. Vol. 5. N.p. Edited by Roy P. Basler, Marion Dolores Pratt, and Lloyd A. Dunlap. Ann Arbor, Mich.: University of Michigan Digital Library Production Services.

Manual of the Church of the Nazarene: 2009-2013. 2009. Kansas City: Nazarene Publishing House.

Mason, Steve. 2003. *Josephus and the New Testament*. Second ed. Peabody, Mass.: Hendrickson.

McCarthy, Dennis J. 1965. "II Samuel 7 and the Structure of the Deuteronomic History." *Journal of Biblical Literature* 84:2, 131-38.

McEwan, David. 2002. "Being Holy Is Being Christlike: To What Extent Is This a Definable and Useful Model in an Australian Context?" Pages 65-82 in *The Challenge of Culture: Articulating and Proclaiming the Wesleyan-Holiness Message in the Asia-Pacific Region*. Edited by David A. Ackerman. Taytay, Rizal, Philippines: Asia-Pacific Nazarene Theological Seminary.

Miles, Jack. 1995. *God: A Biography*. New York: Knopf.

Miller, J. Maxwell, and John H. Hayes. 2006. *A History of Ancient Israel and Judah*. Second ed. Louisville, Ky.: Westminster/John Knox.

Mitchell, Christine. 2006. "The Ironic Death of Josiah in Chroniclers." *Catholic Biblical Quarterly* 68:3 (July 2006), 421-35.

Modine, Mitchel. 2009a. *The Dialogues of Jeremiah: Toward a Phenomenology of Exile*. Piscataway, N.J.: Gorgias Press.

_____. 2009b. "Hope Complete: Ezra and Nehemiah." *Adult Faith Connections Leader* 33:2 (Winter 2009-10), 5.

Myers, Jacob M. 1965a. *I Chronicles*. Anchor Bible, vol. 12. New York: Doubleday.

_____. 1965b. *II Chronicles*. Anchor Bible, vol. 13. New York: Doubleday.

Nelson, Richard D. 1981. *The Double Redaction of the Deuteronomistic History*. JSOTSup 18. Sheffield, England: University of Sheffield Press.

Newsom, Carol A., and Sharon H. Ringe, ed. 1998. *Women's Bible Commentary*. Expanded ed. Louisville, Ky.: Westminster/John Knox.

Nielsen, Kirsten. 1997. *Ruth*. Old Testament Library. Louisville, Ky.: Westminster/John Knox.

Pritchard, James B., ed. 1969. *Ancient Near Eastern Texts Relating to the Old Testament*. Third ed. Princeton, N.J.: Princeton University Press.

Purkiser, W. T. 1983. *Called unto Holiness: The Story of the Nazarenes*, vol. 2: *The Second Twenty-Five Years, 1933-1958*. Kansas City: Beacon Hill Press of Kansas City.

Rasmussen, Carl G. 2010. *Zondervan Atlas of the Bible*. Revised ed. Grand Rapids: Zondervan.

Rehork, Joachim. 1982. "Postscript to the Revised Edition." Pages 433-38 in Werner Keller, *The Bible as History*. Second rev. ed. New York: Bantam.

Reuther, Rosemary Radford. 1983. *Sexism and God Talk: Toward a Feminist Theology*. Boston: Beacon.

Roth, Martha T. 1997. *Law Collections from Mesopotamia and Asia Minor*. Second ed. Edited by Piotr Michalowski. Writings from the Ancient World Series. Atlanta: Society of Biblical Literature.

Rupp, E. Gordon. 1970. "The Study of Church History." Pages 105-21 in *What Theologians Do*. Edited by F. G. Healey. Grand Rapids: Eerdmans.

Seow, Choon-Leong. 1999. *The First and Second Books of Kings*. New Interpreter's Bible, vol. 3. Nashville: Abingdon.

Septimus, Bernard. 2007. "Literary Structure and Ethical Theory in *Sefer ha-Madda*." Pages 307-25 in *Maimonides after 800 Years: Essays on Maimonides and His Influence*. Edited by Jay M. Harris. Cambridge, Mass.: Harvard University Center for Jewish Studies.

Shanks, Hershel, ed. 1992. *The Rise of Ancient Israel*. Washington, D.C.: Biblical Archaeology Society.

Shao, Joseph Too, and Rosa Ching Shao. 2007. *Ezra and Nehemiah*. Asia Bible Commentary. Edited by Bruce J. Nicholls and Sang-Bok David Kim. Singapore: Asia Theological Association.

Smith, Timothy. 1962. *Called unto Holiness: The Story of the Nazarenes*, vol. 1: *The Formative Years*. Kansas City: Nazarene Publishing House.

Smith-Christopher, Daniel. 2002. *A Biblical Theology of Exile*. Overtures to Biblical Theology. Minneapolis: Fortress.

Sparks, James T. 2008. *The Chronicler's Genealogies: Towards an Understanding of 1 Chronicles 1-9*. Academia Biblica 28. Edited by Steven L. McKenzie. Atlanta: Society of Biblical Literature.

Strange, John. 1975. "Joram, King of Israel and Judah." *Vetus Testamentum* 25:191-201.

Sweeney, Marvin A. 2001. *King Josiah: The Lost Messiah of Israel*. Oxford: Oxford University Press.

Tolstoy, Leo. 1869/2010. *War and Peace*. Translated by Amy Mandelker. Oxford World's Classics. New York: Oxford University Press.

Van der Toorn, Karel. 2007. *Scribal Culture and the Making of the Hebrew Bible*. Cambridge, Mass.: Harvard University Press.

Varughese, Alex, and Mitchel Modine. 2010. *Jeremiah 26-52: A Commentary in the Wesleyan Tradition*. Kansas City: Beacon Hill Press of Kansas City.

Waltke, Bruce K., and M. O'Connor. 1990. *An Introduction to Biblical Hebrew Syntax*. Winona Lake, Ind.: Eisenbrauns.

Wesley, Charles. 1992. *The Unpublished Poetry of Charles Wesley, Volume III: Hymns and Poems for Church and World*. Edited by S. T. Kimbrough Jr. and Oliver A. Beckerlegge. Nashville: Kingswood.

Wesley, John. 1761/1991. "The Repentance of Believers." Pages 405-17 in *John Wesley's Sermons: An Anthology*. Edited by Albert C. Outler and Richard P. Heitzenrater. Nashville: Abingdon.

Westermann, Claus. 1984. *Genesis 1-11: A Continental Commentary*. Translated by John J. Scullion. Minneapolis: Augsburg.

Wilcock, Michael. 1987. *The Message of Chronicles: One Church, One Faith, One Lord*. The Bible Speaks Today. Edited by J. A. Motyer. Downers Grove, Ill.: InterVarsity.

Williamson, H. G. M. 1977. *Israel in the Books of Chronicles*. Cambridge: Cambridge University Press.

_____. 1982. *1 and 2 Chronicles*. New Century Bible Commentary. Grand Rapids: Eerdmans.

INTRODUCTION

A. The Importance of Chronicles

The study of history is the study of the past, but also of the present and the future. On the importance of history as a record of human life, Russian novelist and essayist Leo Tolstoy (1828-1910) wrote:

> History is the life of nations and of humanity. To seize and put into words, to describe directly the life of humanity or even of a single nation, appears impossible. The ancient historians all employed one and the same method to describe and seize the apparently elusive—the life of the people. They described the activity of individuals who ruled the people, and regarded the activity of those men [sic] as representing the activity of the whole nation. (1869/2010, 1270)

Writers of history often tell their stories in particular ways, and the investigation of those methods often yields quite a bit of insight not only into the events being described but also into the worldview of the one describing them. One should proceed with caution in this attempt, however, as Steve Mason notes: "History does not lend itself easily to argumentative analysis. Yet we know that ancient writers wrote history to teach lessons. And even with a narrative we are not without important clues as to what those lessons might be" (2003, 65).

A particular genre of history writing is the national chronicle. Chronicles, or records of events, are of indispensable importance for human history. Though they may be at times cumbersome to read, and though they may be filled with incredible amounts of seemingly minor details, they contribute to the construction of a people group's essential self-understanding. Umberto Eco writes that "if the Italians still use the word *cronaca* to define the local-news page in the papers, it is because chronicles have gone on being written over the centuries" (1983, 520). Thus, though they may at first be off-putting because of their detail, they cannot be ignored.

The importance of a chronicle as a vehicle to communicate the history—or the story; in German they are the same word—can also be seen in the OT. The books of 1 and 2 Chronicles are Israel's historical record reaching from the first human to the end of the Babylonian exile. These books were considered one in antiquity, having been divided more on account of the physical length of a scroll than on any substantial thematic, historical, or theological basis. This commentary assumes that they should not be considered in isolation from one another, except perhaps for when one is reading a specific passage from either. They both complement and provide an alternative version to the history of Israel found in other parts of the OT. Most importantly, they are inspired Scripture. This means that while they are "just" history, they also give evidence of a particular kind of history writing, namely, theologically inspired history. The last thing that should be said is that history is boring. History is only boring if human life is boring.

William Dever, a preeminent archaeologist who conducted extensive digs at sites throughout Israel and other places in the ancient Near East (ANE), disagrees with this basic assumption. He writes: "The word 'history' does not even occur in the Hebrew Bible. The Bible is not history; it doesn't pretend to be. It is literature, and a peculiar brand of *theological* literature at that. It is a reconstruction of the past after the past was essentially over" (1992, 28). Admittedly, he comes at the question from the standpoint of someone who works with material evidence in addition to—or perhaps, in preference over—textual witness.

That being said, the present writer believes that texts like the Bible are still important pieces of evidence, because at the very least they show what ancient Israel claimed about itself. Whenever it was finally written down seems to be of less importance than the fact that it *was* written down. Even if it is not the kind of evidence admissible for historical reconstruction, it is nonetheless genuinely authentic ancient material and should be considered as such. Though the archaeological record is quite different from the textual record, and though the textual record is of course affected by the ideological and theological commitments of its creators in the way that material remains are not, the textual record is a historical artifact. The textual record is, therefore, part of history. The Bible is, therefore, history—theological history, perhaps, but history. Joachim Rehork magnificently affirms this idea when he writes:

> It [the Bible] is, or rather, it was an historical work, but not such as we understand the term. It is an account of a people and its god, whose powers his worshippers came to know in the course of history. The Bible does not attempt to be a neutral, objective account of the events it relates. It is far too committed for that, much too rooted in its own times, in the times of which it speaks the language. This, too, must not be forgotten—the Bible uses descriptive methods which are by no means always those we employ. (1982, 437)

It should also be said that there is no such thing as "just" history. Contrary to increasing popular opinion—at least in the West—history is not the stuff of dry, dusty libraries. Instead, one's history, and especially the history of one's tribe, nation, ethnic group, and so on, constitute a vital part of one's identity. It will not do to ignore history. Worse, it is a great tragedy to extend from Chronicles' nature as theological history to leave historians out in order to make room for just another theologian pretending to do history. Neither, for that matter, is there any such thing as "just" theology. One can make a mistake on both ends of the spectrum, to be sure, and both have equally tragic consequences. So this commentary aims to keep in tension the facts that Chronicles is *theological* history and that Chronicles is theological *history*. As one reads Chronicles, therefore, one must remember that the Chroniclers arranged the material they had for both chronological and thematic reasons. Whenever the two were in tension, the Chroniclers as creative writers of theological history often felt free to downplay one of these dimensions in favor of the other. Though the thematic dimension seems most often to win, this is not always the case, as will be made clear at various points.

While keeping this tension in mind, the commentary nevertheless assumes that Chronicles is primarily historical rather than theological. The Hebrew title of Chronicles is perhaps the most convincing evidence for seeing Chronicles in this way. This title is *dibrê hayyamîm* or "words of the days." Some examples of this phrase in the OT are Esth 6:1 ("book of the chronicles"); 1 Kgs 14:29 ("book of the annals of the kings of Judah"); 1 Kgs 15:31 ("book of the annals of the kings of Israel"). Each of these other examples occurs with the word *sēpēr* (book). The books of Chronicles, therefore, are the books of the words of the days of Israel, or the book of history.

Yet this title also presents a problem. The editors of the OT placed this "book of the words of the days" not in the Prophets section alongside Joshua-

Kings but instead in the Writings section alongside Ezra-Nehemiah. In fact, according to many arrangements of the MT of the Hebrew Bible the books of Chronicles may be found at the very end. By contrast, English Bibles—following the Greek Septuagint, the Latin Vulgate, and others—place the books of Chronicles directly alongside the other Historical Books of Joshua, Judges, Samuel, and Kings. (English Bibles also include Ruth and Esther in the Historical Books. However, these two books are more properly understood as historical short stories or morality tales than historical records like Joshua or 1 and 2 Chronicles).

One gets the impression from the placement in the Hebrew Bible that Chronicles, Ezra, and Nehemiah are not as important as Joshua through Kings. Leslie C. Allen comments, "In Christian tradition these books have long suffered by being placed behind 1 and 2 Samuel and 1 and 2 Kings as if they were some pale shadow instead of an epic work in their own right" (1999, 299). Nothing could be further from the truth, however. It is ultimately unclear why the "second history" (itself a problematic term) is not in the history section of the Hebrew Bible. One interesting option was taken by the Septuagint (Greek) translation of the OT. The Septuagint calls Chronicles *Paralipomenon*, or "things left to one side." The obvious reference is to Samuel-Kings. Thus, from this perspective, Chronicles must include material that Samuel-Kings leaves out, and that is why there are two versions. However, as will be seen throughout the commentary, one might rather see it the other way around, for Chronicles actually leaves out a great deal that Samuel-Kings includes!

The place of the so-called Deuteronomists in creating the OT is a matter of considerable debate. This commentary assumes that the final editors of at least many of the books of the Hebrew Bible were probably in sympathy with the Deuteronomistic Historians (writers/editors of Joshua-2 Kings who evaluated and interpreted Israel's history from the perspective of the theology of blessings and curses in Deuteronomy), though this matter is the subject of considerable debate. They themselves were not the Deuteronomists, however, because as will be noted below, as much as three centuries passed between the completion of the Deuteronomistic and Chroniclers' Histories. Perhaps another three centuries or so passed from the writing and editing of Chronicles to the writing of Daniel, which some consider the latest book in the OT. The Deuteronomists, if a group identifying itself as such ever really existed, were long dead and (probably) forgotten by the time the OT was completed. It does not seem likely, therefore, that the final decision to locate Joshua-Kings in one place and 1 and 2 Chronicles in another was made for Deuteronomistic reasons.

One often encounters, in reading historical writing, the issues of objectivity and reliability. At least since the Western Enlightenment, historians, scientists, and scholars have reached for the goal of objectivity. In recent years, the possibility of an absolutely objective stance has been questioned. According to postmodern scholarship, the standard of objectivity cannot be reached, because all written documents have interests or agendas to defend. This realization can be taken too far, however. On one side, a cynical reader may suggest some kind of sinister attempt to deceive the readers into thinking that the writers do not have an interest and are objective. On the other side, a naive reader may refuse to admit the presence of these interests or agendas. The more excellent middle way is to admit that Joshua-Kings, Chronicles, and Ezra-Nehemiah do in fact have their separate interests to advance. However, both their historical reliability and later interpretation of the texts seem to escape unharmed.

However, another dimension of reliability must be taken into account with regard to the Bible. Joachim Rehork states the issue simply: "The Bible can claim another form of 'rightness,' however, insofar as it brings nearer to us its times and the people of its times with their ways of thought and behaviour" (1982, 438). In other words, it is anachronistic to judge the reliability of the Chroniclers' historical witness according to modern or postmodern standards (if such even exist) of reliability. The Chroniclers faithfully—and more or less "historically"—recorded Judah's history. They worked within a particular intellectual frame of mind and attempted to serve particular interests. While their mind-set and interest may have been different from the Deuteronomists, so that they at times sharply disagreed with the earlier history, this in no way means that either Joshua-2 Kings or 1 and 2 Chronicles must be considered right or wrong. Putting it simply, both are right, considered within the parameters of their times.

B. The Place of Chronicles in the OT

The books of Chronicles deserve to be honored as the great historical epic that they are. This is in contrast to the view voiced by Peter C. Craigie and probably held by the majority of people. Craigie writes: "Some [OT] books are splendid when viewed as literature (for example, Job), whereas others have a more mundane character (for example, Chronicles)" (1986, 20). Though it is perhaps a quite natural, and for many a quite familiar, procedure for biblical interpreters to compare biblical books to others of similar genre, this may in the case of Chronicles lead to a bit of a misunderstanding. On the one hand, the most clearly relevant comparative material for Chronicles is to be found in the Deuteronomistic History of Joshua-2 Kings. Yet, on the other hand, that the editors of the Hebrew Bible placed 1 and 2 Chronicles in the Writings section (and, in most versions, at the very end of the book) while keeping

Joshua-Kings among the Prophets would tend in the direction of making the Deuteronomists' epic history seem more important than the Chroniclers' epic history. It is true that the arrangement of the Hebrew canon reflects the relative importance given to its various sections by the editors of the Hebrew Bible. Shaye Cohen writes, "The scrolls of the Torah are more sacred than those of the Prophets, which in turn are more sacred than those of the Writings, just as the Torah is more authoritative than the Prophets, and the Prophets are more authoritative than the Writings" (2006, 173). Though this may have been true for the editors of the Hebrew Bible (and for Judaism in general), Christian readers need to resist the temptation to assign levels of authority to the canonical books. By doing so, we may see more clearly the unique contributions of Chronicles to emerging Hebrew/Jewish theology and identity, which in turn would provide great insight into the worldview at least of some of those who were active and writing during the Second Temple period.

Similarly, reading Chronicles alongside Ezra-Nehemiah has many problems. This issue will be dealt with at length below, but a few comments will suffice here. Put simply, both Chronicles and Ezra-Nehemiah come from the Second Temple period and, as such, exhibit certain linguistic and theological features in common. However, this does not mean that they had to have been written by the same person or even emerged out of the same group. In other words, the similarities between them could simply stem from the fact that they were both written in the same general era, rather than a common authorship. This commentary will therefore operate under the assumption that Chronicles and Ezra-Nehemiah came from different hands, intending to respond to different situations.

Reading Chronicles over against or in light of Joshua-Kings or Ezra-Nehemiah does a great disservice. While comparative readings between the Chroniclers' and Deuteronomistic Histories may shed light on particular situations, one must always remember that Chronicles can be understood in its own right. Failure on this point has led scholars ancient and modern to question the place of Chronicles in the canon, its theological outlook and supposed deficiencies in it as compared with the Deuteronomists, and its original contribution in the context of the emerging Second Temple literature, language, and theology.

C. Chronicles and Kings as OT "Synoptics"?

The interpreter of Chronicles sometimes encounters a particular approach that views Chronicles and Joshua-Kings as OT "synoptics." This methodology draws an analogy to critical study of the first three Gospels in the New Testament. In basic form, the Synoptic theory is this: Mark, being written first, was available as source material for Matthew and Luke. These later Gospels also apparently drew on a second source, available to both of them, but containing material that does not appear in Mark. This hypothetical source has been called Q, short for *Quelle*, the German word for "source." In a further development on the theory, scholars have suggested that Matthew and Luke both had sources—independent of Mark, Q, and one another—for their unique contents. These have been called M and L.

A recent example of this methodology is the 1998 volume *Chronicles and Its Synoptic Parallels in Samuel, Kings, and Related Biblical Texts* edited by John C. Endres, William R. Millar, and John Barclay Burns. This book examines the Chroniclers' reuse of many biblical texts, not just in Samuel and Kings. As such, it is a helpful summary. However, methodologically speaking, the analogy to NT studies is misleading. The view taken in this commentary is that a "synoptic" view of the relationship between the Deuteronomistic History and the Chroniclers operates on the faulty assumption that this kind of relationship must have been necessary. In other words, the Chroniclers' use of the Deuteronomists' work need not have been any sort of reworking or copying. The Chroniclers could have, instead, written an entirely different historical work, but while not failing to consult previous sources. In a sense, all new writing on a given topic is dependent upon what has gone before, but this does not mean that new writing has to make a conscious attempt to revise old writing.

The view taken here is based on five reasons. First, Mark, Matthew, and Luke are far closer to one another in time than are the Deuteronomists and the Chroniclers. Whereas perhaps twenty to thirty years—at any rate less than a generation—passed between the writing of Mark and the writing of Luke, as much as three centuries may lie between the two canonical versions of Israel's history. While this does not in itself rule out a kind of synoptic relationship, it certainly does strain the definition.

Second, as was mentioned above, Chronicles never says it is a revision of Joshua-Kings. It could simply be a new version of the history for a new time. By contrast, Luke may in fact say he is revising the Gospels of Mark and Matthew (see the prologue in Luke 1:1-4). Though Luke does not make this explicit, the implication is surely there. Andrew Hill comments similarly: "The Chronicler may be favorably compared to the New Testament Gospel writer Luke as both a historian and a theologian" (2003, 42).

Third, the significant differences between the two histories render the synoptic methodology problematic. These differences are far more than the sometimes stylistic differences between Mark, Matthew, and Luke. On the one hand, the northern kingdom of Israel does not show up in the Chroniclers' work after the "rebellion" (on which see below). On the other hand, while the Deuteronomists were not shy to admit the faults of God's favorite kings, the Davidides, according to the Chroniclers the Davidides can do no wrong. To note just one example, there is no mention of the Bathsheba/Uriah incident (see below). In the late nineteenth century, P. C. Barker argued along the same lines. He wrote:

> The difference between the contents of [1-2 Chronicles and Samuel-Kings is] . . . a subject quite distinct from the question whether the compiler of Chronicles adopted direct from them those parts of his own work which are exactly similar to them—the negative reply to which question seems by far the most probable to us. (1890, xi)

Fourth, the identities of the prophets who come into the foreground in the different versions of the history trouble a synoptic methodology. A significant stream of scholarship on the Deuteronomistic History maintains that Jeremiah at least had some influence over its writing, if not direct control. In any event, the Deuteronomists have exercised considerable influence over the editorial process of most of the latter prophets. However, this approach falls into difficulty when one notices that Jeremiah is not mentioned at all in 2 Kings, even though he was alive and actively preaching during, of all things, the Josianic reform so praised by the Deuteronomists. By contrast, several of Jeremiah's prophecies having come true are a repeated theme of 2 Chronicles (see 2 Chr 35:25; 36:12; 36:21-22). Problems with these ascriptions will be dealt with at appropriate points in the commentary. However, based simply on mentions, Chronicles is far more concerned with Jeremiah than is Kings!

Finally, the analogy between the Gospels and the OT histories breaks down over the question of sources. Both the Deuteronomists and the Chroniclers name a lot of their sources, including the annalistic things already mentioned, as well as things like the Book of Jashar (Josh 10:13; 2 Sam 1:18), the Book of the Wars of Yahweh (Num 21:14), and a few others. In contrast, the supposed Q source for the Gospels of Matthew and Luke, drawing from Mark as well as their own unique material, is never mentioned. This alone should sink the analogy, but especially when combined with the others it renders such a methodology impossible.

D. The Relationship Between Chronicles and the Deuteronomistic History

However, that the Chroniclers and the Deuteronomists do not see eye-to-eye (syn-optic) does not mean that there is no relationship between the two of them. The Chroniclers were certainly aware of the Deuteronomists, even if only through the massive document they left behind for posterity. This is so even though the Chroniclers do not mention the Deuteronomists or their work at all. (For that matter, the name Deuteronomists never appears in the

OT or any extrabiblical source from the relevant time frame. It may be, after all, a construct of scholarship rather than of history. Space and relevancy concerns prevent full consideration of this idea.) One of the axioms of historical-critical scholarship on the OT is that, if text A is not mentioned in text B, then the authors or editors of text B could not possibly have known about text A, which probably means that text A was in fact of a later origin than text B, even though text A (the Deuteronomistic History) comes before text B (the Chroniclers' History) in the canon. This idea is built on a faulty assumption, as exposed by Jione Havea, an OT scholar from the Pacific island of Tonga. Speaking of the relationship between early Christian and Jewish exegetes, she writes: "I imagine that the fathers knew something about their Jewish neighbors and their view of Scripture. That most fathers did not mention Jewish/rabbinic literature does not mean that they did not know (of) these writings" (2003, 137, n. 11). Indeed, this is not a difficult thing to imagine; rather, the alternative, that the Chroniclers did not know Joshua-Kings, is unfathomable.

So what, then, is the relationship between the Deuteronomistic History and Chronicles? Four different options seem to present themselves. First, Chronicles may be seen as "volume two" or a supplement to the Deuteronomistic History. Second, Chronicles may be seen as a conscious attempt to respond to the earlier work. Such a response may try to correct errors, omissions, or perceived misinterpretations or misstatements in the earlier work. Third, Chronicles may be seen as a complement to the Deuteronomistic History, presenting the story from a different angle or a different agenda. Fourth, one could read Chronicles entirely independently from the Deuteronomistic History. Although it is undeniable that the Chroniclers had access to Joshua-2 Kings before sitting down to write, and that they made certain changes to the source material as were necessary for their own purposes, there need not have been a conscious attempt at revision.

Chronicles is much more than a simple supplement to the Deuteronomistic History. This is clear from the fact that the Chroniclers did not pick up where the Deuteronomists left off. Second Kings ends with the release of Jehoiachin from prison. If Chronicles were volume two, as it were, then it should begin with where it ends, namely, the Edict of Cyrus allowing the Jews to return to their homeland. Ezra and Nehemiah, often considered part of the Chroniclers' History, do in fact continue the story after the return from the exile. However, these are certainly a supplement to 2 Chronicles, not to 2 Kings.

Neither are these books to be seen as an alternative, competing version of the history. Such an alternative version would attempt to correct errors, misstatements, excisions, misinterpretations, and so on. Sometimes, these new histories are simply the attempt to get the story better, as E. Gordon Rupp maintains:

> The student of history takes as little as possible for granted, is ready to question himself [sic] at every turn, submits his tentative conclusions to the rough criticism of the learned world, and like his fellow historians is ready to re-open any case on the submission of fresh evidence. (1970, 109)

Evidence in favor of this interpretation—that Chronicles is a revision of Kings—may be found. For a few examples, one may mention the absence of the northern kingdom from the history and the much more positive view of the history of the Davidides. Although some later works having to do with the same time period as earlier ones do indeed compete, to think this about Chronicles vis-à-vis Kings would be misleading.

Third, Chronicles is not a complementary version of the history, from a different angle. Histories written in this way often supply significant missing information. This information, once "restored" to the history, completes, or comes closer to completing, a rounded picture of the historical record in question. If, for example, Chronicles revealed some of the internal history of the northern kingdom of Israel, then it would provide a key complement to the Deuteronomistic History. All would depend on how the information is presented. In particular, in this scenario, Chronicles would likely not consider the withdrawal of the northern tribes from the authority of the Davidic monarchy as a "rebellion." Alternatively, might it be called a "liberation"? Such counterfactual questions, at the end of the day, may be interesting but have no real bearing on the interpretation of Chronicles itself.

The final possibility mentioned above is the one under which this commentary operates. The Chroniclers' History should be viewed entirely independently from the Deuteronomistic History. It may well be unsatisfying to see Chronicles as simply a new version of the history without being a conscious updating. Nevertheless, at present that seems to be the most viable option. Michael Wilcock seems to be in agreement with this position when he writes that Chronicles "is more than an alternative history. It is . . . a sermon. Its object is the fostering of a right relationship between God and his people" (1987, 14). Thus, while Wilcock emphasizes the theological aspect of the history, nevertheless he recognizes that Chronicles is long overdue a place in the church's attention.

Naturally, in the intervening centuries between the Deuteronomistic History and the Chroniclers' History, many different things will have happened in order to make a separate history not only possible but necessary. New written sources may have come to light. Israel's theology developed as well, which can be particularly seen in 2 Sam 24 and 1 Chr 21. Moreover, a new history was needed because time had moved on. It would not have been sufficient for Chronicles to have picked up the story. Instead, going back to what had been dealt with before was necessary, for historical writing is never good enough for all time.

E. The Relationship Between Chronicles and Ezra-Nehemiah

An older traditional model of scholarship saw 1 and 2 Chronicles as a unit with Ezra-Nehemiah. This theory had one positive effect and one negative effect. Positively, it definitively separated Chronicles-Ezra-Nehemiah—called the Chroniclers' History or something along those lines—from Samuel-Kings by showing how a different version of the history worked by extending both backward and forward from what the Deuteronomists had done. Negatively, it tied Chronicles to the concerns of Ezra-Nehemiah, which may not be a legitimate connection.

This old scholarly consensus that Chronicles, Ezra, and Nehemiah all belonged together was definitively rejected by Sara Japhet in a 1968 article titled "The Supposed Common Authorship of Chronicles and Ezra-Nehemiah Investigated Anew." H. G. M. Williamson followed Japhet with *Israel in the Books of Chronicles* in 1977. Japhet states that "at the end of the 19th century it was accepted as general knowledge" that Chronicles, Ezra, and Nehemiah belonged together (1968, 330). Only later, so ran the theory, had the books been separated and Chronicles placed in an illogical position following Ezra-Nehemiah with its later subject matter. (The theory further assumes that the Greek ordering in the LXX is correct.) Japhet goes on: "An immediate result was that each book was dealt with in constant reference to the other, and the consequences for the understanding of the books, the historical period they describe and the religious concepts they contain were enormous" (1968, 331).

Japhet writes that the assumption of a connection between Chronicles and Ezra-Nehemiah rests on four pillars. This summary is echoed by H. G. M. Williamson (1982, 5). This is perhaps reminiscent of the four sets of three bulls Solomon had placed under the bronze altar in the Jerusalem temple (see 2 Chr 4:4). First, there is a linguistic connection between 2 Chr 36:22-23 and Ezra 1:1-3. Jack Miles comments, "The repetition of the first words in Ezra at the end of II Chronicles may well be an accident, but its effect is nonetheless to turn these last four books of the Tanakh into a musical round" (1995, 392). Yet if, as Williamson argues, vv 22-23 are secondary to 2 Chr 36, the repetition loses its importance for canonization, no matter how neat it might be literarily speaking. Allen suggests that 2 Chr 36:22-23 is a quote of Ezra 1:1-3. He cites this among other examples of quotes of Ezra-Nehemiah in Chronicles as evidence for his position that "Chronicles appears to have been written after the bulk of Ezra-Nehemiah" (1999, 300). Jacob Myers agrees with this last statement of Allen. Myers writes:

> The separation of Ezra from Chronicles may have resulted from the incorporation of Ezra-Nehemiah into the Bible as a supplement to the story of Samuel and Kings, which occurred after Samuel and Kings had been canonized and therefore could no longer be tampered with. Chronicles, then, was added later. (1965a, xvi-xvii)

Myers thus also anticipated Japhet's critique of the consensus position in important ways (but see below).

The other three arguments Japhet cites are, in turn, literary, linguistic, and theological. On the literary angle, there is an overlap not only between 2 Chronicles and Ezra, but with 1 Esdras as well. In addition, it has long been recognized that Chronicles joins Ezra-Nehemiah and a few other OT books on the level of Late Biblical Hebrew. Finally, there is a supposed strong theological connection between Chronicles and Ezra-Nehemiah. Japhet concludes her summary by stating, "Most weight is given to the last two arguments, which are internal and relate to the main elements of the literary unit" (1968, 331-32).

In her critique, Japhet's direct targets are "the [supposed] linguistic and stylistic resemblances of the two books," and she writes that the theological angle needed treatment on its own (1968, 332). Against the third item mentioned above, Japhet suggests that this link has been overemphasized, such that a rather illogical leap has been taken. The similarities between Chronicles and Ezra-Nehemiah, undeniable as they are, could be effectively explained without recourse to a common author, and therefore this argument fails to offer the support it was once thought to. The studies in support of this theory neglected differences between them, of course, yet "study of these differences, both linguistic and stylistic, will show that on the background of late Biblical Hebrew each book exhibits strong and distinct traits of its own, some of which reveal a true linguistic opposition and could not have been written by one author" (1968, 332-33). The remainder of Japhet's article is devoted to technical comparisons of the Hebrew used in Chronicles with that used in Ezra-Nehemiah. These discussions are perhaps inaccessible to the general reader. For the present purposes, one may jump to Japhet's conclusion:

> It seems rather that a certain period of time must separate the two [Chronicles and Ezra-Nehemiah]. We are certain that a further study of the literary characteristics, the attitude to the sources and their use and the theological conceptions of the two books will greatly support our conclusions. (1968, 371)

From the Ezra-Nehemiah side of the argument, brief comments from a recent commentary deserve mention. The authors of the volume on Ezra-Nehemiah in the Asia Bible Commentary divide Chronicles and Ezra-Nehemiah primarily on thematic lines. Though their arguments are not as technical as Japhet's linguistic ones, nevertheless their work has the benefit of suggesting that the older, linked understanding may in fact be a Western conception. Citing Japhet's article and Williamson's monograph, the Shaos note that their "basic findings have become the accepted norm that Ezra-Nehemiah and Chronicles are two different works" (2007, 4). On the one hand, they note that Chronicles emphasizes the Davidic dynasty and the immediate retribution for sins, themes that Ezra-Nehemiah ignore. On the other hand, Ezra-Nehemiah include themes that the Chroniclers leave to one side (see above!): the exodus traditions, and in particular the return from exile as a new exodus (see Jer 16:14-15; 23:7-8); the avoidance/severance of so-called mixed marriages; the use of "Judah and Benjamin" as a designation for the people over against the Chroniclers' "Israel"; inward focus; and Sabbath regulation (Shao and Shao 2007, 4-5). Thus one sees that, from both linguistic and theological perspectives, the theory of common authorship between Chronicles and Ezra-Nehemiah is untenable.

Nevertheless, voices are still to be found on the opposite side of this question. In other words, many have either ignored or remain unconvinced by Japhet's broadside. Among these are Andrew E. Hill, who seems to prefer the traditional association, though he does not say so explicitly (2003, 41). Also, the older commentary by Edward Lewis Curtis maintains the nineteenth-century consensus, calling as further witnesses the Talmud and unnamed "Church fathers" (1910/1976, 3-5). Roddy Braun agrees with the older position but dispenses with the arguments for it by stating simply, "These two books are counted as one in the Hebrew canon, where they normally stand at the end . . . of the Writings . . . preceded somewhat anomalously by Ezra-Nehemiah, commonly considered their sequel" (1986, xix). Jacob Myers assumes the consensus position (1965a, xviii).

F. Who Wrote Chronicles?

Regarding most of the books of the Bible, the question of authorship has often been a difficult one. Over the past fifty years or so, the impossibility of identifying authors of biblical books with certainty has led some scholars to abandon the quest altogether. The present writer believes such a move may be an overcorrection. Naturally, the question of authorial identity goes rather well with the question of authorial intent, and perhaps it is in the desire to free oneself and one's interpretive methodology from the latter that this group of scholars—a diverse lot indeed—have jettisoned the former.

This commentary will assume, with a dominant stream of contemporary scholarship (see, for example, van der Toorn 2007), that the creation of the Chroniclers' History was a communal affair. Ancient authors, it seems, were not nearly as concerned with what may be called "author credits" as are contemporary writers, such as the writer of this commentary. With regard to Chronicles scholarship, it was common among historical critics to refer to the author as "the Chronicler" and the text (whether or not it included Ezra-Nehemiah; see above) as "the Chroniclers' History." Typically, the writer is supposed to have been male, and hence "the Chronicler" could be referred to by the masculine pronoun "he," and the "Chronicler's History" as "his history." This usage is owing to the patriarchal nature of ANE societies in general and Israel in particular. The fact is, however, that scholarship simply does not know who the author of Chronicles was, and probably there was not a single author anyway. In order to reflect this, and also in order to avoid being forced into gender-exclusive language, this commentary will adopt plural nouns throughout. In other words, the creators of the text will be called "the Chroniclers" (esp. as opposed to the Deuteronomists) and the books of 1 and 2 Chronicles together as "the Chroniclers' History." No attempt will be made to "correct" the statements of others in this regard; in other words, if scholarly works cited refer to "the Chronicler" in the singular and "him" or "his," these references will be left standing. Incidentally, this is also the approach adopted by John Jarick in his recent commentary (2007), though Jarick calls the authors "the Annalists." He justified this by writing:

> I am also attracted to the homonymous relationship between the word "Annalists" (designating a school of chronographers) and the word "Analysts" (designating professionals or others who apply analytical skills to their tasks). The people responsible for telling the story of the kingdom of Judah . . . put forward an account which scrupulously insisted on their line of analysis. (2007a, 2)

G. Chroniclers' Presentation of Yehud/Judah/Judea

Yehud is the Persian name of the colony that included Jerusalem. From a postcolonial perspective, interpreters may not want to use the word "Yehud" because this is the language of the colonizers. Yehud, in basic terms, was a district within a province within one of the larger satrapies, numbering twenty-two. These were initially developed by King Darius. Something similar to this is mentioned in Dan 6, but there the number of satrapies is nearly six times what was historically the case.

The satrapy into which Palestine fell was called *'eber nahara'* ("beyond the Euphrates River"), the river in question being the Euphrates, and the point of view from Babylon westward. The area included "Phoenicia, Syria called Palestine, and Cyprus," according to the ancient Greek historian Herodotus (Miller and Hayes 2006, 516). It should be noted that "beyond the Euphrates River" has a different meaning in texts like Josh 24:2. First, the Hebrew is slightly different, *'eber hanahar*. Second, the Hebrew perspective is from west to east. In other words, "beyond the Euphrates River" is east of the Euphrates. However, the Persian perspective is from east to west. This makes "beyond the Euphrates River" west of the Euphrates.

The Bible's perspective, as the reader might expect, puts Israel in the center of the world. The other nations serve, theologically speaking, as a backdrop or larger dramatic setting for what is going on in Israel and Judah. Moreover, in the case of the Chroniclers, even Israel is part of the larger "stage decoration" for Judah. As the text is primarily concerned, therefore, with what God is doing in and through Judah, the perspective that comes to the foreground is wrapped up in Judah.

This is not a complete picture, however, of how the Bible and more specifically Chronicles present Judah in its west Asian environment. For Chronicles, as has been said, seems primarily to be a work of history rather than a work of theology. That is, while theological explanations for historical events are found all throughout 1 and 2 Chronicles, in terms of historiographical methodology these theological dimensions are part of the backdrop rather than the main action.

There seem to be, then, two different ways of viewing the Chroniclers and their work. As *theological* history, the events that are recounted in the books are cast in such a way that the work of God comes to the front, and the wider historical and sociological contexts of Israel and Judah are paid little attention. As theological *history*, however, Chronicles pays much attention to the wider events of ANE history. The history covers a span of some five hundred years—except for the genealogies, which purport to go all the way back to creation—and, since these five centuries were a momentous time of different empires, the larger historical context is considered in rather great detail.

H. The Importance of the Temple

One of the dominant concerns of the Chroniclers' History is the centralization of worship in the Jerusalem temple. In certain ways, this is similar to the Deuteronomistic History, but in other ways this concern is amplified by the Chroniclers to a greater degree even than the Deuteronomists with their favor for Josiah and his great reform of temple worship. Concern for the temple, moreover, was a distinct concern in the period following the return from the Babylonian exile (see, for example, the prophecy of Haggai).

When the Chroniclers' History is viewed alongside other writings from the Second Temple period, this concern for temple worship is brought into high relief. For example, comparing the prophecies of Haggai—who, incidentally, is the most securely dated prophet in the entire canon—to the Chroniclers is quite fruitful. On the one hand, Haggai is quite concerned to excoriate the people for dithering about with regard to reconstruction of the temple. On the other hand, the Chroniclers expend many words, in many different sections of the document, detailing who was fit for temple service, and from whom they had descended, and who had been established by Solomon in their respective places. The Chroniclers are also quite in harmony with Ezra-Nehemiah on this point, though it should be remembered (see above), that Chronicles and Ezra-Nehemiah are separate documents that share similar concerns.

Beyond the almost excessively or obsessively detailed descriptions of worship in the temple, another way in which this concern for temple worship is demonstrated is the very lengthy genealogy given for the descendants of Levi in 1 Chr 6:1-81 (5:26—6:66 HB). Genealogies of the Levites and their divisions of labor are also given in 1 Chr 23—27.

This concern for the temple is interesting in light of the emphasis given to Jeremiah and his prophecies in Chronicles (see 1 Chr 35:26; 36:12, 20-21, 22), including credit given to Jeremiah for the words of Second Isaiah about God stirring up the spirit of King Cyrus (Isa 44:28; 45:1). This connection is odd for the simple fact that, of all the writing prophets, Jeremiah is perhaps the most critical of temple worship (see Jeremiah's famous temple sermon in Jer 7:1-15). The Christian interpreter may have difficulty with this emphasis on a particular place to worship, as if it were possible that God could only be worshiped in one place. Two things must be kept in consideration, however. On the one hand, this represents an earlier stage in Jewish religion. The destruction of the first temple by the Babylonians made necessary a change, as did the later Roman destruction of the second temple. These changes profoundly altered not only the Jewish community and their thoughts about proper worship but also their very thoughts about God. On the other hand, particular locations, rituals, formulas, and so on, are not bad in themselves; in fact, such things are very good in the access they give to God, the feeling they engender in the worshiper. They only become inappropriate when they come to be treated as an end in themselves, rather than as a means toward the end of making possible a renewed relationship with God. Jesus' conflicts with the

Pharisees in the NT reflect this reality: the Pharisees' zeal for the Law was good and righteous; it only became a hindrance when they became (from Jesus' perspective) so focused on the Law that they forgot the Source of the Law.

I. Theological Issues

Four principal theological ideas seem to inform the Chroniclers' History. Chief among these is the concern with the southern kingdom of Judah. This is also one of the characteristic differences between the two great historical epics in the OT. This focus on Judah sets Chronicles further apart from some of the prophets who predicted a reunification of Judah and Israel. Examples of this prophetic view can be seen in Jer 50:4-10 and Ezek 37:15-28. Lying behind these predictions is the conviction that the breakdown of the united kingdom was a "rebellion" on the part of the north, in need of being healed through repentance and turning again to Yahweh. This possibility certainly sounded a hopeful note in Jeremiah and Ezekiel, two major prophets whose work centered around the exile. The Chroniclers, by contrast, show very little concern for the northern kingdom of Israel, as will be apparent throughout the course of the commentary.

Second, the Chroniclers are concerned with matters involving the Israelite priestly caste. This emphasis comes to the fore early on, through the considerable amount of attention paid to the descendants of Levi in the genealogies of 1 Chr 1—9. In addition, Chronicles deals with many matters related to the proper worship in the temple (see the previous section), and those primarily responsible for such matters in ancient Israel were the priests and Levites. This does not necessarily mean that priests and/or Levites edited the work or added to it in any significant way. Historical-critical exegesis was concerned in particular to distinguish between the original work of the Chroniclers (usually assumed to be a single author; see above, "Who Wrote Chronicles?").

This theological issue connects nicely with a third, namely the matter of religious reform. In contrast to the Deuteronomists, who emphasize the reform conducted by King Josiah as the high point, so to speak, of history, the Chroniclers detail no less than four reforms, carried out by the kings Asa, Jehoshaphat, Hezekiah, and Josiah. Moreover, they do not suggest, as the Deuteronomists do, that the discovery of the book of the law in the temple began Josiah's reform (see 2 Kgs 22). Instead, according the Chroniclers, this discovery took place much later in the process, after Josiah began to seek Yahweh in the eighth year of his reign and purged the land of alien religious objects four years later. A major implication of this is that the Chroniclers are not as keen to present Josiah as the greatest king since David—indeed, perhaps even greater than David—as 1 and 2 Kings are wont to do.

The fourth theological theme that seems to lie behind Chronicles is the idea of Yahweh as the Lord of History. This idea also plays a role in the background to Jeremiah, whose prophecies are important for the Chroniclers near the end of their history. Throughout the history of the world and of the nation, and in particular when the survival of the nation is threatened, demonstrations of how Yahweh is directing everything are invaluable. Thus it is Yahweh who stirs up King Cyrus of Persia to restore the Jews to their ancestral homeland (see 2 Chr 36:22-23). Though this end to the history leaves the reader looking for more, the assumption is that the God who led history in the past will continue to do so in the future.

COMMENTARY

THE BOOK OF FIRST CHRONICLES

I. THE HISTORY OF THE WORLD (IN BRIEF) (I CHRONICLES 1:1—9:44)

▶ Overview

The genealogical record in Chronicles is long, detailed, and somewhat confusing. It has led many people to ignore Chronicles entirely. The genealogies seem at many points even to be repetitive. Those brave enough to devote close attention to them have often found themselves frustrated with the constant intertwining of the lines that fed into ancient Israel. This frustration may cause such persons to wind up, like those who ignored Chronicles in the first place, no less knowledgeable but worse for wear, having been defeated by the difficult material confronting them in 1 Chr 1—9.

However, the difficulty readers may have with this material should not lead them to ignore it. Close attention, by contrast, to the details reveals some interesting results. At the end of the day, the genealogies of Chronicles are part of inspired Scripture. That they were included in Scripture, of course, makes a big difference for their interpretation. Even if that were not the case, however, the fact that a historian decided they were worth mentioning is significant, since they were, after all, a key part of the story. One may, then, recall what was said above about theological history in studying this section.

Perhaps more famous to most readers among biblical genealogies are those included by Matthew and Luke. Both of these serve a particular purpose, namely to show how Jesus Christ fit within the stream of Jewish history. Matthew 1 goes back to Abraham, the father of the faith. From there, the first Gospel puts together a stylized account of fourteen generations between Abraham and the exile and between the exile and Jesus' birth.

Taking a different approach, Luke 3:23-38 tells the genealogical story in reverse order. Not concerned as much for style as Matthew apparently was, Luke's "orderly" account is actually closer to that found in Chronicles. While not calling Adam "the son of God" as Luke does, the Chroniclers go all the way back to the beginning to show how this version of the history fits within the overall story of God's people.

Aside from this theological interpretation, reading Chronicles as a historical document yields a different kind of importance for the genealogies. Inclusion of a genealogical record in a historical document is not surprising at all. By contrast, that the Deuteronomistic History does not have at least some kind of genealogy—beyond the patrimony of the various kings—makes it seem quite unusual among historical writings. The way in which the story is told gives particular insight into the standpoint of the historian. In this way, the genealogies of Genesis, with their descriptions of the very long life spans of the ancestors, appear quite different from those one finds in Chronicles. The genealogies are, perhaps, more interesting for what they leave out than what they include.

The genealogies in 1 Chronicles may also reveal something significant about the way in which the Chroniclers wrote. This is particularly so with regard to the use of source material. James T. Sparks comments, "If it is determined that the Chronicler had before him a particular written document while he completed his work, then this may help determine the origin of some of the Chronicler's material which, although not a direct quote, has certain affinities with other Biblical material" (2008, 294).

In addition to this, the way in which the Chroniclers present the genealogies gives great insight into the historical methodology being employed.

Put very simply, the Chroniclers give what is most important for their own purposes, and this often leads them to present information somewhat out of order. Sometimes, the "most important" father is presented last, as is the case with the three sons of Noah (1:4). However, at other times the most important father is presented first, as in the sons of Hezron, Ram and Jerahmeel (2:9). In addition, a great many of the names one encounters in this genealogical prologue serve as the progenitors of the inhabitants of cities, nations, and even large portions of the world. These eponymous ancestors whom the Chroniclers name thus stand in as fulfillments of the command to "be fruitful and increase in number; fill the earth and subdue it" (Gen 1:28; see 9:1).

A. Adam to the Sons of Israel (1:1—2:2)

BEHIND THE TEXT

The Chroniclers begin, as it were, at the beginning. The history goes all the way back to Adam, the first human. Doing so gives an insight into philology, the relationship between language and culture. The Hebrew word 'adam means both the proper name "Adam" and "humanity." This situates the story being told within the overarching story not just of Israel but also of humanity in general. As such, it yields an important insight for what the Chroniclers are trying to achieve. As has been repeatedly said, this is theological history, and in the genealogies the historical dimension is probably more in focus. However, even if this is the case, the theological dimension is by no means excluded.

Sparks notes, "The Genealogies contained in 1 Chr 1 have numerous parallels to those contained in the book of Genesis, with most of the genealogies contained in Genesis making an appearance in the Chronicler's opening chapter" (2008, 296). As will be seen, the Chroniclers put these genealogies to a specific purpose, and the way in which 1 Chr 1 reports the genealogical record contributes significantly to that purpose. Sparks ultimately concludes, "It is evident that copying of the Genesis material by the Chronicler took place" (2008, 297). He demonstrates this conclusion through charts detailing the extensive amount of parallel passages between Genesis and 1 Chr 1, including some lengthy consecutive sequences of copying of exact words. Even with a few minor spelling differences, the copying is remarkable.

Sparks's ultimate conclusion is that "the Chronicler had the text of Genesis before him as he wrote, and he copied much of the data contained in 1 Chr 1 from it. Although at times the Chronicler slightly modified his source, he did not substantially change any of the content which he found within Genesis" (2008, 319). This conclusion appears essentially correct, with respect to the genealogies. However, Genesis also includes a great deal of narrative that accompanies the genealogical record. The Chroniclers omit this for the most part. By presenting the genealogies the way they do, without the accompanying narratives, the Chroniclers give evidence of changing the source material in Genesis by way of summarizing a great deal of material. In the commentary that follows, when divergences are noted from the text of Genesis, for the most part attention is being paid to these summaries of the accompanying historical narratives.

Brief mention may be made of spelling variations between the genealogies in 1 Chronicles and the source material in Genesis. There are far too many of these to make mention of each one in the course of the commentary, but a few basic items can be noted. The Hebrew letters *dalet* and *resh*, transliterated by the English *d* and *r*, look quite similar to one another. Often, a name appears spelled with a *resh* in Genesis and a *dalet* in Chronicles, or vice versa. In addition, the letters *vav* and *yodh*, transliterated as *v* and *y*, also look similar. The only difference between them is that the *vav* is slightly longer. The commentary that follows assumes that these spelling differences do not in any respect indicate different persons.

IN THE TEXT

■ **1** In v 1 one notices a difference from the history reported in Genesis. Following the stories of the first family, including all of the events in the garden of Eden and the first murder, Gen 5:1-32 gives the genealogical record from Adam to Noah, with additional details of the ages at which the fathers had the sons. In a way, Gen 5 tells Adam's story again, but without many of the details. Chronicles, by contrast, does not include any stories of Adam and his descendants, mentioning only their successive names until the founding of the monarchy under Saul (ch 9).

Also left out is the story of the first murder. Thus the story of the first two sins—the eating of the fruit by the parents and the killing of the son by his brother—are not included. On the one hand, one might expect the line to continue through Seth—Abel being killed and Cain having moved to "the land of Nod" (Gen 4:16). This is in line with the genealogy given in Gen 5. On the other hand, leaving out the reason why it was the third son and not either of the other two is interesting. As an aside, Seth's name is spelled in Hebrew *Sheth*. Such a change happens frequently when Hebrew names are translated to English, most notably with Solomon (Heb. *šelomoh*) later on in the narrative. The change is most likely due to Greek (the language of the Septuagint) not having a letter representing a *sh* sound. The Greek OT most often uses a simple *s* in such cases.

The reader should also notice in this verse the names of both Adam and his grandson Enosh are words for "human." Whereas Adam's name is also the common Hebrew word for humanity, Enosh's name is the common Aramaic word for humanity. This word occurs with a slight spelling variation in Dan 7:13, a verse famous for its messianic implications (one of Jesus' titles is Son of Man; see, e.g., Luke 9:58).

■ **2-4** The six generations (see below) represented in these two verses also diverge somewhat from Gen 4. The descendants of murderous Cain, according to Gen 4:17-22, were Enoch, Irad, Mehujahel, Methushael, and Lamech. To Lamech were born Jabal, Jubal, and Tubal-Cain. These names are similar to the descendants of Adam in 1 Chr 1, yet, as has already been seen, Cain is excluded from the genealogy. The names are spelled differently in Hebrew. On this basis, Claus Westermann suggests that the two genealogies should be distinguished (1984, 348). This is in contrast to James Sparks, who believes that the differences between Chronicles and Genesis are only made for specific rhetorical purposes (2008, 319).

In the attempt to achieve greater clarity, the NIV makes a couple of additions to vv 3-4. First, **Noah** is added to the end of v 3. Second, the phrase **The sons of** is added to the beginning of v 4. The latter change follows the Septuagint. These additions are not necessary, however. One may, instead, see this first part of the genealogy as a kind of flowchart. Once the generations get down to the children of Noah, the line splits into three branches. This is in contrast to the formulaic genealogy in Gen 5, which indicates that the various fathers had other sons and daughters aside from those through whom the genealogy continued. Having only the relevant sons listed in 1 Chr 1 in no way indicates that these are the only sons born to the fathers. The point is rather that the Chroniclers are using the genealogical record for a particular point, just as the writers of Genesis, Matthew, and Luke do.

With 1 Chr 1:4, the simple presentation of names comes to an end. The remainder of the genealogy grows increasingly complex. In addition, many of the names in the genealogical record are also names of cities and territories. This indicates that something more is going on in these genealogies than a list of names.

■ **5-7** While the sons of Noah are listed in their birth order in v 4—Shem, Ham, and Japheth—their descendants are listed in reverse order. Verses 5, 8, and 13, therefore, form something of a ring structure with v 4. In addition, the sons of Noah become the patriarchs of three main divisions of the world. This makes it likely that the Chroniclers had Genesis ready to hand when composing the genealogies of ch 1. As James T. Sparks correctly notes, "The Genealogies contained in 1 Chr 1 have numerous parallels to those contained in the book of Genesis, with most of the genealogies contained in Genesis making an appearance in the Chronicler's opening chapter" (2008, 296).

As has been noted, the Chroniclers also used the genealogies of Genesis for a specific purpose, namely to show where Israel fit in the history of the world. By waiting to list the descendants of Shem (or the Semites) until last, even though Shem was Noah's firstborn according to Genesis, the Chroniclers saved what was most important until last. On the last being first, Jewish medieval commentator David Kimchi (also known by the abbreviation "Radak") notes, "The reason that the text begins by presenting the progeny of the youngest is that the only important part of the account concerns Abraham, and it is in connection with him that it will present the genealogies at length" (2008, 30).

■ 8 Here the reader sees the first of many names used throughout the Chroniclers' genealogies that are also the names of regions, cities, nations, or ethnic groups. The name of Noah's second son, **Ham**, is also given to the region of the world basically identical with the region bordering the Mediterranean Sea on the southeast. It is even used in a synonymous parallel chain in Ps 105:23, "Then Israel entered Egypt; Jacob resided as a foreigner in the land of Ham." With one exception, the names of Ham's children cement this assertion. First, **Cush** generally refers to Ethiopia (see Gen 2:13; Num 12:1; 2 Chr 16:8 [paired with Libya]). Second, *Mizraim* is the exact spelling of the Hebrew word for **Egypt** (thus NIV's translation is justified, if somewhat misleading; see also Gen 10:6). Third, **Put** is not credited with any descendants in either 1 Chr 1 or the source material in Gen 10. Fourth, **Canaan** becomes the father of those inhabiting the most important land in the Bible.

■ 9-16 The grandsons of Ham, like their fathers, become the patriarchs of people groups important for subsequent biblical history. What is important to note about this information is the suggestion of common ancestry for all the peoples of the world, as the Hebrews understood it. This certainly says something important about how the Chroniclers viewed the world and Israel's place in it. Specifically, the entire history of the world, as told through the genealogy, is preparing for the coming of Israel, which first appears in 1 Chr 2:1. The theology being proclaimed here is one of election: Israel is God's chosen people and, coming at the right time, their lives (and especially the life of the nation) bring about a new chapter in God's relationship with the world.

Many of the names appearing here, people groups growing out of the patriarchy of Canaan, figure in earlier OT stories. So, for example, in 1:13-15 **the Hittites**, the **Jebusites, Amorites, Girgashites**, and **Hivites** are some of the people whom Israel, according to the tradition, was destined by God to replace (see, among others, Exod 3:8 and Deut 7:1). The **Arkites** will appear later on in the story of David, with one of their number, "Hushai the Arkite" being called "the king's confidant" (1 Chr 27:33).

■ **17-26** Next, and last, come the sons of Shem, the firstborn of Noah. This collection of descendants will lead to one of the most important men for Israel's history, Abraham the father of the faith. Abraham is given his own verse in v 27, indicating his particular importance as the grandfather of the twelve patriarchs. Interesting in this text before Abraham is the first person whose name is explained. **Peleg** (v 19), one of the sons of Eber, was so named **because in his time the earth was divided**. It is unclear what is meant by this phrase, though it does indicate something of a regular practice. Children were often named for significant events occurring just before or simultaneously with their births, and, at least according to the Chroniclers, this Peleg is the first to have been so named. It may not be the case that Peleg was the first, but at least he was the first about whom the Chroniclers commented.

■ **27** Coming around to Abraham, the Chroniclers once again very quickly pass over a large portion of the narrative from Genesis. From Gen 12:1 to 17:4, the father of the faith is called "Abram," which means something like "exalted father." In a dramatic experience recorded in Gen 17:5, God changes his name to "Abraham," which means something like "father of a multitude." Here, however, the Chroniclers indicate merely that **Abram** and **Abraham** are the same person, without any mention of the change effected and what it might have meant in Abraham's life. This is again within the Chroniclers' intent throughout the genealogies—to tell the "backstory," as it were, of Israel and Judah under the Davidic monarchy. Radak also noted the connection with Gen 17: "The text says 'Abram' in keeping with the way [one presents] genealogical lines; and 'that is Abraham'—the famous one, whom God loved and whose name He aggrandized (Gen 12:2), making him the father of many nations (Gen 17:5)" (Kimchi 2008, 33).

■ **28-54** The two sons of Abraham and their descendants, as is well known from Genesis, have always existed in tension with one another (see especially Gen 16). The text presents the sons of Abraham in a chiastic or ring structure. First, 1 Chr 1:28 tells us that the sons of Abraham were **Isaac and Ishmael**, though, of course, Ishmael was the firstborn. Radak does not delay much on this, stating merely that "in the course of presenting the lines of Abraham, the text provides the lines of his son Ishmael and the sons of Keturah, and after that states 'Abraham fathered Isaac' (1 Chr 1:34), since he is the essential one" (Kimchi 2008, 33-34). In this way, the presentation of the descendants of Abraham is similar to that regarding the descendants of Noah earlier in vv 4-27. Radak's recognition of Ishmael as Abraham's son is a key point, however, for according to law 170 of the Code of Hammurabi, the official recognition by a father of sons born to a maidservant or a concubine was sufficient to allow those sons to claim a share of the inheritance (see Deut 21:15-17).

Wives and Concubines in Ancient Near Eastern Law

A significant number of Hammurabi's laws deal with the relations between sons born to a man's multiple wives and/or a maidservant given by the wife to the husband as a surrogate mother. Two of these laws, numbered 170-171, seem to have direct relevance to the story of Abraham. Law 170 reads, in part: "If . . . the father during his lifetime then declares to (or: concerning) the children whom the slave woman bore to him, 'My children . . . ,' after the father goes to his fate the children of the first-ranking wife and the children of the slave woman shall equally divide the property" (Roth 1997, 113-14). Law 171 addresses the opposite situation: "But if the father during his lifetime should not declare . . . 'My children . . . ,' the children of the slave woman will not divide the property of the paternal estate with the children of the first-ranking wife" (Roth 1997, 114).

Other law collections from the ANE could be cited here as well. Samuel Greengus, for example, cites the Laws of Lipit-Ishtar (especially Laws 25-26). Greengus writes:

> These cases establish the principles that a son of a slave woman could become a member of his father's family or an heir to his father's estate in two ways. One was if he was formally "legitimized" by the father even if his mother was not ranked as a wife; the second was if his father took his mother in marriage. (2011, 78)

1:28-54 The issue with regard to Abraham, Sarah, Hagar, Ishmael, and Isaac turns, therefore, on whether Abraham recognized Ishmael as his son. On the one hand, the Genesis text seems to suggest that he did not do so; instead, he apparently left the decision entirely up to Sarah (Gen 16:6). However, Gen 16:3 ("wife") and 16:15 (named "the son") and "his son" in 17:23-27 and 21:11—all suggest Abraham's recognition of Ishmael as his legal son, though Sarah sees him as the son of her slave girl!

This ring structure is not quite correct, however. This is because the sons of the concubine Keturah are inserted in between the lines of Ishmael and Isaac. Nevertheless, Radak is correct that the most important line of descent from Abraham for the Chroniclers is the line of Isaac, and the best is left for last. Interestingly, the headings of the NIV call these sections, respectively, the descendants of Hagar, Keturah, and Sarah. On the one hand, this usage might have been unfamiliar to the original hearers/readers of Chronicles, aside from the note that **all these were *the sons* of** Keturah (v 33). On the other hand, it does perhaps help modern readers keep the story a bit straighter. Finally, the second mention that Abraham was the father of Isaac, as Radak noted, also forms an inclusion with v 28.

A couple of the descendants of Esau are interesting in other contexts. **Eliphaz** and his firstborn son **Teman** (v 36) remind the reader of one of Job's three friends/accusers, Eliphaz the Temanite. Inscriptional evidence from Kuntillet 'Ajrud in the Negev desert links Yahweh with the city of Teman (see also Hab 3:3). In addition, a distant descendant of Esau also has relevance for Job. First Chronicles 1:42 states that **Uz** was a son of **Dishan**. Uz is the land from which Job came, said only to be somewhere in "the East" (Job 1:1, 3).

Following the descendants of Esau and his connection with Edom and Mount Seir, the Chroniclers then turn to a discussion of kings who ruled **in Edom before any Israelite king reigned** (1 Chr 1:43). Radak notes that after the Israelites established a monarchy the Edomites "did not have kings . . . because they were under the control of David—until the sins of the Judean kings facilitated their rebellion against [Judean] rule (2 Chr 21:8-11)" (Kimchi 2008, 35). Again, however, the Chroniclers' main purpose is not to make all the cited details align with historical reality, but instead to pave the way for the emergence of Israel. This emergence is saved for ch 2, when the descendants of Abraham's grandson Israel come into focus.

■ **2:1-2** As noted above, the Chroniclers save the best for last. Everything has been building up to the point at which Israel emerged on the world scene. At the same time, however, the Chroniclers once again omit a significant piece of backstory. For here there is no selling into slavery of the favored son Joseph, no famine driving the patriarch and his family down into Egypt, no oppression, and no crossing of the Red Sea. On top of that, the sons of Israel are not given in the order of their birth (see Gen 30 for the correct order). The six sons of Leah are given first, like the other sixteen lists of the sons of Jacob (Sparks 2008, 286). Then 1 Chr 2:2 lists the sons of Rachel bracketed by those of her servant Bilhah. Finally, the sons of Leah's servant Zilpah are given. Scholars are generally at a loss to explain why the Chroniclers did what they did. For example, Sparks comments only that this ordering of Jacob's sons is "unique within the Hebrew Bible" (Sparks 2008, 270). Moreover, "the Chronicler's order in his genealogical section has been based upon criteria other than birth order, or whether the son descended from a wife or a concubine" (Sparks 2008, 287).

FROM THE TEXT

Chronicles, like the rest of the OT, has no "doctrine of original sin," at least in the way this term is understood in the NT. Though there are hints here and there of such a doctrine (see, for example, Ps 51:5, "Surely I was sinful at birth, sinful from the time my mother conceived me"), no OT writing builds its hamartiology upon reflection on what happened in the garden of Eden. This was left for Paul to do in Rom 5, though it is consistent with the trajectory of meaning in Gen 3.

The reader might perhaps wonder why such an "important" piece of history should be left out. To find an explanation for this, one needs to carefully consider the overall structure of Chronicles. The Chroniclers treat the related ideas of sin, punishment, repentance, forgiveness, and restoration—themes encountered again and again throughout the Bible—in their own way. In other words, they knew that sin existed; telling the story of how sin began lay outside of their goals. They wanted to present the history of the world in such a way as to prove God's ultimate direction of history. This was an important note to sound in their postexilic context, when it seemed as if all of the important theological anchors of Jewish life had been taken away, even as "Jewish life" as such (for it is only after the exile that the Israelites may properly be referred to as "Jews") was beginning.

However, one should be cautious about comparing the Chroniclers with other, earlier bodies of literature in the OT. One temptation here, naturally, is to suggest the older ones are better and the newer ones deficient. The Chroniclers and the writers of Genesis have very different motivations. Genesis was perhaps concerned to be more theological, and this is why it includes more historical details alongside the genealogies. Chronicles, by contrast, was excited to get to the "important stuff" and used the genealogies merely as a device to get to Israel. Yet even this is not quite an accurate statement, for the Chroniclers could well have begun with David and ignored everything else. At the end of the day, the interpreter must acknowledge that the genealogies serve more than just background, though their details somewhat defy precise explanation.

B. The Israelite Tribes (2:3—9:1)

▶ Overview

The majority of the genealogical record, as is perhaps to be expected, is devoted to the tribes of Israel. As will be seen, some tribes receive far more coverage than others. This is undoubtedly due to the fact that the Chroniclers' interests lie with particular tribes, especially the tribe of Judah, to which attention turns first. Structurally, it is interesting that the two tribes that receive the longest treatment—Judah at one hundred verses and Levi at eighty-one—in fact get more than all of the others following them in the text. Moreover, the advantage Judah has over the ones following it is greater than that of Levi over the ones following it. The shorter genealogies after Judah receive a total of forty-four verses after Judah's one hundred. This is in contrast to the shorter genealogies after Levi, which at a total of seventy-nine verses are only two verses shorter than the priestly tribe's eighty-one.

I. The Tribe of Judah (2:3—4:23)

BEHIND THE TEXT

Though Judah is not the firstborn of Jacob/Israel, according to the Chroniclers he is the most important. This is because the most favored Davidic royal line comes from the tribe of Judah. Radak supports this assertion: "The author begins by presenting the progeny of the sons of Judah, because the book is primarily about the Judean kings" (Kimchi 2008, 38). The source material for this tribe's genealogy comes from a number of different places within the Pentateuch, most notably in Gen 46, as well as other places in the OT. Two places in particular outside Chronicles are of interest. First, the reader finds a most interesting story of Judah and his descendants is told in Gen 38, seemingly an interruption in the Joseph cycle of Genesis. Second, almost as a response to this story, one may find the dual genealogies of David in Ruth 4. The first proceeds forward from the marriage of Boaz and Ruth, then the second looks all the way back to Perez, the son of Judah by Tamar. In her commentary on Ruth, Kirsten Nielsen suggests that Ruth 4:18-22 is meant specifically to counteract what happened in Gen 38, or, in other words, to correct an ancient sin done to the Canaanite(?) Tamar through the honoring of the Moabite Ruth (1997, 17).

James Sparks, however, questions the assumption that David is at the center of the Judahite genealogy. He argues instead the case for Jerahmeel. His primary evidence for this claim is the fact that this man's name appears not less than six times in 1 Chr 2 (vv 9, 25, 26, 27, 33, 42). The person or persons responsible for producing a work like Chronicles certainly needed both significant training and significant financial resources, not to mention access to the many sources that appear to lie behind the epic. The backing probably came from a prominent or rich Judean family, which may or may not have been excited at the prospect of the return to the Davidic monarchy. Sparks writes: "Such a return, if successful, would diminish their own power and prestige, while a failed attempt to return to Davidic rule would result in their deaths or, at the least, loss of power and prestige at the hands of the Persians" (2008, 245).

The ultimate value of such a move, according to Sparks, is to demonstrate that hope perhaps should not lie with the return to the way things were before the disaster that had come upon Jerusalem. Sparks writes further:

> Jerahemeel [sic] in the centre is an attempt by the Chronicler to encourage the people to look to other than David for their political authority and hope. David is thus de-centred . . . [Therefore,] although the people may have had a hope of a restored Davidic monarchy, the Chronicler himself did not share it. (2008, 246)

This is an intriguing possibility that awaits further study and clarification. One central implication is the need to reevaluate why Judah is the first listed genealogy. A possible answer to this is that, even if David is not the central concern, Jerahmeel is also a son of Judah. If Sparks's suggestion is true, finally, it may shake the traditional understanding of Chronicles, as represented by Radak, at its foundation, but it now seems too soon to make a decision.

IN THE TEXT

■ **3-4** As has already been seen, the Chroniclers have a habit, when giving the genealogies, of leaving out much information that the source materials found important enough to include. First, the identity of Judah's wife is left out, for she is only called **a Canaanite woman, the daughter of Shua**. Admittedly, Gen 38 is also unclear as to why **Er . . . was wicked in the LORD's sight** (v 3). However, that chapter goes on to explain, perhaps in somewhat shocking detail, how **Onan** was also evil in the sight of Yahweh. John Jarick comments simply that Onan "is not assessed in the Annals (though he is—rather salaciously—in Genesis 38:8-10)" (2007a, 39). Onan fails to live up to his duty to his dead brother Er, providing him an heir through the barren Tamar. In response to this failure, Yahweh kills Onan as well. Judah then, perhaps wisely—but nonetheless deceitfully and wrongfully—deceives Tamar into thinking that he will give her his third son **Shelah** when the latter is grown to maturity. Tamar ultimately has her revenge, however, and though she finally fades into obscurity, assumedly as a widow in her father's house (Gen 38:11), through her the line is continued that, in the due course of time, produces the great King David. Chronicles, like Genesis, is unconcerned with what happens to Tamar (though Gen 38 does report that Judah "did not sleep with her again" [38:26]). This is, of course, not much of a consolation, for the value of women was largely in their production of heirs; if Judah never slept with her again, she could naturally no longer perform her "function."

■ **5-12** The Chroniclers agree with the version of the genealogy in Ruth 4, except with fuller detail. Whereas Ruth is concerned only to name the direct ancestors of David, Chronicles gives the entire line from Perez to Jesse and after this proceeds to give all the sons of Jesse. The omission, of course, from the Chroniclers' account is the most favored convert, Ruth the Moabite. Again drawing a link between Ruth and the story of Tamar, Nielsen comments: "Admittedly the Old Testament contains only these two stories of childless widows who set out to create offspring for their deceased husbands, but in both cases the genealogy attributes the child to the biological father" (1997, 96-97). In both of these cases, then, there is a failure of the levirate law as originally intended. In Ruth 4, the nearer redeemer declines his obligation. So also in Gen

38, first Onan refuses to complete the act then Judah refuses to give his third son to Tamar. Though one should be cautious in drawing conclusions from such meager evidence, perhaps there is in fact more to the levirate marriage law than is stated in Deut 25. In any event, these two similar stories excite the mind engaged in intertextual exploration.

■ **13-15** The sons of Jesse are then named, with **David** of course being **seventh** and last (v 15). This detail disagrees with the story of the anointing of David as king in 1 Sam 16, which has David as the eighth son (vv 10-11). Nielsen suggests, citing the work of Jack M. Sasson, that "genealogies prefer to put important persons in particular places in the family order: the places in question are number 7 and number 10" (1997, 97). In Ruth 4, Boaz is in seventh position and David in tenth. The point could be brought to bear here as well, because David is moved up from eighth—where he belongs according to 1 Sam 16:10-11; 17:12. Roddy Braun concurs with Nielsen's suggestion (1986, 35). Radak attempts to get around this problem by suggesting "it is possible Jesse had a son from another wife, and that in the book of Samuel, the text counts them all when saying 'seven of his sons' and then 'There still remains the smallest one.' But here, it refers to the seven that were of the same mother as David" (Kimchi 2008, 40). This explanation is unsatisfactory, however, since the Chroniclers do not mention a second mother—not even a first!—whereas they did so with regard to the five sons of Judah, three from the daughter of Shua and two from Tamar. Resolution of this will have to await further illumination.

2:5-17

■ **16-17** With **Zeruiah**, one finds the first reference to a woman being the ancestor of three sons, without mentioning also the identity of the father. While this comes from the Chroniclers' source material in such places as 1 Sam 26:6 and 2 Sam 2:18, it is a nonetheless interesting anomaly. Curtis suggests that Zeruiah and Abigail "are recorded for the sake of their distinguished sons" (Curtis 1910/1976, 88). Myers indicates similarly that these two women were mentioned solely because of their connection to a man, this time David: "Only here do we learn that Zeruiah and Abigail were sisters of David (I Samuel xvi 6; II Sam xvii 25), brought in because they figure in the history of the latter later on" (Myers 1965a, 14). Alice Laffey echoes the note of her male counterparts, pronouncing with a nearly audible sigh that "thirteen of the references are to women named only here [in the genealogies]. When one asks why they were included in the Chronicler's account, one can only surmise that they and their children add to the prestige of their husbands" (1998a, 120).

■ **18-24** In what seems to be an interruption in the foregoing, the Chroniclers turn attention next to the descendants of **Caleb**. This is not the spy, who was a contemporary of **Bezalel** (v 20), this Caleb's great-grandson. Verse 18 has a serious textual problem, in that MT's **Caleb had children by Azubah, a woman, and Jerioth** is undoubtedly corrupt. The NIV correctly follows the Syriac, Targum, and Arabic versions to add a pronominal suffix to *woman,* yielding **by his wife Azubah (and by Jerioth)**. This reading is supported by the evidence of v 19, according to which Caleb took another wife after the death of Azubah, which he would not have needed to do had Jerioth also been his wife. However, Williamson goes on to suggest that retaining **and** is misleading (the third person masculine suffix "his" and "and" are created with the same consonant in Hebrew). His suggestion is to take the verb *hôlîd* as having a double accusative, making **Jerioth** into the daughter of **Caleb** and **Azubah** (1982, 53). Radak disagrees, saying both women "were [Caleb's] wives, and he had children from both of them. But the text keeps the genealogical lines brief[!], mentioning the sons of just one of them, namely, Azubah" (Kimchi 2008, 43).

Here, as elsewhere in the genealogies, the Chroniclers make mention of many people who will eventually become the eponymous ancestors of important places. Included among those names well-known from elsewhere in the OT are **Gilead** (v 21), **Jair** (v 22), **Geshur**, and **Aram** (v 23). This demonstrates one of the tasks the Chroniclers set out to accomplish in the genealogies, namely, to populate the known world. This was seen earlier with reference to the sons of Noah being the ancestors of the three main divisions of the Mediterranean/Mesopotamian world, and here in the genealogy of an otherwise unknown **Caleb** the same thing is happening on what is closer to a microscopic level.

■ **25-33** With the descendants of **Jerahmeel** (v 25) the text again follows something that has become familiar: presenting descendants of brothers out of their birth orders. Radak reminds that "Ram . . . is the one who is essential for presenting the family of David" (Kimchi 2008, 46). However, this part of the genealogy also displays an interesting feature not encountered elsewhere in Chronicles. In vv 30 and 32 one finds the tragic note that **Seled** and **Jether died without children**. Thankfully, the line did not stop with these two men, or else no King David and no Davidic monarchy. That each of them had one—but only one—brother to carry out the line surely, to the Chroniclers, was further evidence of the specialness of the Davidic line. Given that it was almost wiped out generations before David, it must therefore be important. In other words, God's hand must be active in preserving the line that will eventually result in the "man after his own heart" (1 Sam 13:14).

■ **34-41** In 1 Chr 2:34, the reader comes to an apparent contradiction. This part of the genealogy reaches back into the descendants of Jerahmeel in the previous section. Verse 31 reports that "Sheshan was the father of Ahlai." However, v 34 says **Sheshan had no sons—only daughters**. The NIV's rendering, incidentally, obscures the problem by its uneven handling of the genealogies, sometimes translating the phrase *ben PN PN* (which literally means "the son of PN was PN" in the form "PN was the father of PN"). Radak's solution is far better, for he suggests that "Ahlai died in his father's lifetime, and there was no son or daughter left by him" (Kimchi 2008, 47).

Sheshan having no sons—or perhaps no living sons—calls for creative means to extend the line. Radak points out that this was technically against the Torah in Deut 23:8-9, since **Jarha** was a first-generation Egyptian convert. He goes on to say that having done this might have led to a rather dark time in Israelite history, "for there are sixteen generations from Jarha until Ishmael son of Nethaniah" (Kimchi 2008, 48). Ishmael son of Nethaniah was the assassin of the Babylonian-appointed governor Gedaliah (see Jer 41:2). Although Ishmael may have been a patriot in the eyes of some, he certainly was a terrorist in the eyes of others, and the giving of Sheshan's daughter to Jarha may have unwittingly prepared for a tragedy.

■ **42-55** Radak suggests that this section "proceeds to complete the progeny of Caleb, whatever was not recorded above (vv 18-20)" (Kimchi 2008, 48). Several sons mentioned here bear the same names as important cities in Israel. This may perhaps indicate eponyms for these cities, as has been seen elsewhere. First, **Ziph** and **Mareshah** (v 42) are also the names of cities fortified by King Rehoboam (2 Chr 11:8). Second, **Hebron** (1 Chr 2:42) is the city where David was proclaimed king (11:3). Third, Caleb's second wife **Ephrathah** (2:50) was the grandmother of **Bethlehem** (v 51). These two names together form a famous address in the prophecies of Micah (Mic 5:2), often interpreted by Christians as a prediction of Jesus. Fourth, **Kiriath Jearim** (1 Chr 2:50) shares the name of the place from which David brought the ark of the covenant to Jerusalem (13:5-6; 2 Chr 1:4). Finally, not belonging in the list of apparent city names but still worthy of mention are **the Rekabites** (1 Chr 2:55). This group was a sect of ultra-pious Israelites with whom the prophet Jeremiah had some interaction several centuries later (see Jer 35).

■ **3:1-9** Though continuing with the tribe of Judah, the text here seems to make something of a great leap forward in discussing the sons of David. Aside from the fact that this summary of David's progeny maintains an old distinction between David's activity in **Hebron** (v 1) and **Jerusalem** (v 4), the Chroniclers once again betray their sympathy toward the Davidic kings, clearly the most important players in the entire history of Israel. Radak summarizes this change a bit differently, saying that here the text returns to complete the family of Ram after the seeming interruption of the family of Caleb (Kimchi 2008, 54). Nevertheless, the reader should not be surprised at the somewhat confused nature of the genealogy of Judah, for as James Sparks drily comments, it "is at once the longest and most convoluted of any of the genealogies within 1 Chr 1—9" (2008, 215).

Leslie Allen uses this information of David's later genealogy as the last in a succession of points to support a late-Persian period dating of Chronicles:

> The same impression of a dating late in the Persian period is given by the post-exilic continuation of the Davidic genealogy in 1 Chr 3. The exact number of generations involved cannot be ascertained, but the genealogy extends into the fourth century BCE. (1999, 301)

Whatever the reason for it, that this material is difficult is an understatement. The difficulty is further compounded, certainly, by the vastly different report of David's offspring in 1 Chr 14 (see below). However, this material was clearly important for the Chroniclers, so again the difficulty of understanding should not be a reason for throwing up one's hands in despair, even though this may seem to be the only comprehensively logical reaction.

It is interesting, in the presentation of David's offspring, that nearly all of the principal women are mentioned as the mothers of the various sons. The importance of the queen mother in ancient Israel is well known also from the Deuteronomistic History, which fails in only a few cases to mention her identity. Further, among the mothers mentioned, especially striking is the order of birth given for **Bathsheba** (v 5). First, it should be pointed out that the majority of Hebrew manuscripts read ***Bath-shuah daughter of Ammiel***, whereas 2 Sam 11:3 calls the mother of Solomon "Bathsheba, the daughter of Eliam." This is most certainly not more than an odd textual variant. The name Bathshua would be more appropriate for the unnamed wife of the ancestor Judah (Gen 38). Second, the names are not given in birth order. This is probably due to what has already been seen in Chronicles: the tendency to hold the most important until the end.

A further note deserves mention here. Most Hebrew manuscripts read ***Elishama***, a name that occurs twice among David's sons in this text. The NIV has followed a divergent manuscript tradition, reading **Elishua**. While it is certainly not out of the realm of possibility that David could have given two different sons the same name, it is more likely an error in reporting. A different textual tradition lying behind 1 Chr 14:5-7 (→; see also 2 Sam 5:15) corrects the apparent error.

Finally, 1 Chr 3:9 exhibits a particular late Hebrew construction. The expression is translated **besides his sons by his concubines**. The **besides** is the Hebrew *milləbad*. Features like this assure the relatively late dating of the composition, while at the same time not giving as much credence as was once thought to the theory of a strong authorial connection between Chronicles and Ezra-Nehemiah.

■ **10-16** These verses list the remainder of the Davidic kings through the end of Judah's independent existence. The Chroniclers are fond, in the genealogical section, of summarizing great bits of information in this way. Of course, as is also familiar by now, the Chroniclers focus only on the most important of the offspring in question, in this case Solomon, "since the kingship belonged to him and to his children after him" (Kimchi 2008, 58). This could be said of the information throughout the summary, since none of the many other children the various kings had are considered important enough to mention. The point, after all, in this section is to demonstrate the continuity of the Davidic kingship, rather than to present a comprehensive historical record.

It is not until the end of the story, that is, with the sons of Josiah, that this methodology is broken, again for specific purpose. The final four kings of Judah all come from the family of Josiah. He is first succeeded, briefly, by **Shallum** (v 15), who takes the throne name Jehoahaz. However, since the Egyptians killed Josiah, they took the opportunity to put on the throne in Jerusalem someone who would be loyal enough not to interrupt their plans as Josiah had. So they deposed Jehoahaz and replaced him with Eliakim, who took the name Jehoaikim. After Jehoiakim's death was his son Jehoiachin, who was exiled by the Babylonians. (Jehoiachin's release forms the ambiguous note of hope at the end of 2 Kings and Jeremiah.) Finally, the last king was Josiah's son and Jehoiachin's uncle Zedekiah. The son-brother-son-uncle sequence is unique in Judah's history.

■ **17-24** As a complement to the summary of the Judean kings, the last few verses of ch 3 pick up after the exile to describe the governors taking charge of Yehud after the Persians replaced the Babylonians as the world power. That there is no discussion of genealogy during the exile is not surprising given the Chroniclers' general feeling about the exile. This general feeling is that the land, having been emptied (though, → 2 Chr 36:21), rested from having been inhabited. In a sense, then, the exile was an interruption not only in the life of the land but also in the life of the people. Therefore, there was no need, at least at this point, to record the succession of fathers and sons who were born, lived, and (at least some of them) died while in exile.

Famous from elsewhere in Scripture is **Zerubbabel** (1 Chr 3:19). This governor appears many times in Ezra and Nehemiah, as well as being one of the principal human subjects of the prophecies of Haggai and Zechariah. There is some debate as to whether Zerubbabel's claim to Davidic lineage is authentic, mainly coming from sociological circles. For example, Jon Berquist writes: "There is no clear evidence that Zerubbabel was the grandson of Judah's last king, or even that he was Davidic" (1995, 63). Regardless of the position one takes on this issue, however, for the Chroniclers the issue was clear, and Zerubbabel as a son of David was thus an important person with an important genealogical pedigree. Through Zerubbabel, the most favored Davidic line was reestablished, and thematically that was of importance, even if later sociologists would call the claim into question.

■ **4:1-23** Having concluded the summary of the Davidic leaders, the text now returns to filling in the remainder of the descendants of Judah. This is in line with the typical practice of the Chroniclers: spending a great deal of time on those considered most important, then returning to fill out the historical record with those considered of lesser importance. The judgment of importance, once again, has to do with the contribution of the persons under consideration to the overarching theme of the story. In a way, therefore, the additional personages mentioned may fall into a category of "other people": important as a part of the people of God, but not important in the sense of not having a particular leadership role to fill.

In spite of the recognition that these other descendants of Judah are not important to the Chroniclers in the grand scheme of history, nevertheless deserving brief mention is **Jabez** (vv 9-10). The famous best-selling self-help book based on the so-called prayer of Jabez found its inspiration here. The NIV footnotes suggest that the name Jabez sounds like the Hebrew word for "pain," though the pun is not quite as clear as in other, similar namings in the OT. **Jabez**, in Hebrew, is *ya῾bēts* and pain is *῾etseb*. In other words, the pun requires reversing the final two letters of one of the roots. This problematizes the pun somewhat, though Radak suggests that simple transpositions or other alterations between a name and its supposed source are in fact quite common in Hebrew wordplay (Kimchi 2008, 63). Nevertheless, v 10 goes on to record that Jabez prayed to be **free from** the **pain** in which his mother apparently conceived him.

FROM THE TEXT

The OT is often misused and abused (see Bright 1967/1975 for a classic treatment of this issue). "Prosperity theology," in particular, is often guilty of such misuse. Elevating what happened to Jabez into a universally applicable formula for success in Christian faith or in life is especially dangerous. This is dangerous primarily because it equates material success with spiritual success. In other words, prosperity theology teaches that a Christian's personal wealth, health, happiness, and so forth, is a measure of the authenticity of that person's walk with Jesus.

The book of Job sounds a particularly harsh note against such thinking. God does indeed promise reward for faithfulness. This reward does indeed sometimes take the form of material blessings. Job, after all, was rewarded with twice what he had lost at the end of the book. However, it is illegitimate to argue that God always rewards in this way. To believe so is, essentially, to fall to the challenge presented by Satan in Job 1! By contrast, Christians from other, poorer countries—Papua New Guinea, for example—generally do not equate material wealth with spiritual health. This seems to be a particular disease of Western Christianity, especially from wealthy countries like the United States, and one wonders if it might not properly be called heresy.

2. The Tribe of Simeon (4:24-43)

IN THE TEXT

■ **24-43** Joshua 19:1-9 and Gen 49:7 suggest that the tribal territory of the Simeonites was, in certain ways, carved out of the tribal territory of Judah. Radak combines the three texts to claim the Simeonites "did not have their own portion as did the other tribes" (Kimchi 2008, 70). John Bright recognizes further that although "the number 'twelve' was rigidly adhered to, it appears that component members could fluctuate . . . Though Reuben early lost significance, and Simeon was absorbed into Judah (Josh 19:1-9), both continued to be reckoned as full clans" (1959, 143).

Allen makes an interesting suggestion on the basis of the two notices of **to this day** in vv 41 and 43 at the end of this section on the Simeonites. He writes:

> Did the chronicler regard the two districts . . . as still occupied by Simeonite families? He might have assumed the contemporary validity of the source. If so, he was maintaining membership in the people of God not only of returned exiles, but also of those who were not deported. (1999, 337)

If this argument has any validity, as it seems it does, then it should be marshaled as further evidence for the separation—along ideological lines—of Chronicles and Ezra-Nehemiah. This is so because of the latter's insistence (along with a large amount of other literature from the exilic and postexilic periods) that the only true Israelites were those who had undergone, or whose parents and grandparents had undergone, the trauma of exile. Such a view is expressed, for example, in Jeremiah's vision of the baskets of figs in Jer 24:1-10. Jeremiah, in that passage, argued quite persuasively, if not convincingly, that avoiding exile was not any cause for rejoicing, for only with the exiles did hope remain for the future (Modine 2009a, 172-75).

3. The Tribe of Reuben (5:1-10)

IN THE TEXT

■ **1-10** Like the tribe of Simeon, the tribe of Reuben seems, at various points in the OT and the history of Israel, effectively to disappear from the scene. Though the number of the tribes remained fixed at twelve (→ 1 Chr 2:1), the names associated with the particular tribes fluctuated a great deal. Though **Reuben** was the firstborn of the sons of Jacob/Israel, as has already been seen the Chroniclers are willing to present genealogies outside of the birth order if such practice suits the purpose. That purpose seems to be to present the most important first (or last, in the case of Shem, Ham, and Japheth, the sons of Noah [1 Chr 1:4-17]).

Another reason to dethrone, as it were, Reuben from the honored place that should have been his as the firstborn is that it was a punishment for sin. Verse 1 of ch 5 goes on to indicate something of what Reuben had done. In this way, the Chroniclers recount the "blessing" given by the dying Jacob to Reuben: "Turbulent as the waters, you will no longer excel, for you went up onto your father's bed, onto my couch and defiled it" (Gen 49:4).

The curse upon Reuben continues in 1 Chr 5:2, with the note that **the rights of the firstborn belonged to Joseph**, even though Judah should have been next in line to be counted as the firstborn since he **was the strongest of his brothers and a ruler came from him**. Simeon and Levi, the second and third sons of Jacob, had been similarly dispensed with as had Reuben, though it was because of violence in their case rather than adultery. Why the birthright should have gone all the way down to eleventh-born Joseph is unclear. A note on the translation might give some illumination, however. Radak applies the phrase **so he could not be listed in the genealogical record in accordance with his birthright** to Joseph, not to Reuben (v 1). Resulting from this is a further explanation:

> When [Jacob] gave [Joseph] the birthright, it was not for Joseph to be reckoned as firstborn in all respects and to be called Israel's firstborn; for had that been the case he would have had the kingship also, just as the rule would have dictated that Reuben have everything. (Kimchi 2008, 73)

The assigning of the birthright to Joseph takes place in Gen 48:22. Radak's explanation seems plausible given the general difficulty of rendering one language into another. In other words, perhaps the NIV is translating the Hebrew phrase *velo' lĕhityaḥes labbĕkorah* as complementary to the main thought of the verse, whereas Radak takes it as complementary to the secondary thought about Joseph. Radak's sense is therefore "Joseph was given the birthright, *but* he was not otherwise considered the firstborn." Justification for this could also be found in the double deception necessary for Jacob to get the favored status from Esau: first swindling his older brother out of the birthright (Gen 25:27-34) and then deceiving his father into giving him the blessing (Gen 27:1-29).

4. The Tribe of Gad (5:11-17)

IN THE TEXT

■ **11-17** The **Gadites** divided the territory of **Bashan** with the half-tribe of Manasseh that lived on the other (east) side of the Jordan (see Deut 3:13 and → 1 Chr 5:23-26). The part of Bashan that was controlled by the Amorites is here compared to that which was controlled by King Og (called the "king of Bashan" in Num 21:33). The latter was given to the half-tribe of Manasseh, the former to the Gadites.

Another possible way to eliminate any confusion is suggested by the editors of the *BHS*. Their suggestion is to insert "in the land of Gilead and" before "land of Bashan." This would, admittedly, further specify which part of Bashan had belonged to the Gadites. The suggestion is apparently made on the basis of v 16, where the same phrase occurs. No textual evidence is given for the insertion, so on that basis it is probably to be rejected.

The note in v 17 that the two-and-a-half trans-Jordanian tribes **were entered in the genealogical records** relates to the "war against the Hagarites, Jetur, Naphish and Nodab" (v 19). Through relative chronology, it can be established that the **Jeroboam king of Israel** (v 17) being referred to is Jeroboam II, son of Joash, not the first king who rebelled against Judah (or liberated Israel, depending on one's perspective; → 2 Chr 10:16-19).

5. The Israelites on the East Side of the Jordan (5:18-22)

IN THE TEXT

■ **18-22** This section does not seem to have a careful structure; the section begins with a statement of the two and a half tribes who lived on the east side of the Jordan, though the Reubenites and the Gadites have already been introduced in the previous section, and the half-tribe of Manasseh is waiting to be introduced (vv 23-25). The two and a half tribes will be mentioned again at the end of the next section (see v 26). The insertion of the half-tribe of Manasseh in this section along with the Reubenites and the Gadites suggests that the aim of the Chroniclers at this point was to compile a summary statement concerning God's help to them **(they were helped)** in their battle against their enemies when **they cried out to him during the battle** and **trusted in him. God delivered** their enemies **into their hands** (v 20) because the **battle** they fought **was God's** (v 22). This is a striking note in light of the stance of silence the Chroniclers generally take when they deal with the northern tribes. The reason for their exile is explained in the next section, which introduces the half-tribe of Manasseh. The Chronicler may have been using at this point "whatever material was available to him" to create a summary statement about the two and a half tribes that lived on the east side of the Jordan (Williamson 1982, 66). **The exile** referred to in v 22 is probably the deportation of these tribes some ten years before the fall of Samaria, around 734 B.C.

The Northern Kingdom of Israel in the Southern Historical Works

Truly, the northern kingdom does not fare well in either of the two great epic historical works coming from the southern kingdom of Judah. In the Deuteronomistic History (Dtr), the kings of Israel are univocally condemned for having followed after the sin of Jeroboam I, the son of Nebat, which is how Dtr defines the dispute that resulted in the divided monarchy. Yet, there are a few positive notes about Israel in Dtr, like 2 Kgs 14:23-27. That text is interesting for a couple of reasons: first, it is the only mention of the prophet Jonah son of Amittai outside of the book of Jonah in the OT. Second, it mentions Jeroboam II, who was seen above in a positive light. This note about the two and a half tribes living east of the Jordan serves, for the Chroniclers, as one of the few mentions in the history of the northern kingdom. It is striking that one of these few mentions is positive. Evidence like this should perhaps cause one to question the ages-old consensus that, from the perspective of the south, the north could do no right.

6. The Half-Tribe of Manasseh (5:23-26)

IN THE TEXT

■ **23-26** The Eastern portion of the tribe of Manasseh shared the territory of **Bashan** with the Gadites, one of the two tribes who lived completely on the eastern side of the Jordan. In this passage, the Chroniclers return to the characteristically negative portrayal of the northern Israelite tribes, in indicting them for idolatry and suggesting that God allowed them to be destroyed because of their worship of **the gods of the peoples of the land** (v 25). The use of a pagan king by Yahweh to punish the people is certainly not a new concept. The prophet Jeremiah uses this idea well (see Jer 25:9; 27:6; 43:10). Isaiah also employs the concept, using it in a positive way in 45:1-8. There the servant is King Cyrus, who is called by Yahweh to release the captive Israelites from Babylonia (see also 2 Chr 36:22-23).

Pul/Tiglath-Pileser III

The name **Pul** has been a subject of debate among scholars. *Tiglath-Pileser III* was indeed king of Assyria, and one reads about his activity in Israel in 2 Kgs

15:29, though there the focus is on the land of Naphtali rather than the Transjordanian tribes. Pul appears to have been a name taken by Tiglath-Pileser III upon his takeover of Babylon. Thus it was a Babylonian throne-name, as Bright argues (1959, 252). Further support for this comes from a text in *ANET*, which T. R. Hobbs says "makes clear that Tiglath Peleser and Pul are the same person, the latter name being given to him after he seized the throne of Babylon" (1985, 198; *ANET* 1969, 272). Kenneth Kitchen, however, disagrees, suggesting that Pul was an "alias" of unknown origin (2003, 38). Choon-Leong Seow writes in his commentary on 2 Kgs 15:29 that Pul was "an alternate Hebrew name for Tiglath-peleser III" (1999, 248). Of the three options (Pul as Babylonian throne name, as an alias of unknown origin, or as an alternate Hebrew name) the first seems the most convincing.

7. The Tribe of Levi (6:1-81)

BEHIND THE TEXT

The tribe of Levi is given almost as much space by the Chroniclers, eighty-one verses, as is the tribe of Judah at one hundred verses. This surely reflects the strong emphasis on the temple and on cultic faithfulness. As Leslie Allen correctly notes, "The chronicler wrote his history to promote the interests of the temple. He leaves readers in no doubt about his convictions that the temple merited the community's unstinting support and that worship should be conducted in a traditional and proper manner" (1999, 344). Though the addition of verses and therefore, the number of verses, was a later addition, this comment nevertheless holds true. Concern for the temple, moreover, was a distinct concern in the period following the return from the Babylonian exile. The prophecies of Haggai especially, and only to a slightly lesser extent Zechariah, are filled with admonition to complete the second temple and re-begin the proper worship of God in the proper place. The Chroniclers, in telling the story this way, are surely looking back to an idealized past from which the community has fallen and to which it can be restored through the grace of God and the faithfulness of the people.

IN THE TEXT

■ 1 The English and Hebrew verse numbers differ in this text. Whereas in English ch 5 ends with v 26, in Hebrew it continues through v 41. This means that the English 1 Chr 6:1-15 is 5:27-41 in Hebrew. Alignment between Hebrew and English verse numbers is restored at the end of ch 6, which in English has eighty-one verses but in Hebrew only sixty-six. Bearing in mind that the verse and chapter divisions were added later saves the interpreter from confusion. Care must be taken, however, so that one's further hearers and readers do not themselves become confused.

■ **2** One interesting feature of the genealogy of the Levites is the repeated listing of "the sons of Levi" in vv 1 and 16, with a variant spelling for "Gershon" (v 1) and **Gershom** (v 16). The NIV has "Gershon" in both cases, while the NRSV has "Gershom" in both cases. Radak comments simply that "in names, *mem* and *nun* are equivalent" (Kimchi 2008, 83). Allen writes: "Gershom is the chronicler's preferred form; the variant Gershon used in priestly texts of the Pentateuch appears here as a reflection of his source, reverting in v. 16 to Gershom" (1999, 344). In the view of the present writer, the harmonization is unnecessary, though some readers would indeed be tempted toward confusion.

Aside from the variant spelling, it is interesting that the Chroniclers would restate the genealogy they were working on. This is a unique feature among all the genealogies. Of course, only the tribe of Judah had a similarly lengthy genealogy, yet the device is not employed even there. Perhaps it was necessary to recapitulate that the descendants in vv 16 and forward were also Levites, but this remains uncertain.

■ **3-15** It appears that even though the genealogy is lengthy, it still is not complete. The Chroniclers do not mention that other priests were descended from **Ithamar** (v 3), a fact that is noted in 1 Chr 24:1-4. Again, this is likely due to the specific purpose for which the Chroniclers were using this genealogy, namely to legitimize the Jerusalem priesthood and the temple in which it served. Even though the temple was destroyed at the time of the writing of the Chroniclers' History, it was expected to be rebuilt, and eventually it was, though needing some significant prophetic encouragement from Haggai and Zechariah.

Verse 3 lists the important leaders of the Exodus, the siblings **Aaron, Moses and Miriam**. The explanation for Miriam being mentioned last, although she was born second, is likely to be found in the usual spot: males—especially male children—were, in general terms, thought of as more important than females. However, this genealogical note is balanced somewhat by the story of Moses' birth in Exod 2, with the vital role his sister played in securing Moses' knowledge of his true ethnicity. Though Pharaoh's daughter recognizes that "this is one of the Hebrew babies," nevertheless being raised at the Egyptian court should surely have obliterated, or threatened to obliterate, Moses' awareness of the fact.

The Bible in the Movies

The 1998 animated film *The Prince of Egypt* presented the story of Moses and the Exodus in a manner designed for children to readily understand. This project was fine in itself, but along the way the film, perhaps unintentionally, created some misconceptions. For example, Moses' mother Jochebed is not involved at all in his upbringing, having separated from him forever when she places him in the basket in the Nile. Miriam, for her part, has no communication with Pharaoh's daughter. As a result, once they become adults, Moses's appearance surprises Miriam, who then becomes bold enough to convince him who he is—over Aaron's strenuous objections. The biblical record, however, rather clearly shows that Moses knew of his cross-cultural identity all along.

On another level, the VeggieTales version of Esther (2000), finds a creative way to deal with the violence of Esther. Haman, in the children's version, desires to send Mordecai and his people to a place called the Island of Perpetual Tickling. This certainly provides a good way to avoid difficult subjects like death and warfare. However, the downside of this sanitation is that it may mask a questionable methodology that believes children are not "ready" for the full truth. The present writer feels that there must be a way to deal with these violent stories—of which the OT in particular is well-known to be filled—that takes due regard for children's sensibilities yet does not have the side effect of misunderstanding and confusion.

In v 10, the reader comes up against an interesting note. The text says that **Johanan . . . served as priest in the temple Solomon built in Jerusalem**. On the face of it, this is in direct contradiction of 1 Kgs 1:34, which notes that the high priest under Solomon was Zadok. Zadok, for his part, had replaced the deposed Abiathar, sent back to his hometown of Anathoth by Solomon (see also 1 Chr 29:22). Later, Jeremiah the prophet, so important to the Chroniclers, would come from Anathoth. (Though there is no apparent connection between Jeremiah and Abiathar, it is an interesting coincidence.) One would certainly not expect such an error from one so concerned about accuracy in history, and particularly with accurate reporting of the history of the all-important Jerusalem temple, as the Chronicler. However, this difficulty is not quite so severe as it seems. Since the text does not claim that **Johanan** was high priest during Solomon's reign, one should not assume that this is what the Chroniclers are saying.

Finally, in v 15, one finds the first reference to Nebuchadnezzar King of Babylon as the agent of God's punishment of the people of Judah. This punishment took the form of the exile, which occupies a significant place in the thought of the Chroniclers, as well as Second Temple Judaism as a whole. Elsewhere reference had been made to "Jehoiachin the captive" (see 1 Chr 3:17), who was exiled by Nebuchadnezzar, but here it is made explicit for the first time. Just as the line of kings was taken all the way down to the exile and beyond in 3:10-24, here the line of the priests—some high priests and some others—is extended down to the exile, though not beyond, in this chapter.

■ **16-30** As noted above, 6:16 returns to the beginning, as it were, and restates that the Chroniclers are describing **the sons of Levi**. The NRSV has harmonized the spelling of **Gershom** here with that of "Gershon" in v 2, though this seems to be an unnecessary correction (see the quote from Radak above). It seems certain that the Chroniclers wanted to give the genealogy of the Levites here up until the point of David, as v 31 begins a new section with an emphasis on the identities of those installed as temple musicians.

■ **31-49** The following passage gives a list of temple musicians whom David installed, and Solomon maintained, to make music first in the tabernacle and later in the temple. That David established these musicians doubtlessly further speaks to David's high reputation in the eyes of the Chroniclers. David, who could and, in fact, did do no wrong. For more on this idea, see 1 Chr 20:1-8 and 28:1-7.

The musicians are divided into families, the **Kohathites** (vv 32-38), the ***Asaphites*** (vv 39-43), and the **Merarites** (vv 44-47). The name Asaph is also known from the book of Psalms, with many songs in the collection attributed to Asaph, though of course it is highly doubtful that the same person is being referred to. On the one hand, the dating of individual psalms varies widely. On the other hand, there may well have been many individuals named Asaph who were connected more or less directly with the temple. For that matter, the psalms attributed to Asaph may or may not have actually originated with anyone of that name, just like the psalms attributed to David. If the Asaphite psalms are pseudonymous, the likelihood still remains strong that this particular name was chosen because of his association with temple musicians, a fact confirmed by the Chroniclers' depiction of him as such.

■ **50-53** This text, which may be a redactional addition, restates the succession of high priests up until the time of David. A difference between what one reads here and the beginning of the chapter is the correct listing of **Zadok** (v 53) in place of Johanan (v 10). Allen says that this new list "does not involve a new role. Its intent was to illustrate from a priestly perspective the shift from tabernacle to Temple" (1999, 346).

■ **54-81** The final text in the chapter deals with the allotment of cities within the territories of the various tribes for the Levites. This information recalls Josh 21. With the exception of an original introductory note in 1 Chr 6:54*a*, the Chroniclers have adapted this material completely from Josh 21:4-39. The description moves from south to north, with the southern cities summarized in 1 Chr 6:55-60, the northern cities summarized in vv 61-63, and the northern cities given in detail in vv 64-81. As a kind of refrain throughout this text, each city is given **with their pasturelands** (vv 60, 69, 71, 73, 75, 77, 79, 81). This phrase certainly indicates the point of assigning these cities to the Levites: since the Levites were not given a tribal portion among the rest of the tribes, they needed some source of income to support themselves other than the occasional offerings brought to the various holy places, the tabernacle, and the temple. The surrounding pasturelands of all of the cities mentioned fit this need admirably, so that the Levites would not go hungry among the Israelites, and thus sacrifice some or all of their effectiveness as ministers between Yahweh and Israel. The care needed for the Levites fits in with care taken for religious workers throughout history. God does not let his workers go without support, and the genealogy of the tribe of Levi bears that belief out.

8. The Tribe of Issachar (7:1-5)

IN THE TEXT

■ **1-5** Verse 1 of the Issachar genealogy more or less directly quotes the source material in Num 26:23-24. Two other parts, 1 Chr 7:2 and vv 3-5, list Issacharites according to the number of soldiers ready to go to war. Allen suggests that the Chroniclers might have had in mind David's census in ch 21, with a parallel in 2 Sam 24 (1999, 352). This sounds a bit odd, however, given the condemnation that the census brings down on King David and the nation of Judah. The condemnation is made even more severe in the Chroniclers' version of the story, for in ch 21 David is following the leadership of Satan rather than God! Nevertheless, the Chroniclers are certainly drawing off some source, and the total in 7:5 seems to include those counted from v 1 as well.

9. The Tribe of Benjamin (7:6-12)

IN THE TEXT

■ **6-12** Allen suggests two reasons why Benjamite material is included here rather than with the rest of the tribe of Benjamin's genealogy in ch 8 (1999, 352). First, there is the connection to the military list given for Issachar in the immediately preceding passage. Alternatively, the Chroniclers may be drawing on the tradition of certain members of the tribe of Benjamin living among the northern tribes. The present writer feels the first of Allen's suggestions to be the stronger one, as the passage does bear some structural relation to the preceding passage. Three eponymous ancestors are given, as opposed to four for Issachar. In both families, one of the ancestors has only one son. In addition, the fighting men are listed in separate numbers. With Issachar, it is unclear whether the second, larger number includes the first. With Benjamin, however, it seems clearer, though still not certain, that the different numbers are not ultimately meant to represent a total.

10. The Tribe of Naphtali (7:13)

IN THE TEXT

■ **13** The shortest of the genealogies is interesting for its recognition of Jacob's concubine **Bilhah** as the ancestor of the tribe of Naphtali. Allen concludes that the Chroniclers did this to "augment [their] scanty source material" (1999, 352). It may be nothing more than that. However, it seems always worth noting when the biblical text gives a prominent place to a female ancestor. This is especially so since it does not happen very often, and not anywhere else in the Chroniclers' genealogies.

11. The Tribe of Manasseh (7:14-19)

IN THE TEXT

■ **14-19** Whereas in 5:23-26 the Chroniclers detailed the genealogy of the half-tribe of Manasseh living on the eastern side of the Jordan River, he returns in this text to the other half, the half living with the rest of the tribes on the western side. Diana Edelman confirms that the Chroniclers are in fact dealing with west Manasseh, even though some names like **Machir** and **Gilead** sound very eastern (Edelman 1991, 192-93). The mention of **Zelophehad, who had only daughters** in 7:15 recalls the extraordinary legal matter proposed in Num 27 and resolved in Num 36. So long as the daughters married within their clan, the name of their father would not be forgotten. And so it was not, for the Chroniclers, though doubtlessly drawing on their source material, did not fail to mention Zelophehad, who had only daughters, and thus was in danger of failing ever to be mentioned again in Israel.

12. The Tribe of Ephraim (7:20-29)

IN THE TEXT

■ **20-29** At the end of this text the reader finds a bit more information as to the border of the territory belonging to west Manasseh, but for the most part it is concerned with the tribe of Ephraim. Here one also finds an interesting note about the fortunes of a woman. In contrast to her brother **Beriah** (v 23), who is named because of the misfortune that claimed the lives of his two older brothers, the sister **Sheerah . . . built Lower and Upper Beth Horon as well as Uzzen Sheerah** (v 24). As has been seen, the majority of success stories relate to men, making those relating to women, or telling of the success of women, all the more significant. Sheerah's name may be related to a Hebrew word meaning "flesh," though it is spelled the same as the very significant theological word "remnant" (BDB 984).

13. The Tribe of Asher (7:30-40)

IN THE TEXT

■ **30-40** The genealogy of the tribe of Asher returns to the practice of numbering the tribe in terms of those fit for soldiering. The number of Asherite soldiers is far smaller than the other two given in this chapter (26,000): Benjamin had 42,234 and Issachar 87,000 (taking the last number as a total; → 1 Chr 7:5). This makes plausible Allen's claim that "this listing refers not to the tribe in its northern setting, but to an Asherite enclave in the southern part of the hill country of Ephraim" (1999, 353). This claim is further supported by the names of certain of the cities said here to belong to the Asherites: Gezer and Shechem (v 28) are both located in the Ephraimite hill country.

14. The Tribe of Benjamin (8:1-40)

BEHIND THE TEXT

The final bit of the lengthy genealogy belongs to the tribe bearing the name of Benjamin. It seems appropriate that the Benjamites be given this position, since their patriarch was the last born of the sons of Jacob. At the same time, this perhaps might break a pattern established at the beginning of the genealogies, since the tribe of Judah, being listed first, traced its ancestor to one who was not the firstborn of Jacob. It is also interesting that Benjamin is given the third longest genealogy in terms of number of verses, behind Judah's one hundred and Levi's eighty-one. This certainly means, as it did with Judah and Levi, that the Chroniclers attach particular importance to the line of Benjamin. Judah and Levi had important positions in the Chroniclers' mind, as each in its way gave rise to important personages: Judah was the wellspring of the Davidic monarchy and Levi of the priests serving in God's temple.

The tribe of Benjamin, however, had its own share of important persons in Israel's history. The first legitimate king came from the tribe of Benjamin, and at least one stream of tradition in the OT maintained Jerusalem as a town within the territory of Benjamin (Josh 18:28). Jeremiah was likely also a Benjamite, since his hometown was within Benjamite tribal territory (Jer 1:1). Similarly, in the NT, Paul, the most famous Christian missionary, says he was a Benjamite (Phil 3:5). Thus these three tribes—Judah, Levi, and Benjamin—form a kind of triad of significance for the land of Israel. Though the first (and only) Benjamite king was rejected when he began to lose faith in Yahweh and become paranoid in the presence of noteworthy subjects, nevertheless his rejection by Yahweh paved the way for the acceptance of David, whom, as has already been shown (and will be shown again), was the man after God's own heart (see 1 Sam 13:14). Allen uses a colorful metaphor to describe the relationship between the three tribes:

> So in the chronicler's genealogies Judah and Benjamin stand at either end of a literary rainbow, red and violet, with Levi as the central green . . . The spectrum comprised many more than three colors . . . The southern tribes needed the rest to complete the rainbow. (1999, 356-57)

This idea—that the whole people of God was indeed the whole people of God—at once stands within the stream of postexilic Jewish thought and stands against it. On the one hand, the stream that includes Ezra-Nehemiah seems to have a distaste for the northern tribes, and especially those imported into northern tribal areas by the Assyrians. On the other hand, texts like Chronicles suggest that one of the pivotal marks of the return from exile should, and perhaps must, be the reunification of Judah and Israel, or the healing of a very old fissure. More will be said on this later, but it will suffice to point out two prophetic texts in this connection. First Jeremiah's oracle against Babylon carries a similar idea (Jer 50:4-10 within the context of Jer 50—51; see Modine 2009a, 265-68). Second, Ezek 37:15-28 envisions a similar idea, with v 22 being especially noteworthy: "I will make them one nation in the land, on the mountains of Israel. There will be one king over all of them and they will never again be two nations or be divided into two kingdoms."

IN THE TEXT

■ **1-7** Sparks notes that "there has already been one listing of Benjamin (1 Chr 7:6-12a), [but] the content and purposes of the two lists are different" (2008, 251). On the one hand, the earlier genealogy of Benjamin, standing alongside that of Issachar and Asher, had to do with lists of fighting men. Allen thinks that 8:6 returns to this motif of military commanders, but this is unconvincing (1999, 357). It is probably better to see this list as a complete genealogy, over against the military list of ch 7. The list here more closely follows one of the Chroniclers' sources in Num 26:38-41, which certainly is not concerned merely with soldiers.

■ **8-12** This passage begins with the only mention of divorce (Heb. lit. ***sent away***) in the entire Chroniclers' History work. Ezra-Nehemiah, by contrast, spends a great deal of time on Israelite men divorcing, or refusing to divorce, foreign wives. This is further evidence, so it seems, in favor of the separation of Chronicles from Ezra-Nehemiah that this commentary has advocated, following Japhet, Shao and Shao, and others. One of the sons whom **Shaharaim** fathered after his divorce has an interesting name. **Mesha** (v 9) was the name of a famous king of the nation of Moab who carried out a successful rebellion against Israel (see 2 Kgs 1:1 and, among nonbiblical sources, the so-called Moabite Stone).

The Moabite Stone

The Moabite Stone was discovered by archaeologists at the site of ancient Dibhon in 1868. It is written in the Phoenician language, which is close to Hebrew. This is the longest Iron Age inscription found in the region. In it, King Mesha suggests that Chemosh, Moab's national god, was angry with Moab and allowed Kings Omri and Ahab of Israel to oppress it. Later on, Chemosh turned in favor toward Moab, ordering Mesha to retake many of the areas previously conquered. The similarity of these theological arguments to the OT is illuminating. Of course, the son listed here and the king are not the same person, but it is interesting that they share a name and that v 8 begins with the note that Shaharaim had **sons in the land of Moab.**

Divorce in the OT

Divorce remains, of course, an issue of key concern for evangelical Christians, particularly in the West. Though some recent evidence indicates that divorce rates are falling in the United States, it is still a serious problem. Divorce is mentioned often in the Bible. Some OT laws regarding divorce had to do with prohibitions against Israelite men marrying a woman who had previously been divorced. Examples of this may be found in Lev 21:7, 14; Ezek 44:22. To be included with these are the orders in Ezra 10 to divorce foreign wives because of the corrupting influence they are supposed to have had. Other laws state that if a man had sexual intercourse with an unmarried woman he was forced to marry her and could never divorce her (Deut 22:19, 29). In these latter cases, no one apparently thought to ask the women what they thought about these arrangements. A third type of text places certain conditions on divorced women: if a priest's daughter was divorced, she could return to her father's house and eat his food (Lev 22:13); however, any vow she had made would be irrevocably binding on her (Num 30:9). Further, if she were divorced, remarried, and divorced again, she was not allowed to remarry her first husband a second time (Deut 24:1-4). Extending upon this last, a final, disturbing group of texts has to do with a metaphor of God as a jilted husband rejecting Israel's return to her; such ideas are the exclusive domain of the writing prophets (Isa 50:1; Jer 3:1, 8; Hos 2). Tempering this somewhat is the instruction against divorce in Mal 2:16: "'The man who hates and divorces his wife,' says the Lord, the God of Israel, 'does violence to the one he should protect,' says the Lord Almighty. So be on your guard, and do not be unfaithful." It seems a good thing that divorce is discouraged in Malachi. One may be troubled by the fact that, though referring to a past incident, the Chroniclers treat the problem of divorce casually in 1 Chr 8:8.

8:8-12

■ **13-28** The list includes **Elijah** (v 26), though perhaps not the prophet well known for his confrontations with the followers of Baal. However, citing midrashic sources, Radak suggests that "this Elijah [v 27] is the prophet Elijah and that he had four names." According to these sources, Elijah finally got fed up with endless debates about his parentage and cited this verse from Chronicles to settle the issue on his own behalf (Kimchi 2008, 103). This humorous story highlights something important about Jewish exegesis of Scripture.

Jewish Exegesis

Jewish exegesis is a striking phenomenon, even if obscure to most Christians. These interpreters argue over not just the books, but the pages, the paragraphs, the sentences, the words, indeed, even the very letters making up the words. Just about anything is fair game for interpretation, and meaning can be found just about anywhere, even the most obscure or strange or potentially earth-shattering meaning. These interpretations, however strange or fanciful, have no potential to hurt the sanctity of the text. Jewish scholar Shaye Cohen agrees:

> Once the traditions were established in fixed and unchanging form—that is, once written texts were edited, venerated, and canonized—the imagination was allowed to soar. A free or adventurous interpretation no longer did any harm, since the sacred original was left untouched. (2006, 185)

A few pages later, Cohen knocks over the pins he has set up:

> Perhaps the most radical function of scriptural exegesis was that it allowed Jews to affirm undying loyalty to a text written centuries earlier for a very different society living under very different conditions. They could claim loyalty to the sacred text even as they freed themselves from it by interpreting it. (2006, 197)

■ **29-32** These verses describe a Benjamite family that moved to the environs of Jerusalem to be closer to their extended relations in the clan. Allen suggests that "most of the ensuing family listed in vv. 30-32*a* remained in Gibeon," which was, according to the Chroniclers, named for the Israelite founder of the town (1999, 357). The Canaanite town by that name is of course a good deal older than the Israelite settlements, but one should not fault the Chroniclers for adding a bit of "insider" mythology to the city. After all, this was the place where the ark of the covenant is said to have resided before Solomon completed the temple. Moreover, this was the place where King Solomon had met Yahweh and asked for wisdom (1 Kgs 3; compare 2 Chr 1). Pleased with the king's request, God also gave him riches, long life, and power over his enemies. (For more on this, → 2 Chr 1.)

■ **33-40** The Chroniclers' detailing of the Benjamite genealogy culminates precisely where the reader expects it should, with the family of King Saul. Though David and his descendants were the far better known dynasty, and though the

Chroniclers may have been most concerned for the resumption of the dynasty—though see the quote from Sparks, above, for a different view—this does not minimize or neutralize Saul's importance. Saul was, in fact, the first legitimate king of Israel. The Chroniclers make no mention of Judg 9 and the furtive attempt of Abimelech, son of the judge Gideon, to have himself declared king. This genealogy of Saul, perhaps one of the clearest in the entire collection, is probably so because it is the genealogy of a king. For kings and other hereditary rulers, a clear genealogy was a must. One thing that should also be noted in this text is the correct rendering of **Esh-Baal** in 1 Chr 8:33 and **Merib-Baal** in v 34. The NIV footnote rather blandly suggests these men are, respectively, "Also known as *Ish-Bosheth*" and "Also known as *Mephibosheth*," but this slides over an important theological point. In the Deuteronomistic History, the element of a pagan god's name attached to these men is abhorrent. "Esh-Baal" means "man of Baal" and "Merib-Baal" something like "Baal is contending," similar, in a way, to the etymology of Israel, the name given to Jacob! The Deuteronomists got around this problem by changing the names of these two men, adding a word that meant "shameful" rather than the name of an alien god.

This text and the chapter ends, finally, with a summary statement like the ends of some of the other tribes. Benjamin, last born of Jacob, is the last one whose descendants are numbered. The next chapter will begin with a similar summary statement, though of all the tribes put together.

15. Summary (9:1)

IN THE TEXT

■ **1** The history of the world, or at least that part of it that was important to the Chroniclers to establish their story, is now finished. In a way, the Chroniclers have made it clear who, for them, belongs in the people of God. One way this is done is through repeated use of the term **Israel**, even when the clear reference is to the southern kingdom of Judah. This relationship is made clear later on in v 1 with the reference to **the book of the kings of Israel and Judah**. This source, otherwise unknown, is similar to the sources noted throughout the Deuteronomistic History (→ Introduction). The note, **they were taken captive to Babylon because of their unfaithfulness**, further clarifies that the focus is on the southern kingdom of Judah that was destroyed by the Babylonians in 586 B.C.

FROM THE TEXT

This commentary has repeatedly noted how the genealogical record of 1 Chronicles finally defies complete understanding. The interpreter must, at the end of everything, confess ignorance as to the importance of the ancestry of given individuals in Israelite society. This reticence is partially due to the interpreter's status as an outsider, surely. That the genealogies are important for the overall program of the Chroniclers, however, is beyond doubt. By tracing the ancestors of various tribes, the Chroniclers show that no one is left out of the family tree of the covenant nation; even those who suffered judgment and death receive mention because they belonged to the covenant people of God.

One major implication to be drawn from the genealogies is separation from Ezra-Nehemiah. Chronicles gives a far more expansive answer to the question of who belongs in the people of God than does Ezra-Nehemiah. Allen writes, "The earlier leaders Ezra and Nehemiah had given a minimal answer, understandable in a hard-pressed, relatively new community. The chronicler judged that a broader answer grounded in an ancient tradition could be given" (1999, 354). Thus, as has been said, the Chroniclers reached back to the beginning of the world to ground their history. Ultimately, Israel's story is part of the overarching story of God.

This seems to be the principal reason why the Chroniclers felt it necessary to go all the way back to Adam, all the way back to the beginning, to ground the history of Israel in the history of the world. In contrast to the Deuteronomistic History, which took up where the Torah left off, the Chroniclers wanted to give a new version of history, and often that means telling some of the same old stories all over again, but in new ways. Connecting present experience with the past similarly lies at the heart of all subsequent retellings of the story.

Participating in this reality, Wesleyans recount the stories of the great saints of the past. In some ways, the great faith chapter of Heb 11 is a condensed form of the same idea. Though 1 Chr 1—9 is much longer, and though it serves a somewhat different purpose, namely, to populate the earth and all its various regions, nevertheless by calling to mind the ancestors each successive generation of readers is brought into the community. Though some of the details are hard to follow and difficult to establish, the overarching story is doubtlessly true. Not only do the Chroniclers have an expanded vision of who belongs in the people of God, but also may each reader locate himself or herself in the sweeping story of the ages. "Everyone who calls on the name of the LORD will be saved" (Joel 2:32). This is the great promise for the believer: As God has been faithful in the past, so God will continue to be faithful in the future. The question for the readers is, then, not of God's faithfulness, but the faithfulness (or lack thereof) of human response to that faithfulness.

C. The Exile and Aftermath (9:2-34)

BEHIND THE TEXT

The traumatic experience of the Babylonian exile seems to float just underneath the surface of the majority of the OT. Occasionally, of course, it bobs up to the surface, like in the book of Lamentations with its increasingly chaotic poems. Sometimes the way the exile comes up to the surface can surprise the reader. One such example is the apparent new confession of faith developed in two parallel texts in Jeremiah, Jer 16:14-15 and 23:7-8. The prophet there quotes Yahweh as saying that the confession of faith in him as the One who delivered the people from Egypt will be replaced by one in which he is celebrated for the liberation from exile.

A quite prominent idea—at least judging from the evidence in the Bible—held that the best, if not the only, promise for new life after the trauma of exile lay with those who had actually experienced exile. Both Jeremiah in the Babylonian period and Ezra-Nehemiah in the Persian period argue this point. For Jeremiah (ch 24), the argument takes the form of a vision of two baskets of figs. While some of those who had escaped the first deportation in 598-97 B.C. surely thought they had received a blessing from God by not having been deported, the prophet said that the opposite was the case. Those who were left behind were to be likened to spoiled, rotten figs, which could not be eaten. Those who had been exiled, instead, were those who would eventually be restored to the land, in God's timing.

For Ezra-Nehemiah, this argument took two forms: the command to divorce foreign wives and the rejection of the people of the land (see Ezra 10). Foreign elements were despised, at least in this tradition of emerging Judaism. And those who desired to help rebuild the temple saw their offer rejected, because only those who had come with the authorization of King Cyrus of Persia were allowed to participate in the rebuilding (Ezra 4). This complex of ideas, found in other places in the OT as well, are in direct contrast to more inclusive passages like Isa 56, which allows in many people—including foreigners who voluntarily joined themselves to Yahweh—who were previously excluded.

Chronicles, though separate from Ezra-Nehemiah in most other respects, certainly agrees with that other postexilic historical work on this point. Immediately after a lengthy section of genealogy in which was given an apparently expansive vision of who belonged in the people of God and who did not, the Chroniclers here return to the standard arguments of the Yehudite elites: only those who were exiles, or whose parents were exiles, were allowed to come back in the land, resettle on their own territory, and pick up basically where they had left off. Though it is unfair to judge an ancient document by modern standards, one wonders whether, given the changes in leadership that the Chroniclers may have envisioned, why this particular and arguably most important piece of information was left unchanged. Such a question, unfortunately, can perhaps never be satisfactorily answered.

IN THE TEXT

■ **2** The text that comes under consideration next seems to shock in a similar way, though perhaps not to the same degree. First and Second Chronicles do not talk much about the conditions of the exile in Babylon. Instead, 9:1 notes that the people were exiled for their disobedience, but then this verse skips right ahead to those who were **the first to resettle on their own property**. The point was that exile did not represent a complete separation between the people and Yahweh. Rather, the exile served to clarify the relationship and purify the people so that they could be faithful to God in the future. The Chroniclers do not explain how the people who returned were able to make the claim of **their own property in their own towns**. It is unlikely that these properties remained vacant waiting for their owners to return and resettle.

■ **3-34** This lengthy passage is marked off by "bookend" statements that the people in question **lived in Jerusalem** (vv 3, 34). Many of the names, as was seen in the genealogical record, vary in spelling from other materials. As was noted there, these differences are relatively easy to explain (see Radak in Kimchi 2008, 107-8).

Return from Exile

The notion of a "return from exile" is a problematic one, for it appears that very few of the exiles who returned were ever resident in the land in the first place. [The exile lasted for about sixty years (597-539 B.C.).] On the one hand, the land was never quite emptied of inhabitants, as many of the biblical sources admit, and as the archaeological record testifies. Jeremiah 40:7 is but one example of such passages that indicate a rather sizable population were left behind in Judah after the Babylonians came and carried off the leaders of the citizenry. For that matter, Jer 52:28-30 details a low, but probably close to correct, number of exiles, totaling forty-six hundred. This number represented between 5 and 10 percent of the population of Judah, after whose exile the poorest of the land were given areas to farm for the benefit of the empire. The missing details in the Chroniclers' account make it very difficult to reconstruct the manner in which the people who returned from the exile resettled in their property that had been in the possession of those who were left in the land by the Babylonians. The fact that there were many people who were left behind necessarily creates problems during the postexilic period, as is borne out by a reading of Ezra-Nehemiah and the resistance encountered to rebuilding the land (see also Carroll 1992).

The Chroniclers group these returnees—whatever their experience as regards living in the land and having been exiled from it—in three divisions: laypersons (vv 3-9); priests (vv 10-13); and Levites (vv 14-16). The laypersons belonged to the tribes of Judah, Benjamin, Ephraim, and Manasseh. Verses 17-34 expand the list of the Levites according to their specific functions: gatekeepers who guarded **the gates of the house of the** LORD (vv 17-27); maintenance workers (vv 28-32); and Levitical singers (v 33). Verse 34, as noted above, forms a bookend with v 2 near the beginning of the chapter. The care with which the Chroniclers detail division of the Levites into different jobs makes sense, in light of what has already been said about the Chroniclers' deep regard for proper temple worship. It is somewhat problematic to detail those who serve in the temple at a time when temple worship is not active (i.e., right after the exile), but surely the Chroniclers are looking forward to the time when the temple will be rebuilt and worship restored. If indeed Chronicles as a whole is written after the Edict of Cyrus (as is likely from its inclusion at the end of 2 Chr 36), then what has been written here has been written with the fulfillment of the edict in mind. Of course, the theological assertion is that the one who really made the edict is Yahweh, not Cyrus (compare Isa 45), at least from the perspective of Israel's faith.

FROM THE TEXT

A most interesting realization comes from reading OT texts from the Persian or Second Temple periods. The vision of Israel, and the vision of Israelites, especially the Israelite elites, was not at all unified in this period and perhaps not at any other as well. This is a sign of a vibrant society, rather than one in disarray. The vitality of arguments between those who are passionate, each of whom having what they believe to be the best interests of the community at heart, make for good reading. It is unfortunate when honest disagreements end in a breaking of fellowship. Surely there is a better way. Christians could perhaps take a cue from the ancient Hebrews who struggled so mightily with questions that were so important to them.

D. The Genealogy of Saul (9:35-44)

BEHIND THE TEXT

If the usual interpretation is true and Chronicles has a great sense of regard for the Davidic monarchy, still a sense of historical correctness prevents such a historical epic from failing to mention David's predecessor. That being said, the Chroniclers' treatment of Saul is on the whole quite sparse, particularly when compared with that of the Deuteronomistic History. For their part, the Deuteronomists seem every bit as enthusiastic for David and his successors—and, indeed, more so if the theory of James Sparks mentioned above is correct. Nevertheless, the story of Saul has to be told, and one suspects the reason why is more than just a necessary chore to get out of the way before the epic can deal with what its authors feel is the far more important king, even if they are not especially desirous of seeing that king's line reestablished.

IN THE TEXT

■ **35-44** The text relates some fifteen generations of the line into which Saul was born, beginning from **Jeiel the *patriarch* of Gibeon. Kish** (vv 36, 39) was the name of both the father and great-uncle of King Saul. Naming sons for close relatives has been a common practice in many societies, so while this is interesting it does not indicate a problem with the text (see Kimchi 2008, 105).

In this passage, as in the Benjamite genealogy at the end of ch 8, the name of Jonathan's son is correctly spelled **Merib-Baal** (→ 1 Chr 8:33-40). It remains to be noted here that there is no story of David's kindness to Merib-Baal (Mephibosheth) as one may read in 2 Sam 9. In that earlier story, perhaps in the attempt to shore up the righteousness of David's character (see Halpern 2001; Sweeney 2001), the Deuteronomists claim that David sought out "anyone still left of the house of Saul to whom [he] can show kindness for Jonathan's sake" (2 Sam 9:1). However, this is as has already been seen, namely, that the Chroniclers seem only interested in telling the story in a particular way. The reader has not yet come to proper narrative, which begins in ch 10. Therefore, one should expect a rather great deal of abridgment until the Chroniclers come to that information which is deemed more important. The information that was included in the genealogies is doubtlessly important, but the summary fashion in which it is presented may in fact indicate degrees of importance for the overall plan of the epic historical work.

II. THE HISTORY OF THE UNITED KINGDOM (1 CHRONICLES 10:1— 2 CHRONICLES 9:31)

▶Overview

The next lengthy block of material stretches over more chapters (twenty-nine) than did the genealogies (nine), but in terms of historical coverage it spans far fewer years. The genealogies started all the way back with Adam—an incalculably long time ago—and went to the time of the return from exile. The story of the united kingdom, by contrast, runs a little over one hundred years, from around 1042 B.C. to 931-30 B.C. Many important themes come into play in this section, including perhaps most prominently some of the things that caused the relationship between the tribes to deteriorate to such a point that the kingdoms divided.

As has also been noted, one of the primary differences between the presentations of Israelite and Judean history in the Deuteronomistic History and in the Chroniclers' History is how each treats the northern kingdom of Israel. The Deuteronomists spend significant time talking about the northern kingdom. However, because of their southern bias, most of the reporting—though not all!—is negative. For example, none of the Israelite kings do what is right in the eyes of Yahweh, in contrast to the southern kings, about half of whom do what is right—though not completely. By contrast, the Chroniclers only mention the Israelite kings in the process of synchronizing the reigns of the Judean kings with those of the Israelite kings (see, for example, 2 Chr 13:1). So, if the Deuteronomists have a southern bias, the Chroniclers have a still greater one. The Chroniclers' History is the history of Judah, though Judah is often called Israel, again probably reflective of this same bias.

A. Saul (10:1-14)

BEHIND THE TEXT

The present writer, as noted above, is not convinced by the argument advanced by Sparks that David, and especially the restoration of the Davidic monarchy, is not at the center of the Chroniclers' plan of action. By contrast, the length of treatment given to David's rise to power and time on the throne surely are a testament to the importance of David in the overall sweep of this version of the narrative of Israel's history. Nevertheless, as has also been noted, the Chroniclers are, at base, historians. As such, they had a requirement to present the history as completely as possible. Therefore, although the treatment of Saul is short indeed, it had to be included, if only so that the first legitimate Israelite king could be very quickly delegitimized in favor of the favorite son, David, and his favorite son, Solomon.

Some commentators also seem confused as to what they should do with the very slight treatment King Saul receives in 1 Chronicles. To cite just one example, Leslie Allen combines the genealogy of King Saul in ch 9 with the report of his death in ch 10 (1999, 366-70). The tremendous variation in genre between 9:35-44 and 10:1-14 seem to make this an unworkable strategy. Redeeming himself from this exegetical blunder, Allen is correct in reporting:

> Saul and David are like night and day. They function as models of . . . defeat and victory. The chronicler has given a pointer to their typological meeting by speaking plainly of Judah as first unfaithful to God and so exiled, and then returning to live again in their cities, especially in Jerusalem. (1999, 366)

IN THE TEXT

■ **1-6** It is unclear why the Chroniclers chose to begin the story of Saul with its end. In other words, why did the Chroniclers tell only the story of Saul's death, omitting all the rest of the colorful details of his reign? The Deuteronomistic Historians surely had a similar opinion of David as did the Chroniclers. Yet their earlier historical epic includes a great deal more of Saul than does their Persian period counterpart. True enough, that which the Deuteronomists do include of King Saul show him as an increasingly unstable, even psychologically imbalanced, ruler. However, the Chroniclers seem unconcerned to impugn the character of Saul the way 1 Samuel seems to be.

Saul's story, as short as it is in Chronicles, seems to bear division into two parts. In these verses, one reads the report of the king's death, and in the remaining verses what was done to his body by the uncircumcised Philistines (→ 1 Chr 10:7-14). Having escaped to the top of Mount Gilboa, Saul, apparently mortally wounded, orders his **armor-bearer** to kill him, lest **these uncircumcised fellows abuse** him (v 4). He does not want to be mistreated by the Philistines, and it is likely that the Chroniclers are not at all happy to report that such was the treatment given to Saul after his death. Saul commits suicide, and the armor-bearer follows suit, perhaps because he himself is afraid of what the victorious Philistines might do. An odd statement from v 6 arrests the attention: **So Saul and his three sons died, and all his house died together**. This statement is in direct contrast to 2 Sam 2:8—4:8, which tells the story of the reign of Saul's son Ish-Bosheth/Esh-Baal as king over the northern tribes, and 2 Sam 9, where it is reported that Mephibosheth (Merib-Baal) yet survives long after the deaths of Saul and Jonathan, moving David to care for him. On this verse, Allen (citing Williamson) suggests that the "chronicler has not merely added to his source a negative reference to a possible dynasty, but has highlighted the verse by creating a chiasm" (1999, 368). This statement further contrasts with the report of Saul's suicide in 1 Sam 31:6, where those who died with Saul are called "his men," i.e., his soldiers or perhaps his personal security detail.

Related to this issue in v 6 is a matter of internal consistency. The translation required by the Hebrew construction is **Saul and his three sons died**, as the NIV reads. In addition, the KJV, NASB, NJPS, NKJV, and NRSV all translate both 1 Sam 31:6 and 1 Chr 10:6 so as to give the impression that all of Saul's sons died, which in fact seems to be the rhetorical force of the passage, removing all possibility of continuation of the dynasty. However, 9:39 reports that Saul was the father of four sons, so given that Esh-Baal/Ish-Bosheth was not among the slain in the battle, something must be done to remove him as a contender to

David. Neither the Hebrew nor the Greek allows for a translation like ***three of his sons***, though in context such would seem to be warranted. Hebrew adjectives normally follow the noun they modify, whereas the number three here precedes the noun "his sons." Waltke and O'Connor cite an example of a number preceding a noun with a pronoun suffix, from 1 Sam 16:10 (1990, 277). This text is relevant for comparative purposes, because "his seven sons" there does not include David, who at that point of the story has yet to have been made to pass before Samuel. If one does not translate 1 Sam 16:10 as "seven of his sons," then one should perhaps not translate 1 Chr 10:6 as ***three of his sons***, even though in both cases there is one more son not included in the list. No direct information is given, finally, about the fate of Esh-Baal, though from the later narrative it is clear that he does not pose a threat to David's royal and dynastic ambitions. The Deuteronomists mention the death of Esh-Baal/Ish-Bosheth in 2 Sam 4:8, with a note later on in the same chapter indicating that David punished the murderers of the last living son of Saul in a gruesome, though apparently justified, way.

■ **7-14** Saul's body is in fact mistreated, and so by his suicide he accomplishes only half of what he intended. He did prevent Yahweh's anointed (see 1 Sam 24:6) from being killed by pagan swords. However, he was not spared from mistreatment at the hands of the uncircumcised. In the description of the mistreatment one finds again another discrepancy between the Chroniclers and the Deuteronomistic History. First Samuel 31:9-10 reports that the Philistines "cut off [Saul's] head and stripped off his armor . . . They put his armor in the temple of the Ashtoreths and fastened his body to the wall of Beth Shan." No information is given in the earlier text as to what the Philistines might have done with Saul's head, though the Chroniclers specify that they **hung up his head in the temple of Dagon** (v 10). Radak apparently understood this detail as one of those things that was left to the side (→ Introduction). He writes:

> What is omitted there [1 Sam 31] is filled in here; for they impaled his head in the temple of Dagon and his and his sons' bodies on the wall of Beth-Shan, and the people of Jabesh-gilead then took his and his sons' bodies. They did not, however, take his head from the temple of Dagon. (Kimchi 2008, 114)

The excessively morbid descriptions of what happened to Saul certainly is not what the first king of Israel deserved, even if he **consulted a medium for guidance** (v 13). Radak suggests that Saul's sin for which he was judged so harshly was compounded by not repenting and not inquiring of Yahweh again, but instead going to see the witch to seek a second opinion (Kimchi 2008, 115). That being said, it is necessary for the plot for Saul to be removed, in order that Yahweh could turn **the kingdom over to David son of Jesse** (v 14). It is unfortunate, as has been noted, that Saul merits in the Chroniclers' estimation only a description of his death—as opposed to the Deuteronomists, who treat at great length even those kings that they do not like (e.g., Ahab).

FROM THE TEXT

The short treatment given to Saul illustrates an important tendency not only of Chronicles but also of history writing in general. Put simply, historians have a large role to play in not only the selection of their material but also how it is presented. In other words, since Saul was much less important than David in the course of Israel's history, it was necessary to present him in an unfavorable light. The Deuteronomists and the Chroniclers both accomplished this task, but in different ways, owing to their respective ways of operation. The Deuteronomists characteristically present Saul as a less-than-average military general and king, who eventually develops mental anguish and ends by committing suicide. The Chroniclers, by contrast, even though they leave many of the details out, still present Saul as ineffective.

Theologically, Saul's ineffectiveness could be seen as God's punishment for the Israelites wanting a king in the first place. However, to believe not only says some distasteful things about God but also gives short shrift to Saul. With regard to Saul, though the Deuteronomists do say that Saul's sin ultimately brought him to ruin, the Chroniclers with their abbreviated treatment of Israel's first king leave the story tantalizingly incomplete. With regard to God, it would truly be alarming to suggest that he would anoint for Israel a worthless king, simply to "get back at them" for asking for a king in the first place. Saul certainly could have been a better king, had he not allowed his jealousy of David to get the better of him. God certainly wanted Saul to succeed, and he certainly did not delight in the death of one who turned out to be wicked (Ezek 33:11).

B. David (11:1—29:30)

▶Overview

The remainder of 1 Chronicles is David's story. The large amount of material given to the greatest of the kings should put to rest any speculation about whom might be the focus of the Chroniclers' attention. All of the kings from Solomon to Zedekiah—more than four centuries—are put together into 2 Chronicles. Yet, for all that, the Chroniclers do leave out a good bit of information that the books of Samuel include about David's military achievements, which set in motion David's rise to fame and popularity in the land. As has been repeatedly seen, Chronicles says only what is important to its purposes.

The general picture given of David's reign by the Chroniclers is one of almost complete success. Of course, David's principal failure, according to the Deuteronomists, was the incident with Bathsheba and Uriah. Though it is called "the case of Uriah the Hittite" (see 1 Kgs 15:5), Bathsheba was certainly victimized three times: once through the forced affair, once through the murder of her husband, and once through the death of her apparently firstborn son. Yet, for all the truth of that statement, the Chroniclers leave out all mention of the event, no matter who the victim really was. The point of such an omission, surely, is to lessen negative criticism on the great hero. Isser agrees with this point when he writes, "The sin is admitted in a way that does the least damage, limiting it to a single spot on the image of David as the ideal king" (Isser 2003, 159). The elimination by the Chroniclers even of this one spot cannot but be intentional. Nevertheless, this *is* part of David's story. Whoever the apologists for David may have been—and they are represented in the camps that produced both the Deuteronomistic and the Chroniclers' Histories—they have attempted to strike it out: in the former case by placing the regnal formula reference to sin where it does not belong, and the latter by erasing the episode entirely.

Other odd events in David's reign are "shined up" by the Chroniclers as well. To take what is perhaps the most famous example, the evil census taken in 1 Chr 21 is told in a much different way than the earlier story in 2 Sam 24. This time, the Chroniclers make an attempt to salvage God's reputation, while making a theological development in the process. The earlier story suggests that Yahweh ordered the census for which he then punished David and Israel. The Chroniclers' version, however, puts the blame where it should belong (according to later developments in theology), with Satan. On the evil census and its aftermath, Stanley Isser correctly notes, "While David admits his sin in ordering the census (2 Sam 24:10 [and 1 Chr 21:8]), Dtr's statement in 1 Kgs 15:5 about David's perfection except in the matter of Uriah ignores this episode" (2003, 177).

As has been said throughout this commentary, however, comparisons between the Chroniclers and the Deuteronomistic History falter precisely because of the long gap of time between them. All societies go through changes both small and large over the course of time, particularly over the course of centuries. It is unreasonable to expect later ages to understand, much less agree wholesale with, ideas and modes of expression from far earlier generations. That being said, the view of David is the same, for different reasons, in the two main historical epics dealing with him. (Ezra-Nehemiah is excluded at this time because, though a valid historical work in its own right, does not deal specifically with David.) Both the Deuteronomistic History and Chronicles are quite happy with David, yet the earlier historical epic is willing to admit the mistakes of its favorite son, which for some reason are left out in the later historical work.

1. The Beginning of David's Reign (11:1-9)

IN THE TEXT

■ **1-3** Though comparisons between the Deuteronomists and the Chroniclers are generally unhelpful, a fruitful one can be made here. The Deuteronomists spend a great deal of time detailing how David built up his reputation as a military leader. By contrast, the Chroniclers begin, as it were, right in the middle of things, assuming that this reputation has already been built. On the value of such a literary reputation, Isser writes:

> David was a legendary hero . . . who became a model . . . for the national culture, not unlike Achilles for Greeks and King Arthur for Britons. David appeared in this literature as a charismatic leader, the founder of a kingdom, and yet, also like Achilles and Arthur, a man with flaws and vulnerabilities. (2003, 2)

Thus, once again, the historical work called by the LXX "things left to the side" (→ Introduction) actually leaves to the side many of the things the earlier work includes. The only discussion of David's previous activity is the Hebron elders' admission that David was **the one who led Israel on their military campaigns** (v 2). The reader suspects that at least part of the motive for leaving David's military exploits on the level of "backstory" is to lessen the emphasis on his violent past, in contrast to the Deuteronomists, who were not shy to admit this aspect of David's character. Later on in the Chroniclers' History, the reader will see this violent past catch up to David. This is the reason that the Chroniclers, quoting David quoting Yahweh, give as to why David will not build the temple (1 Chr 28:3). (As an aside, the parallel text in 2 Sam 7 omits this notation.)

Finally 1 Chr 11:3 recounts the anointing of David as king in Hebron. The Deuteronomistic History reports that David reigned in Hebron "seven years and six months" (2 Sam 2:11), and thus at least so far the Deuteronomists and the Chroniclers are in agreement. However, immediately a divergence becomes apparent: 2 Sam 2:4 notes that David was made "king over the tribe of Judah," whereas the present verse suggests that the elders **anointed David king over Israel**. Essentially, the Chroniclers have conflated two anointings into one (see 2 Sam 5:3). This discrepancy can be easily explained through the Chroniclers' repeated use of the term "Israel" to refer to Judah, particularly after the division of the kingdoms (and even more so after Samaria's fall to the Assyrians). However, this explanation bears the mark of being too easy. Whereas 2 Samuel (see chs 2—4) indicates that the early years of David's reign were occupied, among other things, with a civil-war-like power struggle between the house of Saul and the house of David, Chronicles suggests that the transition from Saul to David was a simple one, almost a fait accompli. In a final difference, seemingly less important, though still worthy of mention, 2 Sam 2 does not mention that David's anointing fulfilled the word of Samuel the prophet as does 1 Chr 11:3. This difference is likely due to the vastly more important role prophets play in the Chroniclers' work than they do in Dtr.

■ **4-9** Attention turns next to David's capture of Jerusalem, after which he proclaims it his capital city. According to 2 Sam 5:5, David reigned in Jerusalem "thirty-three years," a note confirmed by 1 Chr 3:4 (→). Verse 5 of ch 11, with the Jebusites' declaration to David, **You will not get in here**, seems to be a kind of "politically correct" version of the story in 2 Sam 5:6, where a fuller taunt by the Jebusites reads, "even the blind and the lame can ward you off." One of the functions of this story is to explain how it was that Joab became the chief of the army. Leaving out certain details of the stratagem by which David and his soldiers take the city, the Chroniclers give only the most important information, namely that **Joab son of Zeruiah went up first, and so he received the command** (1 Chr 11:6). Joab would prove to be a loyal servant of David throughout the latter's life, and even though he balked at the evil census (→ 1 Chr 21), he otherwise served his master without flinching, receiving his due reward for having done so. The text reports here that, after David had completed some reconstruction work on part of the city, **Joab restored the rest of the city** (11:8). Verse 9 reveals the major thrust of the Chroniclers' view of David, in contrast to Saul; David was successful and became a powerful king because **the LORD Almighty was with him**.

FROM THE TEXT

It bears repeating often that comparisons of the pictures rendered of David in Israel's two great historical epics are fruitful for study of the biblical materials, even if comparing the two epics as whole documents is less so. The Chroniclers' version of the history indeed leaves to one side many of the stories included in Dtr that do not serve the purposes of the later work. In the process, the reader receives two vastly different versions of the history. David appears as the hero in both; yet in Dtr, though he is not a tragic hero in the dramatic sense, his character does have some tragic elements to it. According to the theological commitments of both of these great historical epics, David enjoyed success because Yahweh was with him (1 Chr 11:9). Otherwise, he undoubtedly would have failed as had Saul.

2. Identities and Exploits of David's Mighty Men (11:10—12:40)

BEHIND THE TEXT

A twentieth-century American axiom, adopted as a slogan of the feminist movement, opines, "Behind every great man stands a great woman." In the view of the present writer, this phrase is unintentionally pejorative, suggesting that women cannot be successful, but instead only support successful men. However, the principle lying back of the phrase remains valid. Behind all great leaders of human history, so it seems, have stood various support mechanisms. These mechanisms may be systems of government, charismatic personalities, sanguine orientations, highly effective groups of subordinates, or any number of other factors. At least three of these that have been mentioned apply in the case of the unusually effective—according to both the Deuteronomistic and the Chroniclers' Histories—King David. In support of this, the next major section details the identities and some of the exploits of those effective personages who lent even greater effectiveness to David.

Chronicles is a document that, as has been seen, is given the Greek title, "things left to one side." Yet here, however, this title may strike the reader as curious. Although the Chroniclers do include, apparently from the Deuteronomistic source, the stories about the deeds of David's mighty men—with a few changes, mainly in the spelling of names—the similar reputation-building exploits of David have, indeed, been left to one side (→ Introduction, section A, on the Greek title of the book). While this certainly does not mean that the Chroniclers had a higher opinion of David's supporters than he did of David, it is undoubtedly interesting. Perhaps the point is to demonstrate in a conclusive fashion that David's meteoric (in Chronicles, as opposed to steady in 2 Samuel) rise to power was predestined, as it were, in the mind of God to come about.

IN THE TEXT

■ **10-14** This first episode describes, first, the support that **the chiefs of David's mighty warriors** (v 10) gave to David's royal ambitions. Again, the Chroniclers leave these ambitions as backstory, though the details can certainly be supplied from the Deuteronomists. In other words, the Chroniclers are not attempting to suggest that David had the kingship forced on him against his will. Such a statement surely is laughable, in ancient as well as modern times. What is important for the present text is that David had some strong support in his favor, men who distinguished themselves in battle and thus had a right to lead the people as they **gave his kingship strong support to extend** it over the whole land, as the LORD had promised (v 10). Thus these events express once again the Chroniclers' theological slant. Allen notes in this connection, "Military victory was for [the Chroniclers] evidence of divine blessing on obedient kings" (1999, 378).

The episode recounts the deeds of one **Eleazar son of Dodai the Ahohite**, who displayed particular courage of arms at what might be called the battle of the barley field (vv 12-14) or, certainly less imaginatively, the battle of Pas Dammim (v 13). The parallel story in 2 Sam 23 reports that the brave one was "Shammah son of Agee the Hararite" (v 11). Furthermore, in the Deuteronomistic tradition the battle should rather be called the battle of the lentil field. Finally, the Chroniclers suggest that there were many valiant ones who remained in the field during or after the Israelites' retreat, or in any event more than one. This is shown in 1 Chr 11:13*b*-14: **At a place where there was a field full of barley, the troops fled from the Philistines. But they took their stand in the middle of the field. They defended it and struck the Philistines down, and the LORD brought about a great victory.** In contrast, 2 Sam 23:12 makes Shammah son of Agee into Sgt. York, winning the victory by himself, with Yahweh's help, of course. Radak is unfortunately of no help in resolving this difficulty, suggesting only that this text "refers to the three war heroes, and Shammah was the third. It might be, though, that Eleazar was with him . . . Still, Shammah was the main one in that war, as it says in the book of Samuel" (Kimchi 2008, 117-18). It is perhaps better to resort once again to possible divergent traditions. In any case, the existence of different traditions does not do damage to the inspiration of the text in any way, regardless of how such inspiration is to be understood.

■ **15-19** This next section is taken almost verbatim from 2 Sam 23:13-17. Seemingly the only difference between the two accounts is the Chroniclers' explanatory comment in 1 Chr 11:19: **Because they risked their lives to bring it back, David would not drink it**. Allen comments that this story "encapsulates both the devotion of David's supporters and his own devotion to God" (1999, 378). To the present writer, however, this highlights a bit of impetuosity or whimsy on the part of Israel's greatest king. He sends the Three on a death mission to secure water, which he then refuses to drink. It is perhaps only the unyielding, perhaps blindly unyielding, sense of loyalty on the part of David's mighty men that keeps them from murmuring against their captain and king. This is in great contrast to the way in which Israelites are said to have treated their leaders in the past. One need only think of the constant grumbling against Moses and Aaron during the wilderness wandering for a trenchant example. Yet David's mighty men engage in no such grumbling, probably also due in no small reason to David's tendency toward violence. Incidentally, that the Chroniclers bring David into view precisely when he is selected as king, choosing not to take up his days as a guerilla warrior, already colors the picture of David presented to the reader. Furthermore, the absence or alteration of details of the two big sins in David's life further cement the supposition that the Chroniclers want to present David in the most flattering light as is possible.

■ **20-25** Continuing the story of the exploits of David's mighty men, these verses reveal once again their nature as heroic saga. Some of David's mighty men were gathered into a squadron of thirty, while others were the best of the best, elite warriors known as **the Three** (v 20). The NIV correctly capitalizes **Three** in order to indicate that this should be considered as a proper noun. It seems fair to assume such an organization to be accurate, though the lack of any records regarding the organization of the ancient Israelite military outside of biblical record prevents certainty. **Abishai**, further, is regarded as **chief of the Three**. He is **the brother of Joab**, the one whom, according to v 6 of this chapter, was made commander-in-chief of the army after he led the attack on the Jebusites.

Abishai, according to the earlier account of David's story in 2 Samuel, had been loyal to the future king for quite some time (see various verses in 1 Sam 26; 2 Sam 2—3; 10; 16; 18; 19; 20; 21; 23). Among the verses extolling Abishai's loyalty to David is 2 Sam 21:17, which reports Abishai's having saved David's life during an attack by a Philistine wielding a very heavy spear. This note seems similar to one occurring in the next few verses of the current chapter, detailing some of the exploits of **Benaiah son of Jehoiada** (1 Chr 11:22-25). In a text quite reminiscent of David's slaying of the six-cubits-and-a-span (about nine feet, nine inches) tall Goliath of Gath (1 Sam 17), the Chroniclers report that Benaiah **struck down an Egyptian who was five cubits tall** (1 Chr 11:23). The description of the nameless Egyptian's spear almost exactly mirrors that of Goliath's spear in 1 Sam 17:7. One wonders if the two accounts have been conflated in the earlier tradition, in order to ascribe the mighty deed of killing a tall warrior to David. Further evidence for this comes in the ascription of Goliath's death to Elhanan in 2 Sam 21:19 (though the NIV there says "brother of Goliath"; → 1 Chr 20:4-8). Benaiah also figured later in the story of the Deuteronomists as the "hit man" in support of Solomon's rise to the throne, killing a number of those who supported the (perhaps more legitimate) claims of Solomon's half-brother Adonijah, at that time the oldest living son of King David (see 1 Kgs 1—3). For his **exploits**, Benaiah, though **he was not included among the Three**, received a post in David's security detail (1 Chr 11:24-25).

■ **26-47** The final verses of ch 11 give the names of the Thirty, which probably should be considered a proper name by analogy to the Three. Second Samuel 23 has a similar list, though indicating that "there were thirty-seven in all" (v 39). The actual number listed by the Chroniclers is at least forty-eight, assuming that **Hashem the Gizonite** (1 Chr 11:34) had only two sons. Perhaps the difference in numbers is meant to indicate that some replaced others as they were killed or otherwise left the group of the Thirty, though this is not made clear in either 2 Sam 23 or 1 Chr 11. In addition, comparison of the lists reveals a great number of differences in spelling both of warriors' names and their places of origin. One should not treat this as anything other than divergent traditions (for more, → Introduction).

Among those who are mentioned by the Chroniclers, **Elhanan son of Dodo from Bethlehem** (v 26) is the one to whom Goliath's killing will later be ascribed, over against 1 Sam 17. Also, the **Benaiah** of 1 Chr 11:31 may not be the same Benaiah listed earlier as the killer of the tall Egyptian. He may also not be the same Benaiah who supported Solomon, for in 1 Kings his father's name is given as Jehoiada. Finally, the mention of **Uriah the Hittite** (1 Chr 11:41) causes the reader to stop short. This is the only mention of Uriah in the entire Chroniclers' History, he who was so famous as the cuckolded and later murdered husband of 2 Sam 11. The Deuteronomists mention Uriah last in 2 Sam 23:39, in comparison with the Chroniclers' apparent attempt to lose him in the crowd. What for the Deuteronomist is David's greatest sin—and possibly his only one—is thus forcibly forgotten by the Chroniclers.

■ **12:1-22** There is a slight difference in Hebrew and English verse numbers in this passage. The second part of v 4 (starting with the name **Jeremiah** and ending with **Gederathite**) is v 5 in Hebrew. The remainder of the chapter is given vv 6-41 in Hebrew, vv 5-40 in English.

In terms of content, this text reaches back into the past, to give the names of some of David's partisans. That it was in the past that these men attached themselves to David is clear from the reference that this happened **while he was banished from the presence of Saul** (v 1). In other words, Saul was still alive at this time, even though the Chroniclers had already given the details of Saul's quasi-heroic suicide. However, lest the reader accuse the Chroniclers of sloppy chronological arrangement, it must be remembered that the arrangement has both chronological and thematic dimensions, and the Chroniclers as creative writers of theological history often feel free to downplay one of these dimensions in favor of the other (→ Introduction). The thematic dimension is thus at work here. For this passage connects nicely with the following one, indicating persons who joined up with David at Hebron. In the following passage, then, the chronological and thematic dimensions are brought back into alignment, since the setting governing the entire unit beginning at 11:1 is Hebron and the desire of "all Israel" to make David king in place of Saul.

A few other points deserve comment. First, the warriors who joined up with David at Ziklag were very proficient at arms; **they were armed with bows** and were able to shoot arrows or to sling stones right-handed or left-handed (v 2). Ambidextrous archers surely put an army at a great advantage, and as the point of this passage is to demonstrate that Yahweh was behind the attempt to replace Saul with David. The only thing that is missing is the story of the surreptitious anointing of David by the prophet Samuel. Indeed, Samuel is entirely absent from the narrative, as are the chieftains (traditionally rendered "judges") like Deborah and Jephthah. These absences again mark the desire of the Chroniclers to get to David and his dynasty as quickly as possible; in this way the thematic dimension again gains ascendancy.

Second, that many of those who defected to David's side **were relatives of Saul from the tribe of Benjamin** (v 2) had to be an extra burden on the reigning king. The Benjamites are only the first of the tribes to come to David, to be joined later by Gadites (v 8), more Benjamites (v 16), and some Manassites (v 19). Other tribes would join him after he went to Hebron, recounted in the next subsection.

Third, the song of **Amasai, chief of the Thirty** (v 18) is quite interesting. The first two lines in particular will be recalled in a negative fashion by the "rebellion" of the northern tribes against David's grandson Rehoboam (2 Chr 10:16). While here all of Israel is flocking to David to make him king, there all of Israel (north) will be flocking away from Rehoboam, to get a king for themselves.

Finally, 1 Chr 12:19-22 recounts reactions of some people to the activities of David at this time. Recalling an earlier story in 1 Samuel, the Chroniclers report David's attempted defection to the Philistines. The Philistines refused him, though, for they were afraid of a double-cross, surely with amply sufficient reason! However, defectors from the tribe of Manasseh joined him and helped him to build up his army, which the Chroniclers compare to **the army of God** (v 22). The Chroniclers, once again, attempt to legitimize the rise of David as Israel's king who had the support of the mighty and brave warriors of Israel. Comparing David's army to **the army of God** even before he assumed the throne indicates the Chroniclers' view of God's working behind the scene to make him a successful and powerful king.

■ **23-40** The final section of the chapter details the large support base David had from the tribes. This story apparently expands upon the statement in 1 Chr 11:1-3, in which "the elders of Israel" come to make David king. Here, the groundswell of popular support includes soldiers (12:23-38*a*, 39) and the populace (vv 38*b*, 40). Thus the Chroniclers seem to have replaced the story of Samuel's secret anointing of David while Saul was still alive (1 Sam 16) with this second, grander, more publicly visible demonstration of the people's support of David. This is certainly in keeping with the Chroniclers' emphasis on the Davidic monarchy. Perhaps Samuel was left out of the story precisely because his anointing of David could have been seen as an act of treason. The Chroniclers apparently wanted to minimize the hint that the Deuteronomists leave behind that David's rise to power was usurpation. By contrast, in the Chroniclers' presentation, David is no usurper; they do not even allow a hint of such an accusation. David rose to power as he should have risen to power: he simply filled the vacuum left behind by the death of the former king and his sons. The course of history would prove him to be a more able king than his predecessor, an assertion that is difficult to make for a usurper.

FROM THE TEXT

The Chroniclers dealt with the downfall of Saul in a much more abbreviated manner than did their predecessors the Deuteronomists (→ 1 Chr 10). Similarly, they tell of the rise of David different from the earlier history. Specifically, they leave out any mention of the growing conflict between Saul and David, which included such things as Saul throwing his spear at David and Saul's son Jonathan pledging his loyalty to his father's chief rival.

However, again like the story of Saul, the Chroniclers clearly still intend to demonstrate that God had abandoned Saul and had replaced him with David. They needed to demonstrate that God had given his blessing to David, and they did so by relating this remarkable series of successes. The interpreter must bear in mind that it was not because of any special virtue on David's part that he enjoyed this success. However, in the Chroniclers' presentation, it was David's obedience that made him a great king and the father of a mighty dynasty.

3. David's Plans to Build the Temple (13:1—17:27)

▶Overview

Having secured the temporal power through the support of the people, David wanted to secure a divine stamp of legitimacy for his rule by establishing a temple for Yahweh. In the eyes of the ancient world, the modern Western notion of separation between the religious and secular realms would have appeared ridiculous. For that matter, it is only through some debatable interpretation of the U.S. Constitution that such separation is warranted. Indeed, whatever its warrant, it is only imperfectly practiced, since in a country where government and religion are kept separate politicians are still forced to pass some kind of religious test before being admitted into the government. The ancients would not have gotten themselves into such a contradiction, for there was never a question of the separation of religion from politics. For that matter, religion and politics were often forced together, for usually when an army conquered another land they made it a point to destroy or otherwise desecrate the holy structures of the defeated land and also to take the idols or other artifacts related to the deity. Thus the Philistines took the ark of the covenant when they defeated Israel (see 1 Sam 5). Later on, Cyrus and the Persian Empire curried much favor with former Babylonian subjects by restoring many temples throughout the ANE (see 2 Chr 36 and the "Cyrus Cylinder"). It was surely in line with this idea that King David of Israel planned to build a magnificent temple for Yahweh. Though he ultimately would not be allowed to do so, he is correctly credited with establishing the plans for it, to be completed by his son Solomon. The next long section in the Chroniclers' History thus has to do with these intentions of King David and their ultimate frustration.

a. Bringing the Ark to Jerusalem (13:1-14)

BEHIND THE TEXT

The journeys of the ark of the covenant have been many and varied. Though this text is the first time the ark makes its appearance in the Chroniclers' History (because up to this point the history of the world and of Israel has been treated in a summary fashion), it nevertheless assumes a similar place of provenance to that which it holds in the Deuteronomistic History. In a recent book on famous myths from the Bible, Eric Cline wrote that attempts to find the ark will necessarily prove fruitless, since after it is installed in the temple in receives no further mention in the Bible. Cline writes: "The last time the ark was definitely seen by anyone was when Solomon placed it within the Holy of Holies inside the Temple in Jerusalem during the tenth century B.C." (2007, 127-28).

This fact is especially striking in the stories of the Babylonian sack of Jerusalem and the carrying away of the holy objects to Babylon the ark is not mentioned. One example of such texts is Dan 5 that, though it is later, still does not mention the ark of the covenant as among those things stolen from Jerusalem. References are made to the ark in Chronicles and Jeremiah, though Cline suggests that these should be discounted on historical grounds (2007, 128). Perhaps one reason why the ark was forgotten is that it contained many of the things recalling the Exodus, and the Exodus seems, at least in parts of the later biblical tradition, to have been supplanted as the primary miracle of Yahweh on behalf of the people of Israel (see Jer 16:14-15; 23:7-8). The Exodus was not totally forgotten, however, as evidenced by the fact that Passover continues to be celebrated. Yet it seems to have become merely one holiday, one occasion of deliverance among many, even though it was the first. In a similar way, the ark, even though it virtually disappears from the historical record, serves as a quite powerful symbol of God's deliverance accomplished in history. Thus Cline can write, "In short, we could write a book on the entire history of ancient Israel and Judah, as told from the point of view of the Ark of the Covenant" (2007, 149).

IN THE TEXT

■ **1-4** Verse 1 suggests that David did not attempt to move the ark completely on his own initiative, though it clearly was his idea. A peculiar phrase in v 2 serves to highlight the relatively late date of the writing of Chronicles. The NIV reads, **If it seems good to you**, which translates the phrase *'im 'alehkhem tôb*. By contrast, in the earlier Deuteronomistic History the characteristic phrase is *hayašar bĕ'ēnē PN*, which literally translates as "right/upright in the eyes of PN," usually but not always Yahweh. Verse 4 uses the earlier form of the phrase. Further, BDB suggests that one should amend the word *paraṣ* ("divide, spread"), apparently translated by NIV's **far** in the phrase **let us send word far and wide to the rest of our people**. The alternative given is *ḥaraṣ* ("resolute, brave"), which leads to the translation **let us be resolute and send word to the rest of our kinfolk**. The difference is not stark, though it seems that the modified form fits in better with the comment that the people had not consulted the ark during the reign of Saul (see v 3). It is unclear exactly what this phrase means, though Radak attempts to explain it as a further comment reflecting poorly on Saul, and by extension positively on David (Kimchi 2008, 124).

■ **5-10** Following their decision to move the ark to its new home, David and the people begin the process, though it is interrupted by a seemingly strange tragedy. The ark is brought on a cart, and by non-Levites, against specific biblical instructions. Later, Uzzah is tragically killed, although he was trying to save the ark from certain damage. Radak blames David for the death of Uzzah, accusing the king of improper exegesis (Kimchi 2008, 126).

■ **11-14** Allen suggests that the Chroniclers are creatively retelling the story of the ark in this chapter. The Chroniclers, according to Allen, "tantalizingly [leave] loose ends dangling until, like a mystery writer, [they] finally [explain] its twists and turns" (1999, 386). One could indeed see this episode, including the death of Uzzah when he had all good intentions—trying to save the ark from harm—as a foreshadowing of what is to come in the ultimate rejection of David as the one who will build the house of Yahweh. True enough, David gets something better in the exchange. Yet the text both here and in 2 Samuel presents David as someone who wants to pay the ultimate respect to Yahweh. Though his plans are ultimately frustrated, the effort was enough to earn him high praise in both major Israelite historical epics. The final note of the passage, that **the LORD blessed [Obed-Edom's] household and everything he had** (v 14) recalls the prayer of Jabez in 4:9-10. The difference between Jabez and Obed-Edom, however, is that Jabez asked (or one might even say begged) for blessing from God, while Obed-Edom happened to be in the right place at the right time. As a result, Obed-Edom's story is much better from the point of view of extolling the grace of God than is the so-called prayer of Jabez.

FROM THE TEXT

The principal theological lesson from this text is that the things pertaining to God must be respected. Jesus said as much when challenged about paying taxes to the Romans: "So give back to Caesar what is Caesar's, and to God what is God's" (Matt 22:21). On the one hand, this text contributes to a hasty negative view of the OT, since Uzzah was killed trying to prevent damage to the ark. On the other hand, however, Christians may take from this text that issues of form and proper behavior in worship make a difference. In other words, meaning well may not be enough when it comes to doing what God requires. One should remember that Christian tradition is one of the sources on which John Wesley drew. Christian tradition, in particular traditions regarding worship, thus gives a lot of important inspiration for how things ought to be done. This does not mean that innovation can never occur; it simply means that gains made in the past should not be given back merely for the sake of innovation.

b. First Assistance of King Hiram of Tyre (14:1-2)

IN THE TEXT

■ **1-2** This short text introduces a neighboring king who will be a great friend not only to David but also to his son Solomon. In terms of narrative time, this text takes place after the three-month waiting period described at the end of ch 13, during which time the ark had been keeping court at the house of Obed-Edom. The relationship between **Hiram** and the Davidic kings seems to be that of a vassal to overlords. As Allen points out, in 2 Chr 2:14 Hiram refers to David as "my Lord," a typical expression of subservience (1999, 388). This goes to show that with David, and perhaps even more so with Solomon, the kingdom of Israel is well established. Radak also notes that "the other kings were sending [David] gifts," a euphemism for demanded tribute (Kimchi 2008, 127). All of this material, naturally, serves to continue contrasting between King Saul and David.

c. David's Children in Jerusalem (14:3-7)

IN THE TEXT

■ **3-7** This passage returns to the genealogy of David and the list of David's children born during his thirty-three year reign in Jerusalem (1 Chr 3:4). There are a few differences between this list and the earlier one, however. On the one hand, this text lists thirteen sons born to David in Jerusalem, without mentioning any mothers, whereas the genealogy lists four, mentioning the name of Bathsheba, and nine others without their mothers. The number of sons works out the same in either case.

Shammua (v 4) is certainly a variant spelling of Shimei in 3:5 (confirmed by the *BHS* critical apparatus). **Elishua** (14:5) is perhaps not a variant of Elishama in 3:6; recall that the repetition of the name Elishama there was probably a mistake. Apparently, a different textual or historical tradition lies behind the present text. Both names have theological significance: **Elishua** means "my God (or god) saves" and **Elishama** (14:7) means "my God (or god) hears." Before worrying about the integrity of the Bible because of the presence of this inconsistency, it should of course be remembered that the standards of accuracy in the ancient world were nothing like what is required in the modern world. One should in fact not be surprised by differences like this and should pass over them with relatively little concern. Such is also the case with **Beeliada**, whose name appears as Eliada in 1 Chr 3:8.

A final difference between the two lists deserves especial comment. Here **Beeliada** appears as Eliada in 1 Chr 3:8. The NIV footnote comments simply that Beeliada is a variant of Eliada, but this is misleading and weak. It should rather be noted that "Eliada" means "My God (or god) knows" and **Beeliada** means "my master knows." Unlike Saul's son Esh-Baal and his grandson Merib-Baal (→ 1 Chr 8:33-34), this is not an attempt to strike the name of the Canaanite deity Baal from the text, for two reasons. First, the Chroniclers normally have been eager to *restore* "Baal" where it has been deleted by the Deuteronomists. Thus it makes little sense that the Chroniclers would allow such a removal of Baal-elements to stand in 1 Chr 3:8. Second, and more importantly, in Hebrew, possession is often indicated by adding a suffix onto a noun, called a "pronomial (or pronoun) suffix," so that the expression "my God" would be written *ĕli*, literally "God-my." It is generally thought impossible to add such a pronoun suffix onto a personal name, whether that name belongs to a person or a deity. There are potential exceptions to this rule, but these exist only in inscriptions like that of Kuntillet 'Ajrud and not in the biblical text.

d. The Battle of Baal Perazim (14:8-17)

BEHIND THE TEXT

Stanley Isser's 2003 work compares the story of David especially in the Deuteronomistic History to similar stories of heroic figures, many of whom "made their bones" through brave military exploits of one kind or another. David's ongoing battles with the Philistines took up where Saul left off. Indeed, if the sentiment, if not the parallelism, of song in 1 Sam 18:7, "Saul has slain his thousands, and David his tens of thousands" (see also 1 Sam 21:11; 29:5), is correct, then David's reputation as a mighty warrior was already assured at this early period. Such an understanding doubtlessly lies behind the desire of the people to make David king (→ 1 Chr 11:1-3).

Perhaps the reason why this song infuriated Saul so much is that the second line should have read, "The Son of Kish his tens of thousands," in keeping with the typical rhetoric praising the military prowess of kings. Yet a deeper issue remains. This is certainly yet another attempt by the authors or editors of the Deuteronomistic History to demonstrate Saul's ineffectiveness over against David's effectiveness. Even though this song was a compliment to Saul, ascribing an amazingly high "body count" to him, it was a backhanded compliment, for the one taken from the fields surpassed him with an even greater body count. The hyperbole of the song should of course be recognized, but the hyperbole should not conceal the central point: David is replacing Saul, both in the text and in the popular imagination.

IN THE TEXT

■ **8-9** Whenever a new king came to the throne in the ancient world, particularly if a new royal line was being established, tremendous violence often ensued. On the one hand, the new king often needed to dispatch remaining rivals to the throne (see 1 Kgs 1—3). On the other hand, enemy nations often struck at such times, hoping to catch the new king unawares and his realm in disarray, leading to an easy victory. This certainly seems to be the primary motive for the Philistines' decision to attack probably as soon as it became known who had replaced Saul, the immediate heirs also having perished. The Philistines had further motivation, however. They were the ones who had forced Saul off the throne of Israel, even if they did not kill him themselves (→ 1 Chr 10). As the later story plays out, however, they did not know with whom they were dealing in the son of Jesse.

■ **10** The Philistines had raided the Valley of Rephaim. This place was located on the border between the tribal territories of Benjamin and Judah. David seeks an oracle from Yahweh to determine if his military efforts will be successful. Seeking this kind of oracle was a well-known practice from the ANE as well as Greco-Roman times. In the Deuteronomistic History, King Ahab—who, of course, receives hardly any mention at all in the Chroniclers' History—seeks a similar oracle, but Yahweh sends a deceiving or lying spirit into the mouth of the prophets (see 1 Kgs 22). Here, however, Yahweh is not out to mislead David. He tells the new king that the victory is assured, and therefore it is.

When reading passages like this, one cannot help but recall similar stories of Yahweh's action, directing events (or deliberately interfering in them, according to one's perspective), for the working out of his will in history. Thus, for example, in the first battle of Ai (or "the Ai" [Josh 7], Joshua and the Israelites do not seek Yahweh's aid before going to attack the small city. The reason given for their defeat is that Achan stole some of the devoted items, but it may also be explained as resulting from any number of other factors, including blunders in military strategy or not seeking Yahweh's favor to begin with. In support particularly of the latter is Yahweh's promise at the beginning of Josh 8 that the battle has already been decided in Israel's favor. The words given to Joshua then nearly exactly mirror the words given to David now: **Go, I will deliver them into your hands**. With this assurance behind him, David goes out to join the battle.

■ **11-12** The battle of **Baal Perazim** goes quite smoothly and simply for David and the Israelites. The Chroniclers are not concerned with extensive reports of casualties and the like, simply stating **he defeated them** (v 11). The name **Baal Perazim** ("the lord has broken out" or "Baal has broken out") represents a kind of redemption in David's experience. In the last chapter, David's servant Uzzah had been broken out against when he tried to steady the ark. In this chapter, the Lord breaks out against Israel's enemies and destroys them. The enemies destroyed exist on both a human and divine level, for the ***Philistines left their deity statues behind. David said, "Burn them in the fire."*** The NIV translation of v 12 is not preferable, since the phrase **abandoned their gods** [or God, or god] in contemporary language means to adopt a new religious attitude. This is certainly not something the Philistines would have done. Surely, according to their own religious traditions, they would have had to beg forgiveness of the deities whose statues were burned, but they likely would not have converted to the worship of any other deity as a result of this defeat.

■ **13-17** This would not be the first defeat the Philistines would suffer at the hands of David. The enemy raided the Valley of Rephaim again, though this time David's actions are a bit different. A nontheological historical account would probably suggest that David was a skilled commander who employed varying tactics as the situation demanded. However, the Chroniclers being theological historians ascribe this different tactic to Yahweh's leadership. The results of this second battle are similar to the first, with the army having **struck down the Philistine army, all the way from Gibeon to Gezer** (v 16). No mention again is made of how many were killed. Though this is not the typical hyperbole of ANE battle reports, nevertheless complete victory is still being described. As a result of this victory, David's fame is spread far and wide, which is a point emphasized by Isser (2003).

FROM THE TEXT

Throughout the ancient world, nations ascribed military victories—and, for that matter, military defeats—to their gods (→ sidebar at 1 Chr 8:8-12, "The Moabite Stone"). When modern nations do so, the results are often disastrous. The American Civil War, for example, joined other wars in which both sides fought in the name of the Christian God. In more recent memory, wars fought in the name of either Allah or Yahweh have threatened to ignite a devastating class of civilizations. Evangelical pastors sometimes fall to the temptation of equating their nation—the United States, for example—and its intentions with God's purposes for the world. Nations must be very careful about claiming God's approval of wars undertaken for political reasons or gains. Moreover, framing modern wars in religious terms may lead to mistreatment or violence toward members of certain groups, like Muslims for example. Religious violence, or violence done in the name of religion, surely grieves the heart of God, no matter who the target might be.

e. Moving the Ark in the Proper Way (15:1—16:1)

BEHIND THE TEXT

As noted above, the site of David's successful battle against the Philistines, Baal Perazim, put a more positive spin on the tragedy that happened to Uzzah at Perez Uzzah. In the following text, the ark of the covenant is once again moved, though this time in the proper way. By placing the story here, the Chroniclers have repaired, at least in an ideological fashion, the tragedy done to Uzzah. In so doing, David brings the ark to Jerusalem, thus marking out this city as the one that Yahweh has ultimately chosen for his name to dwell. Though such language is not specifically employed by the Chroniclers, a similar idea is surely at work.

IN THE TEXT

■ **1-2** This short introduction to the story orients the reader. In v 1, **After** has been supplied by the NIV translators, apparently for smoothness of English grammar. This seems an unnecessary addition, for the verse could simply be made into two sentences: *He [David] built houses for himself in the City of David. Then he built the place for the Ark . . .* Further, an important textual note in this verse may in fact change the meaning. The text reads *vayyāken* ("he completed"). Multiple manuscripts, including the Syriac and Vulgate, read instead *vayyiben* ("he built"). The NIV follows the reading given in the MT (**he prepared**). In fact, the reading "he built" seems preferable, since a distinction is being drawn between the activity done for the palace and associated buildings, and the creation of a place for the ark. Such an idea accords well with the complaint of David, expressed later in ch 17, that he lives in a house of cedar while the ark *dwells under a curtain* (→ 1 Chr 17). Furthermore, David's reported speech in 17:12 uses a form of the same word, which is not "corrected" by the versions. Verse 2 briefly recalls the tragedy of Uzzah again, with David's recognition that only the Levites are to carry it. Thus the comment on this entire passage is titled "moving the ark in the proper way," something that David failed to do in the previous instance, with tragic results for one of his apparently otherwise orthodox and faithful servants.

■ **3-10** These verses give the numbers of those assigned by David to the task of carrying the ark from the house of Obed-Edom to the site prepared for it in Jerusalem. As with the genealogies, one suspects that this information is given for the sake of historical completeness, though not really advancing a particular theological point. The eponymous ancestors of the clans mentioned are either the sons (Kohath, Merari, and Gershon) or grandsons (Hebron and Uzziel, sons of Kohath) of Levi himself. The only group mentioned here but not mentioned in the genealogies are the ***Elizaphanites***. This clan is mentioned again near the end of the history in 2 Chr 29:13. The oddity is explained by Allen that the Chronicler "cites representatives of the three clans of Levites . . . together with their family heads at the particular time when the list was composed," yet he goes on to suggest that the Elizaphanites were an independent clan, apparently without supporting evidence (1999, 394). Ultimately, it is unclear why the Chroniclers included this group here and not elsewhere, though writing it off as a "mistake" probably betrays too much modern bias.

■ **11-15** These verses are the center of the text, both in terms of verse numbering and theological point. For here, David makes explicit what, as noted above, may occur as a somewhat natural connection between this story and the previous, improper and therefore unsuccessful, attempt to move the ark. The reader may also wonder why, if David in fact knew what the regulations were, did he not follow them in the first instance? The narrator is uninterested in this question, however. The only thing he does say is that the Levites carried out their duty **as Moses had commanded in accordance with the word of the** L<small>ORD</small> (v 15).

■ **16-24** The next unit details the names of the Levites who were appointed to play musical instruments, to be in charge of singing, and to be **doorkeepers of the ark** (v 24).

■ **25-28** After these seeming preliminary matters, the story is finally told of moving the ark. The movement goes as planned, because it is carried out in the proper way. There are no tragedies like there were before. Perhaps the lack of any problems contributed to the joy surrounding the movement of the ark, which included David cavorting around in a display of frenzy. This dancing led to ridicule coming from David's wife, Michal, detailed very quickly in the following verse.

■ **29** The story of Michal's disdain for David is considerably longer in 2 Sam 6. There, one is led to think that, behind her apparently shrill tone, is a concern for keeping the dignity of the king intact, for she says that David was acting "as any vulgar fellow would" (v 20). In a way, she was doing the same thing as Uzzah, trying to save the ark from the certain ruin of having fallen on the ground. This reading has two points in favor of it in fact. First, the Deuteronomists tell both stories together in 2 Sam 6, without the interruption of the list of Levites involved found in 1 Chr 15. Second, both Uzzah and Michal are given a death sentence for what they did, even though they probably did not mean any harm. Moreover, the judgment on Michal is perhaps more severe. In Uzzah's case, he was killed outright, which is certainly bad enough. However, Michal had to live her punishment for quite some time; the text tells us simply that she "had no children to the day of her death" (2 Sam 6:23). This is certainly a case of adding insult to injury.

■ **16:1** The text ends with a short concluding statement. The ark has moved to where it belongs. The people continue the celebration, having brought in various kinds of offerings. Throughout the ANE, the moving of things associated with deities was often a festive affair, but one that had to be done in the proper way. While other peoples were moving their deity statues, the Israelites were moving that which was considered to be God's throne among them. Nevertheless, as David had learned, the right thing must be done in the right way.

FROM THE TEXT

Reverence in worship is a matter that often leads to quite contentious debate. Innovations, particularly the introduction of musical instruments, changing musical styles, different liturgical elements, and the like, often cause lines to be drawn, dividing the house of God. This is most tragic, particularly due to the fact that form and content should be complementary. This complementarity means that a particular form should not be allowed to keep one from engaging with the content of the Christian faith. Once the church, or a denomination, or a particular local church, puts form in too high a position, then content is always lost. Even if the intentions are good—for example, to make apparently outdated worship forms more palatable for a contemporary audience—content should not be sacrificed in the process. At the same time, neither should content be allowed to assert too high a place, for meanings of words do in fact change over time, and ancient formulations sometimes do not speak to those with more modern sensibilities. As David relearned the lesson about how to treat the ark of God with respect, so contemporary Wesleyans should relearn what it means to strike a middle way, whether that be between Calvinism and antinomianism, between Catholicism and Protestantism, or between hymns and praise choruses.

f. Appointing Some of the Ministers (16:2-6)

IN THE TEXT

■ **2-6** Having moved the ark to Jerusalem, David appoints some to minister before it. This is the final step in conquering the city of Jerusalem. Not only is this called the City of David (2 Sam 5:7; 1 Chr 11:5), but it is now the City of Yahweh. As has already been noted, the principal city belonging to a given deity—whether Yahweh, Baal, or any of the thousands of others known from ancient texts—typically housed the principal shrine to that deity. As has also been noted, while Jerusalem was not the only place where there were active shrines to Yahweh (others were Arad in southern Judah, and probably also Bethel and Dan in Jeroboam's Israel), it was the preeminent place, particularly after Solomon finished the work of building the temple (→ 2 Chr 8:12-18).

An interesting point is the distribution to all who were in attendance of **a loaf of bread, a cake of dates and a cake of raisins** (1 Chr 16:3). The second of these two terms is especially difficult to translate. BDB suggests it is of uncertain etymology and meaning, and the NJPS translates it as "a cake made in a pan," which does little to alleviate the confusion. The term certainly had a precise meaning to the Chroniclers; the fact is that this meaning is now obscure.

Verse 4 outlines the functions of the Levites; they were appointed **to minister before the ark of the** LORD, **to extol, thank, and praise the** LORD, **the God of Israel**. Verse 5 includes playing **the lyres and harps** and sounding the **cymbals** as part of the ministry of the Levites. The priestly duty included blowing **the trumpets regularly before the ark of the covenant** (v 6).

g. David's Song of Praise (16:7-36)

BEHIND THE TEXT

The text of David's hymn of praise before the ark is essentially the same as portions of three different psalms. Verses 8-22 are quite similar to Ps 105:1-15 with some variations. The next few lines, 1 Chr 16:23-33, parallel Ps 96:1-13. The final part of the hymn, 1 Chr 16:34-36, is similar to Ps 106:1, 47-48. One should be careful in assigning relative dates to these compositions. On the one hand, there is the long-standing traditional connection between David and the book of Psalms. Though this connection has been questioned by much modern scholarship, going at least as far back as Sigmund Mowinckel and Hermann Gunkel, it still indicates one way certain psalms can be read. On the other hand, simply because Chronicles comes later in the canon (earlier in English Bibles) certainly does not mean that the Chroniclers had to have borrowed from the psalmist. Neither does it mean that the psalmist had to borrow from the Chroniclers, however. Determining the relative ages of compositions that mirror each other in this way is a modern preoccupation; the ancients would simply have been unconcerned with this question. By contrast, ideas such as those expressed in this psalm in 1 Chr 16, or the psalms in Pss 96, 105, and 106, were simply "in the air," or in other words were a part of the general line of thought in ancient Israel or the ANE more generally. If this is the case, one might not be able to identify the precise originator of the idea, even if one were inclined to try to do so. An explanatory analogy can be drawn to patriotic sentiments or "common sense," which are both products or intellectual constructs of a given cultural environment.

Radak suggests that the differences between this hymn and Ps 105 "do not affect the meaning" of the text (Kimchi 2008, 133). The present commentator disagrees. While Radak's statement does indeed hold true for *most* of the differences between this text and Ps 105, some of the differences are in fact rather significant. In the remainder of the commentary on the chapter, these differences will be laid out with some comment as to what difference they may or may not make for the meaning of the psalm.

IN THE TEXT

■ **7** The narrative introduction to the psalm immediately raises problems for the traditional association between David and the Psalms. The authorship of the Psalms is a matter of some debate, which is incidental to the present point. Briefly, however, **Asaph**, along with **David**, is among those to whom psalms are ascribed—whether or not they actually put pen to paper being beside the point. Ten poems in the Psalter are ascribed to Asaph: Psalms 50, 73, 75, 76, 77, 79, 80, 81, 82, and 83. It is unclear whether the Asaph mentioned here is the same as the one who is supposed to have written these ten psalms. Two points are interesting in this connection. First, the three psalms that this one echoes are not included among those ascribed to Asaph. Second, this psalm is not a psalm of David in the way that phrase is normally understood. David merely commissions Asaph and the others to sing. So, while the king provides the impetus for this song, it must be recognized that his influence in the creation of this particular psalm is, at best, secondary.

■ **8-13** The first six verses of this poem are almost the same as Ps 105:1-6, with some slight variations. They invite people to praise God, a typical first section of the hymn of praise in the Hebrew Bible. A series of imperatives urge people to *give thanks* and **sing praise** to God, activities assigned to Levites in 1 Chr 16:4 (vv 8-9). These verses also direct worshipers to **seek his face** (v 11), a challenge that will be repeatedly advocated later in Chronicles (2 Chr 7:14; 14:4; 15:2; 16:12; etc.).

There is a slightly different spelling at the end of the phrase *the judgments of his mouth* (NIV: **the judgments he pronounced**) (1 Chr 16:12). Aside from the NIV inexplicably changing the noun phrase to a verb phrase, the difference comes in the spelling of **his mouth**. Here, **mouth** is spelled *piyhv* whereas is Ps 105 it is spelled *piyv*. It is unclear whether the letter *he* has dropped out of 1 Chr 16 or been added to Ps 105. Either it is a variant spelling, of which the reader will notice some further examples later in the poem, or else it is evidence of a linguistic shift.

In v 13, the phrase **descendants of Israel** corresponds to "descendants of Abraham" in Ps 105:6. This difference seems an exception to Radak's claim mentioned above that the differences make no difference. This is so because of the supposed "erasing" from the history of the northern tribes, who were "in rebellion against the house of David" (2 Chr 10:19). The northern tribes were known, collectively, as the nation of Israel or the "Jacob tribes" after the division. Israel is the name given to Jacob in Gen 32:28. Moreover, Ps 105:6 has a less exact parallelism than does 1 Chr 16:13. In other words, **descendants of Israel** goes much better with **children of Jacob** than does "descendants of Abraham."

■ **14** There are no significant differences between the two versions of the poem in this verse. The NIV, however, seems too committed to basic meanings of Hebrew terms when it translates **his judgments are in all the earth**. A better translation would be *his judgments concern all the earth*. The Hebrew preposition *bĕ* in its basic meaning does in fact meant "in," but its semantic range is larger than simple location.

■ **15** Another significant difference occurs here. Asaph and the singers, at David's influence, are issuing a command (assumedly to the people assembled or to all Israel) to remember Yahweh's covenant. Psalm 105:8, however, renders this as an indicative: "he remembers his covenant." Radak suggests: "When the text here says, 'be mindful,' it means: Always be mindful of His covenant, which is with you forever" (Kimchi 2008, 136). In other words, the commandment here is to remember that which Yahweh always remembers. Yahweh cannot forget his covenant, and the reader recalls Isa 44:21 in this context: "Remember these things, Jacob, for you, Israel, are my servant. I have made you, you are my servant; Israel, I will not forget you." One may consider also Deut 4:31: "For the LORD your God is a merciful God; he will not abandon or destroy you or *forget the covenant with your ancestors*, which he confirmed to them by oath" (emphasis added). Warnings against the people forgetting God abound throughout the OT. For just one example, consider Job 8:11-13: "Can papyrus grow tall where there is no marsh? Can reeds thrive without water? While still growing and uncut, they wither more quickly than grass. Such is the destiny of all who forget God; so perishes the hope of the godless."

■ **16** This verse has a different spelling of **Isaac** than that in Ps 105. It appears here as *yiṣḥaq* with a *tsade*, as the name appears in Genesis. Psalm 105:9 reads *yisḥaq* with the letter *sin* (seen). One suspects this is a difference of dialect, not unlike the shibboleth/sibboleth incident in Judg 12:6.

■ **17-18** There are no significant differences here. The only difference at all is that Ps 105:11 has the definite direct object marker before **the land of Canaan**, while 1 Chr 16:18 does not. This is a stylistic variation.

■ **19** This verse reads *we were few in number* while Ps 105:12 has "they were but few in number." Here the NIV improperly harmonizes the two versions of the poem and translates **they were but few in number**. The alteration between they-language and we-language is typical in covenant renewal formulas in the OT. See Deut 26:1-11 for many examples.

■ **20** Again, here there are no significant differences. The verse recalls the nomadic existence of the Israelites prior to settling down in the promised land. The Chroniclers' likely first readers were themselves not settled in the promised land, so they would resonate with the experience of their ancestors.

■ **21-22** The version here reads **he allowed no man** (*'iš*) to oppress them while in Ps 105:14 one reads **no human** [*'adam*] **to oppress them**. This makes more of a difference to modern readers than it would to an ancient Israelite audience. In both cases, the NIV translates simply **he allowed no one to oppress them**, again a harmonization, though with more justification than the previous example. The statement in 1 Chr 16:22 is often misused. Sometimes, pastors or other church leaders suggest, on the basis of this text, that they should not be subjected to criticism or question by the laity. Martin Allaby discusses this with regard to corruption among Evangelical church leaders in the African nation of Zambia. Allaby writes:

> Informants described . . . [a] theology that undermine[s] accountability and honest behaviour. [It] teaches that since the pastor has been anointed by God he [sic] should be accountable only to God and not subject to any scrutiny by others in the church. (2013, 138)

Gender Inclusive Biblical Translations

The 2009 General Assembly of the Church of the Nazarene authorized the following statement on gender inclusive language:

> The Church of the Nazarene affirms and encourages the use of gender inclusive language in reference to persons. Publications, including the *Manual* and public language should reflect this commitment to gender equality . . . Language changes shall not be applied to any scriptural quotations or references to God. (*Manual* 2009, 372)

That the Bible has a bias toward the masculine is true without doubt. However, this reflects the general usage in the historical contexts out of which it arose, both in the ANE and in the Greco-Roman world. For that matter, the need for gender inclusive language is a relatively recent development in intellectual history. Still, the condition of the world has changed, and it is an important step to banish gender-based discrimination—even if it is unintended—from thoughts and spoken and written public discourse. Moreover, the Bible does at least attempt to make some improvements on the situation, including even some feminine metaphors for God, though not feminine pronouns and not any terms like "Mother" or "Queen." Women are certainly included in the biblical understanding of what it means to be created in the image of God (Gen 1:27). In general terms, the Hebrew word in 1 Chr 16:21 usually refers to humans of the male gender, while that used in Ps 105:14 usually refers to humans of both genders. Adam as the name of a particular male human occurs only after the creation of the woman. However, the Hebrew word '*adam* is used more frequently in Gen 1—4 for humans in general, both male and female, both before and after the creation of the woman.

■ **23-33** Here the text of Ps 105 is left entirely. First Chronicles is now following Ps 96. Actually they are, in a way, following the instruction of Ps 96:1, to "sing to [Yahweh] a new song." Throughout this part of 1 Chr 16, many lines from Ps 96 are rearranged: 1 Chr 16:23 begins with the second line of Ps 96:1, 1 Chr 16:24 skips the first line of Ps 96:2, and 1 Chr 16:30-33 rearranges Ps 96 in a number of ways, though most of Ps 96 does appear here. First Chronicles 16:27 has different vocabulary from Ps 96:6. The LXX, Syriac, Vulgate, and the NIV harmonize. **Joy** is read here, in comparison to "splendor" is Ps 96. Perhaps these are different aspects of the same theological point. As to which should be chosen, the answer that immediately leaps to mind is "both"; certainly both the unknown poet of Ps 96 and the Chroniclers chose these ways to express their common thoughts for their own creative reasons. A further difference is **dwelling place** vs. "sanctuary" in Ps 96. In 1 Chr 16:29 one finds a minor difference between **come before him** and "come into his courts" (Ps 96).

■ **34-35** The final three verses quote from Ps 106:1, 47-48. Verse 35 includes the liturgical direction **Cry out**, clearly indicating that this text was to be used in a worship setting. Verse 35 also reads **Save us, God our Savior** compared with "Save us, LORD our God" in Ps 106:47. The former expression may be earlier, since it lends itself to a more generic understanding of which god might come in answer to the prayer. The reader must remember that the OT came into being in a polytheistic context, and many of its statements are directly in response to/correction of this context and conception of deity.

■ **36** The final verse has the longer version of the command *Praise Yahweh*. The shorter form in Ps 106:48 is the most well-known Hebrew word grafted into many modern languages: "Hallelujah." They mean the same thing, of course. Also 106:48 is the end of Book Four of the Psalms, so it is interesting that David (or Asaph) would quote this, or the Chroniclers would quote David (or Asaph) quoting this.

FROM THE TEXT

The people of God have been using music and poetry to praise him from the earliest days of the faith. It is truly unfortunate that the form and style of music has often been a source of contention in Christian history, particularly recently. Whether particular music styles or lyrics are appropriate in worship can only be judged with great care. This evaluation must be undertaken very carefully, however. It is perhaps insufficient to accept all forms of music so long as they are employed in the proper spirit. Doubtlessly also insufficient is allowing any form of music that "works" to bring someone closer to God. At the end of the day, both the criteria used to judge and the judgments made are matters that should be subjected to the most rigorous examination, and in no case should anyone else's piety be challenged on this basis.

h. Leaving the Ministers to Their Work (16:37-43)

IN THE TEXT

■ **37-43** Having finished the great psalm of praise (whether or not he sang it himself), David departs the scene. In essence, the psalm of praise was a kind of introduction for **Asaph and his associates**, who are then charged to do their work, **according to each day's requirements** (v 37). In light of v 39's note that **Zadok the priest and his fellow priests** were left **in Gibeon**, it is clear that Asaph was not a priest. In any event, there is already a distinction being drawn between certain classes of people in Yahweh's service. This probably reflects ancient practice. It is most interesting that the foreigner **Obed-Edom and his sixty-eight associates** are put in such a position (v 38). Moreover, Obed-Edom is not just a foreigner but a Philistine! The Chroniclers have already suggested that "the LORD blessed [Obed-Edom] and everything he had" (13:14) because the ark remained in his house for a long time. In a way, therefore, this is yet another reversal of the tragic outcome at Perez Uzzah: the ark was left at Obed-Edom's house because of the danger involved in moving it. As a result, Obed-Edom and all of his household were blessed. However, once the ark was moved the blessing on this foreigner did not end, for he and his sixty-eight associates were given a place—assumedly one with hereditary continuation like the priests, although this is not made explicit—to serve before the ark. The final verse of the passage seems like a grand exeunt in a drama. The scene has reached its climax in the bringing of the ark to its resting place, accompanied with an appropriate musical number. The denouement of the scene is the appointing of Asaph, Obed-Edom, Zadok, and all the rest to their places. Finally, everyone leaves and the story changes direction yet again. A great accomplishment has been made—the ark of God is now in Jerusalem—so the Chroniclers, or perhaps in this case the playwright, now moves on to a new scene.

i. You Will Not Build a House (Temple) for Me, but I Will Build a House (Dynasty) for You (17:1-27)

BEHIND THE TEXT

The metaphor of a drama seems to work quite well in this part of Chronicles. Though the scenery has changed, the story is advanced in exactly the way it should be. Comparison with the famous story in 2 Sam 7 reveals very few differences, which seem only to be minor. Again, this does not mean that the Chroniclers took the story entirely from the Deuteronomists. Rather, it is much more likely that this story was part of the common, oral tradition. Interpretation of the text naturally turns on the ambiguous meaning of the Hebrew word *bayit* ("house"). In the first sense, David means temple, a dwelling place for God. But Yahweh, speaking through Nathan the prophet, means dynasty, an enduring line of kings (which, in the later history, was virtually unbroken until the Babylonian exile).

As for the importance of this text for the history as a whole, an important connection can be drawn here to 2 Sam 7. In an important article from 1965, Dennis McCarthy considers this speech to be of primary importance. McCarthy draws on the work of Martin Noth, who had described the structure of the Deuteronomistic History by considering the speeches of several major characters. McCarthy believes that this speech delivered by Nathan the prophet, at Yahweh's orders, to King David should be included in such a presentation. McCarthy writes, "This famous passage fills the same function as the key passages picked out by Noth; more, in conjunction with the others it sets in relief a carefully worked out over-all structure for the deuteronomic history as a whole" (1965, 131). Incidentally, the present writer believes that Nathan's confrontation of David in 2 Sam 12 is an even better speech for McCarthy's point; indeed, the two should be considered together. It is doubtful that this speech in 1 Chr 17 and others like it function in precisely the same way for the Chroniclers, especially since its companion (the confrontation after the sin with Bathsheba) is missing. However, 1 Chr 17 does represent at least the beginning of an important shift in the narrative, moving from David to Solomon. Indeed, a considerable amount of time and words will be spent on this transition: a sure indication that it is important for the author.

IN THE TEXT

■ **1-2** The first two verses are a narrative introduction. The only thing "missing" from the narrative is a note that this happened "once upon a time," although the word **After** at the beginning of v 1 hints in this direction. It is incidental to the point of the story to know how much time passed between 16:43 and 17:1. The story is structured in a familiar way. The king desires to do something and consults a prophet to see if the undertaking will be successful. Whether the task in question was a war or a building project, sovereigns in the ANE often sought the advice of whatever deity they worshiped. So David initially seeks the advice of Yahweh through Nathan. **Nathan**, of course, had a highly visible role at David's court. Nathan showed up at three critical junctures in the Deuteronomistic History. The first was 2 Sam 7, the equivalent text to this one in 1 Chr 17. Second was 2 Sam 12, the confrontation after the sin with Bathsheba. Third was 1 Kgs 1, where Nathan conspires with Bathsheba to convince addled old David that he made a promise for Solomon to succeed when he apparently had never done so. The latter two of these speeches are absent from the Chroniclers' version of the history, and this absence will be dealt with at the appropriate points below. Here, however, Nathan initially gives David a go signal: God is with David, so essentially whatever David proposes should automatically align with what Yahweh proposes.

■ **3-6** Immediately, however, it becomes clear that David's proposal is not in line with Yahweh's will. The revelation of this discrepancy to Nathan introduces the narrative tension on which this story in 1 Chr 17 feeds. The mention of **a house of cedar** in v 6 nicely parallels the speech of David in v 1. There, he was lamenting that he was in a house of cedar while the ark of God was in a tent, but here Yahweh says he never asked anyone to build him a house of cedar. The "mobile" nature of Yahweh's presence with Israel has always been a key feature. At least in some fashion, the attempt to "localize" Yahweh in a temple, even the grand one that David was apparently contemplating, represents something of a digression from an old standard. One must be careful, however, in saying that present circumstances are always worse than what has come before, for such is not always the case (see Eccl 7:10).

■ **7-15** In the revelation given to Nathan, Yahweh does not provide a specific reason why David should be disqualified from building the temple. David himself will suggest a reason in 1 Chr 22:8 (→), namely that he has **shed much blood in the land**. Yahweh's speech also turns, of course, on three different meanings of the word **house** (vv 1, 4, 10). David has built his own house (palace) and desires to build a house (temple) for Yahweh. Yahweh, however, does not desire a house (temple), but instead will build David a house (dynasty). The NIV correctly leaves all instances of the Hebrew word *bayit* as "house." Although there is always something lost in translation when moving from one language to another, it would be a tragic mistake to attempt to "correct" the Chroniclers' language by translating the successive uses of *bayit* as "palace" (v 1); "temple" (vv 4-6, 12); and "dynasty" (v 10). The Chroniclers, as has already been shown, are writers of great skill, and words were available in Hebrew for each of these specific concepts. However, the Chroniclers chose to use the same term in three different ways, and translators should respect the creativity of the authors. It is up to interpreters to explain the three uses, which is not, in the end, a difficult thing to do.

■ **16-27** David gives another long prayer, reminiscent of his song of praise in the previous chapter. Along the way, David recalls many of the key themes from Israelite theology. One finds notes on the unworthiness of Yahweh's servants (v 16); the uniqueness of Yahweh (v 20); Israel as the chosen people (v 21); and Yahweh's redemption of Israel with mighty acts (v 21). David sees himself as part of the nation Yahweh has redeemed, and he is humbled to have been given such a high position. He prays that Yahweh will confirm and ensure the word he has spoken (v 23). This does not express a lack of confidence in Yahweh, or the need repeatedly to convince Yahweh to do something. Indeed it is the very opposite, for in making this request of Yahweh, David already knows that it will be fulfilled, because it was Yahweh who made the promise in the first place.

4. More Events in David's Reign (18:1—21:17)

▶Overview

The Chroniclers' treatment of David's reign is long and detailed, as the reader might expect for a king who was thought to be the greatest ever to rule. Though this greatest king is not to be the one who will build Yahweh a house, nevertheless it is clear that the Chroniclers wish to present him as one who could do no wrong. The remainder of David's long reign is presented in a series of episodes. These episodes seem to fall into three general categories. First, David cements his reign through various military and diplomatic campaigns. Second, the king works at construction of the temple of Yahweh in Jerusalem, although his work, as has been seen, is preparatory only; it will be left for his successor to finish it. The third and final category has to do with events surrounding the designation of Solomon as David's successor. As will be seen, this designation takes on a decidedly different tone than the so-called Succession Narrative of 2 Sam 9—1 Kgs 2. Analysis of this difference in tone will, perhaps better than any other method, demonstrate clearly the differences in aim between the Chroniclers and the Deuteronomists. As a result, the serious reader of the two histories will have more confidence in explaining why two versions of the history were needed, produced in different time periods with different assumptions and methodologies.

a. Defeating Nations, Capturing and Dedicating Spoils (18:1—20:8)

▶ Overview

The first group of texts having to do with the continuing parts of David's reign summarizes some of the military and diplomatic efforts of the king. The reader sees David grow into the role of a seasoned monarch, as well as the nation grow into a position something like a regional powerhouse. Israel certainly occupied an advantageous position in geographical terms, being situated on major trade routes between Egypt and Mesopotamia. The Chroniclers, working from this information, suggest that under David—and especially under Solomon—the kingdom flourished. The beginning of this flourishing continued what David began at the battle of the barley field (→ 1 Chr 11:13-14). Included in this section are some failures and embarrassments for the kingdom, which are dealt with in a most speedily, and often quite violent, manner.

(1) David's Victory Stela (18:1-17)

IN THE TEXT

■ **1-11** This text is a summary of many nations whom David defeated. Summaries like this were common in the ANE. Often, information of this kind was put onto victory stelae, or large stone slabs, proclaiming the greatness of a particular king. Archaeologists have dug out of the earth many examples of this kind of thing, a fair number of which mention Israel. The function of these stelae was, naturally, to command respect for the king being honored. However, a further purpose surely was to extol the virtues or blessings of the particular deity worshiped by the great king. Thus, for example, the stela of King Merenptah, an Egyptian pharaoh in the late fourteenth century B.C. Merenptah claims to have utterly defeated, among others, Israel. Though in point of fact Israel was not completely wiped out as Merenptah boasts, the hyperbole evidenced by this stela is typical of such documents from the ANE.

Though no stelae of this type have been found for Israelite kings, it may be profitable to read certain biblical texts as Israelite stelae. These summaries of victories seem to have the same function as physical stelae made from stone, though they are included in the "paper" Hebrew Bible. Besides this text in 1 Chronicles, another example may be found in the list of the kings defeated by Joshua and the invading Israelites in Josh 12. The idea that several kings sent tribute without David bothering to defeat them is similar to Joshua's reputation having gotten through to Canaanites like the citizens of Gibeon who completed a deceitful alliance with Israel (Josh 9).

Finally, 1 Chr 18:2's note that **the Moabites . . . became subject to him and brought him tribute** agrees in outline with another stela from the ANE. This was written by the Moabite king Mesha, which also gives evidence for the general view of the gods held in the ANE. The one against whom Mesha ultimately rebelled was Ahab of the northern kingdom of Israel (see 2 Kgs 1). However, it is within the realm of possibility that Moab was subjected to Israel multiple times. For that matter, Israel may have been subjected to Moab several times, since the balance of power shifted quite often throughout the Iron Age.

■ **12-17** Mention of **Edom** (v 13) ties the two parts of the "stela" together. Like the battle of the barley field above, here one reads an even briefer summary of the battle of the Valley of Salt. Crediting the victory to the general **Abishai** is not unusual; the Chroniclers have established precedent for this in their report of the battle of the barley field and the victory of Eleazar son of Dodai (see 11:12-14). In any case **all the Edomites became subject to David**, so the results of the battle were as expected. Further to be expected is the final line of the "stela": **The LORD gave David victory wherever he went** (18:13). The final four verses give a few more names of David's officials; something similar has already been seen in ch 11.

(2) The Ammonite Incident (19:1-5)

BEHIND THE TEXT

The Ammonites and the Israelites go way back. The relationship between them was one usually filled with varying degrees of acrimony. Of course, the Israelites had in their arsenal a rather salacious story of the Ammonites' origins in Gen 19:29-38. Deuteronomy 2:19 says that God had given the territory of Ammon to the descendants of Lot as an eternal inheritance. The prophets Jeremiah (Jer 49) and Ezekiel (Ezek 25) both pronounced oracles of judgment against Ammon. After the destruction of Jerusalem, the assassin Ishmael ben Nethaniah, who killed the Babylonian governor Gedaliah, apparently had Ammonite backing (Jer 41).

IN THE TEXT

■ **1-5** The embarrassment visited upon David's emissaries, therefore, is nothing out of the ordinary in the relationship between Israel and Ammon. The motif of advisers giving apparently incendiary advice to kings, with disastrous consequences, will be repeated in 2 Chr 10:6-11. In the latter text, Rehoboam the son of Solomon asks what to do and chooses a course of action that leads to the division of the kingdom into two. Here, Hanun decides to humiliate the Israelite advisers, who have apparently come to pay their respects. It should be remembered that the Chroniclers are telling the story from the Israelite perspective, so naturally David's intentions are presented in the best light possible. However, as was seen above, the ascension of a new king was a ripe time for exploitation by nearby rulers. David counsels the embarrassed officials to stay at Jericho until their beards grow back. The parallel text in 2 Sam 10:4 suggests that the beards were shaved half off, which seems to make the embarrassment worse. David's ultimate response, however, awaits, and it will take a military character, in line with what the reader has come to expect of David.

(3) The Defeat of the Aramean/Ammonite Coalition (19:6-19)

IN THE TEXT

■ **6-19** David's revenge comes in the form of an all-out assault on the Ammonites. **Hanun** perhaps realizes that he made a blunder. Even if he did not wish to receive the emissaries from Israel, he realizes that he should not have caused them shame. In believing that the emissaries were sent with hostile purpose, Hanun actually set himself up for the very thing he was trying to avoid, namely a disastrous defeat at the hands of the Israelites. In any case, vv 6-7 report that the Ammonites were not at all prepared to meet David on the battlefield.

Klein points out that the geography of this text is a bit muddled. The difficulty comes after **Joab** divides the Israelite force between his command and that of **his brother Abishai** (vv 10-11). Klein writes that the Arameans' camp at "Medeba is too far to the south to permit the reciprocal emergency arrangements envisioned in 19:12 for the two obviously adjacent Israelite companies" (1999, 416). **Medeba** (v 7) could be replaced with *my rb'* ("the waters of Rabbah"), which would seem to line up more closely with 2 Sam 12:27. The parallel text has Joab reporting to David that he has taken the water supply of Rabbah. The spelling of the two options is quite similar—indeed, it is the same "error" noted repeatedly throughout the genealogies—so it is surely due to a copyist's mistake. Once the mistake is corrected, the story is straightforward: the Ammonites, with their paid Aramean partners, are soundly defeated. Then the ultimate indignity was heaped upon the Ammonites: **the Arameans were not willing to help the Ammonites anymore** (1 Chr 19:19). Hanun and the Ammonites, as the saying goes, could not even buy a victory, and the next passage in fact details their final defeat.

(4) The Defeat of the Ammonites (20:1-3)

IN THE TEXT

■ **1-3** In the first verse, there is a definite change from the earlier narrative in 2 Sam 11. This change makes all the difference in the world with respect to the picture of David that emerges from the narrative. Whereas 2 Sam 11:1 reads, "In the spring, at the time when kings go off to war . . . David remained in Jerusalem," here one reads, **When the time for kings to go out to war returned**. The NIV reads, **In the spring, at the time when kings go off to war**, choosing not to translate the Hebrew word *tĕšubah* (1 Chr 20:1). In either case, the entire story of David's adultery with Bathsheba, her pregnancy, the attempted deceit and subsequent murder of her husband, are left out of the Chroniclers' narrative. This is surely due to the Chroniclers' interest to present the Davidic monarchy in the strongest light possible. Eliminating the scandalous circumstances that lie behind Solomon's succession is part of that goal.

David does in fact go to Rabbah to claim the ultimate victory (as he does in 2 Sam 11). The Chroniclers seem to be playing a double game of "protect the king." On the one hand, David stays home from the battle rather than coming out where he should be. From one perspective, this is cowardice. From another perspective, however, there is security in not risking the king's life unnecessarily. On the other hand, the Chroniclers are protecting the king in terms of his reputation. The authors or editors of the Deuteronomistic History had already attempted to do so by taking the mention of David's sin and "burying" it in 1 Kgs 15:5, but the Chroniclers go one step further. In the process, Uriah and Bathsheba are erased from the narrative. Uriah's murder is forgotten, and what is more the involvement of Bathsheba in Solomon's rise is left completely out by the Chroniclers. It is almost as if she has been erased from existence; surely she has been erased from the story.

(5) Defeating the Philistines Again (20:4-8)

IN THE TEXT

■ **4-8** The Philistines were a persistent enemy for David. This text reports that the events took place **In the course of time**, meaning that it took place *af-*

ter a while (v 4). Three battles are recounted. In the first, the highlight is that **Elhanan son of Jair killed Lahmi the brother of Goliath the Gittite**. The description of a **spear with a shaft like a weaver's rod** (v 5) matches the description of Goliath in 1 Sam 17:7. The earlier, and far more famous, text gives the story of how David "made his bones" according to the Deuteronomists. Also, the Chroniclers in 1 Chr 11:23 describe Benaiah killing an Egyptian who had a similarly heavy spear. The parallel text in 2 Sam 21:19 suggests that Elhanan killed Goliath himself, though the NIV harmonizes the discrepancy by adding "brother of" to the Deuteronomistic text. Radak gives a cryptic comment on this problem: "Goliath the Gittite is the same as Goliath the Philistine . . . And it was not Elhanan who killed *him*, but David (1 Sam 17:49-50)! So there will remain something elusive about the verse in Samuel" (Kimchi 2008, 149-50, emphasis original). Further, 2 Sam 21:19 adds a note of where the battle took place (Gob) and that the father of **Elhanan** was a Benjamite, which leads some to suggest either that Elhanan was another name for David, or else that there are either two Goliaths, Elhanan is another name for David, or it really was Elhanan who killed Goliath and not David (see Japhet 1993, 368). Perhaps a better way through this is to realize that legendary stories like the killing of a giant by a boy often exist in parallel versions with both minor and major differences in detail. After all, the Bible did come to be in a particular literary and historical context; this is, after all, the way they told of the reputation of key leaders like David.

b. The Evil Census (21:1-17)

BEHIND THE TEXT

The story of David's evil census of the army and the punishment exacted for it is a key text in the study of Chronicles, especially the first two verses. This is so for three reasons. First, these verses highlight an important difference between the Deuteronomists' and Chroniclers' versions of this story. Second, the introduction of Satan into the narrative clearly marks Chronicles as a later document. Third, and related to the second, the introduction of Satan indicates something of a profound shift in Israelite theology toward the end of the period where prophecy had its heyday. This is in contrast, of course, to the strong role that prophecy has in the narrative of Chronicles.

IN THE TEXT

■ **1-2** The parallel text in 2 Sam 24 ascribes the impetus behind David's evil census as Yahweh's anger burning against Israel. However, the Chroniclers suggest that this census was taken as a result of Satan rising against Israel. Klein correctly notes, "Whether the chronicler made the change or it had already occurred in his text, it clearly represents theological rewriting" (1999, 421). One may venture to suggest that the Chroniclers—or the source text from which the history drew—attempted to absolve Yahweh of apparent complicity in the carrying out of an act for which he then punished Israel. Alternatively, Radak makes an interesting observation: "This [Satan] refers to what is ingrained in a person's heart from his youth" (Kimchi 2008, 152). While a conception of "original sin" or "total depravity" such as was developed in Christianity is not native to Judaism, this note could reflect some awareness on Radak's part of Christian ideas. (It should not be forgotten that some OT texts, particularly Gen 6:5 and Ps 51:5, hint at an at least inchoate form of the doctrine of total depravity or original sin.) Radak goes on to say that Satan is only a tool in the hand of Yahweh, used to punish Israel, much in the same way that Jeremiah said about King Nebuchadnezzar of Babylon.

Satan in the OT

In the OT, Satan does not play the same kind of role anywhere as he does in the NT. For that matter, even in the NT Satan does not have any kind of existence independent of God. Such an understanding or interpretation violates the monotheistic principles on which the Bible is built. Being monotheistic, however, sometimes requires the biblical writers to ascribe even some manner of evil to God. A statement like this requires careful nuance, of course: ultimately, it means that, though God may allow evil for a time, God's good purposes will always win in the end. This text in I Chronicles is the only place where the term appears in the OT looking like a proper name. In Job 1—2 and Zech 3, the "name" always appears as a noun with the definite article, and so in English one should use a lowercase "s," hence "the satan." Though some languages like Chinese sometimes use a definite article with a proper name, Hebrew almost never does so. That I Chr 21:1 does not use the definite article, therefore, leans in the direction of reading "Satan" as a proper noun with a capital letter, but this is not required, since "Satan" does not do or say anything else in the rest of the chapter. If this was to be understood as a proper name, then it would certainly represent a significant development in Hebrew theology in a dualistic direction. Seeing that "Satan" or "the satan" only appears three times in the OT, however, means that there is insufficient evidence to take a definitive stand.

■ **3-7** Joab, the commander in chief of David's army, initially expresses dignified reluctance to carry out the king's order. The king has ordered him to count the Israelites. It is clear from the text that the object of the census is the number of **fighting men** (v 5), not the whole of the population. The total comes out to be 1.1 million men able to pick up a sword. But Joab apparently did not make a full census, for he **did not include Levi and Benjamin in the numbering, because the king's command was repulsive to him** (v 6). The numbers reported were so large because, as Klein notes, the "chronicler . . . would have appreciated enormous numbers as reflecting the glory of David's reign" (1999, 422). More important than Joab's displeasure is God's displeasure, of course, and v 7 notes that God was in fact unhappy that David had had this thing done. While, by ascribing the blame to Satan, the Chroniclers apparently eliminate the problem of God being angry at David for doing something he, in fact, ordered, nevertheless it is never quite made clear why this was such a bad thing to do. The text only tells us that **This command was also evil in the sight of God; so he punished Israel** (v 7). The phrase **evil in the sight of God** is a common expression in the Deuteronomistic History; though the Chroniclers' usual phrase is somewhat different, here they use the form that was common somewhat earlier.

■ **8-17** The story of the divine response to David's sin is bracketed by David's prayer recognizing that he is the one who sinned. In the first instance (v 8), David admits his guilt. It is not clear what exactly triggered David's expression of remorse. He is not directly confronted with his sin as in the Deuteronomists' story of the matter of Uriah the Hittite. He does not even see the results of Yahweh's anger. Only the second instance of David's repentance (v 17) is given in response to the suffering inflicted upon Israel. The choice given to David is interesting: either **three years of famine, three months of being swept away before your enemies, with their swords overtaking you, or three days of the sword of the LORD—days of plague in the land** (v 12). David chooses what is apparently the least of three evils, yet some seventy thousand people die. A further interesting note comes in v 15: God orders the angel of death to stop slaughtering the people. That the angel **was then standing at the threshing floor of Araunah the Jebusite** sets up the following narrative, which details the selection of the site for the temple (on the place where the angel was ordered to stop) and the resumption of building plans for Yahweh's house.

FROM THE TEXT

Leaders are given the responsibility to do what is right and just for all their people (18:14). This task involves many different aspects, from selecting the best subordinates and allowing them to do their work to resisting the temptation to aggregate more and more power to themselves. Above all, leaders should be careful not to let their responsibility for maintaining the institution allow them to miss or to fail at the responsibility for justice to all persons.

5. Restarting Temple Construction (21:18—22:19)

▶ Overview

Though David will ultimately not be the one to finish the construction of the temple (ch 17), he is very involved in establishing the plans and securing the site for Yahweh's house. An analogy can be drawn between the relationship of David and Solomon regarding building the temple and that between Moses and Joshua regarding entering the promised land. Moses in Deut 1:38 recounts Yahweh's declaration that he (Moses) will not lead the people into the land, but instead Joshua will do so. In context this is clearly a punishment for Moses' sin. Though the language of punishment for sin is not used of David when Yahweh tells him through Nathan that he (David) will not build the temple, Yahweh tells him that it was because of all the blood he shed, which for whatever reason made David unworthy. The Deuteronomistic version of the story attributes a great deal of bloodshed to Solomon, it is true, and so this reason seems odd. At the end of the day, it is unclear why David was set aside for Solomon in this instance. In the narrative, matters related to building the temple will consume a great deal of space, indeed all the way to the end of 2 Chr 7. As things like this have to begin somewhere, they begin here with the purchase of the temple site.

a. Purchase of the Temple Site (21:18-30)

21:18-21

IN THE TEXT

■ **18-19** While in the OT theophanies are often accompanied by tremendous signs and wonders, great advances in piety often follow on the heels of tremendous sin. This is the recurring pattern of the book of Judges, for example. Here, after seventy thousand people succumb to the plague Yahweh sends to punish David, the foundations are laid for the temple, as it were, through the building of an altar to Yahweh. It is interesting to note that it is **the angel of the LORD** who instructs David through Gad to do this, rather than speaking to David directly. Perhaps, though this is not made explicit in the Chroniclers' theology, the sin that had come between David and Yahweh was so odious that Yahweh could not deliver the message directly or even through a prophetic intermediary, but needed to use an additional, angelic "buffer." One should not read too much into this in terms of a developing theology of angels and demons, though such was certainly in the background at this stage in Israel's thought; but it is striking that, in the same chapter in which Satan makes a very brief appearance there is something of a change of the way in which God acts toward the king.

■ **20-21** The sons of **Araunah** hide themselves because they fear, with a good amount of justification, that seeing an angel would be fatal. A fragment of 2 Samuel from the Dead Sea Scrolls restores to 2 Sam 24:20 the note that Araunah was threshing wheat (Klein 1999, 424). It appears that the Chroniclers have corrected a corrupted text. In any event, Araunah stops his threshing work and bows low to the ground when David approaches. His sons have paid proper respect to the angel of Yahweh, and he pays proper respect to the king. In both cases, the ones showing respect know their proper places.

■ **22-25** David's negotiations to buy the threshing floor are interesting from the standpoint of eminent domain. As with other depictions of David in the Chroniclers' History, the intent here is to present King David as much more honorable than others who have sat (or will sit, at this point in the narrative) on the throne. One example of this is the marked contrast between David's honorable dealings here and the dishonest machinations of King Ahab and Jezebel in 1 Kgs 21. There, when Naboth refuses to sell his lands to the king, Queen Jezebel trumps up charges against him to get him arrested and executed.

■ **26-30** David's completion of the purchase of the field and the required sacrifices leads Yahweh to call off the angel of death. Though he had wished the plague fall on him instead of Israel (v 13), it was only through his own penitential action that Yahweh's wrath could be turned aside. David began this mess, and he had to end it. Though Solomon will ultimately be the one to build the temple, David still has a part, as emphasized in the next passage.

b. Gathering Materials and Laborers (22:1-4)

IN THE TEXT

■ **1-4** This short text indicates yet another step in a lengthy process. Klein writes, "David's provision of materials for the future Temple was an ongoing task that he pursued for many years" (1999, 429). The reader might be inclined to ask, if David has already been told he will not be the one to build the house, why he bothers to assemble all the materials.

Two responses may be made to this. On the practical side, David could see himself as preparing the great work that his son Solomon will ultimately complete. One leader leaving work left to be done by the next leader is a timeworn and highly honored motif in the OT. For an earlier example, one may consider the different-yet-similar tasks given to Moses and Joshua. The original commission was given to Moses to lead the people out of Egypt and into the promised land (Exod 3:17). Yet this commission is eventually changed, so that Joshua is given the command to take up where Moses left off (Deut 3:28; Josh 1:6). Yet not even Joshua quite completes the taking of the land; it is a gradual process that apparently lasts several generations (see Josh 13:1-4) and is left for the subsequent generations to complete (see Judg 1).

On the other hand, a close reading of 1 Chr 17 indicates that David is not commanded to stop all work on the temple. Yahweh tells David through Nathan the prophet only that David will not complete the work. Instead, Yahweh will complete the work of making a dynasty for David. In neither case—Moses' not finishing the entry into the promised land and David's not finishing the temple—is the specific reason for not finishing significant for the motif of one leader passing on the responsibility to another. In other words, the earlier generation leader could be barred for sin, as in Moses' case, or for bloodshed, as in David's case. Either way, the principle of passing the work from one significant person to another stands as one of the most important literary (and even theological) themes in the OT.

c. The Charge to Solomon (22:5-16)

BEHIND THE TEXT

The transition from David to Solomon was clearly an important one for the Chroniclers. This importance is demonstrated by the fact that the Chroniclers include at least three different versions of it. The others may be found at 1 Chr 23:1 and 28:1-7. At first glance, this may appear as a degree of inconsistency on the part of the historian. This view is incorrect, however, likely motivated by a particular interpretive presupposition. This line of interpretation presupposes that inconsistency means error, either intentional or unintentional. Intentional error means deliberate deception, while unintentional error means sloppiness. Either seems to throw the authority of the Bible into doubt. Of course, it need not be so.

In point of fact, inconsistency may rather mean importance instead of error. For an example, one may consider various eyewitness reports of a tragic event like a car accident. The eyewitness reports will invariably differ in certain details, but in the main they are consistent, assuming a relative lack of bias on the part of the witnesses. A biblical example may be found in the Gospels, which certainly exhibit some differences in detail but agree on the importance of the central figure Jesus. In the case of the Chroniclers including at least three different versions of the designation of Solomon as David's heir, however, the situation is quite different. The interpreter has to deal with apparent internal inconsistency, which is different from the apparent external inconsistency between, say, Mark and John.

A much better view, however, is to consider these three episodes neither as repetitive of nor as inconsistent with one another. As the commentary will show, each one emphasizes a slightly different aspect. The effect of the whole, therefore, is to indicate the importance of this transition. Theologically, the importance of the transition is that the promise of God continues from one generation to the next. This is consistent with the wider sweep of the biblical narrative. For more examples, one may consider the continuity of the promise from Abraham to Isaac, from Isaac to Jacob, and from Jacob to his twelve sons in the book of Genesis. Literarily, the importance of the transition is that it moves the story along to its desired end, and, along the way, demonstrates that the successor does even better than the predecessor. Solomon's fame and influence will be great indeed, and this is where the story of that greatness begins.

IN THE TEXT

■ **5-8** This version of the transition to Solomon seems to come in three parts. This first part includes David's historical account to Solomon. In other words, these four verses answer the question that may well have been on the minds of those involved in the story: "How did we get here?" Certainly such a question was on the mind of the Chroniclers, or else they anticipated that their readers would have it. The third note of transition, 28:1-7, though slightly shorter than this one in terms of number of verses, will recapitulate some of the same ideas. Chief among the ideas communicated here is Yahweh's statement to David: **You have shed much blood on the earth in my sight** (v 8). It was noted earlier in the commentary on ch 17 that no specific reason is given relative to David why David should not be the one to build the temple. David, by contrast, reports a revelation from God that is more specific, though likely given around the same time. The revelation given to Nathan the prophet earlier concerned Yahweh and his nature specifically as a mobile God, rather than anything David may have done. Again, this serves to give a more complete picture of why it is that David should not be the one to build the temple. An example from elsewhere in Scripture of differently detailed accounts of divine revelation yielding a complete picture may be found in the multiple reports of Paul's conversion in the book of Acts.

22:5-10

Ultimately, regardless of the details, it is not Yahweh's will that David do this. To be sure, an interpreter could take these different details as reflecting different elements or thoughts within society; this is certainly a legitimate line of reasoning. Looking at it another way, a striking note comes to the fore: the content of Nathan's revelation in ch 17 was the promise of Yahweh building a dynasty for David. Here, David reports the name given to him by Yahweh for his successor.

■ **9-10** These two verses make the contrast between David and Solomon more specific. Whereas David had been a man of war, his **son . . . will be a man of peace and rest** (v 9). This statement is a play on Solomon's name, which derives from the noun "peace." The extra *he* on the name may or may not change the meaning of the king's name. It most likely is an unusual form of the third person possessive pronoun, so that Solomon (Heb. *šelomoh*) means "his peace." The pun is repeated in the second part of v 9. This highlights a common Hebrew usage, in which the name of a person is given, followed by a description of circumstances surrounding his or her birth or a prediction for the nature of his or her life. For example, in Gen 38:29, Perez, meaning breach, broke in front and was born after his twin brother had first stuck out only his hand. This feature is also visible in the NT with the etymology of Jesus' name (Matt 1:21).

Moreover, Solomon's importance includes his station as fulfilling the promise made to David (1 Chr 17). Yahweh promises that he **will give** [Solomon] **rest from all his enemies on every side** (22:9). Solomon will thus have the luxury to complete the expensive and lavish building projects he is given to do. If his reign had not been a peaceful one, he most likely would not have been able to build Yahweh a house. This perhaps lies behind the disqualification of David, though this is not explicitly stated.

Therefore, as is proper, David takes it upon himself to give Solomon instruction as to how to follow God's will.

■ **11-13** In this second part of the passage, David turns away from himself, so to speak, and toward Solomon. Most interesting in this charge given to Solomon is the invocation of the name of Moses, the greatest of all the prophets, the liberator and lawgiver. In 2 Sam 7, which, as has been noted, is the great promise of dynastic succession to David (the Chroniclers' version is in 1 Chr 17), the promise is unconditional; though Solomon and his successors may be punished for disobedience, God's love will never be taken away from them, as it was from Saul (2 Sam 7:15; 1 Chr 17:13). Here there is a bit of a conditional element: **Then you will have success if you are careful to observe the decrees and laws that the LORD gave Moses for Israel**. This is a note that is sounded again and again in OT leadership transitions. Just one example is the transition from Moses to Joshua in Josh 1. Moses is already dead, but Yahweh tells Joshua to remain faithful in order to have success. The final link in the chain between Moses-Joshua and David-Solomon is forged in the statement of v 13: **Be strong and courageous. Do not be afraid or discouraged**. In fact, the Hebrew of these texts is nearly identical: Josh 1:9 merely uses a different word for that which is translated **afraid**.

■ **14-16** In the third part, David shifts the focus back to himself very briefly. David details for Solomon the preparations he has made for the work he is giving his son to do. Solomon is one who has "rest from all his enemies" (v 9), so he has the leisure to complete the temple, which will serve as an unfailing monument to Yahweh's peace and protection. He also has an abundance of material: **a hundred thousand talents of gold, a million talents of silver,** quantities of bronze and iron too great to be weighed, and wood and stone (v 14). Finally, he has many skilled workers at his disposal. Everything, it seems, is prepared for him in advance. The upshot of David's charge, then, comes in v 16: **Now begin the work, and the LORD be with you**. This is a much nicer way of saying, "What are you waiting for?!" A similar call will be made by the prophet Haggai during the building of the second temple around the year 520 B.C., when that later project had come to a frustrating standstill (see especially Hag 1:1-4, which uses similar language to 1 Chr 17).

d. The Charge to the Workers (22:17-19)

IN THE TEXT

■ **17-19** Whenever one leader turns over a project to a designated successor, the predecessor often encourages subordinates to follow the new leader in the efforts going forward. As will be shown below (→ 1 Chr 28:1—29:30), the designation of Solomon to succeed David is far more direct and clear—and, perhaps as a result, far less violent—than the version told by the Deuteronomists. To be noted here, though, is the fact that not only does David command **all the leaders of Israel to help his son Solomon** (v 17), but he also encourages them with a theologically laced pep talk. Though the blood that David shed kept him out of building the temple, having done so made it possible for Solomon to do so. In other words, David's work of bringing military victories by the handful and, eventually, rest to the land allowed Solomon the luxury of building up the kingdom in relative security and safety. There was no need for Solomon to engage the army to secure the reign; it had already been secured for him. So David called on the workers to do whatever Solomon told them, just as the previous leader Moses had surely done with Joshua.

6. Divisions of Labor for the Temple (23:1—27:34)

▶ Overview

The reader has, by now, come to expect certain things of the Chroniclers. One of the key expectations of the reader is surely a prodigious amount of detail concerning the names and various tasks of key persons. These persons are both high and low in the social structure. They have many different activities. Without them, important functions would certainly have gone undone. Though in a sense these persons are "extra" characters, not affecting the narrative in a substantive way, nevertheless they are important for the overall picture the Chroniclers are painting. Moreover, it makes sense that the Chroniclers would take time to detail persons important for the temple at this juncture in the narrative, beginning with the boss.

a. Designation of Solomon as Successor (23:1)

IN THE TEXT

■ **1** As has been noted, the Chroniclers include at least three different versions of the designation of Solomon as David's heir. This may be in response to lingering doubt as to Solomon's legitimacy. However, the fact that the Chroniclers were writing during the Persian period, many centuries after the crowning of Solomon instead of his oldest surviving brother Adonijah, mitigates against this interpretation. It is more likely that the Chroniclers emphasized the smoothness of the transition in order to give hope to those living in the period after the exile. It is clear that the easy transition from David to Solomon was Yahweh's doing, and thus the Chroniclers' audience could rest assured that, though things might look bad, nevertheless there was hope to be had.

In any event, the transition from David to Solomon is much more violent in 1 Kings. Indeed, the direct designation is absent in 2 Samuel—1 Kings, even though 2 Sam 9—1 Kgs 1 is called the Succession Narrative. Another point advanced in the way the Chroniclers handle the succession is the building of the temple. The temple, as has been seen, occupies a central place in the Chroniclers' theology, especially in light of the historical context of the temple being destroyed. Similar thoughts may be seen lying behind the prophecies of Haggai. Thus, for the Chroniclers, succession means proper worship more than simply politics. By telling the story in this way, the Chroniclers reveal again their overwhelming concern for the temple, its construction, and the proper worship within it.

b. Assembly of the Officers, the Priests, and the Levites (23:2-5)

IN THE TEXT

■ **2-5** These verses tell of a counting of the Levites who are qualified to serve in the temple. A couple of concerns should be dealt with, and it appears that one answer applies equally forcefully to both. On the one hand, there is an apparent discrepancy between the age requirements for Levites in temple service. Here, the lower age limit for service is set at thirty years. Later in vv 24 and 27, however, the limit is set at twenty years. John Mark Hicks suggests: "Age qualifications may have varied based on the availability of personnel or the nature of tasks assigned" (2001, 221).

On the other hand, this passage at first seems problematic in light of the context of Chronicles. The reader needs to turn back just a few pages to the sinful census of ch 21. Jarick comments on this "seeming discrepancy between this blatant counting of Levites and the episode in ch. 21," concluding that the Chroniclers may have taken Num 1:4 and 3:15 into consideration (2007a, 156). Allen notes, further, that this census is not sinful because it "has a different purpose" (1999, 436). Through it all, it should be borne in mind that ancient documents like Chronicles should never be judged by the requirements of modern logic. This is to say nothing of postmodern thought, which generally "rejects out of hand the premise of any argument based on rationalism" (McEwan 2002, 71). Hicks's ultimate conclusion is spot on. He writes: "The Chronicler left the 'problem' in the text because he did not find it disconcerting" (Hicks 2001, 221). Putting the word "problem" in scare quotes precisely identifies the issue: this is only a problem for moderns; ancients, and probably also postmoderns, are much more comfortable with allowing differing statements to stand side-by-side. Three decades ago, Walter Brueggemann sounded a clarion call for a new way of looking at the Bible. He wrote:

> Dissection of the text . . . requires . . . splitting the elements apart and assigning them to different sources or authors. And that in principle robs the literature of its sophistication and tension which permits communication which is subtle and not flat. (1982, 133)

c. Another Genealogy of the Levites (23:6-24)

IN THE TEXT

■ **6-24** The repetition evidenced by this passage, rather than being pedantic, presents previously encountered information from a different perspective. The perspective adopted in the present text is from family heads, rather than individuals (Allen 1999, 436). In encountering these bits of repeated information, most modern interpreters were keen to isolate sources and eliminate what they concluded were secondary editions to the narrative. Postmodern interpreters, by contrast, are much more willing to entertain the duplications in the text as serving the artfulness of the final form. In other words, in the present intellectual climate of biblical scholarship many see historical questions such as which list was prior to which and which list was copied from or altered, which is precisely irrelevant to the interpretive task.

Allen goes on to comment that this "is not a proper genealogy, but a representative list of family heads current when it was composed, with narrative explanations where the list was incomplete" (1999, 436). Radak makes an interesting suggestion concerning apparent discrepancies between this and earlier genealogical lists. He writes: "It follows, then, that here it includes grandsons with sons: there are many cases like this in the book" (Kimchi 2008, 161-62). Radak further suggests that the name of **Shimei** (vv 9-10) refers to at least two different people. This is an eminently plausible explanation, for there is no reason why the ancient world should be unlike the present world in this regard.

The Chroniclers were willing, and indeed eager, to allow multiple lists with apparent discrepancies to stand alongside one another. In this respect, they were quite similar to the rest of the biblical authors. So, for example, one may read the accounts of the great flood in Genesis and see many differences of detail. Older historical critics tended to resolve this problem by postulating and identifying a myriad of different sources. The phenomenon is perhaps much better explained, however, by the understanding that the scribal culture of the ANE inherited a common stock of tradition, and made creative reuse of this or that part freely, without the restraint of modern logic. Postmodern interpretation, then, working with the final form of the text as the primary datum, has in a sense recaptured something of the way things might well have been composed in the ancient world. Ancient scribes were simply unconcerned with the apparent contradictions; they simply did not see these things as contradictions. In this way, they preserved many parts of the ancient tradition that might have been lost had they had the historical critics' concern to eliminate contradictions on the way to the establishment of a "pure" text.

d. A New Assignment for the Levites (23:25-32)

IN THE TEXT

■ **25-32** At David's command, the Levites are released from an older task and given a newer one. Yahweh had given the nation rest—a situation to be enjoyed mainly under the reign of Solomon. Another implication of this rest was that **the Levites no longer need to carry the tabernacle or any of the articles used in its service** (v 26). That this was done by David's command is made explicit in v 27. This verse also links the section back to the previous one and the counting of the Levites **from those twenty years old or more**. The reader will recall the note from Jarick cited above (23:2-5) that potential confusion about which Levites should be counted, and indeed if they should be counted at all (2007a, 156). Radak had already addressed this "problem" in the following manner: David

> had originally counted the ones who were thirty and above (1 Chr 23:3), in accordance with what is says in the Torah (Num 4:3); but at this point, he figured that since the Levites do not have to carry anything by shoulder, he would appoint the ones who were twenty years old and above also. (Kimchi 2008, 162-63)

This is a plausible explanation, for it keeps before the interpreter of Chronicles the admonition that literary context matters a great deal.

In any event, the Levites were tasked with assisting the priests (***the sons of Aaron***, vv 28, 32) in all things necessary for preparation for the holy work entrusted to the latter. Thus it can be seen that Israel is beginning to settle in to a relatively peaceful existence. According to the dominant theological viewpoint, this peaceful existence represented the blessing of Yahweh upon the chosen people, and in particular upon the Davidic monarchy. Though David was a man of war and shed much blood (see 1 Chr 28:3), the tide is turning now, and Solomon—who was promised as part of the lengthy dynasty to be given to David (see 1 Chr 17:1-27)—will be the primary beneficiary. Yet, even now, the benefit is being extended to the other dominant institution in Israelite society, that of the priests and Levites.

e. Aaronide Tribal Allotments (24:1-31)

IN THE TEXT

■ **1-2** In keeping with what was given to the Levites in the previous text—a new assignment for a new situation—David also reorganized the tribe of Aaron according to shifts. The Chroniclers helpfully remind the reader of a bit of more ancient history when they note that **Nadab and Abihu died before their father did** (v 2). More can be read about the rebellion of Nadab and Abihu in Lev 10:1-3. The crime they committed was to offer something called "unauthorized fire," which in the Leviticus text is not clearly explained. The Chroniclers do not mention why Nadab and Abihu died; for their purposes, it is only important that they died. Hence, the division of the descendants of Aaron is distributed among the lines of Aaron's two remaining sons, **Eleazar and Ithamar** (v 1).

■ **3-5** David reorganized the shifts of the Aaronide priests. This was due, in part, to the relative size of the two families. Radak summarizes this move nicely:

> David saw that the male heads among the descendants of Eleazar were more numerous than those of Ithamar (v. 4). So he took with him one representative from Eleazar and another from Ithamar and added eight shifts. He thus established twenty-four shifts, sixteen from Eleazar and eight from Ithamar. (Kimchi 2008, 164)

Once this division was done, the selection of assignments was done by the time-honored method of seeking Yahweh's will in ancient Israel, the casting of lots.

■ **6** The presence of certain officials overseeing the casting of lots and the assignment of shifts here in v 6 will connect to a similar note in v 31 at the end of the episode. Thus the entire story could be treated as one text, though it seems better to divide into two parts, namely the division of the descendants of Aaron here and the rest of the descendants of Levi in vv 20-31. In point of comparison, the only person mentioned in v 6 who is not mentioned again in v 31 is **the scribe Shemaiah son of Nethanel, a Levite**, who recorded the results of the lots-casting. Scribes like this were very important in the ancient world, as noted ably by Karel van der Toorn (2007).

■ **7-19** These thirteen verses give the exact results of the casting of lots, followed by a concluding narrative summary. Allen notes that "Ithamar's line is made up of numbers 2, 4, 6, 8, 10, 12, 14, and 16" (1999, 441). The other four even numbers and the eight odd numbers, of course, fell to the descendants of Eleazar. It is important to note that David was not establishing a new set of requirements or duties for these priests; such things were already stated in the Torah, as v 19 reminds the reader. David only established "the number and order of the shifts" (Allen 1999, 441).

■ **20-31** The remaining clans of the Levites similarly cast lots to determine their monthly shift arrangements. Verse 31 states more explicitly that it was those who were being assigned who **cast lots, just as their relatives the descendants of Aaron did**. The language was ambiguous in v 5 earlier. However, as noted above, the casting did take place in the presence of—and, as is likely, under the supervision of—**David and . . . Zadok, Ahimelech, and the heads of families of the priests and of the Levites** (v 31). The final note that no distinction was observed between the older and younger brothers will be echoed in 25:8 with the assignment of roles for the musicians. The commentary will note a slight variation in language, though certainly not in principle, at the appropriate time.

f. The Musicians (25:1-31)

IN THE TEXT

■ **1** This chapter begins in a fashion similar to the previous one, with a note that David supervised the division of labor among members of a group of temple servants. The particular servants being assigned positions in this text are the musicians. In addition, the characters who do the setting apart are different from the previous list. Though **David** is of course a constant, none of the priests or Levites are involved, as they were in the assignment of positions for their own group. Instead, and perhaps somewhat oddly, it is **the commanders of the army** who accompany David in the selection of singers by the casting of lots. Dealing with this question, Klein suggests:

> The army officers were presumably present to add formality to the occasion, as "all the leaders of Israel" were in 23:2. It is possible, however,

that the term ... (ṣabâ) refers to the "host" of Levites, as both the noun and its cognate verb are used in Numbers 4 and 8, rather than "army." (1999, 445)

This plausible explanation removes confusion, though definitive information is lacking as to whether it should be adopted. Jarick, for his part, accepts the translation "army" as in the NIV and elsewhere and turns it into an icy comment on domineering or, better, micromanaging leadership:

Notice that it is the king and the military officers who decide who is going to "prophesy" (v. 1), and they have control not only over who does so but also over how and what they prophesy. The end of v. 2—"Asaph ... prophesied under the direction of the king"—is a very revealing comment. (2007a, 159)

The present writer is inclined to follow Klein rather than Jarick here, though it is indeed striking that David does seem to take a more active role in the assignment of the musicians than he did in the assignment of the priests (→ 1 Chr 24).

■ **2-7** The three patriarchs of the musicians, from whose sons David and the "host" (whoever that was) selected persons to fill the assigned roles, were **Asaph** (v 2), **Jeduthun** (v 3), and **Heman** (v 4). These musical men are well known in the traditions of Israelite worship. In fact, several of the psalms are ascribed to one or the other of them. The standard caution against accepting the superscriptions of the Psalms at face value gains some support with the different prepositions used in these particular psalms. Nevertheless, these ascriptions can indeed be valuable clues as to how some in ancient Israel encouraged interpretation and understanding of particular psalms. To **Asaph** are ascribed Pss 50, 73, 75—77, and 79—83. The superscriptions of three psalms—39, 62, and 77—suggest they are for **Jeduthun**. Of these, Ps 39 is traditionally ascribed to David, *lədavid* (so NIV), but the preposition translated "of" David is the same that is translated "for" Jeduthun. Psalms 62 and 77 both read *'al-yəduthun*, which seems more appropriate to translate as "for," "on behalf of," or "concerning" Jeduthun. Finally, Ps 88 is ascribed to **Heman**, there called "the Ezraite," so that it may or may not be the same person (on the name of Shimei, → 1 Chr 23:9-10). A final interesting detail in this section is the Chroniclers' note that **they**, that is, the people being assigned roles, **numbered 288** (v 7).

■ **8** Above, with reference to 24:31, it was noted that the family of the oldest brother among the descendants of the Levites was treated the same as the family of the youngest brother. Here, there is a similar note, but with slightly different language. This verse says **Young and old alike, teacher as well as student, cast lots for their duties**. In both instances, the point is that the people in question submitted without question to Yahweh's will, as revealed in the casting of lots. They did not insist on a high place as, in the one case, descendants of an older son; or, in the other case, as a teacher rather than a student.

■ **9-31** The remainder of the chapter gives the details as to how the lots fell. This is a similar list as was found in 24:7-18. Whereas in the last chapter there was a narrative comment that the persons listed went faithfully to fulfill their duties according to the order in which they had been assigned, such a narrative is not to be found in this chapter. However, nothing at all should be made of this omission—it should, rather, from the context be assumed that the musicians also went faithfully to their tasks, according to how they were assigned.

FROM THE TEXT

It is a well-known bit of biblical tradition that the best form of piety is one that does not seek glory for itself. Examples of this idea abound. Consider Luke 14:10: "But when you are invited, take the lowest place, so that when your host comes, he will say to you, 'Friend, move up to a better place.'" Further, one may consider Rom 12:3: "Do not think of yourself more highly than you ought, but rather think of yourself with sober judgment." The latter thought is echoed in the introduction to Paul's great christological hymn in Phil 2:3-4: "Do nothing out of selfish ambition or vain conceit. Rather, in humility value others above yourselves, not looking to your own interests but each of you to the interests of the others." Incidentally, in Phil 2:4, the earlier version of the NIV makes a common mistake, adding "only" before "to your own interests." The 2011 NIV corrects this error, which blunts the force of the passage. Further comment on this point is of course beyond the scope of the present commentary.

It is a grave error for the church to value position and prestige over piety. Unfortunately, such a grave error is far too easy to commit and has indeed been committed far too often throughout Christian history. Thus certain movements at church renewal, from the Order of Saint Francis in 1209, to the Protestant Reformation in 1517, to the founding of the Church of the Nazarene in 1908, all of these and many others that both preceded and followed them, in part, renewed the church's emphasis on humility in spirit and mission to the poor and outcast of society. In the spirit of the Levites in Yahweh's temple, who submitted to their lot without insisting on a particular higher position because of age or wisdom, the Christian church of the twenty-first century could certainly reduce emphasis on the rewards that come from piety and replace it with emphasis on the renunciation required by piety. After all, did Jesus not say that anyone who gives up life for the sake of the gospel will find life eternal (Matt 10:39)?

g. The Gatekeepers (26:1-19)

IN THE TEXT

■ **1-19** The Chroniclers turn next to the details of those who were assigned to guard the gates of the temple. Unlike chs 24—25, there is no narrative introduction to the identification of the individuals assigned for the task. This can, however, be safely assumed from the foregoing. Verse 13 is reminiscent of the notes in 24:31 and 25:8 to the effect that no distinction was observed between different groups within the gatekeepers. No deference was given to age or experience. Instead, they accepted the will of Yahweh as determined by the casting of the lots. Also, in this text, there is a description of exactly how the lots came out, like was seen in 24:7-19 and 25:9-31. The difference is that, in this text, such description is not nearly so lengthy. The temple gatekeepers were charged with guarding **the storehouse** (26:17), as well as making sure that no one unclean entered the temple grounds. Thus these men are not mere "security guards," at least not in the sense this term is used today. By contrast, they had a decidedly religious function and were, assumedly, duly qualified by Yahweh for such a task. Klein notes: "The condemnation of temple worshipers in Isa 1:10-17 implies that in Isaiah's day this check [of worshipers' holiness by the temple guards] was a perfunctory one" (1999, 452). Other OT texts dealing with such qualification to enter the temple include Pss 15 and 24, the latter including a majestic statement of the holiness of Yahweh as well.

h. Temple Treasurers and Secular Officials (26:20-32)

IN THE TEXT

■ **20-28** While the genealogical record here is unified, the individuals described are split up into two spheres of activity. Those with temple treasury duties are listed in vv 20-28, while the secular officials are listed in vv 29-32. Within the treasury, two types of articles, and thus two types of treasuries, are envisioned. The first, described in 23:7-9, contained sacred vessels and other holy objects used in various worship activities. The second, mentioned in 18:11, served as "a combined bank and museum" (Klein 1999, 452). David donated many valuable items to such a place, from which weapons and other things could be taken out as needed (see 18:11). In general, a treasury like this could be used for maintenance of the temple. Klein continues: "Objects associated with various military campaigns were placed in this treasury, presented as trophies to God's grace" (1999, 452).

■ **29-32** As for the other persons listed here, they had been released from purely religious duties to serve what may be called "secular" functions. This term is put in quotes because it is somewhat misleading. Indeed, all of the people listed in this lengthy section of Chronicles were ultimately religious officials of one sort or another, principally because of their Levitical tribal heritage, but some seem to have been set apart for duties that were not *explicitly* religious in nature.

i. Army Divisions (27:1-24)

IN THE TEXT

■ **1-15** Whereas the army may have been involved in assigning duties for some of the Levites (→ 1 Chr 25:1), now the focus shifts to the army itself. There are a number of differences between this chapter and the ones immediately preceding. First, there is no genealogical record. This is surely due to the fact that the army did not need to come from a specific tribe, as did the temple personnel, all of which had to be Levites. Klein points out that "Levitical involvement in secular work (chap. 26) has eased the transition" from a discussion of temple personnel to the army (1999, 456). Finally, no lots are cast in order to assign this or that general to this or that division. Though Yahweh's will was certainly sought through some kind of ritual action, the specific action taken—prayer, lots, etc.—is not discussed, not least because this kind of ritual action is probably not as relevant to the organization of the military. The interpreter must bear in mind again, however, that there was nothing of the sort of forced separation between religious activities and government in ancient Israel. By way of similarity, the army divisions are still divided along the lines of their assigned months of service, as were the priests and Levites.

Each division consists of twenty-four thousand soldiers, which yields a total of two hundred and eighty thousand. Klein suggests this is a stylized number. He writes:

> It not only adopts a military format, but also reflects the influence of the twenty-four divisions of priests in 24:1-9. Israel is made to march to a priestly tune, like the levitical groups in earlier chapters. This microcosm of divine order provides a pattern for society. (1999, 456)

Jarick, as above, sarcastically turns this into a comment against the Davidic monarchy:

> This twelvefold repetition that there are an equal number of . . . military personnel on duty . . . drives home the point that the king's army is organized for constant alertness. If they are on the alert against non-

Israelite enemies . . . then Israelites at least might relax . . . But are . . . the Israelite people themselves being kept under control? (2007a, 162) The present writer finds these interpretations gratuitous. While the total number may be a bit suspect, nevertheless armies are typically organized into divisions of more or less equal strength.

At least two of the generals' names are interesting from later times. Some of the interesting details of the lives of these men come from the Deuteronomistic History, which, as has been shown, characteristically gives more "side story" details than the Chroniclers generally share. **Benaiah son of Jehoiada the priest** (v 5) was the one credited with killing an impressively tall Egyptian warrior in 1 Chr 11. As was noted there, Benaiah also served, according to the Deuteronomists, as the "muscle" behind Solomon's accession to the throne. This accession is much more muted in the Chroniclers' account, as has already been mentioned. Also, **Abiezer the Anathothite, a Benjamite** (v 12) is worth brief mention. While he is perhaps not as active a character as is Benaiah, his place of origin is important. It is also the birthplace of Jeremiah the prophet, who will cast such a large shadow over the latter parts of the Chroniclers' narrative.

■ **16-22** These seven verses give a slightly different organizational structure for the army. In Radak's words: "To this point the text had listed the warriors who were heads of the divisions, and now it lists the officers who served as tribal heads—one chieftain for each tribe" (Kimchi 2008, 175). Twelve tribes are listed, but the names do not line up with what is expected. First **Levi** and **Aaron** are listed (v 17). The tribe of Levi normally does not appear with other listings of the twelve tribes, because they did not receive a tribal inheritance during the time of Joshua. Also, Aaron is a subgroup of the Levites. Ephraim and Gad do not appear in this list, apparently replaced by Levi and Aaron. In addition, **Elihu, a brother of David** is listed as the chieftain of the tribe of **Judah** (v 18). Elihu had been a warrior for many years, and thus he was rewarded by his royal brother with a significant position over the Judahite warriors.

■ **23-24** A final interesting note comes in the last two verses of the discussion regarding the army. The Chroniclers report a negative situation arising from counting up the number of soldiers. Verse 24 says **Joab son of Zeruiah began to count the men but did not finish. God's wrath came on Israel on account of this numbering**. Radak and Klein both link this back to the account in ch 21, in which it was reported that Joab found the king's order distasteful (Kimchi 2008, 176; Klein 1999, 456). In the commentary on that verse, the striking difference from the Deuteronomists' account in 1 Sam 24 was noted, and it was suggested that this was owing to later theological developments in Israel. Though the story is truncated here, it probably is related to the same sinful counting. If for no other reason, it does not seem to make any sense that David, such a forthright, upstanding, and honest king—according to the Chroniclers—would make the same mistake twice.

j. Other Leadership Positions (27:25-31)

IN THE TEXT

■ **25-31** These verses describe a few of the people involved in administrative tasks for the royal court. Thus the reader finds a fairly consistent progression in the naming of all the people involved in the "executive branch" of Israel during David's reign. It was noted above at the beginning of the present chapter that the priests and Levites were discussed first, then Levites involved in tasks that were not specifically religious, then the army, and now finally strictly "secular" persons involved in strictly "secular" professions. With one more group to discuss in the next text, namely David's inner counselors, the lengthy description of Israelite officials will finally draw to an end, just in time to prepare for the transition from David's reign to that of Solomon.

k. Some of David's Courtiers (27:32-34)

IN THE TEXT

■ **32-34** The eight names listed here seem to form a kind of inner circle of David's advisers. Whereas in the text immediately prior the list had to do with various governmental officials, each of the persons here would understandably have a greater amount of access to the king. Whether they were advising the king or hearing something from him or simply being in his presence, they were clearly highly favored. At least, this is the picture that we get from the Chroniclers. This is the only place where **Jonathan, David's uncle** or **Jehiel son of Hakmoni** are mentioned. Many other Jehiels are mentioned; meaning "God is alive," it was probably a very common name (much like the name Jesus [Joshua] in the first century A.D.). **Ahithophel** and **Hushai** played major roles in Absalom's revolt in 2 Sam 15—16: the former was a defector from David, the latter a double agent for David. Following Hushai's false advice led to Absalom's downfall. The Chroniclers do not mention Absalom's revolt, yet the note that **Ahithophel was succeeded by Jehoiada son of Benaiah and by Abiathar** is indication enough that he was dismissed, for his successors would likely not have been mentioned in this passage had they not also served David. The Deuteronomists report that Ahithophel hanged himself after his advice was not taken by Absalom (2 Sam 17:23). Both father and son had trusted Ahithophel's advice (2 Sam 16:23), except when it mattered the most for the son. **Hushai** was not similarly replaced, indicating that he remained *the Friend of the King* throughout David's reign. *Friend of the King* was an official title

(Allen 1999, 457), a confidant and counselor, but indeed closer to the king than either of those two words denote. **Joab** as the commander of the army is sometimes thought to be a secondary addition, but the present writer feels that it belongs here, since the passage as a whole has been talking about top-level advisers to David, and Joab has been commander in chief of David's army since the attack on Jerusalem all the way back in ch 11.

7. Transition from David to Solomon (28:1—29:30)

▶ Overview

If the Chroniclers think David can do no wrong, the opinion of Solomon is all the higher. That this is the case is surely related to the Chroniclers' insistence on the importance of the Jerusalem temple. If the temple is important, then the king who built the temple is important. With notable exceptions (like Sparks 2008), both historical-critical exegetes and literary critics tend to take note of something that repeatedly occurs in a text. On the one hand, historical critics sometimes summarily dismiss these repeats as interpolations from a later editor, though about as often they take them as clues toward the mind-set and intention of the author. On the other hand, literary critics tend to eschew deleting repeated material. Rather, such things are embraced as important traces of meaning that may then be picked up by the informed reader in the construction of new meaning in dialogue with the text. In other words, literary critics are uninterested in the intent of the author, setting this aside in favor of the tendencies of the text.

In the books of Chronicles, one of the most often repeated scenes or ideas is the transition between David and Solomon as the first—and last—two "good" kings of Israel. Though some of the other kings, especially Asa, Hezekiah, and Josiah (since they each undertook religious reforms of varying size) are considered righteous before God, David and Solomon seem to be without fault. At least, the Chroniclers choose not to emphasize their faults, as the Deuteronomists are in no wise shy to do. The first designation of Solomon as David's successor, apart from the promise that God will build David a dynasty (which implies a successor), was in 1 Chr 23:1. The current section, however, delves more deeply into this transition. How the Chroniclers treat this, and that the text spends so much time on it, demonstrates in a clear way the ideological separation that must be observed between the Deuteronomistic History and 1-2 Chronicles. The Chroniclers put these stories to particular use, and by examining how this is done, one may gain much insight into the interpretation of the history.

a. Designation of Solomon as Heir (28:1-7)

BEHIND THE TEXT

Perhaps contrary to popular opinion and modern practice, royal succession was no simple matter in the ANE. Though it was normally the case that the firstborn son of the king would rule after the king died, this was not always the case. Often, the firstborn would be the target of assassination and other attempts to disrupt the dynasty. Also, in the case of rebellion, if the king was overthrown, all of his surviving sons would be killed as well, in order to prevent the now defeated dynasty from reasserting itself. This was particularly the case when the revolt did not have the support of the people. An example of this can be seen in 2 Kgs 11:1-3 and 2 Chr 22:10-12, where Athaliah, the only queen to rule over Judah, kills all royal claimants, except for one who was hidden. The Deuteronomists were not in favor of Queen Athaliah, and though her reign lasted seven years, the one rival she was not able to kill eventually proved her undoing.

The need to produce a surviving heir, in order to secure the succession of the throne, led to kings throughout antiquity having multiple wives. Though it was typical for the oldest male child to rule after the king was dead, this was not always the case. Sometimes there was usurpation, with a younger son becoming king instead of his brother. It seems that it was something approaching a universal feature that the successor needed to be designated. In other words, while it was typical for the oldest son to succeed, this was not automatic.

It was noted above that the ways in which the respective historical epics handle the transition between David and Solomon demonstrate key differences between them. The bloodiness of Solomon's accession to the throne in 1 Kings has been often noted. This has led some literary critics in particular to question the legitimacy of Solomon's accession. Taking an extreme view is Stanley Isser, who plainly suggests that Solomon usurped the throne that should have belonged to the oldest living brother, Adonijah the son of Haggith (1 Kgs 1:5). Isser writes: "The entire story [of 1 Kgs 1—2] is a transparent justification of Solomon's seizure of the throne and ruthless (though normal for usurpers) elimination of rivals and opponents" (2003, 167). Of course, such a negative opinion of Solomon is not necessary for proper understanding of the text, though it must be acknowledged as warranted.

The Deuteronomists spend a great deal of time describing the elimination of at least three of Solomon's older brothers. Amnon is killed by Absalom, in retaliation for the rape of Tamar (2 Sam 13—14). Absalom is in turn killed, after his almost-but-not-quite-successful attempt to topple David (2 Sam 15—18). The third, Adonijah actually proclaims himself king and garners many important people to support his claim, yet fails to secure the most important endorsement, that of King David himself. This failure proves to be his undoing, and on King Solomon's orders Adonijah is killed (1 Kgs 1—3). The way in which 1 Kgs 1—3 tells the story of Solomon's succession reflects the need for the king specifically to designate who will reign after him. In fact, the court intrigue that surrounds the succession includes a successful attempt by Nathan the prophet and Bathsheba, Solomon's mother, to convince David that he had designated Solomon as an heir (1 Kgs 1:11-27), and Solomon's own successful, in some cases violent, removal of all who would have been potential threat to his kingship (1:28—2:46). The Deuteronomists report the events without making any claim of divine approval/disapproval of Solomon's kingship. Any reference to divine approval of Solomon comes from Solomon himself in his dream encounter with Yahweh at Gibeon (1 Kgs 3:4-9).

By contrast, the Chroniclers, by making the transition from David to Solomon a smooth, bloodless one, seem to make the statement of inevitability even more forcefully. As was shown above, the Chroniclers tend to ignore, or at least severely downplay, those characters that either delay or do not significantly advance the story being told. Thus the reign of Saul, including his pursuit of David, are left to one side, along with the civil war between the house of David and the house of Saul. Something similar was doubtlessly going on behind the decision to leave out all discussion of Amnon, Absalom, and Adonijah. Though all three are mentioned in the genealogical record (see 1 Chr 3:1-3), no stories are told about any of them. This is surely because, having met their deaths before ascending to the throne, they were simply unimportant to the Chroniclers' narrative.

28:1-7

IN THE TEXT

■ **1** In the first, long verse, the narrator reports that David assembled all the key officers in Jerusalem. This is already different from Kings, according to which David is old and feeble, not capable of doing much at all (see 1 Kgs 1:1). As the reader has come to expect, the Chroniclers leave out all of the preliminary information regarding the accession of Solomon. There is no indication of any of the court intrigue, or any of the bloodshed, that one reads in the Kings account. As was seen earlier in 1 Chr 23, the overriding concern was for the building of the temple. This, surely, is the motivation for telling the story in this way. Theologically, it reinforces the idea of Yahweh's election of Solomon.

■ **2-7** The remainder of the passage consists of the reported speech of David. The text follows the expected form of a commissioning. The first part of the form is a historical recollection by the principal actor, in this case King David. For later examples, one may consider the speeches of Paul before the various governors and kings in the NT book of Acts. In these, Paul recounts his experience as a zealous persecutor of the fledgling Christian church, then undergoing a striking change through a confrontation with the risen Lord, and finally becoming a zealous Christian missionary.

David here recounts his long-felt desire to build a house for Yahweh. He experiences a similar transition as does Paul centuries later, though for a different purpose. He reminds his hearers that he made the plans to build the temple. However, he then had a confrontation with Yahweh through the person of Nathan the prophet—indeed a quite important character in the Deuteronomistic version—that steered him off of those plans. In 1 Chr 28:3, David reports Yahweh's reason for not allowing David to build the temple: **you are a warrior and have shed blood.** This point is not mentioned explicitly in 17:1-15. The emphasis in the earlier text is on Yahweh's lack of desire for a permanent structure. Nevertheless, whether David is unqualified or Yahweh doesn't want it, either way David is not to be the one to build the temple. However, David being unqualified makes more sense, for two reasons. First, the obvious contrast between David and Solomon regarding bloodshed ties this text to the smooth transition between the reigns. Second, Yahweh does eventually change his mind and allow Solomon to build the temple. If David had in fact been disqualified because of his being a warrior, then there is no reason why the decision cannot be taken later to have Solomon build the temple. In fact, the charge for Solomon to build the temple is given in the very next passage, so it is perhaps even more important to de-emphasize here that Yahweh had never asked for a temple to begin with. To begin with, the plan was that of David, which now has become Solomon's. Yahweh simply gives his consent, on condition that Solomon would be the one to bring David's desire for a temple to fruition. More than that, the text shows the enduring importance of the dynasty of David through the succession of Solomon—a dynasty that the text claims was willed by Yahweh. On this latter point both the Deuteronomists and the Chroniclers agree.

b. The Charge to Solomon (28:8-10)

IN THE TEXT

■**8-10** After summoning the subordinates to support and follow his son, David turns his instruction to the son himself. In language that sounds so familiar to anyone familiar with the theology of the OT, David tells Solomon that he has been given a dear opportunity. It is dear in two senses. First, it is dear in that it is a wonderful gift from God to be able to build God's temple. Second, it is dear in that the promise comes at great personal cost to Solomon. David says, **If you seek him, he will be found by you; but if you forsake him, he will reject you forever** (v 9). The first part of the sentence reminds the reader of "Second" Isaiah's call in Isa 55:6. In the (canonically) later context, restoration is about to happen. As for the context of the current passage, this is found on two levels. On the first level is the context within the story, namely the instruction of David to Solomon.

On perhaps a more important level, however, is the context of the hearers and readers of 1 Chronicles. They have, at least most of them, recently experienced a restoration, of sorts and to varying degrees, to be sure. Yet, the situating of this promise/threat in the context of a temple about to be built surely has ramifications for the Persian/second temple context of Chronicles. One also thinks of the prophecy of Haggai in connection with this. Haggai upbraided his audience for not undertaking to complete the temple. Though it may not have been as good as the former one (Hag 2:3), the promise of Yahweh rested upon it, because he had willed it to be built. Intertextual investigations of this sort often yield quite valuable results for interpretation of the biblical text.

c. David Gives Solomon the Plans (28:11-21)

BEHIND THE TEXT

Though David was not destined by God to be the builder of the temple, he was nevertheless instrumental in achieving the goal. As noted above in the commentary to ch 22, David testified to Solomon that David's violent life was what prevented him from carrying out this holy task. In literary terms, the transfer of power from David to Solomon was undoubtedly a major turning point in the story the Chroniclers were telling. That this is so is demonstrated by the number of times it appears, each time with significant variation. Rather than being repetitive, however, these retellings are interesting, precisely because of the creative variations.

IN THE TEXT

■ **11-12** The interpreter should be careful not to read too much later doctrine into the language being used here. First, in v 11 there is an interesting expression for the holy of holies: **house of atonement**. Though the noun *kapporet*, meaning something like "atonement stand," occurs in several places, this is the only time in the OT it appears with the noun *bet* ("house") (NIV: **place of atonement** is an acceptable translation). This *hapax legomenon* makes good sense, then, since the holy of holies was where atonement took place. The note in v 12 that **the Spirit had put in his mind** is perhaps to be connected with v

2, where David says, "I had it in my heart" to build a temple for Yahweh (so Klein 1999, 462).

■ **13-21** Verses 13-21 continue the summary of the charges David gave to Solomon. This summary includes the **instructions for the divisions of the priests and Levites** (v 13) and thus essentially duplicates earlier material. David's instruction to Solomon, that he should **Be strong and courageous** (v 20) echoes 22:13 (→ for other uses of the phrase), though adding here the specific instruction **do the work. Do not be afraid or discouraged** (28:20) is a standard instruction given to successors, and especially those called by Yahweh to take up a particular assignment. The reader should be careful not to misunderstand the final part of this verse. It seems on the surface to suggest that Yahweh might **fail you or forsake you** once the work on the temple is finished, though this is clearly not the case. Some of the later kings will go astray after a certain key figure in their lives dies or a certain event passes (→ 2 Chr 24:2 on King Joash). However, Yahweh's provision for Solomon would certainly not be exhausted once this major work was completed. David's instruction merely suggests that Solomon will be able to complete this work without having to worry that Yahweh will fail at any point during the work to support him. This is so because David has already made everything **ready for all the work on the temple of God . . . The officials and all the people will obey your every command** (1 Chr 28:21). This final phrase is reminiscent of Josh 1:18. This earlier text includes an oath taken by the people pledging their lives as guarantee of their allegiance to Joshua. Though that element is not stated here, one may perhaps assume it.

FROM THE TEXT

It is tempting for the reader—and the NIV is complicit in this—to see here, especially in v 12, "the Holy Spirit" of later Christian doctrine. On the one hand, one would of course want to say that the Holy Spirit has always been active in the affairs of the righteous. On the other hand, however, this suggestion is a flat anachronism. The OT writers simply did not have the same conception of the Holy Spirit as did the early Christians. More akin to the Chroniclers' sentiments is the legitimacy of the second temple as compared with the first temple. The first temple, with its plan similar to the tabernacle, made David into a second Moses. Perhaps in the same way, the second temple, with its plan similar to the first temple, made its builders into a second David. The continuity of the inspiration of God—whether that is described in terms of "the Holy Spirit" or something just on the heart of a righteous person, is that which is communicated most forcefully by this text.

d. The People Dedicate Themselves (29:1-9)

BEHIND THE TEXT

The theme of the people of Israel religiously dedicating themselves is found often in the OT. To cite just one example, Joshua orders the people to sanctify themselves prior to crossing the Jordan and taking the city of Jericho in a most unusual way (Josh 3:5). In this text, the dedication of the people comes in the form of donating things for the building of the temple. In the historical context of the Chroniclers, the second temple was being built or had just been built. This new building generated some controversy, as well as a general lack of resolve (see, for example, the prophecy of Haggai). Perhaps a text like this could be meant to encourage those whose courage was failing.

IN THE TEXT

■ **1-5** This text falls rather neatly into two parts. In the first five verses, David recounts for the people what he has done in making things ready for Solomon. Thus the conversation has moved out to a wider audience, so that the reader may be justified in seeing the previous text and the charge to Solomon found there as more of a private affair. After David gives the summary of all that he has done and all that he has given, he then issues the challenge to the people: **who is willing to consecrate themselves to the LORD today?** (v 5).

■ **6-9** The people respond eagerly, and the Chroniclers report vast sums that came in for the building of the temple. Undoubtedly a text like this was originally meant to encourage those who did not have much resource, and who yet were still called on to give of what they had. The interpreter should notice that there is no promise of reward for giving made either explicitly or implicitly in this text. Instead, the people are giving out of the sheer sense of giving. Moreover, they are not giving begrudgingly, out of a sense of obligation, as if they could appease Yahweh and turn away his wrath by contributing a large amount of money to **Jehiel the Gershonite** (v 8) and the temple treasury he managed (see 1 Chr 26:21-22). The whole episode is marked with the attitude of rejoicing at the opportunity to give, and at the willingness to give. The Chroniclers close the episode by stating or, rather, understating, that **David the king also rejoiced greatly** (29:9). Of course David rejoiced greatly, for his fund-raising efforts were overwhelmingly successful. In David's mind, this was an expression of faithfulness to Yahweh, and this expression, moreover, was a response to the previous faithfulness of God.

FROM THE TEXT

Appeals of this sort to the piety of key individuals, for the purpose of raising funds for God's work, are common throughout the history of what may be called, for lack of a better term, "organized religion." Sometimes, these efforts fall into error, as did the Roman Catholic Church of the period just before the Protestant Reformation. It is surely an error in modern times, as well, to encourage faithfulness—and, in particular, faithfulness expressed in terms of giving vast sums of money—through the promise of material reward. The so-called prosperity gospel may, in fact, be the worst Christian heresy to come out of the West in the twentieth century.

Texts like this one in 1 Chr 29 suggest that the giving of faithful individuals is not in the promise of a reward, for such is nowhere mentioned in this text. Instead, it is a response of gratitude for what God has already done. This is the "more excellent way" in describing why it is important for Christians to give of their resources. Moreover, one must always remember the poor widow Jesus observed. He said that this widow, having thrown in her two small coins, too small to amount for much in the grand scheme of things, had really contributed more than anyone else. It is not the size of the offering, and it is not the size of the resources out of which one gives the offering, that matter at all. What does matter is the willingness of the heart to celebrate what God has done. We give, in short, not because we expect a reward, but because we have already received a reward, indeed a greater reward than all of the riches of Solomon and Croesus put together!

e. David's Hymn of Praise and Sacrifices (29:10-22)

BEHIND THE TEXT

The book of Psalms, of course, contains the most extensive collection of prayers in the entire Bible. Similar ideas to what this prayer of David articulates may be found in Pss 41:13; 90:2; 103:17; and 106:48. However, the reader may find many great prayers elsewhere in the Bible. This prayer in particular has had significant influence on later faith, as will be shown.

Old Testament prayers may be grouped into three rather large classes: laments, thanksgivings, and praises. In laments, the worshiper complains to God about some distress (sickness, enemies, etc.) and prays for relief from it. These are by far the most common. Thanksgiving prayers thank God for having delivered the worshiper from whatever distress. In many cases (see, for example, Ps 22), lament and thanksgiving are found together, suggesting that someone—whether a human or God—has given reassurance that the prayer has been heard. Finally, praises usually glorify God for who he is, with or without reference to a specific act of deliverance. The prayer examined here probably belongs in this third category.

The recognition that everything comes from God is a key component of monotheistic belief. If the assumption of this commentary is true, that Chronicles is a document of the Persian period (539-333 B.C.), then it fits in well with the establishment of monotheism in the Jewish popular imagination. Indeed, it was in the Persian period—or, properly speaking, just before its beginning—that one of the greatest statements in support of monotheism flowed from a Jewish pen, that belonging to the so-called Second Isaiah (see, esp. Isa 45:1-8).

IN THE TEXT

■ **10-13** David's prayer in these verses surely belongs with the best of the biblical prayers. Verse 11 finds a near though not exact echo in another v 11, this time in the prayer of the twenty-four elders before the throne in Rev 4:11. In addition, the ascription to Yahweh of **the greatness and the power and the glory and the majesty and the splendor** is somewhat recalled in the wonderful benediction of Jude 25. As with many such thanksgiving prayers, the reasons for giving praise are first described in 1 Chr 29:10-12. With v 13, the text turns toward the overflowing praise itself. Verse 10 also highlights a key point from Israelite theology: Jacob, the father of the nation, is here called **Israel**, which is perhaps meant to highlight continuity between the one who wrestled with God and those who are blessed by God as his descendants. Radak suggests, in part, that this connection is made "because Jacob was the first to say to the Lord that the House of God ought to be built, as it says: 'And this stone, which I have set up as a pillar, shall be the House of God' (Gen 28:22)" (Kimchi 2008, 182).

■ **14-15** David's sentiment about all things coming from Yahweh reminds the careful reader of Job's declaration of faith in the face of his undeserved torment: *I came out of my mother's womb naked, and I shall return there naked. Yahweh has given and Yahweh has taken! May the name of Yahweh be blessed* (Job 1:21). In his theological commentary on Job, well-known Latin American theologian Gustavo Gutiérrez—considered one of the principal founders of liberation theology—forges this link between the present passage and Job 1. He writes: "The believing people is deeply convinced that everything belongs to the Lord and comes from the Lord. This conviction is well expressed in the beautiful prayer of David" (1987, 54).

David's prayer further acknowledges that all wealth comes from God. All that he and the rest of the people are doing is giving back to Yahweh what Yahweh has already given them. This sentiment has the added benefit of driving further away any sort of attempt to manipulate Yahweh into blessing on the strength of the amount given. They are able to give to Yahweh because Yahweh has given to them; they do not give to Yahweh in order that Yahweh should give to them. The alternative, to be sure, finds more of a home in Canaanite religion than in orthodox Yahwistic belief. Klein writes: "The real offerings were spiritual, matters of 'the heart': a sincere motivation to honor God and a readiness to give" (1999, 468).

■ **16-19** The final four verses reinforce the themes already expressed. Verse 18 recalls the beginning of the prayer in v 10, with the use of **Israel** in place of Jacob in the traditional formula "God of Abraham, Isaac, and Jacob" (see, for example, Exod 3:6). The prayer ends with a petition for Solomon. The father prays that the son will be faithful to Yahweh as he himself has been. This prayer is thus a kind of veiled admonishment to Solomon to do what he ought to do. As the reader will see, according to the Chroniclers, for the most part Solomon will disappoint neither his father nor his Father.

■ **20-22** After the great prayer of thanksgiving is finished, David and the people engage in appropriate sacrifices and other ritual acts of thanksgiving. Israelite worship often joined action to word in this way. The important point to note is that, in the same way as the giving of the gifts in the previous text, these sacrifices were offered **with great joy in the presence of the Lord that day** (v 22). It is a great mistake to view ancient Israelite religion as mere formalism or ritualism. To be sure, then as well as now there were likely to be those who performed the rituals in a perfunctory way, then went on about their business once their religious obligations were concluded. However, the history of religion in general reveals that such have never been in the majority. Formality in worship only becomes formalism or ritualism if those who are participating in it allow it to become so. The principal fault in such a case lies snugly at the feet of the leadership. Joyful leaders will likely preside over a joyful flock.

FROM THE TEXT

The recognition that everything comes from God is an important point of which preachers and teachers must never lose sight. Especially when passing on the faith to the next generation, the prayer of parents must be that the children will be faithful. The song "Find Us Faithful," drawing on the image of the "great cloud of witnesses" in Heb 12:1, captures this point well. The difference between that and the sentiment expressed here, however, is that here one finds a note of directness being sounded. In other words, the prayer of David is not so much that Solomon will follow him as he follows God, but that Solomon himself will follow God, which at the end of the day must be acknowledged as a loftier ambition.

This prayer of David (esp. v 11) probably formed the background of the final phrase of the Lord's Prayer (Matt 6:13), though its presence there is disputed by many important NT manuscripts. It is likely that a scribe added "for yours is the kingdom and the power and the glory forever" (NIV footnote) as part of early Christian liturgy. Nevertheless, it is important for modern readers to note that the early church did, in fact, find inspiration from Chronicles. Two major implications flow from this. First, it helps in overcoming the temptation to slide over Chronicles as merely another version of Israel's history, paling in comparison to Joshua-2 Kings. Second, and more importantly, it demonstrates that 2 Tim 3:16, a text famously used (and, perhaps, overused) in early twentieth-century debates over biblical inspiration, speaks to the *fact* of inspiration rather than the *manner* of inspiration. An early scribe reading Chronicles saw God's inspiration therein to such a degree that this person included this phrase as a fitting conclusion to words coming from the mouth of none less than Jesus, God's Son!

f. The Death of David (29:23-30)

IN THE TEXT

■ **23-30** The first volume of the Chroniclers' massive historical work ends, quite appropriately, with the death of Israel's most important king and prepares for the reign of **Solomon, who sat on the throne of the LORD as king in place of his father David.** Most interesting from this is that the throne is said to belong to Yahweh, not to the kings. This indicates something of the Israelite theology of kingship. Whereas in other nations (Egypt and Babylonia, for example) the king was personified as a god (or as a son of the gods, which amounts to the same thing), this is not the case in Israel. As David's prayer pointed out (→ v 11), dominion and glory belongs to Yahweh, and not to any human, not even the king selected by Yahweh. Verses 23-25 provide a kind of summary of Solomon's reign at the beginning of it. While, as has been noted, the transition from David to Solomon is far more violent in 1 Kgs 1—3, the note here that **All the officers and warriors, as well as all of King David's sons, pledged their submission to King Solomon** (1 Chr 29:24) perhaps hints at some kind of struggle. In the Deuteronomistic account, Solomon has one of **King David's sons**, Adonijah, killed because he had asserted himself as king in opposition to Solomon's claim. The Chroniclers make no mention of that, except through this veiled reference. The final note is most interesting: The

Chroniclers report that Yahweh **bestowed on him royal splendor such as no king over Israel ever had before** (v 25). This statement is interesting in light of the fact that the data set included only two individuals: Saul and David. This statement should perhaps be counted as typical ANE language, but it is also reminiscent of certain statements in Ecclesiastes. Ecclesiastes 1:16; 2:7; and 2:9 indicate that the preacher excelled beyond any other king who had reigned in Jerusalem. Of course, Solomonic authorship of Ecclesiastes has been challenged from the earliest times, and for good reason. Nevertheless, the similarity of language is striking.

One should note that the Chroniclers do not call the history "The Books of David," perhaps in order to avoid the oddity resulting from the Deuteronomists' recounting of the death of Samuel the prophet at the end of 1 Samuel, the title character thus no longer being around for 2 Samuel. Many more things are yet to be told after the death of David. Even though the division of the books is somewhat arbitrary, owing to the need to make scrolls only of a certain length in order to ensure portability and usefulness, nevertheless the death of David is as good a place as any to end 1 Chronicles.

The note in v 27 that David **ruled over Israel forty years—seven in Hebron and thirty-three in Jerusalem** differs slightly from the account in 2 Sam 5:5. There, the Deuteronomists report the following: "In Hebron [David] reigned over Judah seven years and six months, and in Jerusalem he reigned over all Israel and Judah thirty-three years." The distinction drawn in the 2 Samuel text takes into account the civil war between David and the house of Saul, after Saul and most of his sons were killed in battle with the Philistines. Further, 1 Kgs 2:11 reports that David reigned over all Israel, "seven years in Hebron and thirty-three in Jerusalem." The Chroniclers are closer to 1 Kgs 2 than 2 Sam 5. However, as has been shown, the reign of Saul was only to be noted in that it prepared the way for David (→ 1 Chr 10:1-14). Either way, the emphasis is on the fact that David is the most important of the kings.

Another interesting note comes in 29:29-30. Beginning with David, the Chronicle will make a note with most of the Israelite (after the division, Judean) kings that more events of the reign can be read about in various sources. Seven times the Chroniclers make an exception to this practice, six for a king and one for Judah's only queen. In each of these cases, the monarch in question was judged to be wicked (Ahaziah, Jehoram, Athaliah, Amon, Jehoahaz, Jehoiachin, and Zedekiah). These negative evaluations are similar to those that the Deuteronomists gave these rulers. In David's case, the sources cited are **the records of Samuel the seer, the records of Nathan the prophet and the records of Gad the seer** (v 29). The citation of these sources is certainly done in order to lend some credibility to the historian's account. It is more than likely that these were real documents, owing to the deep importance of scribal culture in the ANE (see van der Toorn 2007). It is a great loss that these sources are no longer available.

FROM THE TEXT

David lived a long and full life. Most importantly, he was judged faithful before God. Dying at an old age and enjoying wealth and honor are typical expressions for the blessings of a faithful life. One should of course not judge David's faithfulness on the fact of his having enjoyed wealth and prosperity, as some modern teachers tend to do. Instead, one should strive to live one's life not to increase one's material rewards from God, but in order to be judged a "good and faithful servant" (Matt 25:21). Ultimately, God's eternal judgment on the manner in which one lived one's life is far more important than any supposedly "objective" conditions of prosperity or blessedness.

29:23-30

C. Solomon (2 Chr 1:1—9:31)

▶ Overview

The OT has three "multiple volume" works: 1-2 Samuel, 1-2 Kings, and 1-2 Chronicles (Ezra and Nehemiah probably belong together as well, but they are not titled as such). The transitions between the two parts of all three are "clean," literarily speaking, in that a major character's death takes place right at the transition. Saul dies in the last chapter of 1 Samuel and David dies in the last chapter of 1 Chronicles. Second Kings, by only a slight contrast, begins with a reference to the death of King Ahab, which was reported a few verses before the end of 1 Kings. In the case of Samuel and Kings at least, this death prepares for the appearance and rise to prominence of a successor. In this way, the authors demonstrate that the two "volumes" belong together. To a point, the length of biblical books is a function of the amount of material that can be written in one scroll. Nevertheless, the authors or compilers of the biblical documents often were quite intentional in their transitions. In fact, intentional transitions of this type seem to take place more often than transitions that appear, to the untrained eye, to be haphazard or random.

Several examples of this phenomenon may be mentioned. Genesis 50:26 and Exod 1:6 describe the death of Joseph, the latter including the entire generation of the sons of Jacob. This prepares the reader of Exodus for the introduction of the narrative problem, the rising of a new pharaoh "to whom Joseph meant nothing" (1:8). At the end of the Pentateuch, Deut 34:5-9 and Josh 1:1-9 both mention the death of Moses and the divine appointment of Joshua to succeed him and lead the Israelites into the promised land. Joshua 24:29 and Judg 1:1 note the subsequent death of Joshua, the latter going on to suggest a somewhat chaotic situation following his death.

The transition between 1 and 2 Chronicles, however, is somewhat different. It has already been noted that the Chroniclers include several notices of Solomon's succession of David. It has also been noted that the royal succession goes off, according to the Chroniclers, without either hitch or bloodshed, in rather marked contrast to the Deuteronomistic version in 1 Kgs 1—3. However, much more interesting is the fact that David receives only scant mention in 2 Chr 1 (for more on this point → 2 Chr 1:1-17). By violating the expected form in this way, the Chroniclers once again demonstrate that they are creative writers, and hence their work deserves to be considered on its own merits. Interpreters should not venture to guess why this was done, but instead note that it was done and appreciate the unrivaled genius behind it.

I. Solomon Builds the Temple (1:1—4:22)

▶ Overview

In spite of their differences—many of which can be explained through the recognition that they come from different centuries—the Deuteronomists and the Chroniclers are agreed on one fundamental point: the importance of the Jerusalem temple. From a religious standpoint, this is certainly the greatest accomplishment of Solomon's reign. Solomon did many other things, to be sure, as the following commentary will demonstrate. But, given the Chroniclers' emphasis on proper temple worship (→ Introduction), it is natural to expect him to spend a great deal of time describing it. Indeed, the reader will not leave the temple site again until all the way into 2 Chr 9, at the end of which Solomon will follow King David and die righteously.

a. Description of Solomon's Greatness (1:1-17)

BEHIND THE TEXT

The Chroniclers make reference to large numbers (vv 2, 6, 14) and the ready availability of silver and gold and cedar in Jerusalem (v 15). Ancient documents often contain such grandiose statements extolling the virtues of a king. According to modern standards, these statements often defy credibility. However, it must always be remembered that ancient documents cannot be judged by modern standards. In the ANE, the quest for exactness in descriptions, especially in numbers, would have seemed nonsensical. Modern readers should not treat these as intentionally inflated numbers or descriptions but rather as a common practice in the ancient world to call attention to the greatness of a great leader or a king. In cases like these, our focus should be on the message inherent in the text rather than the accuracy of numbers or descriptions. When understood in their proper historical and cultural setting, it becomes clear that such descriptions do not do any harm whatever to the truth of the biblical text.

IN THE TEXT

■ **1** Second Chronicles begins, appropriately, where 1 Chronicles leaves off (see 1 Chr 29:22*b*-25). It was noted above that 2 Chronicles is unique in its transition. No further reference is made here to David's death (for more on these transitions → Overview to 2 Chr 1:1—9:31). Here, David is only mentioned in the phrase **Solomon son of David**. As was noted in the introduction, the division between 1 and 2 Chronicles is more likely a function of the length of a scroll than any particular thematic or theological concern. In point of fact, in the Jewish canon these two books are considered one—as are 1-2 Samuel, 1-2 Kings, and the twelve Minor Prophets. Nevertheless, the division is not completely without thematic freight, for David is in fact gone from the scene when 2 Chronicles begins. Therefore, the focus rightly turns to Solomon, who will do even greater works than his father, David (see 1 Kgs 2—3 for the Deuteronomists' perspective on how Solomon established his kingship and became great).

■ **2-6** Verse 2 does not record Solomon's words, though the translation **Then Solomon spoke to all Israel** is a technically correct translation of the Hebrew. A more preferred reading, **Then Solomon summoned all Israel**, makes more sense since vv 2-3 report the pilgrimage of Solomon and his commanders and leaders to Gibeon. It is interesting that, in this text, the Chroniclers begin the description of Solomon's greatness by saying first that he was religiously great. In other words, the first thing he does is seek Yahweh. In the parallel story in 1 Kgs 3, the Deuteronomists seem a little embarrassed that the great king would worship at an improper shrine like this. By contrast, as Klein mentions, the Chroniclers "had no such misgivings. Elsewhere [they distinguish] between sincere worship of the Lord and idolatrous religion at the high places" (1999, 473). In the movement of the history, of course, it was not yet possible for Solomon to worship in the proper place, as it was not yet built! The section ends with an amazingly large sacrifice on the altar. After David had brought the ark to Jerusalem, he had never returned to **Gibeon** but had left the priest Zadok in charge of what went on at the high place. Ultimately, **the bronze altar** had to join the ark in Jerusalem once the temple had been built. This historical detail is probably included to indicate the indubitable importance of the event. For the religious activity here, and especially the theophany that will follow, will spell the end of one era (the era of worshiping Yahweh in a mobile shrine) and the beginning of another (worshiping Yahweh in a grand, fixed structure).

■ **7-13** Yahweh comes to Solomon in a dream.

Dream-Theophany in the OT

Yahweh often comes to key people in the OT through dreams. Abram, whose name was later changed to Abraham, had God meet him in a dream in Gen 15. Connected with the story of Abraham, the Canaanite king Abimelek was warned who Sarah was—Abraham's wife, not his sister—by God in a dream (Gen 20). Later on, Jacob had an encounter with God in a dream at Bethel (Gen 28). Laban, Jacob's uncle, also has God come to him in a dream to give him a command concerning his nephew (Gen 31). In both Genesis and the apocalyptic book of Daniel, dreams and their interpretation play a big role in the narrative.

The dream-theophany that Solomon experiences in the present text thus serves the function of putting the king in the long line of persons whom Yahweh has visited at night. In this instance, **God appeared to Solomon and said to him, "Ask for whatever you want me to give you"** (v 7). The Chroniclers drew off the common tradition here, showing the virtue of Solomon in that he did not choose unlimited wealth or immortality or something like that. Yet there is a deeper and more interesting dimension to this story. Israelite theology, by including in its tradition a story of the deity appearing before a ruler with, as the saying goes, a blank check, makes a strong statement. In Israel, the king is not the personification of the deity, as in Egypt. In other words, though Yahweh does have a special relationship with Israel (see Exod 19:1-6), the ruler of the people is not higher, in Yahweh's eyes, than the rest, even though he has been granted authority. Though Solomon does not choose anything for himself, but instead **wisdom and knowledge, that I may lead this people** (v 10), "all these things" (Matt 6:33) are added to him as well! (2 Chr 1:12). While the Chroniclers leave out the colorful story demonstrating Solomon's wisdom—two prostitutes, one living baby, one dead baby (1 Kgs 3:16-28)—nevertheless they are convinced that Solomon was a great king indeed. God also promises Solomon great wealth, which actually turns out to be his downfall, according to the Deuteronomists, since ultimately he takes his eye off the one who blessed him with the wealth and instead looked exclusively to his own interests.

■ **14-17** The description of Solomon's wealth is amazing, even though he is a king. The Chroniclers seem somewhat critical of Solomon here. Although they certainly attribute Solomon's wealth to Yahweh, they do not fail to point out that the king also engaged in elaborate import and export operations in order to make himself wealthy. Nevertheless, the Deuteronomists are keener on describing Solomon's abuses in full than are the Chroniclers. Both groups of historians, however, surely noted at least to themselves how their description of Solomon's wealth, and in particular his horses, would perhaps be in violation of the "law of the king" (see Deut 17:16; → 2 Chr 9:13-28). It must be recognized, however, that overall the picture painted of Solomon is a positive one. While intertextual comparisons like this one are illuminating, they may ultimately distract one from perceiving the full message.

b. Dialogue with King Hiram (2:1-18)

BEHIND THE TEXT

As will be discussed further below with regard to the accession of Rehoboam, Solomon's son (→ 2 Chr 10), a new king coming to power often included a reevaluation of old relationships. For example, conquered or otherwise unwilling subjects might be more likely to rebel in the period of time—sometimes short, sometimes rather longer—when the new king is getting everything established and secured. This establishing and securing regularly involves wholesale slaughter of the rivals to the throne (for an example, see 2 Kgs 10).

With the accession of Solomon, however, at least one of the relationships that his father, David, enjoyed remained intact. This solid relationship was with King Hiram of Tyre. Earlier this was described as a ruler/vassal arrangement, and such a description probably remains valid for the relationship between Solomon and Hiram. Hiram had already sent and, in the course of the narrative, will continue to send, much materials and many laborers for building the house of Yahweh in Jerusalem. That a pagan king would spend so many resources for one who, for him, is an alien god at once testifies to the charisma of David and Solomon and to the sense of compulsion lying back of the action. Nevertheless, the Chroniclers are quick to point out that Solomon has plenty of help in accomplishing what will be the signature achievement of his reign: building a permanent house for the One who had dwelt in a tent for so long (see 1 Chr 17:1).

IN THE TEXT

■ **1** The first thing one notices about this text is an issue with verse numbers. What is 2 Chr 2:1 in NIV and other English versions is 1:18 in Hebrew. As in other cases where this has happened, the commentary that follows uses the English verse numbers. Verse 1 indicates the order in which the two buildings, **a temple for the Name of the LORD and a royal palace for** Solomon, are to be built. Naturally, given the Chroniclers' emphasis on the temple, far more space will be given to the description of its building process. In fact, 2 Chr 9:3 is the only place where the building of the palace is mentioned, and then only in passing.

■ **2** Perhaps more important for the later history, however, is 2:2, which makes reference to Solomon conscripting a total of 153,600 men for various tasks such as **carriers**, **stonecutters**, and **foremen**. Verse 2 is essentially a duplicate of vv 17-18, where the Chroniclers add that the conscripted workers came from a census taken of "all the foreigners residing in Israel." The Deuteronomists, however, add that Solomon conscripted 30,000 laborers from "all Israel"; Deuteronomists also report that Solomon had a labor force of 153,300 (300 less than the Chroniclers' number), but do not connect them to a census or foreigners living in Israel. Solomon's conscription of forced labor will, in time to come, be a point of contention among the northern and southern tribes. When the former bring a grievance against King Rehoboam, he will fail to listen to them, and this failure leads, unfortunately, to the rupture of the kingdoms. As a labor strategy, what Solomon does is commendable in its efficiency and organization. As a people strategy, however, it may have been less than good, especially as it planted such a deep root of resentment.

2:1-10 ■ **3-10** These verses record the letter that Solomon sent to **Hiram king of Tyre** (v 3). The occurrence of the name here is interesting. In Hebrew it is **Huram**. The difference is likely due, as the variations in the genealogies of 1 Chronicles, to a stylistic variation. There is no indication that a new king had come to the throne, whose name differed from his predecessor in only one vowel. In Hebrew, the names "Hiram" and "Huram" (also found in 2 Chr 2:11-12) are even closer than they are in English, requiring only an extension of the *yod* in "Hiram" to create the *vav* in "Huram." This is the only difference; it must be remembered that in the original Hebrew manuscript no vowel points were included.

This letter assumes a well-known feature of ancient societies, namely that when a new ruler comes to power, old relationships are reevaluated. With his letter, Solomon informs Hiram that the old relationship will continue. It is not at all unusual for someone in Solomon's position to say that **the temple I am going to build will be great** (v 5), for he clearly wants to give honor to his God. However, it seems strange that he would, in a letter to a non-Yahwist, use the expression **our God is greater than all other gods**. At first glance, this gives evidence that, at the time of the events of the story at least, belief in the existence of many gods but worship of only one (henotheism) was still common in Israel. Works like the Chroniclers' History and the so-called Second Isaiah, in part, contributed to a concerted effort at rooting out such a position in emerging Jewish theology, and they were of course ultimately successful.

A further point to notice is that Solomon assumes Hiram would acknowledge the greatness of Yahweh in comparison to all other gods. Two options seem to present themselves to the interpreter. First, it may be that Solomon expected Hiram, his vassal, to acknowledge Yahweh's greatness and worship the God of his overlord (to convert to the religion of his overlord). Later on, in Hiram's response to Solomon, he praises Yahweh "the God of Israel, who made heaven and earth" who established Solomon as Israel's king (vv 11-12). This response may have been what was expected of a loyal vassal, and may not necessarily be a reflection of Hiram's genuine faith in Yahweh. Both the Deuteronomists and the Chroniclers promote the view that Solomon extended the kingdom of his father farther and wider than David could have imagined, which shed some light on this way of interpreting this text.

Second, Solomon may have made this statement without respect to Hiram's religion. That is, Solomon—and probably the Chroniclers as well—may have been unconcerned whether Hiram was a Yahwist or a worshiper of the Tyrian Baal as was Queen Jezebel somewhat later. Other languages may prove a help here. Tagalog, one of the official languages of the Philippines, where the present author currently serves, has different second person plural pronouns ("we," "our," etc.). One set includes the hearer of the message and the other does not. In a popular Tagalog translation—actually, the Tagalog equivalent of the Good News Bible—Solomon uses the version of **our God** that *does not* include Hiram. He feels free to order Hiram to do things because Hiram is his vassal. However, he acknowledges—according to the Tagalog—that Hiram is not a worshiper of Yahweh. The most convincing support of this option is that it does not require Hiram to have converted, as the first option seems to.

2:3-16

One further item deserves comment. Solomon's repeated emphasis on "the temple I build/I am going to build" is interesting. Is he building this temple to show his greatness or to show the greatness of God? He questions, "Who am I?" but then "brags" about his plan to build a "large and magnificent" temple! The Chroniclers display great subtlety here, for even while they marvel at the magnificence of the temple, they do not spare Solomon from critique.

■ **11-16** King Hiram's response to his master Solomon comes in two parts. The first part, in v 11*b*, is very short: twelve words in English and seven in Hebrew. It thus has the character of a postcard or a congratulatory note. It is striking that Hiram uses the proper name **Yahweh**, whereas Solomon did not in v 5, giving the impetus to the discussion above. The second part of the letter, in vv 12-16, begins with even more praise of Israel's God. Verse 12 includes a familiar doxology, again perhaps more suitable on the lips of Solomon than of the pagan king Hiram. The main body of the letter, vv 13-16, answers the specific request of Solomon in vv 7-10. He indicates that the skilled laborer being sent has an Israelite mother, or at least one who came from **Dan**. The final two verses of the letter are a request back to Solomon. Hiram asks for goods in exchange, indeed goods that Solomon had **promised**. This indicates something of the extent of this conversation, as well as the long established relationship between Hiram, Solomon, and David.

■ **17-18** (→ v 2) It is unclear whether **the census his father David had taken** (v 17) refers to the evil census, incited by Satan, in 1 Chr 21. What is clear is that this particular census is not evil in Yahweh's eyes as was the previous one. Second Chronicles 2:17 gave the total number of workers, while v 2 listed by groups, as in v 18. The stage is now fully set for the building of the temple, with materials and workers firmly in place.

c. Description of the Building (3:1-17)

BEHIND THE TEXT

One should perhaps expect a lengthy section such as this, considering the importance the Chroniclers attached to the Jerusalem temple. As has been discussed elsewhere in this commentary, the Chroniclers likely had support of the second temple in mind as they lovingly lingered over the descriptions of the preparation of the site, the building, the furnishings in the building, and the dedication of the first temple. The second temple began operation as a place of sacrifice in 515 B.C., but it is unclear whether the Chroniclers' History as a whole should be dated before or after the completion of its construction. According to the prophet Haggai, who preached during the year 520 (and his is the most securely dated of all of the writing prophets' ministry), the prevailing opinion was that the second temple's splendor paled in comparison to that of Solomon's temple. Nevertheless, the leaders are encouraged to have hope, for Yahweh was behind the building and would see it through to a grand conclusion (see Hag 2:1-9).

Jesus and the Temple

In the NT, Jesus frequently got into debates with opponents—usually the Pharisees—about the importance of the temple. In John's version of the cleansing of the temple (which takes place at the beginning of Jesus' ministry, while for the Synoptic Gospels it is at the end), Jesus' opponents claim that the temple has taken forty-six years to build. Therefore, Jesus' contention that he could, after it was destroyed, raise it up again in three days was, for them, ridiculous (John 2:19-22). The evangelist comments that Jesus was talking about the temple of his body, and "after he was raised from the dead, his disciples recalled what he had said" (John 2:22). In the Synoptics, Jesus' statement is used against him by those mocking him as he hung dying on the cross (Matt 27:40; Mark 14:58).

It is likely that the Chroniclers had a similar view of the second temple as did Haggai, believing that the glory of the second temple would eventually surpass that even of the first. First, however, the immediate task was to describe the building effected by Solomon's leadership, and that is the focus of the present section.

IN THE TEXT

■ **1-2** The first two verses orient the reader both theologically and historically. Theologically, the site of the temple is **Mount Moriah**, long a significant place in Hebrew tradition. This was the place on which Abraham had been called to sacrifice Isaac, only prevented from doing so at the last minute. The Chroniclers indicate that the building of the temple began **on the second day of the second month in the fourth year of his reign**. Such precision as this further contributes to the importance the Chroniclers attached to the temple. Moreover, they attached particular importance to Solomon as the builder of the building that they considered the most significant in Israel. This led eventually to them giving very little attention to the other buildings Solomon built. Also, it led them to give very little attention to Solomon's foibles, of which the Deuteronomists, by contrast, do not spare any details. This further difference between the two historical epics indicates once again that each group of authors or compilers did their work for their own purposes, even as they sought to give a faithful and orderly account of the events of the past (see Luke 1:3).

■ **3-17** The remaining verses give a striking amount of architectural detail for the temple. The text contains general reference to the foundation, portico, and inside walls, but the focus is on the most holy place (vv 8-13) and the two pillars (named Jakin and Boaz) in front of the temple (vv 15-17). There is not sufficient reason to doubt the accuracy of the description found in this text, even if it cannot be conclusively proven through archaeological investigation. This is so because digging on the Temple Mount is forbidden for political and religious reasons, since three of the world's major religions consider this among the holiest places on the earth. Thus the existence and architectural features of the Jerusalem temple cannot be viewed by archaeologists. Nevertheless, the plan of the temple as described here and elsewhere in the OT is consistent with abundant archaeological evidence of temples and shrines located throughout the ANE and dedicated to various gods and goddesses. The nature of the account must always be kept in mind, in order to avoid much confusion.

159

d. Temple Furnishings (4:1-22)

IN THE TEXT

■ **1-22** This chapter gives the description of the furnishings that Solomon and Hiram made for the temple. The apparent change in subject might cause some confusion. From vv 1-10, Solomon is assumed to be the subject of the action. Then, from vv 11-16, the subject seems to change to Huram/Huram-Abi, the skilled worker Hiram sent (see 2:13 and 3:16). Finally, from 4:17 until the end of the chapter, Solomon again assumes center stage. Moreover, the level of organization necessary for such a large labor force—one hundred and fifty thousand workers with their thirty-six hundred overseers—staggers the imagination. The precise descriptions of the furnishings in this chapter mirror the similarly precise descriptions of the building itself in the previous chapter. For later readers, these details may seem a bit overdescriptive. However, later readers must never judge the text by modern standards of literary quality. It was, in fact, a feature of ANE literature generally to include somewhat repetitive and overly descriptive depictions of those things that were held to be important. The Jerusalem temple certainly fits this bill. This means that the modern reader must approach the text with humility, recognizing that it comes from a different historical context. This point, perhaps like the description of the temple, bears constant repeating as one seeks to understand the text. As one reads with this stance of humility, one also must see beyond the excessive description into the sense of wonder that certainly lies back of this description. The temple was ornate, and its furnishings were ornate, by design—and the design was naturally to give the greatest honor to the greatest among the gods; indeed, according to the Chroniclers' own theology, the only God!

2. Dedication of the Temple (5:1—7:22)

▶ Overview

After the lengthy description of the building of the temple, the narrative next turns to an equally lengthy account of the dedication of the temple. Examples of dedicating holy buildings abound in many societies, both ancient and modern. Often, these rituals are highly structured, even within traditions that normally eschew "ritualism," however that term is defined. While archaeological investigation has not yet found clear, convincing evidence of Solomon's temple—and probably never will, due to politically and religiously charged restrictions on digging in that area of Jerusalem—its description makes perfect sense. Other examples of holy shrines in the ANE have the same three-part pattern that is described for the temple of Yahweh in Jerusalem: outer court, holy place, holiest place. Two examples will suffice. The first is the Iron Age Syro-Hittite temple at 'Ain Dara, northwest of the modern city of Aleppo, Syria. The second is the Israelite temple at Arad, a small city near the Negev Desert. The Jerusalem and Arad temples differ from others located outside of Israel, of course, in the respect that the others would have a statue of the deity to whom the temple is dedicated. One example of this idea is found in the Bible, concerning the temple of Dagon in the Philistine city of Ashdod. This is the place to which the ark was taken (1 Sam 5) and where the head of King Saul was displayed after his suicide on Mount Gilboa (1 Chr 10). The latter text includes a reference to "the temple of their gods" (v 10), without specifying which deities.

The movement of this section is rather similar to the Deuteronomists' presentation in 1 Kgs 8—9. First, the ark is brought to the temple. Second, both historical accounts report Solomon's long dedicatory prayer, and predictions of (or reflections upon) exile are included in these prayers. Third, Yahweh appears to Solomon again, giving further divine blessing to his reign. As has been repeatedly shown, however, close connection between the two accounts should not lead the reader to think that the Chroniclers merely repeated what the Deuteronomists had to say.

a. Bringing the Ark to the Temple (5:1-14)

BEHIND THE TEXT

The commentary to 1 Chr 13:1-14 above noted that the history of the ark of the covenant was a varied one. This is by no means, however, to suggest that the history of the ark has not been important, nor that the ark itself has not been important. In other words, the ark is no mere box. In fact, one of the Talmudic tracts suggests that "common people perish . . . [because] they treat the holy ark as a box" (*Shabbat* 32.1).

At the end of the 1 Chr 13 text, the ark of God remained at the house of Obed-Edom the Gittite. It was left there because of the tragedy that befell poor Uzzah. Uzzah tried to steady the ark to keep it from falling, but even this was considered an illegal touching, which merited the death penalty. In 1 Chr 15, the ark was finally moved to Jerusalem. This time, proper care was taken so that Uzzah's tragedy would not be repeated. Now, however, the time has come for the ark to come to its proper resting place, in the Jerusalem temple. The reverence paid to the ark might naturally lead one to think that it was considered divine, for throughout the ANE such reverence was in fact often paid to divine cult images. The Deuteronomists recount an example of considering the ark as the image of Israel's God in 1 Sam 5. In that account, the Philistines had defeated Israel and had taken the ark as a trophy. Having installed it in the temple of Dagon (the Philistine god of grain) in Ashdod, they and their gods experienced tremendous punishment as a result. Israel, however, has been consistent throughout its history in barring images of Yahweh—or of anything else for that matter—from its worship. The ark, in that case, really is simply a box! True enough, it is a symbol of ongoing divine-human communication, and thus it is sacred—but it is not in itself intended to be a representation of Yahweh.

IN THE TEXT

■ **1-10** The chapter can be profitably divided into two sections of unequal length. The first ten verses give the specific story of the ark's installation in the temple. The first verse gives a summary statement, reporting that Solomon **brought in the things his father David had dedicated . . . and he placed them in the treasuries of God's temple**. The **treasuries of God's temple** were the repository of all the holy objects dedicated to the service of Yahweh, along with a great amount of silver and gold. These were sometimes emptied, often to pay off various foreign rulers (see 2 Kgs 16:8; 18:15; 2 Chr 16:2). Sometimes the foreign rulers took them by force, as in Dan 5:3. The ark is clearly not included in this summary, perhaps because it is the most important of the objects in question. Tribal and family representatives, representing the entire nation, came together in Jerusalem to witness and participate in the transportation of the ark from **Zion, the City of David** (2 Chr 5:2) to the temple. The ark is called **the ark of the LORD's covenant**, which is a fuller name, perhaps because the ark contained, among other things, the two tablets of the covenant stipulations. Solomon and the assembly of Israel marched ahead of the ark carried by the Levitical priests, sacrificing sheep and cattle too numerous to **be recorded or counted** (v 6). This statement is more than likely a rhetorical overstatement meant to capture some of the glory and significance of the event. This was indeed a significant liturgical act in the life of the nation, and the Chroniclers did not waste any effort in describing it as such. The solemnity of the ritual is evident in the fact that only the priests who carried the ark entered the most holy place to place the ark **beneath the wings of the cherubim** (v 7), already installed in the innermost sanctuary (2 Chr 3:10-13). Thus the wings already on the ark itself (see Exod 37:6-9) perhaps fit under those already made for the sanctuary. Further, in 2 Chr 5:9, the suggestion is made that the poles used to carry the ark **could be seen from in front of the inner sanctuary, but not from outside the Holy Place; and they are still there today**. The final phrase in particular is striking, since the Chroniclers are undoubtedly writing at a time when the ark and the poles used for carrying it had long been lost to history.

Therefore, not only could the poles not be seen at the time the Chroniclers created their history, but the ark itself was no longer definitely seen once it was placed in the holy place by the priests. This is not to suggest that the story is fiction; more probably it actually happened just the way it is recorded. However, that the ark very quickly moved off the pages of history and into the pages of folklore cannot easily be denied.

As for the contents of the ark, both v 10 and 1 Kgs 8:9 report that **there was nothing in the ark except the two tablets that Moses had placed in it at Horeb**. According to popular tradition, the two tablets of the Law were accompanied by Aaron's budded staff and a jar with an omer of manna. These items are mentioned in Heb 9:4 (the staff) and Exod 16:32-34 (the manna). Ultimately, the specific contents of the ark are not as important as the ideological importance of the symbol.

■ **11-14** The last four verses of the chapter discuss the withdrawal of the priests **from the Holy Place** (v 11). This was the second major division of the temple. They had completed the task set before them, and so they no longer belonged where they were. Moreover, only one person could ever enter the most holy place, and him only once a year. The person so authorized was the high priest, and the occasion was the Day of Atonement. It is no surprise, therefore, that the ark does not appear much at all in the rest of the history. The priests withdrew from the holy place while the Levitical musicians were playing various instruments and one hundred and twenty priests sounding trumpets, and the singers singing praises to God. The short doxology, **He is good; his love endures forever** (v 13; see Ps 136:1) concluded the ritual placement of the ark in the holy of holies. After the song, the cloud—which was a symbol of God's presence in Exodus—descended upon the temple **and the priests could not perform their service because of the cloud** (2 Chr 5:14; see a similar report about the cloud covering the tent and the glory of Yahweh filling the tabernacle in Exod 40:34). The chapter ends with a striking phrase bringing together the holy name of God with his title: ***the glory of Yahweh filled the Temple of God***. For the Israelites, the name Yahweh and the title God in all cases referred to the same divine person. This is all the more the case with a document like Chronicles, which is throughout so concerned with the holiness of God.

FROM THE TEXT

Discussions about the place of ritual in worship are common on the contemporary landscape. The options range across the entire continuum from absolute rejection to absolute embrace. Pastors, worship leaders, Christian educators, and others responsible for making decisions in this area must balance theological and practical concerns, which is often a difficult balance to achieve. If theological and historical concerns are overemphasized, then worship experiences may be meaningful and deep to those aware of theology and history, but may confuse laypeople if proper education does not take place. On the other hand, if practical concerns are emphasized, worship experiences may degenerate into entertainment, with little knowledge of or concern for the place the local congregation holds in Christian history. This decision must therefore be taken with the needs and condition of the community in mind. Ritual does in fact have a place in worship, for through adherence to ritual the faithful can accomplish the work of God and express the piety required of the task. Everything is done in this text with the precision, order, and formality required by an act of worship. Finally, ritual ends with doxology. Public worship need not embrace ritual for ritual's sake, but it must never degenerate into mere entertainment.

Furthermore, contrasts between Judaism and Christianity are inevitable, undoubtedly because of the latter's roots in the former. In the NT, the book of Hebrews in particular stresses many of the differences between Christianity and Judaism. Principal among these differences is the discussion of the role of the high priest, performing the functions of the Day of Atonement in the holy place (see esp. Heb 9:1-10). Such distinctions are only helpful to a certain degree. That is, it is important to understand that Christianity is, in fact, different from Judaism. However, it does not and should not follow from this that Jews are damned. From the Christian perspective, naturally, Judaism is incomplete because Jews fail to recognize and confess Jesus as the Messiah. However, according to no less a figure than the Apostle Paul, God certainly has not rejected or "un-chosen" his chosen people (Rom 11:1). The discussion between Christianity and Judaism could be far less acrimonious than it is if both sides would recognize the value of the other and the genuine contributions that each has made to human history. Such an approach is many steps removed from the nasty, negative rhetoric that has often characterized Christian attitudes toward Judaism, as well as Jewish attitudes toward Christianity.

b. Solomon Recites What Yahweh Has Done (6:1-13)

IN THE TEXT

■ **1-2** The final stage of the temple's dedication is told over the next two chapters. It takes place in four parts, which combine action and speech. The first part (vv 1-11) includes a short speech by Solomon, with two different addressees (vv 1-2, 3-11). In v 1, Solomon states a theological maxim from the past, namely that **The Lord has said that he would dwell in a dark cloud**. God's presence in "a pillar of cloud" and in "thick darkness" is part of the Exodus tradition (see Exod 13:21-22; 20:21). This verse also recalls 1 Chr 17, the message given by Yahweh to Nathan. There, Yahweh said that he had never asked for "a house of cedar," but instead Yahweh was content to go around with the people rather than being located in one place. Solomon, however, does not stop after having recalled this great theological truth from the past. In 2 Chr 6:2, the addressee changes to Yahweh (apparently the people had been addressed in v 1). Solomon says, **I have built a magnificent temple for you, a place for you to dwell forever**. An alternative reading of Solomon's building project suggests that, through this phrase, Solomon is domesticating Yahweh, so that Solomon might proceed about his kingly business without respect or concern for Yahweh. While such a skeptical reading is possible, there is nothing in particular to commend it to the interpreter. One would do well, however, to note that the building of the temple does, in fact, mark a significant change in the way Yahweh has dealt with his people. Some quarters of contemporary church practice are moving away from the need to have church buildings as a sign of religious legitimization, but in the ANE a great temple built to the greatness of one's god was indispensable.

■ **3-13** The address turns back to the people in the final eleven verses. These verses represent a historical summary of the events that have transpired. The theological assumption behind this retelling is that all of these events were done at Yahweh's behest. This is, as has been shown, the dominant theological stance of the Chroniclers, and indeed much of postexilic Jewish theology. For it was only in the postexilic period that Judaism finally left behind the idea that many gods existed, each one having responsibility over one particular nation. Verse 9 recalls the promise made to David as recorded in 2 Sam 7:13 and 1 Chr 17:12: **your son, your own flesh and blood—he is the one who will build the temple for my Name**. Halpern suggested, as noted above, that Solomon may have been the son of Uriah (2001, 404). At least, such a rumor might have been spreading at the time of Solomon's birth. A text like this would surely have served to combat such speculation. Moreover, both 2 Sam 7:12 and 1 Chr 17:11 say the same thing. All three use slightly different terminology, which leads strongly in the direction of credibility. In this issue, like others, it never ceases to amaze how often close attention to the details of the text puts idle—and certainly ideological—speculation to rest. Solomon also makes clear to his people that the temple he built for **the Name of *Yahweh***, the God of Israel, is his faithful response to the fulfillment of God's promise to build a house for David (v 10; see 1 Chr 17:10-14). The Chroniclers leave no doubt in the mind of their readers the intrinsic relationship between the temple and the dynasty; the temple is a visible representation of the legitimacy of the Davidic dynasty; the Davidic dynasty is a visible representation of the faithfulness of God who dwells in the temple.

c. Solomon's Prayer of Dedication (6:14-42)

BEHIND THE TEXT

The quest to understand the present text becomes, if not easier, more comprehensive when comparing it to other similar prayers within the Chroniclers' History. In fact, one finds that the best intertextual "join" to Solomon's prayer of dedication is nothing other than David's prayer in 1 Chr 17:16-27 (→). Especially given the Chroniclers' lengthy and repeated treatment of the passing of leadership from David to Solomon, it is not surprising that Solomon should make in this prayer so many references to David and the promises that Yahweh made to David. No fewer than three references are made to these promises, and at the same time the prayer looks forward to the continued faithfulness of Yahweh to the descendants of David—Solomon, of course, first among them—provided that they remain faithful to Yahweh.

One may also compare this prayer with its equivalent in 1 Kgs 8:22-53. The major difference between the two is that the prayer ends in 1 Kings with reference to the Exodus. By contrast, the Chroniclers' version ends with a citation of Ps 132:8-10. Thus the emphasis in the Chroniclers shifts from the Exodus to the Davidic covenant. This is consistent with the Chroniclers' appreciation of the Davidic monarchy and their hope for its reestablishment in their own day.

IN THE TEXT

■ **14-17** One finds the primary references to David and Yahweh's promise to David in these first four verses, which serve as a kind of "introduction" to Solomon's prayer of dedication for the temple. These verses also amplify a key theme of the Chroniclers, namely the importance of the temple. The building of the temple helped cement the promise of Yahweh to the Davidic dynasty. Although Yahweh told David, through the prophet Nathan, that he would not build the temple, this did not mean that the building was unimportant. In other words, Solomon's fulfillment of this task was a supreme fulfillment of the theological idea common to both the Deuteronomists and the Chroniclers. Both groups of historians believe there is a more-or-less simple correlation between Yahweh's blessing and human faithfulness to Yahweh's commands. This means that, even though Yahweh had never asked for a house of cedar (1 Chr 17:6), nevertheless the permanent house Solomon built represented a supreme act of faithfulness to Yahweh. Three times in these verses Solomon cites the promises given to his father, David, imploring Yahweh to keep these promises. His final plea in this section is directly to the point: **And now, LORD, the God of Israel, let your word that you promised your servant David come true**. His specific reference is to the promise of a dynasty, which of course is, by extension, a promise to Solomon. Therefore, Solomon is included both in the promise and in the obligation, and the primary way he fulfills the obligation is through the building of the temple.

■ **18-21** Klein suggests simply that the "rest of Solomon's prayer is about prayer" (1999, 496). This prayer can be divided into seven sections. The first, in these verses, states Solomon's proper attitude of humility before Yahweh. He recognizes how shocking is the idea that Yahweh should dwell with humanity on the earth. The **temple I have built**, even with all its magnificence, is nowhere near equal to the task (see Mark 13:1-3). Nevertheless, Yahweh has brought himself down to call this temple a home. This idea is similar to that which is seen in other ANE religions with the building of temples and, particularly, with the construction of divine cult images ("idols"). Rarely, if at all, would the devotees of this or that deity believe that the idol or the divine cult image *was* the deity. Rather, elaborate rituals and prayers accompanied the creation of a divine cult image. These rituals and prayers were designed to implore the deity, either god or goddess, to allow the cult image that had been created to be a reasonable representation of the deity. Of course, representation of Yahweh had been forbidden from Mosaic times, even if the written injunctions against it (as seen, for example, in the second commandment) may have come later. Therefore, Solomon saw neither the temple nor the ark of the covenant as direct representations of Yahweh. However, both of these things were certainly seen, at least by the official religious establishment, as definite and more-or-less clear representations of the presence of Yahweh with the people and their king. Later on, in the Chroniclers' own context, they were perhaps encouraging the building of the second temple, which would again, in their minds, serve as an impressive symbol of the presence of Yahweh with the people and of his blessings extended toward them.

■ **22-23** The second through the sixth sections of Solomon's prayer introduce supplications to Yahweh. Each of them begins with a case including some sort of condition, followed by a plea for what Yahweh should do should such a condition occur. The secondary function of these supplications is to sanctify the various parts of the temple and its furnishings. For example, these verses reflect the practice of oath-taking before the altar in the temple. Deuteronomy 6:13 enjoins the people to swear oaths only in the name of Yahweh. The principal place where such oaths would be taken, naturally, is in the temple. Solomon prays that Yahweh will judge fairly between Israelites when they have a dispute between them. Temples often served as a place where legal disputes could be adjudicated. Solomon cements this idea in his prayer when he declares that Yahweh's declaration of innocence or guilt establishes the fact of innocence or guilt. Though this may not line up well with modern standards of jurisprudence, it was well in line with ancient practice, and therefore the statement is to be judged plausible. This is in line with the criteria applied by Werner Keller (see Keller 1965/1980).

■ **24-25** The third section of Solomon's prayer confirms a well-known principle of ANE theology. It was a general characteristic of ANE societies—Israel included—to accept as a given the existence of many gods. Often, however, only one god was worshiped in a particular place. Even in places where more than one deity was worshiped (Egypt, for example), most often one of them served as the high god. Thus Amun-Ra (or briefly, Aten) was the chief deity in Egypt, Marduk in Babylon, Qaus in Edom, Chemosh in Moab, Yahweh in Israel. Coming along with this idea was the supposition that warring armies were represented in the heavens by warring deities. While the victorious army usually proclaimed the superiority of their god, the defeated army usually proclaimed that their god (or goddess, as the case may be) had turned away from them. Thus, in Israel and other nations, when the nation was defeated, the usual practice was to proclaim that Yahweh was angry with them for this or that misstep. Another example of this view from the ANE is expressed in the Moabite Stone (→ sidebar at 1 Chr 8:8-12, "The Moabite Stone"). These two verses enforce this theological idea, imploring Yahweh to **hear from heaven and forgive the sin of** his **people Israel** (v 25). This note will be sounded again in the following chapter when Yahweh appears to Solomon, generating one of the most famous memory verses from the book of 2 Chronicles.

■ **26-27** The fourth section of the prayer is directly related to the previous one. Here, however, the scenario imagined is not punishment through military defeat but punishment through natural disaster. Such was also a well-known feature of ANE theology. At times, the punishment took the form of a drought, but at other times the form of a flood. Many societies today ascribe natural phenomena like this to the anger of God or the gods, which emphasizes human sin again. Solomon's prayer here is for the restoration after the drought, specifically that Yahweh would teach them the right way to live. The Chroniclers could possibly have had in mind here historical experiences of drought such as that which occurred during the time of the prophet Elijah, or like the famine that formed the literary setting of the book of Ruth.

■ **28-33** This fifth section details two different scenarios, again related to worshipers of Yahweh seeking forgiveness after having been punished for sin. The first scenario, in vv 28-31, deals with Israelites having experienced **famine** or plague . . . or blight or mildew, locusts or grasshoppers (v 28) in addition to a siege by an opposing army. The latter is essentially an echo of that treated in vv 24-25 above. Verse 29 indicates something of a proper stance for prayer, suggesting that the worshiper seeking redress from Yahweh should **stretch out the palms of the hands toward this temple.** It is perhaps beside the point to inquire whether this was actual practice in Israel. This is assumed in the prayer, and that is sufficient evidence for credibility in the present context. The second scenario is perhaps more interesting. This is so because it involves a **foreigner who does not belong to your people Israel** (v 32). Even such a one as this should be heard and forgiven by Yahweh. This is something of a bold statement by the Chroniclers. The Deuteronomistic version in 1 Kgs 8:41-43 gives a reason why foreigners may call out to Yahweh, namely that they have heard of the reputation of Israel's God in their faraway places and have come to pray. In the postexilic period, there was considerable debate between the returnees and those who had never left Judah to begin with as to whom, precisely, constituted the true Israel. Each side claimed the other as a foreigner, outside of Yahweh's concern. Perhaps a text like this functioned, like the so-called Third Isaiah (see esp. Isa 56) and the books of Ruth and Jonah, to advance the argument that Israel's God was in fact God of all the nations of the earth, and therefore that all nations could approach Yahweh and Yahweh would grant their righteous requests.

■ **34-39** These six verses are the reverse of the notes having to do with warfare in vv 24-25 and 28b. That is, this supplication has to do with Yahweh's positive action in favor of the Israelites going to war, as opposed to defending themselves from enemy attack. As the army goes out to war, they pray to Yahweh, and Solomon asks that when such a thing happens Yahweh would **uphold their cause** (v 35). This is to be the case when the cause is just. However, if the cause is not just—if there is sin in the community—then the people will be given over into their enemies' hands. More specifically, this is a kind of prediction after the fact of the exile, as v 36 makes clear. Yet the prayer is that Yahweh would not leave his people alone in **a land far away or near** (v 36) but instead would **hear their prayer and their pleas** (v 39) and restore them to the land Yahweh had sworn on oath to give them. This is surely a reflection of the Chroniclers' original audience, who in fact were those who had been returned to their land by Yahweh. They had had **a change of heart in the land where they** were **held captive** (v 37), and Yahweh had in fact restored them. They were beginning a new life with meager conditions, but at the very least they were no longer in exile. The final verses of the Chroniclers' History (2 Chr 36:22-23) will return to this theme, leaving the question of the return still somewhat open, though it was promised.

■ **40-42** The final segment of Solomon's prayer, like the opening segment in vv 14-17, returns to unmitigated praise of Yahweh (more or less a quote from Ps 132:8-10; see above). The NIV sets off 2 Chr 6:41-42 as poetry, a practice not observed by the *BHS*. These verses are a bit of rhetorical flourish and are certainly analogous to enthronement ceremonies that were accomplished on a yearly basis throughout the ANE. Though specific evidence for such an annual enthronement festival is lacking with regard to ancient Israel, nevertheless the matter of "moving God in" to the temple was a very serious one indeed. Its seriousness is indicated by the accompanying rhetoric of chosenness. The city has been chosen as a place for the temple to be built, to be a **resting place** for Yahweh (v 41). The temple was not only a place of rest for the ark from its days of wandering but also a symbol of rest/peace for the nation (as mentioned in 1 Chr 22:9). Yahweh's rest thus anticipates "rest" for the people (see Heb 4:9 for a similar idea). The **ark of your might** (2 Chr 6:41) has been chosen as a symbol of the divine presence. The **priests** have been chosen as those who will minister before the presence of Yahweh for all time. God's **faithful people** have been chosen to participate in the benefits of his graciousness, so long as they remain faithful to him. Finally, Yahweh's **anointed one** (v 42) is not rejected, as Yahweh is called upon to **remember the great love promised to David your servant**. Even in the case where hope seemed still to be awaiting fulfillment, that it would be fulfilled was never a matter open to question.

FROM THE TEXT

This prayer can serve as an important model of prayers for church dedications. Calling a place of worship "the house of God" has important connection to tradition, so long as one retains the theological principle that God is not contained in such a "house." In addition, this prayer also shows how a place of worship can be more than a place where rituals are done. It can also be a place for comfort in times of crisis and distress. This is a practice engaged in throughout the world, in many different situations. Finally, prayer does not submit well to analysis. Instead, it most often expresses genuine, spontaneous emotion. Nevertheless, models can be found in the tradition, and even those experiencing spontaneous emotion can be helped by written prayers used in the past by the faithful people of God.

d. Solemn Assembly and Sacrifices (7:1-10)

IN THE TEXT

■ **1** In various OT texts, divine acceptance of prayers is often clearly displayed through "special effects," chief among them being pyrotechnics. An important intertextual connection to the present text is the theomachy (battle between the gods) that takes place on Mount Carmel in 1 Kgs 18. In that Deuteronomistic text, the question is which of the two gods (or one goddess) is able to send fire from heaven and consume a sacrifice. By extension, Yahweh, Baal, or Asherah—whoever was successful—would be believed capable of ending the drought then being experienced by the northern kingdom of Israel. Naturally, Yahweh proved superior: "Then the fire of the LORD fell and burned up the sacrifice, the wood, the stones and the soil, and also licked up the water in the trench" (1 Kgs 18:38). Here, then, Yahweh's support of and pleasure with the temple and the prayers that King Solomon has offered is demonstrated when **fire came down from heaven and consumed the burnt offering and the sacrifices, and the glory of the LORD filled the temple** (2 Chr 7:1). The latter phrase has another intertextual hook to the great vision of the prophet Isaiah in the temple: "In the year that King Uzziah died, I saw the Lord, high and exalted, seated on a throne; and the train of his robe filled the temple" (Isa 6:1).

■ **2** The careful reader may find further intertextual connections in this verse. In suggesting that **the priests could not enter the temple of the LORD because the glory of the LORD filled it**, the Chroniclers make an allusion to the ancient tabernacle. Exodus 40:35 reports that "Moses could not enter the tent of meeting because the cloud had settled on it, and the glory of the LORD filled the tabernacle." Furthermore, that the Deuteronomists do not include these details surely says something interesting about a comparison between the two epics. In addition, the Chroniclers do not mention the Exodus here either (see 1 Kgs 8:62-66). True enough, the Deuteronomists do give a slightly fuller account of the sacrifices Solomon makes at the dedication of the temple, but this text yet again shows the Chroniclers' gift as creative writers. They decide to hold off on the vast numbers of sacrifices until 2 Chr 7:5, a move certainly designed to meet their own theological purposes in writing or rewriting Israel's history.

■ **3** The amazed response of the Israelites to Yahweh's pyrotechnic display elicits, as one might expect, a reaction of awe and wonder. Just as the fire falling upon Elijah's sacrifice on Mount Carmel resulted in the ecstatic utterance of the people that Yahweh, not Baal or Asherah, was indeed God (1 Kgs 18:39), so the fire falling here upon the elaborate sacrifices brings forth from the people a poetic response. The words **He is good; his love endures forever** are exactly the same as in Pss 106:1; 107:1; 118:1, 29; 136:1. Each of these five occurrences in the Psalms are the reason why the people should follow the command to "Give thanks to the LORD." This phrase is used two other times in the Chroniclers' History. In 1 Chr 16:34 one finds the phrase exactly the same as the Psalms references. Also, in 2 Chr 5:13 this phrase (in the form here, without the summons to give thanks) at the bringing of the ark into the temple.

■ **4-5** As noted above, the Chroniclers decided to leave off the description of how many bulls and goats Solomon offered until now. The numbers given, **twenty-two thousand head of cattle and a hundred and twenty thousand sheep and goats**, exactly mirrors those given in 1 Kgs 8:63. A key difference comes in the end of the same verse. Whereas the Deuteronomists summarize "So the king and all the Israelites dedicated the temple of the Lord," the Chroniclers instead write **So the king and all the people dedicated the temple of God**. However, though this is a linguistic difference, it is not a theological difference, since the name "Yahweh" and the designation "God" are considered the same by the Chroniclers, as noted above. The convergence between the two probably reflects the realization cemented in Jewish theology around this time that Yahweh really was the only God throughout the entire world. Whereas the Deuteronomists needed perhaps to be sure to which God the temple was being dedicated, the Chroniclers' situation has changed, and they do not need now to be so specific.

■ **6-10** The final five verses of this text describe the continuing festive activities that accompanied the dedication of the temple. The making of sacrifices, together with the declaration of the people that Yahweh's love endures forever and Yahweh's glory filling the temple, formed the climax, so to speak, of the dedication ceremony. Verse 6 echoes the theme of Yahweh's love enduring forever. Verse 7 makes the bold claim that **the bronze altar . . . could not hold the burnt offerings, the grain offerings and the fat portions**. This is likely the same kind of inflated rhetoric that has been seen throughout, but again was customary in the ANE, especially in stories detailing the dedication of a holy place to an important deity. The festivities last for a total of fifteen days, according to v 9, **for they had celebrated the dedication of the altar for seven days and the festival for seven days more**, with the fifteenth day being given over to a solemn assembly. The people eventually go home, **joyful and glad in heart for the good things the Lord had done for David and Solomon and for his people Israel** (v 10). This text briefly recalls David's celebration and sacrifices after bringing the ark to the house of Obed-Edom. At the end of that earlier time, David had given "a loaf of bread, a cake of dates and a cake of raisins" to everyone in attendance. Solomon does not give such gifts to the people here—at least, such gifting is not explicitly mentioned. Sadly, though perhaps not surprisingly, the king who has spent all the resources of the land to display his strength and power has nothing to give to the poor. Oftentimes, generosity ends where self-aggrandizement begins! Nevertheless, the grand story winds down here, only to be ramped up again immediately.

e. Yahweh Appears to Solomon (7:11-22)

BEHIND THE TEXT

Theophanies, or miraculous appearances of God, occur often in the OT. The typical function of theophany stories was to identify the one whom God visited as a particularly significant individual in the course of Israel's history. Thus venerable men such as Abraham and Moses both had God visit them in this way (see Gen 15 and Exod 3). In addition, many important women enjoyed visits from God, including the non-Israelite Hagar (Gen 21). Sometimes theophanies happen with "special effects," as in the appearance to Moses in a flaming bush that is never consumed. However, in at least one case—the journey of the prophet Elijah to Horeb—God sets aside the special effects for a greater purpose (see 1 Kgs 19). Given this tradition, it is not at all surprising that Yahweh should visit Solomon on the occasion of the dedication of the temple. Thus the visit recounted in this passage serves the typical function of theophanies. Not only does it proclaim the obvious importance of Solomon, but it also does so for the act of building the temple. Sociologically, the reign of Solomon represented a high-water mark in terms of exploitation of the populace by the central ruling authority. Theologically, however, Solomon's reign was seen by the Chroniclers as the high-water mark in terms of the blessing of Yahweh upon the chosen people.

IN THE TEXT

■ **11-12** In the first two verses of the passage, Yahweh gives a brief introduction. This is similar to what was seen in Solomon's great prayer of dedication in 6:14. Yahweh's opening speech gives a summary statement, as it were, of Yahweh's blessing of Solomon and what he has done: **I have heard your prayer and have chosen this place for myself as a temple for sacrifices** (7:12). This statement functions, for Israel, similarly to how the prayers for the dedication of divine cult images in other ANE societies functioned. The typical recital of such prayers included the confirmation of the deity in question that the image thus constructed and dedicated could, in fact, serve as a faithful and accurate representation of the deity. This idea, of course, does not play a role in Israelite theology, though the temple, and especially the ark of the covenant within it—served as a visible, if not touchable, symbol of God's presence with the people. Curiously, the divine speech makes reference to the temple as **a temple for sacrifices**, not a "resting place" for God. This may mean that God refuses to be domesticated by Solomon.

■ **13-16** The next four verses of Yahweh's speech include what is perhaps the most well-known verse in 2 Chronicles. Unfortunately, however, v 14 is often memorized without any recognition of the context in which it occurs. The illumination that comes from this "contextualizing" (a term that is put to different use in different theological disciplines) is striking. Specifically, vv 13-14 recall the language of Solomon's prayer in 6:26-27. In both cases, the punishment for sin is the withholding of rain necessary for farming. That droughts, floods, and other extreme weather events represent the judgment of God against various sins is a well-attested, ancient motif in many religious traditions. While such a connection may or may not be relevant in modern times, it is helpful to recognize that the ancients made it, for it provides an excellent insight into both official and popular religion of the ancient world. Solomon prayed in this connection that Yahweh would "teach them the right way to live, and send rain on the land you gave your people for an inheritance" (6:27). Yahweh says in response, **Now my eyes will be open and my ears attentive to the prayers offered in this place** (7:15). Though the answer is not precisely the same as the prayer, it does indicate something important regarding the Chroniclers' theology, namely, that knowledge of and faithfulness in the proper worship of the temple are coextensive with doing the will of Yahweh in the land.

■ **17-18** In these two verses, Yahweh recalls the conditional promise given to David in 1 Chr 17 and 28. The earlier promise, given through the prophet Nathan, seems to have been unconditional (see 1 Chr 17:13-14; 2 Sam 7:14-15). In other words, Yahweh's promise of an heir to always sit upon David's throne was not contingent upon the faithfulness of the sons who would succeed him. Yahweh's speech here, however, makes clear that the establishment of Solomon's **royal throne** and the promise of an eternal dynasty that God **covenanted with David** (2 Chr 7:18) are contingent upon Solomon's faithfulness and obedience to God's decrees and laws. When David passes on the charge to Solomon in 1 Chr 28:9, he adds the element that Solomon must be faithful in order to enjoy Yahweh's continued faithfulness (see 1 Kgs 2:4). Both the Deuteronomists and the Chroniclers seem to hold this unconditional-conditional character of the Davidic covenant in tension with each other. We are reminded here that while God's promises may come with or without any conditions, obedience to God is the most appropriate way to relate to God for those who are recipients of his promises.

■ **19-22** The final section of Yahweh's speech to King Solomon details the curses that will surely follow on the king's disobedience to Yahweh's will. The principal promised punishment is exile from the land, the ultimate rejection of the temple Yahweh just approved as a dwelling for his name and the offering of sacrifices back in v 12. Of course, the Chroniclers are writing in a retrospective mode, for in their experience—or at least, that of the previous generation or two prior to their experience—Yahweh has already rejected the temple and expelled the people, only to bring them back again and allow them a chance to rebuild. So, ideologically speaking, they are "transferring" the threat given to Solomon to their own time. In other words, they believe Yahweh has given the people a second chance, and they maintain the threat previously given, in the belief that the same punishment will happen again if the same sins are continued. It is also interesting to note that the threat of punishment is not extended to the royal dynasty; the dynastic promise will continue to have its validity, a theme found in both the Deuteronomists and the Chroniclers (see 1 Kgs 9:6-9).

The motif in vv 21-22 of **All who pass by** being **appalled** is a well-attested usage in the ANE. For example, Jer 22:8-9 gives "a non-specific prophecy of persons viewing the destruction of the city and wondering why it has come about" (Modine 2009a, 211). A text from *ANET* refers to a similar prophecy about Arabia and the god Enlil: "'On account of what have these calamities befallen Arabia?' (they answered themselves) 'Because we did not keep the solemn oaths (sworn by) Ashur'" (*ANET* 1969, 300; quoted in Modine 2009a, 212). Thus, again, the OT is proven to reuse traditional ideas from the ANE environment, always making sure to "contextualize" them into proper Hebrew idiom and theology.

3. Solomon Secures His Reign (8:1-18)

▶Overview

The next chapter details some of the things Solomon did to secure his reign. Kings throughout history have had to make bold moves for this purpose. This is a particular need with regard to dynastic successors, for there are always rival claimants to the throne. The material here mainly duplicates the version in 1 Kings, although it should of course be remembered that the two accounts must be read on their own merits. Comparison between them is helpful, so long as it is not done in terms of the one being a more or less perfect copy of the other.

Solomon's royal activities are accomplished in the reverse order than what his father, King David, did. David secured his reign, fought wars, and built his palace before turning to the building of Yahweh's temple. Solomon, by contrast, attended first to the building of the temple—as has been shown throughout all of the previous lengthy section of the book. Only after the temple was built and dedicated did Solomon turn his attention to matters of state, so to speak. This is perhaps due to the fact that Solomon did not need to engage in much costly and time-consuming military action in the same way that David did. While certainly there were some military matters to attend to, on the whole it seems that Solomon's reign was a time of nearly unparalleled peace and certainly unparalleled prosperity.

a. Fortification of Key Cities (8:1-6)

IN THE TEXT

■ **1-6** The first thing Solomon does to secure his reign is to fortify the five important cities. One suspects that this action was undertaken in order either to prevent or to prepare for any military activity that Solomon may have had to lead. The location of **Hamath Zobah** (v 3) is uncertain, though it may be in the Beka Valley near Lebanon. **Tadmor in the desert** (v 4) was located in the north Syrian desert and served as a caravan stop. Improving this city would have helped Solomon control some of the lucrative trade passing through the area. Exactly what location is meant by **all the store cities he had built in Hamath** (v 4) is not certain. However, **Upper Beth Horon and Lower Beth Horon** (v 5) were both located some two miles apart. They were on a ridge at the entrance of the central hill country, thus forming an important barrier between the area surrounding Jerusalem and the coastal plain, lately the stronghold of Saul and David's longstanding enemies the Philistines. Finally, **Baalath** (v 6) is an earlier name for the city of Kiriath Jearim, where David had brought the ark so many years previous (see 1 Chr 13:5-6; 2 Chr 1:4). Thus this was an important city for Israel's history.

b. Foreigners and Israelites Treated Differently (8:7-11)

BEHIND THE TEXT

The remaining existence in the promised land of various non-Israelite populations is a vexing problem throughout the history of Israel (see v 7). The careful interpreter of the two great historical epics—the Deuteronomistic History and Chronicles—must approach this reality with caution, for if improperly handled it can yield interpretations that are quite misleading. On the one hand, many readers assume a dispute between Joshua and Judges as to the fate of the other nations. According to the typical reading, Joshua maintains that all of the nations were ultimately driven out before Israel (see, in particular, Josh 24:18). By contrast, Judges is quite clear that several of the tribes were not successful in driving out all of the previous inhabitants of the land (see especially Judg 2:23; 3:1). Yet a closer reading of Joshua reveals that all was in fact not well; there were many groups of Canaanites who remained in the land (see Josh 13:13; 17:13). This evidence is, of course, aside from the fact that Joshua's reports that all the people were killed are certainly examples of the hyperbole typical of ANE battle reports.

On the other hand, the archaeological record, if it really confirms or disconfirms any of the Bible's claims, rather supports the picture of Judges and the careful reading of Joshua over against the naive reading. Moreover, the differences (ethnic, cultural, religious, social, and so on) between the Canaanites and the Israelites were probably somewhat minor. William Dever concludes similarly:

> In short, if you had been walking in the countryside of central Palestine, especially in the hill country, in the 12th or 11th century B.C.E. and had met several people, you could probably not have distinguished Israelites from Canaanites or Canaanites from Philistines. (1992, 54)

There should be little doubt, however, that the Israelites knew they were Israelites, the Canaanites knew they were Canaanites, and the Philistines knew they were Philistines. It must be recognized, however, that "the kinds of things that now enable us to talk about ethnicity will have disappeared from the archaeological record" (Dever 1992, 54).

IN THE TEXT

■ **7-8** At first glance, this note concerning the treatment of those persons who **were not Israelites** (v 7) seems to be much improved over previous such notes. For example, Judg 3:2 maintains that Yahweh left the other nations in the land "to teach warfare to the descendants of the Israelites who had not had previous battle experience." Though, as indicated above, the situation recorded in Judges is probably a lot closer to actual reality than that recorded in Joshua, nevertheless it is presented as a negative situation with negative results. Here, however, the treatment of the other nations is a little more just—though not completely so!—in that they are put to forced labor rather than the sword.

■ **9-10** In a somewhat startling contrast to what will come later on in the story, the text reports that **Solomon did not make slaves of the Israelites for his work** (v 9; see 1 Kgs 5:13 for the Deuteronomists' report). Nevertheless, the Israelites will ask for leniency from Solomon's son Rehoboam. Not desiring to grant this leniency, Rehoboam sees the northern tribes rebel, tearing the majority of the kingdom away from the Davidic monarchy. This is one of the great tragedies of the history of Israel, and it will receive its due treatment. It is here sufficient to note that Solomon gave the Israelites honored place. Against this idea, naturally, is the tendency already noted, quite common in Chronicles, to call the Judeans after the division of the kingdoms Israelites. In other words, perhaps those who are reaping the benefits are actually Judeans.

Nevertheless, what is more important is the seemingly more positive treatment of the other nations.

■ **11** Solomon continues what by now is time-honored practice and excludes his foreign wife from the palace. Though Solomon comes into heavy criticism from the Deuteronomists for building shrines to the gods of his foreign wives (see esp. 1 Kgs 11:1-13), the Chroniclers here present him in a more favorable light. The reader has come to expect such from this version of Israel's history. The Chroniclers apparently did not think it such a problem that Solomon was married to these foreign wives. At least, from his perspective, he did not defile the temple of Yahweh or the holiness of the city where **the ark of the LORD has entered** by allowing these foreign women and their supposed "corrupting influence" to remain in the palace of King David located in the City of David. One may assume that the palace he built for his Egyptian wife was outside the city limit. This is one place where the Chroniclers appear more astute in the ways of the world and, in the process, less naively theological, than their historical predecessors.

c. Solomon Finishes All the Work (8:12-18)

IN THE TEXT

■ **12-18** In the Chroniclers' History, the account of the building of the temple lasted four chapters. Following that, the account of the dedication of the temple lasted four chapters. This second major section ends here, with the summary comment that ***all of Solomon's work was finished*** (v 16). This follows on a description of the daily work of the temple. It seems that, after the temple was built and dedicated, Solomon's work was indeed concluded. The king, though he certainly had an important role to play, was not to usurp the authority of the religious establishment. In the Deuteronomistic History, one of the reasons why King Saul was ultimately rejected was due to just this kind of usurpation, with Saul performing a sacrifice without waiting for Samuel the prophet to arrive (see 1 Sam 13:7-15). The Chroniclers make clear that altar upon which Solomon offered/officiated sacrifices was outside the holy place, and that he appointed priests and Levites to carry out their specific duties (2 Chr 8:12, 14). However, the king burning incense on the altar of incense in the holy place would have been considered by the Chroniclers as a defiant act (see 2 Chr 26:16-21). Though one should avoid the anachronistic (and often misapplied) term "separation of church and state," nevertheless it does seem to be the case that, in Israel, the king and the high priest—as representatives, respectively, of the government and the religious establishments—largely stayed out of one another's affairs. Encroachment did frequently take place, though almost exclusively from the side of the "church" invading the "state." An exception to this is the improper sacrifice offered by King Saul, which brings forth great rebuke from the prophet Samuel (see 1 Sam 13). This was sometimes done by priests, but more often by prophets. Thus the prophet Jeremiah, whose work was quite important for the Chroniclers, had many dealings with the kings, often committing what look like very bold attacks upon the power of the sovereign. In the final two verses, after the note that Solomon had gotten everything done, the Chroniclers report that the king went about securing more wealth for the royal coffers, a note that will be sounded again in the next chapter as the account of Solomon's reign will draw to a close (see 9:13-28).

FROM THE TEXT

Solomon's completion of the work entrusted to him by David and, ultimately, by God surely carries a great lesson for all those who have been commissioned by God to fulfill a given task. The first part of such a lesson is that the work God commands one to do should be done with all one's might (Eccl 9:10). Second, one must recognize when the work is done. Though some work is never really finished, sometimes one can hold on to a particular task so long that it becomes an obsession. In Solomon's case, although his wealth eventually spelled his downfall, nevertheless he moved on to other things after having completed work on the temple. Concluding one's work often involved entrusting it to others, and this is what Solomon in fact did when the proper time had come.

4. The End of the Reign of Solomon (9:1-31)

▶Overview

The Chroniclers have three more things to say about the lengthy reign of Solomon. The first two of these will be descriptions of the king's influence and wealth. The influence of the king will be described through a story of the state visit of a monarch from the mysterious land of Sheba. The wealth of the king will be described evocatively, even if somewhat less imaginatively. Finally, the Chroniclers will report on Solomon's death, using a formula established in the report of David's death and followed throughout the rest of the history. The few notable exceptions to this pattern should startle the reader and will be dealt with in due course.

a. The Visit of the Queen of Sheba (9:1-12)

BEHIND THE TEXT

The visit of the Queen of Sheba to the court of King Solomon is the stuff of which legends are made. Though the text is clearly designed to talk up Solomon's prestige, particularly as an interpreter of riddles and so on, the king's dialogue partner is interesting. One might expect such repartee to go on between men, particularly men in a wisdom school or scribal house, but here it is a woman who arrives to test Solomon. Attempts at identifying the mysterious Queen of Sheba and the location of her territory have been largely disappointing, with options ranging from the southwest Arabian Peninsula to the horn of Africa, near modern Djibouti (Rasmussen 2010, 298). The specific location of her land, however, is less important than the exchange related in the text. This story is plainly intended to bolster the reputation of Solomon. Thus it fits in nicely with the other texts in this section. In other words, though the episode with the two prostitutes and the babies is not included (1 Kgs 3:16-28), this text nevertheless shows how wise Solomon is. In addition, a long-standing tradition holds that Solomon and the Queen of Sheba were lovers. Some in Ethiopian society, for example, believe that the child born of this union served as the first king in a Solomonic dynasty in Ethiopia. Of course, such a suggestion probably lies beyond verification or falsification. It seems most likely that this theory has to do with national or ethnic pride on the part of Ethiopians who subscribe to it, desiring to establish for their people a most noble ancestry.

IN THE TEXT

■ **1** The tribal name **Sheba** occurs three times in the genealogies of 1 Chr 1. In v 9 of that chapter it occurs alongside a similar, but differently spelled, Seba. It also occurs in vv 22 and 32. Jarick notes that the first of these, in v 9, is of Cushite origin, while the other two are Semitic (2007b, 56-57). Rasmussen suggests that the queen's visit **with a very great caravan** reflects "her interest in maintaining good relations with Solomon so as to expedite the passage of her caravans through his territory" (2010, 144). On this interpretation, the visit is purely political and economic. While it is plausible that this was the only reason the Queen of Sheba came to visit, one must not out of hand discount the theory mentioned above, namely that the queen meant to establish a relationship of a decidedly more personal nature. After all, as has been noted at various points throughout this commentary, the human characters in the Bible were flesh-and-blood people with flesh-and-blood desires, wants, and needs.

■ **2-4** The Queen of Sheba is overawed and perhaps more than a little intimidated by the wisdom of Solomon and the opulence of his court. The wisdom test she gives him, and the fact that **Solomon answered all her questions** set her back. According to the text, **nothing was too hard for him to explain to her** (v 2). In 1 Kgs 4:32, the Deuteronomists report that Solomon "spoke three thousand proverbs and his songs numbered a thousand and five." This summary statement surely includes the display given to the Queen of Sheba, which is related in the earlier epic in 1 Kgs 10.

■ **5-9** The Queen of Sheba gives a speech in which she praises Solomon for his wisdom and for the grandeur of his court. She says she had heard of the reputation of Solomon all the way back in her home country, so she, as the saying goes, had to see it for herself. Yet, when she saw it, she could not believe it. The reports were not even adequate to describe what she found there. Though, in one sense, this is typical royal flattery, in another sense this serves what was undoubtedly an important need in Persian-period Judah. That is, the people trying to rebuild the country after the trauma of exile needed a certain amount of ideological boost. A story like this could easily fill the bill: if, once upon a time, Judah was so great that foreign kings and queens came to marvel at it, perhaps it could be so again (see Hag 2:9 for a similar sentiment regarding the temple).

■ **10-11** These two verses seem out of place. King Hiram, with whom Solomon had dealings earlier in the narrative, suddenly shows up again without having been reintroduced. The link between them and the context comes in the note that the things Hiram brought were of such eloquence that **Nothing like them had ever been seen in Judah** (v 11). This line echoes v 9 and also the queen's report in v 6. The last of these reflects Hiram's comment in 2:11, thus reinforcing the link. The NIV appropriately marks 9:10-11 off as a parenthetical comment, which seems to be a reasonable solution.

■ **12** The diplomatic détente concluded, Solomon sends the queen back to her home country. That she left with **more than she had brought to him** fuels the ethnic speculation noted above. Again, a statement like this is probably unprovable. For that matter, it is not probable that evidence would ever be found so many thousands of years later to definitively *disprove* the suggestion, either. Thus the wisest course of action is to mention it without comment as to whether it might be true.

b. The Wealth of Solomon (9:13-28)

IN THE TEXT

■ **13-28** The Chroniclers celebrate in these verses Solomon's incomparable wealth and fame perhaps to stir up the imagination of their readers that a future filled with glory and wealth is a possibility under future Davidic rulers.

666 Talents of Gold and Intertextuality

The note that the annual revenue of gold flowing into Solomon's coffers **was 666 talents** might fuel speculation regarding possible connections to the so-called number of the beast in Rev 13:18. It might even be said that the Deuteronomists at 1 Kgs 10:14 and the Chroniclers here have intentionally included this information just before describing how Solomon fell into sin. Therefore, so the reasoning goes, the number of the beast is an active concept even in the OT. This, it seems, is an example of how intertextuality can be taken to absurd and misleading extremes. Proper intertextuality, by contrast, after noting an apparent connection (sometimes called a "trace" or an "echo") of another text, then examines how the common term or idea is used in both (or all in the case of multiple examples) texts in order to gain a wider field of reflection on which to construct a meaning for the term in question.

In other words, that the Chroniclers include the data that Solomon received an annual income of **666 talents** of gold is a datum for consideration and interpretation. The Deuteronomists at 1 Kgs 10:14 agree with this data, thus giving a second datum. Finally, this number does in fact occur again in Rev 13:18, making this a third datum for consideration. However, when one honestly and forthrightly examines the respective contexts of 1 Kgs 10, 2 Chr 9, and Rev 13, one cannot help but see that each of the three texts employs the number 666 differently. It seems that both the Deuteronomists and the Chroniclers use this number as part of praise of Solomon. However, the Deuteronomists go on from the description of Solomon's wealth to describe the king's fall into idolatry because of his one thousand wives and concubines. The Chroniclers steadfastly refuse to include any of this information, though the omission is in no wise to be judged as deliberately deceptive or willfully ignorant. In Revelation, however, there is no mention whatever of Solomon. In fact, the beast to whom the number refers is a mythical creature come out of the sea, a typical motif for apocalyptic literature. Thus, even though the number occurs in all three texts, each of them uses it differently. Therefore, theological correlation between them—doubtlessly based on the ideological power the number of the beast holds in certain Christian circles—is at best idle speculation. At worst it is a heretical misreading of Scripture and a misleading of the people of God.

Solomon seems to have made gold the standard symbol of economic prosperity and as a result, **silver was considered of little value in** his day (v 20). Hence, naturally the king would desire the most valuable materials for his palace. Indeed, Solomon seems to have contributed to the devaluation of silver, as he **made silver as common in Jerusalem as stones** (v 27)! This does raise other problems, however, particularly from the standpoint of sociological criticism. Stated as directly as possible, at what cost to the people of Israel did Solomon decorate his palace—and indeed, his palaces, as v 16 suggests? Jarick comments that **the Palace of the Forest of Lebanon** was

> presumably a grand hall for spectacular regal occasions, probably constructed with the best quality timber from Lebanon and perhaps furnished with pillars and roof-beams that artistically replicated the appearance of a forest. The name of this structure . . . might also be

intended to suggest the expansion of Solomon's realm into the area of Lebanon. (2007b, 59)

The point of all of this information is to demonstrate that **King Solomon was greater in riches and wisdom than all the other kings of the earth** (v 22). This is doubtless the same kind of ANE rhetoric seen in such places as the Merenptah stela mentioned earlier (→ 1 Chr 18:1-11). It is common in modern times, when ranking the top ten of whatever, to include precise details and rankings. This practice would not have been understood in antiquity. In other words, Israelite scribes would naturally say an Israelite king was the richest ever or the wisest ever, while Egyptian scribes would naturally say an Egyptian king was the richest ever or the wisest ever. An intertextual trace of this note may be found in Job 1:3.

It was mentioned above that sociological criticism does in fact raise a concern with regard to Solomon's wealth. This is especially the case for 2 Chr 9:25-27, and in particular the notes about Solomon's horses. Israel never seems to have developed a strong equestrian tradition. In fact, the horse may well have served as a rather powerful symbol of oppression by an outside force. Brueggemann writes:

> We have ample evidence to suggest the social function of horses and chariots for kings . . . The Bible characteristically associates horses and chariots with royal power, which is regularly seen to be oppressive . . . Yahweh's hostility to horses and chariots bespeaks Yahweh's hostility to the social system that requires, legitimates, and depends on them. (1994, 305-6)

Brueggemann cites Josh 11, which describes the Israelites' victory over a heavily armed cavalry, as prime evidence for this. Other evidence may be found in the so-called law of the king in Deut 17:16. This verse specifically forbids going down to Egypt for horses, as 2 Chr 9:28 suggests Solomon did. Also, the prophet Samuel warns that a king will be oppressive, particularly with regard to horses, in 1 Sam 8:11-12. It may well be, then, that the Chroniclers do attack Solomon precisely under the guise of praising him: in getting all this wealth, Solomon made the people suffer. Sociological insights like this can be very helpful in illuminating the meaning of—or constructing new meaning with—biblical texts.

c. The Death of Solomon (9:29-31)

BEHIND THE TEXT

At long last, the Chroniclers come around to the death of the great King Solomon. Like that of his father, David (→ 1 Chr 29:23-30), Solomon's death marks a key transition in the narrative. Comparing the two leaders is difficult, since the situations they faced were different. Perhaps it is best to say that each rose to the occasion presented him and through it proved himself to be a great leader. David's exploits did in fact pave the way for Solomon's, bringing a relative degree of peace and stability to Israel. Not having to defend himself from without, Solomon was then free to expand, as the narrative demonstrates.

IN THE TEXT

■ **29-31** Verse 29 continues a practice established by the Chroniclers with the story of David's death in 1 Chr 29. The Chroniclers suggest that **other events of Solomon's reign, from beginning to end** are written down in a couple of sources. The information is written **in the records of Nathan the prophet, in the prophecy of Ahijah the Shilonite and in the visions of Iddo the seer concerning Jeroboam son of Nebat**. The first of these was also cited in connection with David. As for the Deuteronomists, when they come to the death of Solomon they cite a source called "the book of the annals of Solomon" (1 Kgs 11:41), which is certainly meant to indicate official royal records. The third source is interesting, because its main figure is Jeroboam son of Nebat, who will eventually become the first king of the northern kingdom of Israel (2 Chr 10). The material of the obscure prophet Ahijah from Shiloh apparently had to deal mostly with Jeroboam as well, since this prophet is mentioned again in 2 Chr 10:15.

The note that Solomon reigned **in Jerusalem over all Israel forty years** (v 30) is a well-known stylistic feature. The number forty is frequently used in expressions of time in the Bible (Gen 7:4; Exod 24:18; Num 14:33; Deut 9:11; 1 Kgs 19:8; Matt 4:2; Acts 1:3). However, though this may refer to a nonspecific length of time, it is not completely impossible that Solomon did, in fact, reign for forty years. This is so because of the peace and prosperity of the kingdom over which he ruled. Kings, in the ancient world, tended to live longer than other people anyway, since (just like today) the wealthy and powerful have access to better resources for the maintenance of life. Such resources include food, certainly, but also protection in the form of armed guards and laborers to do the difficult work of farming, and so forth, for them.

FROM THE TEXT

As the reader will see, things begin to fall apart quite quickly after Solomon's time. Indeed, the great kingdom that David and Solomon labored to build will be torn into two during the reign of Solomon's son Abijah. Of course, the only direction to go after the heights reached by Solomon is down. However, the lesson that should perhaps be derived from this is that living in the glory of the past is not an effective strategy for going forward. The preacher of Ecclesiastes warns: ***Do not ask why the good old days were so much better than these. It is not smart for you to ask such things*** (7:10). Whether King Solomon wrote these lines or, more likely, not is beside the point. What is more important is that Rehoboam was not as wise as his father, and his lack of wisdom had disastrous consequences for the nation.

The Chroniclers seem to have an overall positive view of Solomon. They certainly do not give any negative evaluation of him. However, they do seem to suggest a way of life that is ambiguous. They represent Solomon as pious, yet opulent. This divided way of life sets the nation on a downhill journey. As will be apparent in the subsequent commentary, things fall apart quickly from the so-called golden age represented by Solomon.

III. THE HISTORY OF JUDAH AFTER THE DIVISION OF THE KINGDOMS (2 CHRONICLES 10:1—36:23)

▶ Overview

Another area in which the southern bias of the Chroniclers comes into play is the way in which the division of the kingdoms is presented. On the one hand, both the Deuteronomists and the Chroniclers seem to agree on the point that the division was really a "rebellion" (2 Chr 10:19). On the other hand, one may find in each an at least grudging acceptance of blame on the part of Rehoboam and the Judeans. The division between the kingdoms created a significant ideological problem, with implications running throughout the OT. The prophets Jeremiah and Ezekiel both have visions for the reunion of Israel and Judah after the exile (Jer 51; Ezek 37).

One more item deserves mention at the outset. The majority of the Judean kings after the division of the kingdoms get relatively short treatment by the Chroniclers. In fact, most of their stories are contained within one chapter. Though the chapter divisions are of course secondary to the creation of the text and somewhat arbitrary, nevertheless this is an interesting point to note. In 2 Chronicles, the following kings' reigns last more than one chapter: Rehoboam (10:1—12:16), Asa (14:2—16:14), Jehoshaphat (17:1—21:1), Hezekiah (29:1—32:33), and Josiah (34:1—35:27). Queen Athaliah (22:10—23:21) belongs on the list because of the space given her. However, she is an oddity because she is not favored by the Chroniclers. A comparison with the Deuteronomists is helpful here. Of these six kings, Rehoboam and Athaliah are judged to be wicked. Asa, Jehoshaphat, Hezekiah, and Josiah, by contrast, are judged positively. Five other kings (Jehoram, Joash, Amaziah, Uzziah, Jotham) are judged positively by the Deuteronomists but do not receive more than a chapter of coverage from the Chroniclers. Surely the principal reason why Asa, Jehoshaphat, Hezekiah, and Josiah received such long treatment in comparison to the other "good kings" is that, in addition to being good, they also undertook great religious reforms. In what follows, the commentary will return to this topic at appropriate points.

A. The Reign of Rehoboam (10:1—12:16)

▶ Overview

Things begin to fall apart very quickly. From the greatness of King Solomon, the only way for the fortunes of Israel to go was, unfortunately, down. Indeed, they went down in quite a hurry. For, as the following commentary will show, Rehoboam was not nearly as wise as his father. Though it is true from a certain point of view that Solomon's empire was built through a degree of oppression, Rehoboam is much worse. In fact, he is defiantly worse. His defiance, lacking in wisdom, tact, and prudence, lead rather directly to the dissolution of the kingdom his father, Solomon, and his grandfather, David, had worked so mightily to establish. While it is certainly not always true, this kind of dissolution happens rather often in a number of different empires of differing natures. As the old American phrase runs, "A chain is only as strong as its weakest link." King Rehoboam, most unfortunately for Israel, proved to be a very weak link indeed.

The Chroniclers' version of Rehoboam's story falls into two uneven "halves," with a much greater amount of material being devoted to the second part. The break between these two halves is, of course, what one expects, namely the most important event to take place during the reign of Rehoboam.

This is the rebellion of the northern tribes, which eventually results in the division of the promised land into the land of Israel in the north and the land of Judah in the south. After the division, of course, the Chroniclers spend far more time in Judah than in Israel. Indeed, as has already been noted, the Chroniclers tell far fewer stories of Israel even than the Deuteronomistic History. This is surely a reflection of the northern kingdom having long been a destroyed memory, but also it represents the theological view that the rebellion and division together formed a sinful break in Yahweh's plans for the nation. This is the rhetoric of Judah, to be sure, and the interpreter may be able legitimately to ask how the Israelites might have viewed the question. The commentary that follows will make some educated guesses along these lines, though in the main it will stick to a principal investigation of the text as it stands in 2 Chronicles.

1. From the Beginning of Rehoboam's Reign to the Division (10:1-19)

▶Overview

The first half of Rehoboam's reign runs from his accession to the division of the kingdoms. These events, divided into four scenes, take a very short time to transpire. What is important for the interpreter to note in these scenes is the presentation of the characters as three-dimensional, flesh-and-blood characters. The last thing the Chroniclers apparently want to do is show the characters who populate their history as automatons. Automatons, by their nature, respond in predictable ways to given situations. For example, presented with a challenge such as that given to Rehoboam, an automaton's response may have taken the following character. If concerned with the preservation of the institution of the Israelite monarchy—already known by that time as the house of David—then perhaps the automaton would placate the complainers. However, in a real-life situation, a king like Rehoboam is concerned with establishing and securing his reign, goals that are compromised by taking a weak-kneed approach to those who give criticism. Even if Rehoboam is ultimately presented as unwise when compared with his father, nevertheless he does what is necessary to preserve what he has been given and follows the course he believes Yahweh has set him on.

a. Appeal from the Northern Tribes for Leniency (10:1-5)

IN THE TEXT

■ **1-5** Whenever a new king came to power, all old relationships may be reevaluated. This principle seems to underlie the events related in the present text. Jeroboam, who **had fled from King Solomon** into Egypt, apparently in the hopes of reestablishing his favored status in the new court. At the very least, now that Solomon is dead he hopes not to remain under the sentence of death. Jeroboam was a respected leader of the northern tribes, and thus he acts as their representative in the court of Rehoboam. Their request, surely, is a reasonable one. They ask that the burden of forced labor, which Solomon imposed on them for the building of the temple and the royal palace, be lessened. Without using the specific word, it seems that the northern tribes are proposing a covenant-style agreement between themselves and Rehoboam. If the new king grants their request, they will serve him faithfully. The implicit threat is that, of course, they will react negatively toward Rehoboam if he responds to their request negatively. At least at first, Rehoboam acts wisely, telling the petitioners to come back in three days' time. He intends to use this time to deliberate over their request. Of course, the tendency of the reader is to interpret this text in light of developments later on in the chapter. This will not do, however. It is far better to interpret each segment of the text on its own.

FROM THE TEXT

10:1-5

Transitions in leadership are important for all organizations. New leaders usually have both the responsibility and the opportunity to reevaluate the policies of their predecessors. Either to continue or to discontinue old policies, without sufficient critical reflection, is to slight the responsibility and squander the opportunity. Once critical reflection is engaged in, however, the new leader must be resolute in the decision taken, whether it lies on the side of continuity or the side of adaptability. Strong organizations and institutions are able to withstand either. Both leader and followers can come out of this process of evaluation stronger and more effective, provided it is done well. If it is done poorly, however, great pain can result. Leaders and followers need to respect each other in order for the relationship to be healthy. This applies not only in politics and the business community but also in the church. A heavy-handed pastor can turn the flock against him or her quite quickly, while recalcitrant followers can stagnate the growth of the congregation. It is important to remember that the enemy of God can use people to accomplish his or her ends just as much as God can do so. Therefore, whenever leaders or followers are faced with a decision, due, careful, critical evaluation must be undertaken in order to assure that the decision taken is the right one.

b. Rehoboam Seeks Counsel (10:6-11)

IN THE TEXT

■ **6-7** King Rehoboam first goes to the elders for advice as to how he should proceed. Deference to elders, and the wisdom that comes from age and experience, is a characteristic feature of Asian societies both ancient and modern. Thus, in the book of Job, the first of Job's "friends" to speak is the surely aged Eliphaz the Temanite. True enough, when one comes to the Elihu speeches beginning in Job 32, the assumption that wisdom only comes with age is called into question. This point will be noted again below in the commentary on Rehoboam's unwise answer (→ 2 Chr 10:12-15). The reader may ask the obvious counterfactual question. In other words, what might have happened had Rehoboam followed the advice of the elders? Cyrus the Great, king of Persia, had a similar opportunity presented to him when he took over control of the Babylonian Empire in 539 B.C. Cyrus was much more liked than his Babylonian predecessors, even in Babylonia. This was so because he instituted a policy of restoring the shrines that had been decimated by the Babylonians throughout their conquered domains. This was done in order to curry the favor—and the willing subjection—of the territories he inherited. At least in the OT, there seem to be no complaints about Persian rule, whereas there are plenty about Babylonian rule (see esp. the books of Daniel and Habakkuk).

■ **8-9** In the end, however, such counterfactual speculation is "merely academic." Rehoboam in fact **rejected the advice the elders gave him** (v 8). According to modern Western ways of making decisions, "getting a second opinion" is not rejection of the former opinion. The former opinion is not rejected until the decision is made. However, the logic operating in the text assumes that, by doing anything other than immediately acting in accordance with the elders' instructions, he is by definition rejecting what they have to say.

■ **10-11** The phrase **My little finger is thicker than my father's waist** (v 10) is an obvious euphemism. The reader should not be surprised to see a vulgar comment like this in the mouth of a biblical character. Though the text presents a "sanitized" version of the conversation, the actual conversation probably was rather crude, because it had to do with deep questions of authority. Moreover, the Chroniclers apparently assume that the decision was wrong. Though it ultimately was in God's will that these events take place (see v 15 of this chapter), that does not make Rehoboam's decision wise. As demonstrated throughout the Bible, God can use even wrong decisions by humans to carry out his will. By suggesting the answer they do, the brash young men convince Rehoboam that he should make things even worse for the northern tribes. Thus he not only fails to follow the elders and grant the request of the northerners, but he goes to an even further extreme. Perhaps the kingdom would still have been divided had Rehoboam made a different decision. Nevertheless, this was the decision he did in fact make, with disastrous consequences that will become immediately apparent.

FROM THE TEXT

Charles Wesley, brother of theologian and preacher John, was a skillful preacher and biblical interpreter in his own right. Whereas John took to the pulpit, Charles took to the pen. In all, Charles contributed some nine thousand poems of both religious and secular verse to the rich history not only of Methodism but also of English literature. He often turned to Scripture as a source of inspiration for his poetry. When he did so, his intent seemed not merely to explicate Scripture but to engage in the same kind of "prophetic" meaning-making that has been discussed above in the Introduction.

To cite just one instance of this, Charles seems to have been bitterly opposed to brother John's ordination of ministers for the Methodist Church in America. This was seen by Charles and many others as a schismatic break between the Methodist movement and the established church. Though opinions may differ on whether or not such a move was necessary, all sides agree that it represented a definitive paradigm shift. The discussions between Rehoboam and the northern tribes inspired an image embedded in one of Charles's poems on the issue:

> A troop of Jeroboam's priests appears
> For, after a long life of fourscore years,
> Poor John had Rehoboam's Counsellors. (Wesley 1992, 92)

Charles puts the image to creative use here, indeed intentionally mixing up the metaphor. In so doing, he interprets the break of the northern tribes from the house of David as the sin of Rehoboam, not the sin of Jeroboam. This is so even if Jeroboam did commit a great sin in going on to establish the unauthorized shrines in Bethel and Dan. To put it another way, he likens John to Rehoboam and Thomas Coke—one of the first Methodist bishops in America whom Charles seems to have particularly disliked—to Jeroboam. John had steadfastly refused to ordain Methodist preachers for many decades, until finally he turned into error and did this very thing, as Charles further laments:

> Christ our merciful High-Priest,
> With the people's grief distrest [sic],
> Help us for our guide to pray,
> Lost in his mistaken way:
>
> By a show of good misled

Lest he farther should proceed,
Stop, restrain him, and defend,
Till the hour of darkness end.

Hide him from the thing design'd
Not according to thy mind;
Save him from the purpos'd Ill
After his, but not thy will. (Wesley 1992, 93)

These citations, which may be multiplied, show how the biblical text can be used for new situations that the biblical writers could never have intended. A complete understanding of biblical inspiration includes the belief that God's inspiration of Scripture does not end with the end of the writing of Scripture. In other words, God inspired the readers as well. Preachers and teachers in the Wesleyan tradition should therefore feel bold to take their lead from the poet Charles Wesley, himself no doubt an author inspired by God, even if what he wrote was not Scripture!

c. Rehoboam's Unwise Answer (10:12-15)

IN THE TEXT

■ **12-15** In a move that would prove unfortunate for the later history of Israel, Rehoboam decides to follow the counsel of the young and restless rather than the old and experienced. Though wisdom is not always found with experience (see Job 32:9), in this case it surely would have been wiser to give a little back in order to keep everything. In other words, if King Rehoboam had submitted himself to their request, there would never have been a need for a King Jeroboam. Thus, a reading of this encounter from the perspective of the northern tribes, who consider themselves to have been slighted, yields the understanding that this is a renewal rather than a rebellion. The last verse of the exchange is interesting from a theological perspective: **this turn of events was from God, to fulfill the word the** Lord **had spoken to Jeroboam son of Nebat through Ahijah the Shilonite.** This agrees with 1 Kgs 12:15. In other words, within the text of both historical epics the seed may already be found of the alternative reading being proposed. Though all of the northern kings will be considered evil because they persisted in Jeroboam's "rebellion," nevertheless the division itself was by the will of Yahweh. One might be curious as to why such a disastrous event may be the will of Yahweh, but ultimately one confesses with Second Isaiah that Yahweh's thoughts are above human thoughts, as has already been shown (see Isa 55:9-11).

d. Beginning of Israel's Rebellion (10:16-19)

IN THE TEXT

■ **16-19** The northern tribes, with Jeroboam as their representative, respond precisely as might be expected to Rehoboam's unwise answer. The poetic exclamation **What share do we have in David, / what part in Jesse's son? / To your tents, Israel! / Look after your own house, David!** (v 16) is also found in 1 Kgs 12:16. A shortened form, with slightly different vocabulary, may be found 2 Sam 20:1. The context there is the rebellion of a Benjamite named Shebna against David. Whereas 2 Chr 20:16 and 1 Kgs 12:16 read the first line as a question, Shebna's version is a negative declaration: "We have no share in David, / no part in Jesse's son!" Further, Shebna's version reads "Every man to his tent, Israel!" thus combining the last two lines into one.

The reuse of this old poem highlights a couple of important things about the "rebellion" of the northern tribes. First, there is no reason to suggest that this is not an authentic utterance. Second, the Israelites who said this knew their history. This poem was likely every bit as annoying to the Davidic kings as was **Saul has killed his thousands / David his ten thousands** to Saul (1 Sam 18:17; 21:11; 29:5). Third, though the original utterance of Shebna was addressed to David, the reuse applied to his grandson cemented the idea of corporate identification. In other words, any descendant of David—normally referred to as the "son of David"—was the same as David himself.

The northern Israelites back their bravado with violence, killing **Adoniram, who was in charge of forced labor** (2 Chr 10:18). Rehoboam apparently was unwilling to do so, thus proving himself yet again to be ill suited to the situation. By listening to and following the wrong advice, he got himself into a situation for which he was unprepared. The Chroniclers' understated comment that **Israel has been in rebellion against the house of David to this day** (v 19) is important as well, for two reasons. First, except for scattered references, the Chroniclers do not deal with Israel again throughout their historical epic. Instead, they often refer to Judah with the term "Israel." Second, they did not attempt to update their source material—likely the Deuteronomistic History—on this point. They were writing in the Persian period, as has been noted. At that time, Israel had long been destroyed and largely forgotten. This was the case even for the Deuteronomists. Indeed, it is even possible that for both the Deuteronomists and the Chroniclers the "northern" part of the land remained as a symbol of resistance/rebellion against the Davidic dynasty, though history is being written at a much later time, long after the end of the northern kingdom.

FROM THE TEXT

As was noted in the commentary to 1 Chr 5:11-17, the question should remain open as to whether Jeroboam I's rebellion was, in fact, rebellion or liberation. Naturally, both the Deuteronomistic History and the Chroniclers' History, having a distinct bias toward the southern kingdom of Judah, represent this as a revolt, an unnecessary breaking away of the north from the south. A more even-handed assessment, however, should recognize that King Rehoboam did shoulder the lion's share of the responsibility in this question. Even though he thought he was doing the right thing, and even though the Chroniclers suggest that this came from God, ultimately the division did happen, and the interpreter must be careful. God is, of course, able to turn even the worst of human choices toward God's ends. It must be remembered that God lives outside of what humans in their limited perspective refer to as "history," so that the question of whether God's foreknowledge means that things had to have been determined in advance is speculative and subject to theological scrutiny. Every moment in the history of the world is immediately present to God at any time and at all times. Though Wesleyans would surely want to avoid questions of predestination, especially as regards salvation, divine foreknowledge seems to be another matter entirely. With respect to the current question, could the division of the kingdoms have been avoided? At that moment in history, had Rehoboam paid attention to the wise counsel of his elders, the kingdom would have remained in the house of David. If it had been the case, then something else would have been in the mind of God than what happened in this text (2 Chr 10:15), and so the text and this commentary would have been different.

2. Rehoboam After the Division (11:1—12:16)

▶ Overview

As noted above, the most important thing for the history of Israel that happened during the reign of King Rehoboam was the division of the kingdom into the northern kingdom of Israel and the southern kingdom of Judah. Thus, the second half of Rehoboam's reign in the Chroniclers' History is devoted to the events that followed the division. As things for the Davidic dynasty fell apart quickly, so also it seems that things fell apart quickly for Rehoboam. For though he enjoyed a fair amount of success in the immediate term following the revolt of the northern tribes, the last major event in his reign was a devastating attack from outside by the Egyptian Pharaoh Shoshenq I (called Shushak or Shishak in the text). Rehoboam is ultimately judged wicked in the eyes of Yahweh by the Deuteronomists (see 1 Kgs 14:22-24), a judgment with which the Chroniclers would likely ultimately agree, even though they do not explicitly say so.

a. Preparations for War Turned Back (11:1-4)

IN THE TEXT

■ **1-4** Rehoboam's initial response to what might be termed the "Shechem incident" or the "encounter at Shechem" is the expected one. Leaders whose rule has been rebelled against often attempt to respond violently. The aims of such a response, according to the government, are typically expressed in terms of reestablishing order in society or combatting terrorism. From the perspective of the resistance, oftentimes the government is accused of various kinds of atrocities and criminal overreaction. The truly unfortunate ones are those caught in the middle, namely the peasantry or ordinary members of society, those who neither sit in the seat of government nor hold any particular sympathy for the rebels.

In the present text, Yahweh tells Rehoboam, through the otherwise unknown prophet **Shemaiah the man of God**, to turn back his preparations for war. The reason given for this command is not the suffering that will be inflicted on the general population—spoken of, in military language, with the dreadful euphemism "collateral damage." Such suffering was likely on the minds of at least some of Rehoboam's ministers and other witnesses to the escalating tension. Instead, Yahweh commands Rehoboam and the Judeans, **Do not go up to fight against your fellow Israelites**, a phrase in itself that indicates something significant. Though, as has been noted, the Chroniclers repeatedly refer to the nation of Judah—the collective name for the southern tribes after the division—with the name "Israel," here they stress the close connection between the northern and southern tribes. Other situations throughout history that threatened to become, or became, civil wars have been warned against in just such terms. President Abraham Lincoln, for example, wrote that his preeminent goal was to prevent Americans from going to war against Americans. In a letter to Horace Greeley, Lincoln wrote: "If I could save the Union without freeing *any* slave I would do it, and if I could save it by freeing *all* the slaves I would do it; and if I could save it by freeing some and leaving others alone I would do also that" (Lincoln 1862 [emphasis original]).

Perhaps, therefore, Rehoboam's chief goal was to preserve the union. Of course, in his case, to preserve the union meant preserving his own royal authority, but this does not necessarily impugn his motives. Nevertheless, Yahweh orders him to turn back, **for this is my doing**. This means, as the previous chapter suggested, that the division of the kingdoms, terrible as it was, was to be interpreted as God's will. Even though a great deal of ideological and cultural suffering resulted, the people could take solace in the fact that Yahweh was directing events. This is a principle that lies behind much of the Chroniclers' History, and therefore the reader will certainly encounter it again.

FROM THE TEXT

It is well known, and should be even better known, that violence begets violence. In other words, when human violence breaks out, whether it is war or religious persecution, a violent response rarely, if ever, corrects the situation. The injunction against violence can be extended back further, however, to prevent the outbreak of violence to begin with. This is the call expressed in this text: Rehoboam has been wronged—though he carries the lion's share of the blame—and he attempts to respond violently. Whatever the wrong, a violent response is far inferior to a nonviolent one. Though governments often respond in violent ways to perceived wrongs against them, the church and Christians should turn the other cheek, as Jesus reminds us (Matt 5:39; Luke 6:29). Discretion is the better part of valor, and this is never truer than when the course of events, though one might perceive them as an injury, are nevertheless orchestrated by God (see Jonah 4 for a similar idea).

b. Rehoboam's Fortifications (11:5-12)

IN THE TEXT

■ **5-12** Having been ordered by Yahweh not to make war against his erstwhile subjects, Rehoboam instead turns his attention to fortifying certain key cities in the nation of Judah. Verses 5-10*a* report that **Rehoboam lived in Jerusalem and built up towns for defense in Judah**. The list of the cities reminds the reader of the lengthy list of genealogies. First Chronicles 1:1-4, in particular, list persons in groups of three. Fifteen key cities are listed, many of which are otherwise quite well known from the biblical record. **Bethlehem** (2 Chr 11:6) was, of course, the city where David (and, in the NT, Jesus) was born. **Tekoa** (v 6) was the hometown of the "wise woman" who was sent by Joab to admonish King David for not bringing his rebellious son Absalom back to Israel (2 Sam 14). **Adullam** (2 Chr 11:7) was the city where Judah the patriarch went after he separated from his brothers. The events that transpired there included the incident with Tamar (Gen 38). **Gath** (2 Chr 11:8) was the hometown of the giant Goliath, whom David killed with a slingshot, lending historical background to a key bit of Western civilization in the process (1 Sam 17). **Lachish** and **Azekah** (2 Chr 11:9) are tied together not only in the biblical record but also in extrabiblical sources. The key item is Lachish Letter IV, written from one Hoshaiah to his commander Joash—who was in charge of Lachish—for instructions during the Babylonian campaign against Judah. Azekah had apparently already fallen at this time, since Hoshaiah reports: "We can no longer see [the fires of] Azekah." Finally, **Hebron** (v 10) was the seat of David's throne over Judah during his civil war with the remaining supporters of the dead King Saul. According to 2 Sam 2:11; 2 Sam 5:5; and 1 Chr 3:4, David reigned in Hebron for seven years and six months before moving to Jerusalem, where he reigned for the remainder of his forty years on the throne. These fifteen cities are situated at key points throughout the tribal territory of Judah and Benjamin. Rehoboam fortified these particular cities because, as the Chroniclers summarize, **Judah and Benjamin were his** (2 Chr 11:12).

c. The Priests and Levites Support Rehoboam (11:13-15)

IN THE TEXT

■ **13-15** At first glance, it seems that Rehoboam is, in fact, in the right. This impression is gained from these three verses and the following two, both of which passages describe those who fall into line to support Rehoboam after the division. Here it is **priests and Levites** who flock southward. Previous generations of scholarship associated such things as the Exodus traditions with these Levites who moved south at this point and, especially, later after the destruction of Samaria and the northern kingdom in 722-21 B.C. While this theory has much to commend it, it lacks decisive evidence. At any rate, these verses are a textual witness to a plausible tendency of the religious establishment to "vote with their feet," as it were. Some of these Levites, however, were forced to leave, **because Jeroboam and his sons had rejected them as priests of the LORD** (v 14). While the Chroniclers do not devote nearly as much attention to the "alien shrines" that Jeroboam set up in Bethel and Dan (see 1 Kgs 12:25-33), they do leave behind a hint of this in 2 Chr 11:15. They report that Jeroboam **appointed his own priests for the high places and for the goat and calf idols he had made**. The idol in the shape of a goat is not mentioned by the Deuteronomists, but here it serves to reinforce the religious nature of the division, according to the Chroniclers. What the Deuteronomists call "the sin of Jeroboam son of Nebat" (see, for example, 1 Kgs 15:34), in other words, was much more than a political rebellion. It amounted, instead, to religious treason, for the kings took on themselves the authority to appoint priests to serve in their temple. On the other hand, Jeroboam may well have intended his shrines to be shrines to Yahweh. This assertion cannot be proven, however, since no writings from the northern kingdom have survived—except, of course, those like the Exodus traditions, which eventually made it into the Bible.

d. Others from Israelite Tribes Support Rehoboam (11:16-17)

IN THE TEXT

■ **16-17** Apparently, the support of Israelites for Rehoboam does not come only from the religious establishment. The Chroniclers assign a particularly religious motivation for these laypersons' decision, namely that these were the ones **who set their hearts on seeking the LORD, the God of Israel** (v 16). The assumption behind this is clearly that there is only one proper place in which to worship the true God. Though this notion will be challenged by Jesus (see esp. John 4), it fits in nicely with its historical context. In other words, at the time described in this text, it was eminently appropriate for religiously minded Judeans to believe that Yahweh could only be worshiped in one place. For the historical context of the writing, moreover, the importance of the second temple comes through in this text as well. Events such as the exile would of course make a reevaluation necessary, for many exiled Judeans and their descendants stayed behind in Babylon and other places and established thriving centers of Jewish culture and learning. That later historical reality should not blind one to the fact, however, that the worship of deities throughout the ANE was often confined to particular locations or buildings.

Those who moved from northern Israel to southern Judah could, moreover, have had motives in addition to the religious one. The Chroniclers only mentioned the religious motivation because that was what was most important to them. In truth, the reasons why people both ancient and modern make particular decisions of loyalty and allegiance are complex. While they can be explained by appeal to this or that limited factor, one should perhaps never suppose that a particular discovered reason is the only reason something happens. To do so is to fall into a logical booby trap. Recognizing this does not harm the Chroniclers' reliability, but it is helpful to recognize that other reasons could explain the move. Regardless, Rehoboam seems to have enjoyed a broad base of support, at least for the **three years** in which the people were **following the ways of David and Solomon** (v 17).

e. Rehoboam's Wives and Sons (11:18-23)

IN THE TEXT

■ **18-23** These six verses list the wives and sons of King Rehoboam. This information is important for two reasons. First, a historical work like Chronicles would clearly need to document this kind of information, especially when the Chroniclers spend so much time on the reign of Rehoboam. True enough, they will not do so with regard to many of the other kings. However, as will be seen, only four other kings receive treatment longer than a chapter from now until the end of the history: Asa, Jehoshaphat, Hezekiah, and Josiah. The distinguishing feature of those four kings is not the list of their wives and sons, but rather that each of them instituted an important religious reform. For that matter, the list of Rehoboam's wives and sons is not particularly significant in terms of the wider sweep of history. Of course, the most important event during the reign of Rehoboam was the division of the united kingdom into the "untied" kingdoms. Nevertheless, though women and children are without a doubt essential to continuing a royal line, they are in fact not mentioned very often. This is not the only reason why it is interesting that the Chroniclers would linger over this information, though it certainly belongs near the top of the list.

The second reason why a list of Rehoboam's wives and sons is important for the history is the illustration this gives about how Israelite kings conducted themselves in the world. As noted above, the wives and sons of other kings are not often mentioned. However, it is perfectly reasonable to suppose that each of them, particularly those who reigned the longest number of years, would also have taken on many wives and borne many sons. Yet, somewhat curiously, the Chroniclers fail to mention this practice. Even Solomon, notorious from 1 Kings for having three hundred wives and seven hundred concubines, takes only two wives according to the Chroniclers. (By contrast, according to the Deuteronomists Rehoboam only takes one wife!) Klein suggests that "Solomon's harem was passed over because of the sinister interpretation the deuteronomist had put on it" (1999, 522). Jarick, however, is a bit more sarcastic: "No reference to producing more than their heir is made in the cases of the other ten successors of Rehoboam, so he stands head and shoulders above all his descendants in this achievement." Playing off the meaning of the king's name, Jarick ends his work on this section with a biting comment: "Thus no-one comes close to the efforts of the 'Expander of the Nation' to expand the royal household, even as he reigns over a considerably shrunken kingdom" (2007b, 96).

It is not at all striking that only a few of the sons, and none of the daughters, are named in this section. It is well-known that the ANE societies were, perhaps without exception, patriarchal. This is particularly true for the purposes of royal succession. In addition, the two wives singled out for special mention come from the extended royal family. This serves to solidify the line, and such a practice has long been a staple of royal families both in the ancient and modern worlds. Thus **Mahalath** was both Rehoboam's first cousin on the side of her father **Jerimoth** and his third cousin on the side of her mother **Abihail** (v 18). Similarly, Rehoboam's second wife (of those mentioned) is **Maakah daughter of Absalom** (v 20), thus also his first cousin. Finally, in a principle noted above regarding the transition to Solomon, because **Rehoboam** loved Maakah . . . more than any of his other wives and concubines (v 21), he designated her firstborn son **Abijah** (v 22) to become king after him. This significant decision being based on the king's love for his wife should give women, as well as men, reason for rejoicing, for light here breaks through the dark of patriarchalism.

f. Attack of Pharaoh Shushak (12:1-12)

BEHIND THE TEXT

The relationship between archaeology and the Bible is a spotty one. Often, certain well-meaning individuals claim to have "proven" this or that element from the Bible on the basis of an archaeological find. Usually, such finds have to do with the sensational stories in the Bible, like Noah's ark or the ark of the covenant. Also usually, the public and the press react with varying degrees of enthusiasm while the scholarly establishment defers and dissembles, seeking more certain proof or else writing the process of discovery off entirely as a hoax or some other kind of fraud. Once in a great while, however, archaeological finds shed the clearest light possible on events recorded in the Bible. Thus it is with the Egyptian invasion of Judah that took place during the reign of King Rehoboam.

The Egyptian pharaoh who founded the Twenty-Second Dynasty was named, in English characters, Shoshenq I. Five other kings are named Shoshenq in the Twenty-Second and Twenty-Third Dynasties, but none of them, according to the best of scholarly knowledge, had any business in Syria/Palestine. Shoshenq I, however, "has left us explicit records of a campaign into Palestine" (Kitchen 2003, 30). Shoshenq I ruled Egypt around 945-924 B.C. Dates for Egyptian pharaohs, it should be noted, are for the most part secure. Among other things, Shoshenq left behind a victory monument in the city of Megiddo, as well as a massive monument in the Great Temple at Karnak describing his successes in Palestine. Rehoboam's dates are around 931-914 B.C. Even though Shoshenq does not mention either Rehoboam or Jeroboam by name, this seems to be insufficient reason to doubt that Shushak from the Bible (→ v 2) and Shoshenq are one and the same.

IN THE TEXT

■ **1** In keeping with the general theological tenet that world events happen exclusively by the will of Yahweh, the Chroniclers begin the story of the Egyptian attack by suggesting that it came about because Rehoboam **and all Israel with him abandoned the law of the** LORD. The specific sin is not mentioned here. By contrast, the Deuteronomists list a number of religious errors committed during the time of Rehoboam (see 1 Kgs 14:22-24).

■ **2-4** A marginal note in the *BHS* suggests that the name of the pharaoh should be spelled **Shushak** rather than **Shishak** (v 2). This is the reading adopted in the LXX. In further support of it is the fact that "o" and "u" are closer to one another than are "o" and "i." Therefore, the conversion of Egyptian "Shoshenq" into Hebrew Shushak is more probable linguistically.

Shushak comes into Palestine with an impressive force. The Chroniclers report that the foot soldiers were **innumerable** (v 3), and it certainly must have appeared that way at the time of the invasion. The infantry is made up, first, of **Libyans**, unsurprising because Shushak/Shoshenq was himself of Libyan descent, as were many other pharaohs throughout Egypt's long history. Also coming with the pharaoh were people known as **Sukkites**. According to Kenneth Kitchen, these were "scouts, Libyan auxiliaries known in Egyptian texts from the thirteenth/twelfth centuries onward." This detail is something that, Kitchen continues,

> we owe exclusively to the Chronicler and his (nonbiblical) sources. Thus, overall, the very differently composed Egyptian and Hebrew sources usefully complement one another, to produce a fuller picture of a particular historical occasion. (2003, 34)

The final group of soldiers are **Cushites**, a somewhat general term that refers to people of the Upper Nile region, perhaps Ethiopians.

■ **5-8** The prophet **Shemaiah** was first seen in 11:2-4. In the earlier episode, he communicated Yahweh's will to Rehoboam and his officers that they should not try to retake the northern tribes' territory by force. This was so because the events that had taken place were to fulfill the promise made to Jeroboam. Incidentally, Shoshenq I was probably the pharaoh who gave safe haven to Jeroboam before the latter was able to return to Jerusalem and eventually be made king of the northern kingdom of Israel after the division (see 1 Kgs 11:40).

In this scene, Shemaiah informs Rehoboam and his advisers that the attack of **Shushak** is due to their sinfulness: **You have abandoned me; therefore, I now abandon you to Shushak** (v 5). Immediately the events relating to Shushak's campaign are telescoped somewhat, because the Chroniclers next move on to the obeisance Rehoboam and the advisers make, saying, **The LORD is just** (v 6). Recognizing that the punishment that comes from Yahweh is just is a well-known feature of Israelite/Judean religion, at least on the official level; another example may be seen in the great penitential Ps 51, esp. v 4. Seeing the humility of the humans, Yahweh indicates that Jerusalem will be spared, but that Judah **will . . . become subject to him** [Shushak], **so that they** may learn the difference between serving me and serving the kings of other lands (2 Chr 12:8).

■ **9-12** As confirmed in Shoshenq's own records, Jerusalem is in fact not sacked by the Egyptian ruler. However, Jerusalem is forced to pay heavy tribute. All this is well-matched in the Egyptian materials, so that one only doubts it in the face of overwhelming evidence, perhaps in support of a preconceived notion that the Bible could not possibly reproduce historical facts. Though the opposite extreme—that everything in the Bible is perfectly historically accurate—is probably also not true, there is no reason to suggest that the decision must be all or nothing. When the external records do, in fact, confirm the biblical account, the Bible's interpreters must not fail to recognize the reality that stares them in the face.

g. The Death of Rehoboam (12:13-16)

IN THE TEXT

■ **13-16** Coming to the end of Rehoboam's life, the Chroniclers give a summary evaluation of the king. Rehoboam is the first king whom the Chroniclers judge negatively in this manner. As noted above, though the Chroniclers were not shy to point out Solomon's faults, they downplayed them somewhat. They are not so reticent with Rehoboam. In fact, they are even more direct in their criticism than the Deuteronomists were. In support of this statement, one may consider v 14: **He did evil because he had not set his heart on seeking the LORD**. The Deuteronomistic version reads, "Judah did evil in the eyes of the LORD" (1 Kgs 14:22). Thus the blame is removed from the king by one step. One might be more inclined to follow the Chroniclers here, for ultimately the one who has the power entrusted to him is charged with making the decisions and owns all of the implications of the decisions he makes. That being said, however, it at first seems odd that Rehoboam is not criticized precisely on the point of one of his most significant decisions, namely the discussions that led up to the division of the kingdoms. This is so because, as the Chroniclers maintained, this was done in accordance with Yahweh's word spoken through Ahijah the Shilonite (2 Chr 10:15). In other words, because it was Yahweh's will for the kingdoms to be divided, Rehoboam's contribution to it cannot be considered a sin, even if it was unwise. The final note regarding Rehoboam is the citation of two lost sources, **the records of Shemaiah the prophet and of Iddo the seer that deal with genealogies** (12:15). **Iddo the seer** is also known from the superscription to Zechariah, wherein that prophet is called "son of Berekiah, the son of Iddo" (Zech 1:1). Of course, it cannot be determined with certainty if this is the same Iddo referred to here. If it were, then "son" in Zech

1:1 should be understood as "successor" rather than biological offspring (see above for "son of David"), since the prophet Zechariah in the fifth century B.C. could not possibly be the grandson of the prophet Iddo in the tenth century. Rehoboam, finally, is given a burial due kings and other important persons, even though he is judged negatively. Such good treatment will not be afforded all of the kings of Judah, as will be seen in due course.

B. The Reign of Abijah (13:1—14:1)

BEHIND THE TEXT

In the introduction to the reign of David above, it was noted that both groups of historical writers in ancient Israel took pains to reduce or eliminate blemishes on the record of David. The principal way in which the Chroniclers accomplished this task was by eliminating all mention of what Israel's great king did to Bathsheba and Uriah. The Deuteronomists, by contrast, do describe these events, particularly in 2 Sam 11—12. However, it is not until the reign of Abijah that they give the customary judgment on David's reign, similar to the ones used for other kings: "For David had done what was right in the eyes of the LORD and had not failed to keep any of the LORD's commands all the days of his life—except in the case of Uriah the Hittite" (1 Kgs 15:5).

IN THE TEXT

■ I In the Deuteronomistic version of the history at 1 Kgs 15:1-8, **Abijah** is called by the name ***Abijam***. There is no conclusive evidence behind any theory attempting to explain the difference. However, it is important not to pass over it in silence, because it is of a different character than the simple spelling variations encountered, for example, in the lengthy genealogical section of 1 Chronicles. One possibility is that this represents a theological "fix" not unlike the Deuteronomists' changing the names of Saul's sons Esh-Baal and Merib-Baal to, respectively, Ishbosheth and Mephibosheth (→ 1 Chr 8:33-34). **Abijah** means "Yahweh is my father." However, the name "Abijam" could mean "Yamm is my father." Yamm was the Canaanite god of the sea and a one-time opponent of Baal in certain Canaanite mythological texts from the city-state of Ugarit. Thus, in its original form, the name of Rehoboam's son may have carried the name of a pagan god. If this were true, it would need to be eliminated. The inconsistency between changing Abijam's name and not Esh-Baal's name finds a simple explanation: the former became king whereas the latter did not.

The beginning of the reign of Abijah is indexed to the kingship of Jeroboam I of Israel. This device is known as "relative chronology" and is quite familiar from 1-2 Kings. In the Deuteronomistic History, there are many such regnal formulae for both Israelite and Judean kings (see Nelson 1981, 29-42). After the fall of the northern kingdom of Israel, a few of the Judean kings' reigns are indexed to the reign of rulers from other countries (see, for example, Jer 25:1). This is the only time the Chroniclers preserve a relative chronology also found in Kings. It is probably mentioned here because of the war between Abijah and Jeroboam, the description of part of which dominates the chapter (2 Chr 13:3-20).

■ **2a** As noted above, comparing this verse with Abijah's regnal formula in 1 Kgs 15 yields some interesting results. First, his mother's name is spelled **Maakah** in the LXX and NIV, but ***Micaiah*** in the MT. Quite often, the text refers to two people by the same name. Radak writes: "Many such cases can be found in this book, where the text refers to one person by two [different] names" (Kimchi 2008, 226). Second, the name of his maternal grandfather is different in the two versions, Absalom in 2 Chr 11:20 but **Uriel of Gibeah** here (13:2*a*). Klein unhelpfully comments: "The different patronymic represents another tradition" (1999, 530). Radak applies the same principle to Abijah's grandfather as he did to his mother. Third, as noted above, there is no mention of David here as in 1 Kgs 15:3-5. The primary elision here is to "the matter of Uriah the Hittite" (KJV).

■ **2b-3** This segment begins with the summary statement **There was war between Abijah and Jeroboam** (v 2*b*). Verse 3 details the forces with which each king took the field. Though the Chroniclers do not explicitly mention Abijah's intention, it certainly had in the main to do with an attempt to reunify the now divided monarchy. What Rehoboam was prevented from doing (11:3-4), Abijah now attempts to do. By the end of the story, the reader will see that although Abijah had many victories, he still did not meet the primary goal. Therefore, at best, the war turned out to be a stalemate, though one might not have predicted such given that the Israelite army (**eight hundred thousand able troops**) outnumbered their Judean opponents (**four hundred thousand able fighting men**) two to one.

■ **4-12** With these verses the Chroniclers effect a major diversion from the Deuteronomistic account. First Kings passes over this rousing, enthusiastic speech by King Abijah in silence. This is likely due to their tendency to write off the kings with whose religious policies they disagreed as abject failures, no matter what good they may have done. The content of the speech makes a mockery of Jeroboam and his associates, calling the latter **worthless scoundrels** who **gathered around him and opposed Rehoboam son of Solomon** (v 7). Abijah claims that the kingship was given **David and his descendants forever by a covenant of salt** (v 5). On the latter phrase, Jarick says it was "an expression denoting a particularly sacred and binding agreement" (2007b, 103). He cites Num 18:19 as an example. This text suggests that the principle of giving a portion of sacrifices to priests for their support "is an everlasting covenant of salt before the LORD for both you and your offspring." Finally, Abijah appears quite orthodox in his suggestion (2 Chr 13:10) that the Judeans **have not forsaken** Yahweh, as the Israelites have apparently done. This is a veiled reference to the "pagan" shrines that Jeroboam set up in Dan and Bethel, an act that does merit explicit mention from the Chroniclers. Even when the Deuteronomists do mention these shrines (1 Kgs 12:25-33), however, the attentive reader wonders precisely what Jeroboam intended by building them.

■ **13-20** The Deuteronomists also eliminate any mention of the battle itself. The battle goes the way of most of the battles reported in the OT: **Judah** (v 13), in this case, is faced with overwhelming odds, but after crying out to Yahweh they are able to overcome a bit of strategic trickery in order to defeat the armies of Israel. The Deuteronomists record the use of a similar stratagem in the second battle of Ai (Josh 8:1-29). In that earlier battle, Joshua took a small detachment of soldiers and plundered the city while the enemy army had been lured out of the gates by the main part of the Israelite army. Here, however, Jeroboam has divided his forces in order to attack Judah from both sides. Somehow—and the Chroniclers here give tantalizingly sparse details— **God routed Jeroboam and all Israel before Abijah and Judah** (2 Chr 13:15). The victory was decisive enough that **Jeroboam did not regain power during the time of Abijah** (v 20). Along the way, although Abijah did not accomplish his main goal of reunifying the nation under his leadership, he did take three key cities, including **Bethel**, in which one of the two shrines Jeroboam had set up as rivals to Jerusalem had been established (v 19).

■ **21—14:1** The numbering of verses is off by one here. Second Chronicles 14:1 in English is 13:23 in Hebrew. The difference is perhaps due to the mention of **Asa** (14:1), the son of Rehoboam, in the second part of the verse. Also, as for the Deuteronomists, they give the same summary of Abijah/Abijam's reign that is found here (1 Kgs 15:7-8). Although Jeroboam faded away and died, **Abijah grew in strength** (2 Chr 13:21). The Chroniclers report his successes in securing his reign through the production of children, **twenty-two sons and sixteen daughters** in all. Though Abijah is not nearly as prolific as was his father, Rehoboam, in this respect, nevertheless he certainly accomplished his fair share. After reporting that he had done so, the Chroniclers direct the reader to further information **in the annotations of the prophet Iddo** (v 22), who has appeared before (see 2 Chr 9:29). If the **Iddo** referred to here is the same one as before, then one is most likely dealing with the disciples of

Iddo, though the possibility that multiple prophets had the same name should not, of course, be excluded.

C. The Reign of Asa (14:2—16:14)

▶ Overview

King Asa, as previously noted, gets significantly more "text time" than does his father, Abijah. (This is so even in light of the longer treatment the Chroniclers give Abijah when compared to the Deuteronomists.) This is probably due to the fact that he receives a positive evaluation from both the Chroniclers and the Deuteronomists (see 1 Kgs 15:11). King Asa's story will be told in five separate episodes, each of which shows a different part of the reason why Asa was evaluated positively. However, like his son Jehoshaphat—who gets mixed reviews at the end of his life and is rather frankly scolded by one of Yahweh's prophets—Asa does come in for a bit of criticism, when he turns his eyes off of Yahweh and toward political allegiances. Thus the reader sees the continuation of a theme that had developed with Solomon, though as was noted above the negative implications were somewhat muted by the Chroniclers at that point in the narrative.

A rather interesting interpretive issue with regard to the reign of Asa is the religious reform in which he engages. It is significant especially in light of the fact that his son Jehoshaphat will also undertake a similar reform. One wonders, of course, why the reform of Asa did not "stick"; nor, for that matter, did that of Jehoshaphat, since Hezekiah later and Josiah later still both reformed the religion of Judah. Below, it will be suggested that the reforms did not last because of the endurance of human sinfulness. Though this is certainly a contributing factor, it seems less than satisfactory. In any event, the interpreter, particularly the Christian preacher, must avoid any semblance of anti-Semitism. Such negative attitudes might take the form, for example, of excoriating the Jews for their failure to maintain the true worship of Yahweh, and even more so for failing to recognize Jesus as the Messiah.

Another distinguishing feature of the Chroniclers' report of Asa's reign has to do with two military victories. Each of these is followed by an encounter with a prophet. The first of these is positive, with the prophet Azariah encouraging the king. The second, however, is negative, with the prophet Hanani scolding the king. This ambiguous relationship to Yahweh through his prophets reflects how the Deuteronomists and the Chroniclers evaluate Asa. Although he gets a positive general evaluation, there is a qualification in that "he did not remove the high places" (2 Chr 15:17; also 1 Kgs 15:13-14).

1. Asa's Reform (14:2-7)

IN THE TEXT

■ **2** Unlike Abijah, the year of whose accession was noted in comparison to the years of King Jeroboam I of Israel (2 Chr 13:1; see also 1 Kgs 15:1), there is no such comparison listed for his son Asa. First Kings 15:9 reports that he became king in "the twentieth year of Jeroboam king of Israel." As for Jeroboam, the Chroniclers left open the question of when he died. In any event, "the country was at peace for ten years" (2 Chr 14:1) of Asa's reign. The Chroniclers also do not say, like the Deuteronomists, that Asa reigned for a total of forty-one years (1 Kgs 15:10). For whatever reason, this detail was unimportant to them.

Far more important for the Chroniclers is what Asa accomplished in the way of religious reform. Though, as has been noted, the reform seems not to have been very long-lasting (since Jehoshaphat, the next king, will accomplish a similar reform), it nevertheless is an important event in the history of Judah. It earned Asa the judgment that he **did what was good and right in the eyes of the Lord his God**. This phrase is a variation of similar positive commendations throughout both the Deuteronomistic and Chroniclers' Histories.

■ **3-5** These three verses succinctly describe the reform undertaken at the command of King Asa. The **foreign altars** (v 3) likely represented either shrines to other gods or shrines to Yahweh other than the temple in Jerusalem. Although the temple was the only place to worship Yahweh for about the last forty years of its existence, the establishment who supported it were generally not in favor of other, rival shrines—perhaps like those that Jeroboam set up in Israel. The **high places** were low hills or raised structures for the offering of incense and sacrifices. King Solomon, prior to the temple's construction, had gone to such a high place in Gibeon (2 Chr 1:5) in order to receive a word from Yahweh. Finally **Asherah poles** were some kind of tall, thin pole dedicated to the Canaanite goddess Asherah. Indirect evidence for Israelite worship of Asherah has been found by archaeologists at the Kuntillet 'Ajrud site in the Negev desert. There inscriptions were found referring to "Yahweh and his Asherah," but the precise meaning of the phrase remains uncertain. After removing all of the paraphernalia pertaining to other gods, Asa **commanded Judah to seek the Lord, the God of their ancestors, and to obey his laws and commands** (14:4). The presence of a leader encouraging or commanding faithfulness to God is a well-known motif in the OT. A prime example is the book of Deuteronomy, which purports to be the last words of Moses before the Israelites went into the promised land.

■ **6-7** The final two verses of the section describe what Asa was able to do **since the land was at peace** (v 6). These activities include fortifying several important cities and increasing the wealth of the country. In ancient times as well as modern, having rest from enemies is a key point in being able to accomplish such expansion, and Asa did not waste the opportunity he had been given. This turned out to be a wise strategy, since before long the peace Judah enjoyed in the early years of his reign was to be interrupted by war with a neighbor to the south, Zerah the Cushite.

2. Victory over Zerah (14:8-15)

IN THE TEXT

■ **8** The stories of Asa's two military victories begin here, appropriately, with a description of Asa's forces. The description is specific, and it undoubtedly serves to demonstrate the somewhat miraculous nature of the victory against an overwhelming force. Asa's army overcoming tremendous odds through Yahweh's help links back to Abijah's decisive victory over the forces of Jeroboam discussed above. There, the Israelite army outnumbered the Judeans two to one. Here, the Judean force is even smaller, **three hundred thousand men from Judah . . . All these were brave fighting men**.

■ **9-15** The Deuteronomists do not include an account of this first of Asa's two military victories. Instead, after the qualifiedly positive evaluation of Asa's reign (→ 2 Chr 14:2—16:14 Overview), 1 Kgs 15:16 moves right on to the war between Asa and Baasha of Israel (→ 2 Chr 16:1-6). The Chroniclers' story sets up dramatic tension by indicating that **Zerah the Cushite marched out against them with an army of thousands upon thousands** (14:9). Above, in ch 12, the Chroniclers described the invading army of Pharaoh Shushak in a similar fashion. Though Shushak prevailed over Judah—even without sacking Jerusalem—Zerah ultimately does not. The Judean victory comes about as a direct result of Asa's prayer to Yahweh in 14:11. The chief plea of Asa appeals to Yahweh's divine nature: **do not let mere mortals prevail against you**. Of course, this statement does not suggest that such a thing would be possible. Rather, it merely asserts that Yahweh must be the one to fight for Judah. He appears and does do so, with the result that **Such a great number of Cushites fell that they could not recover** (v 13), an expression that refers to the condition of the army rather than the condition of particular soldiers. An innumerable army has once again been defeated by a vast, though limited and much smaller, army. Yet the Judean forces and King Asa had Yahweh on their side, so that in spite of their material and personnel disadvantage the day was theirs. Finally, though it may at first sound strange that after all their success and plunder, the Chroniclers report that **They returned to Jerusalem** (v 15). One way to look at this would be with suspicion, since successful armies in the ancient world often pressed the issue as far as they could take it rather than

14:6-15

voluntarily withdrawing. A more likely explanation, however, is that the Judeans were only interested in removing the threat from their homeland since, after all, it was Zerah who mobilized first.

3. Asa Is Encouraged by the Prophet Azariah (15:1-19)

IN THE TEXT

■ **1-8** The Deuteronomists do not include this episode. For that matter, the Deuteronomists exclude any mention of prophetic interaction on the part of King Asa. As suggested above, the two meetings Asa has with prophets seem to function for the Chroniclers to demonstrate the somewhat ambiguous results of Asa's reign. The Deuteronomists, for their part, gave qualified praise to Asa, saying that, in spite of all the good things he did and in spite of the faithful attitude he adopted toward Yahweh, he did not remove the high places. As they consistently argue against any shrine other than that in Jerusalem, they surely considered this a devastating critique. Nevertheless, for the Chroniclers this episode serves to bolster Asa's confidence. In addition, by saying **The LORD is with you when you are with him** (v 2) the Chroniclers sound an important theological note, namely that Yahweh does not abandon those who are faithful. Verses 4-6 form a familiar historical reminiscence. **Azariah**, in thus encouraging Asa to remain faithful to the faithful God, essentially gives a theological lesson from his own name. Though this is not explicit in the text, it is helpful to see what he says in this light. His name means "Yahweh has grasped," and the essence of his mini-sermon in this text is that Yahweh will not release his grasp on Judah, so long as Judah does not squirm and struggle to be free through disobedience and turning away from Yahweh. The last verse of this section seems to repeat, or at least extend, the story told earlier about Asa's religious reform. The king thus desires to live out the promise contained in the prophet's name.

■ **9-15** As a further consequence of his religious reform, Asa **assembled all Judah and Benjamin** (v 9) along with some from the northern tribes who had defected to him when they heard of his faithfulness. This is one of the few times the Chroniclers use the phrase **Judah and Benjamin**, but they do so in order to parallel the tribal identifications **Ephraim, Manasseh and Simeon**. This great assembly makes many sacrifices to Yahweh in order to renew the covenant. This wonderful story of faithfulness has a dark side, however, since **All who would not seek the LORD, the God of Israel, were to be put to death, whether small or great, man or woman** (v 13). Though similar ideas have been expressed elsewhere (see, for example, Josh 1:18), it is and perhaps should be disturbing. Rosemary Radford Reuther labels such attempts to control theology by violence as abstractionism. She defines this term as the attempt, sometimes deliberate, but usually not, to deal with people according to principles, irrespective of their true identity. She writes:

> To burn the body of the heretic in order to save "his [sic] soul" ... [is] abstractionism. The ability to do violence to others is built, psychologically, on this ability to extract oneself from real contact and shared feeling with existing human reality. (1983, 179)

In spite of the discomfort this text gives the modern reader, however, Yahweh seems to give approval to this drastic action, for **the LORD gave them rest on every side** (v 15).

■ **16-19** The last four verses summarize a few more things that **Asa** did in connection with his great religious reform. He removed **his grandmother Maakah** because of her religious infidelity. Apparently he did not subject her to the same punishment detailed in v 13, above, yet it is disturbing all the same. The rub of this note is that Rehoboam had loved Maakah the best out of all his wives (2 Chr 11:21). Somehow, the **queen mother** had gotten into what the Chroniclers believed to be an inferior religion, or perhaps she had always been a closet "Asherian" without even her doting husband, Rehoboam, knowing it. In contrast to this, Jeremiah's foes in Jer 44, the women who worshiped the Queen of Heaven (whoever she was), did what they did with the full knowledge—and, assuming they needed it, the full approval—of their husbands (Jer 44:15, 19). The section ends with a final, resounding note of Yahweh's approval of what Asa has done, even though **he did not remove the high places from Israel** (2 Chr 15:17; "Israel" here means "Judah"). Asa and Judah had rest from war for the first ten years of his reign, and then they experienced **no more war until the thirty-fifth year of Asa's reign** (v 19). The text is ambiguous concerning how long the battle with Zerah the Cushite took, but in any event it and the following event were but momentary interruptions in a long reign otherwise characterized by divinely authorized peace.

4. Dispute with King Baasha of Israel (16:1-6)

IN THE TEXT

■ **1-6** As stated above, this is the only episode that the Deuteronomists and the Chroniclers have in common. For the Deuteronomists, this is most likely due to their lack of real, sustained interest in any of the Judean kings except David, Solomon, Hezekiah, and Josiah. These four kings are praised as being close to God, although, as has been noted, David and Solomon are both called in for a critique that is lacking in Chronicles. **Baasha** picks a fight with Judah by fortifying the city of **Ramah to prevent anyone from leaving or entering**

Judah. This act could certainly be seen as an act of war. The Deuteronomists clearly have this view (see 1 Kgs 15:16). By contrast, the Chroniclers apparently see this rather as a diplomatic dispute. Neither account suggests that Asa himself engages in military maneuvers in order to break the blockade. However, he does send **silver and gold out of the treasuries of the LORD's temple . . . to Ben-Hadad king of Aram** (2 Chr 16:2) in order to convince the latter to intervene on his behalf. **Ben-Hadad**, like many other ANE kings, is named after a deity. In his case, it is Baal-Hadad, and his name therefore indicates that he is the favored son of the god. (The warrior Benaiah, by contrast, is named "son of Yahweh" [1 Chr 11]). Ben-Hadad conquers a number of cities in Israel, causing Baasha to withdraw. The section ends with a note that, although King Asa and Judah did not directly participate in the fight, nevertheless they took the spoils, for **they carried away from Ramah the stones and timber Baasha had been using** (2 Chr 16:6). In a way, Asa used Ben-Hadad as a foreign proxy to steal away building materials from his neighbor to the north. This action, in itself, is not critiqued by the Chroniclers or by the prophet who confronts the king in the next episode. Nevertheless, Asa will in fact be excoriated for relying on force of arms rather than on Yahweh, and this is perhaps the most important point with which the interpreter should walk away from this text.

5. Asa Is Scolded by the Prophet Hanani (16:7-10)

IN THE TEXT

■ **7-10** As noted above, **Asa** has contact with prophets after both of his victories. However, the interaction with **Hanani the seer** (v 7) is not nearly as comfortable as the previous one with Azariah. The first thing to note about this passage that, like the story of the battle with Zerah the Cushite above, this episode is unique to the Chroniclers' History. Second, one should note the near-equivalency of the terms "prophet" and **seer**. Apparently, in Israel these terms had been used interchangeably for some time (see 1 Sam 9:9). While Azariah was not himself called "prophet," his word was called "prophecy" (2 Chr 15:8). The seer Hanani calls the king in for some serious critique. The specific sin complained of is that Asa **relied on the king of Aram and not on the LORD his God**. As a result, **the army of the king of Aram has escaped from his hand** (16:7). Passed over in silence is a second sin, emptying out the temple treasuries to bribe Ben-Hadad. However, this was likely not far from Hanani's mind. Third, King Asa's response to the challenging prophetic word is one of anger: **Asa was angry with the seer because of this; he was so enraged that he put him in prison** (v 10). Throughout the history of Israel and Judah, prophets speaking truth to power often did so at tremendous personal risk. The clearest example of this is Jeremiah, the remembrance of whose prophecy will be important in the later chapters of the Chroniclers' History. On the other side, the kings who oppressed the prophets in this way almost always also oppressed the people. Asa is no exception in this regard. No specifics are given as to the manner in which **Asa brutally oppressed some of the people**, nor is there any indication which people were oppressed. However, some conjecture may be made. After all, complaints about oppression of the poor are a common theme of the prophets. Perhaps the best example of this is the book of Amos, which accuses the rich of selling the poor for a pair of shoes (Amos 2:6). Without either confirming or contradictory evidence, then, one may assume that those whom Asa oppressed are those whom the leaders and the wealthy (and the wealthy leaders) are always in danger of oppressing, and often unwittingly so.

FROM THE TEXT

Those to whom God has entrusted leadership have a special responsibility. They must, above all, remain humble. Proverbs 16:18, among many other biblical texts, warns of the deadly dangers attending unchecked pride. Leaders must also sometimes follow the advice of those who have been placed under them, because sometimes the subordinates may see dimensions of a problem that leaders cannot, whether due to their many responsibilities or to a lack of a certain ability or realm of knowledge. More often, God places just the right subordinate under the right leader, and if the latter follows the advice of the former—or if the advice is merely sought in the first place—a grievous error can be avoided. Asa did not do this, and so even though a great victory was achieved, he missed the chance for an even greater one.

Wholehearted commitment is what God requires from humanity (Ps 86:11; Prov 3:5-6; Ezek 11:19; Matt 5:48). Reliance on others or, worse, exclusive self-reliance is a frequent subject of prophetic critique in the OT. Rehoboam failed this key test, and it seems especially the case that when leaders begin to think they did things all on their own (Deut 8) that they subject not just themselves but all who serve under them to peril. Leadership given by God is a great responsibility, and leaders should guard their faithfulness most closely.

6. The Death of Asa (16:11-14)

IN THE TEXT

■ **11-14** The negative note on which the account of Asa's reign ends leads one perhaps to expect that he will, or should, die a painful death. What happens to Asa, therefore, confounds expectations. His death is not as ignoble as that of the later King Jehoram, noted in 2 Chr 21:20 (→). Instead, his passing is recorded in the usual way, with the Chroniclers suggesting more information can be found **in the book of the kings of Judah and Israel** (16:11). This lost source is also cited in 1 Chr 9:1; 2 Chr 25:26; 27:7; 32:32; 35:27; and 36:8. A final story is told of King Asa, which may in fact conform to the expectations of a death filled with judgment. The king contracts some mysterious foot disease. Jarick gives several possibilities as to what this might have been. He writes:

> We are spared the medical details of this disease, though we might imagine something like chronic gout or lameness, or even a venereal disease—due to the word "feet" (*raglayim*) sometimes being used in biblical Hebrew as a euphemism for the genitals. (2007b, 115)

Regardless of what this was, however, the point is that **even in his illness he did not seek help from the LORD, but only from the physicians** (16:12). One should be careful not to make too much of this, since it is only in extreme forms of faith healing that medical assistance and **help from the LORD** are set in tension with one another. The Chroniclers believe the king should have sought Yahweh, and for them this is emblematic of the problems and temptations King Asa faced throughout his life.

D. The Reign of Jehoshaphat (17:1—21:1)

▶ Overview

Like Asa before him, Jehoshaphat is given quite a lot of space by the Chroniclers. This is significant, with the general absence of the northern kingdom of Israel from the Chroniclers' History, with respect to what the space is given over to. In the Deuteronomistic History, Jehoshaphat appears near the end of 1 Kings. In fact, he is the last Judean king described before 2 Kings begins. The Deuteronomists report that he did everything right in the eyes of Yahweh, which is the standard by which the earlier historical epic judges the faithfulness or effectiveness of the kings.

In general terms, both the Deuteronomists and the Chroniclers evaluate Jehoshaphat similarly. This is seen in the "but" that is attached to his positive evaluation, by the Deuteronomists at 1 Kgs 22:43*b* and by the Chroniclers at 2 Chr 20:33. An important difference of opinion as to what this "but" entails will be discussed at the appropriate point. Yet so far, however, the interpretation already advanced holds true in this case: the kings about whom the Chroniclers have a good opinion receive a large amount of space, while those of whom they have a negative opinion get relatively short shrift in their treatment. This latter will become all the more prominent with the last few kings of Judah prior to the destruction by the Babylonians.

Jehoshaphat will also engage in a serious religious reform, as his father, Asa, did. Later on, Hezekiah at the end of the eighth century and Josiah at the end of the seventh century will also reform Judah's religion. The last of these four reforms is the most well known from the Deuteronomistic History, but from the standpoint of the Chroniclers they all seem to be on rather equal footing. The interpreter might of course be tempted to ask why reform never really took in Judah. This is a legitimate question, though it may lead rather far afield. Certainly sociology and anthropology could help explain or clarify matters further, but most people will need no further explanation than the deep-seated wickedness of the human heart (Gen 6:5). It is a blessing from God that reform movements do come along from time to time, rather than humanity being left in the darkness without light (2 Cor 4:6; 1 John 1:7).

1. Description of Jehoshaphat's Administration (17:1-19)

BEHIND THE TEXT

Jehoshaphat's name means "Yahweh has judged," "Yahweh has decided," or even "Yahweh has ruled." The noun form of this root is used of the "judges" or, perhaps more properly, "chieftains" in the premonarchical period. At least in part, Jehoshaphat lives up to his name. As noted above, he engages in the second of the four great religious reforms discussed by the Chroniclers. Through this, he submits to Yahweh's will. However, at the end of his life his reign over Judah is evaluated in mixed terms (→ 2 Chr 20:33-36). The present text describes some of the features of his royal administration. While all of the kings, of course, developed and were supported by a bureaucracy, that operating during the reign of Jehoshaphat seems to be one of the most complex in the history of Judah.

17:1-19

IN THE TEXT

■ **1-6** As they did in their treatment of his father, Asa, the Chroniclers devote far more space to Jehoshaphat than do the Deuteronomists. In fact, 1 Kings only gives ten verses to this king, in contrast to the nineteen that the Chroniclers devote just to "narrative setup," as it were. The first six verses are given over to the by-now standard evaluation of the reign. Verse 2 maintains that he **stationed troops in all the fortified cities of Judah . . . and in the towns of Ephraim that his father Asa had captured**. This means that he solidified the gains Asa made, thus giving further strength to the nation of Judah. Throughout most of its history, Judah was far inferior to its northern neighbor Israel. Though, as has been repeatedly noted, the Chroniclers are interested in Israel in only a cursory fashion, knowledge of the "facts on the ground" are helpful in the quest for a more complete understanding. Further on in this section, the Chroniclers indicate something of what they will deal with more extensively later, namely the reform that Jehoshaphat instituted in Judah. The wonder this causes with respect to the reform accomplished by Asa has been noted above. The Deuteronomists explain it by suggesting that Asa went far, but not quite far enough: "He [Jehoshaphat] rid the land of the rest of the male shrine prostitutes who remained there even after the reign of his father Asa" (1 Kgs 22:46). Second Chronicles 17:5 reports expected information, namely that Yahweh blessed Jehoshaphat for his faithfulness. Verse 6, however, causes the careful reader to stop short, for the second part of the verse—**furthermore, he removed the high places and the Asherah poles from Judah**—is in direct contrast to the report of the Deuteronomists in 1 Kgs 22:43, which reads: "In everything he followed the ways of his father Asa and did not stray from them; he did what was right in the eyes of the LORD. *The high places, however, were not removed*, and the people continued to offer sacrifices and burn incense there" (emphasis added). The present judgment finds confirmation in the mouth of the prophet Jehu son of Hanani in 2 Chr 19:3 (→ 2 Chr 19:1-3). Radak and Jarick offer no help in resolving this difficulty, and Klein's comments strike one as intentional sidestepping: "As in 14:3, the chronicler is writing idealistically and so does not use 1 Kgs 22:43, which he will cite later in 20:33" (1999, 546). Klein understates the issue, for the Chroniclers not only did not use 1 Kgs 22:43 but also directly contradicted it. One wants to steer far clear of accusing either the Deuteronomists or the Chroniclers of dishonesty, so perhaps a solution may be found in the suggestion that, as the reform of Asa did not "stick," so also did the reform of Jehoshaphat not "stick." In other words, what from the dominant biblical perspective were "alien religions," "other gods," "idolatry," or whatever similar label may be attached, the fact is that the Judeans were constantly exposed to a variety of religious traditions from a variety of places. Yahwism, competing for the devotion of the populace in such a situation, was bound to have varying degrees of success in claiming the exclusive status its most ardent supporters championed. Therefore, one might in fact be able to agree with both the Chroniclers and the Deuteronomists, in the respect that Jehoshaphat did remove the high places, but he was not able to keep them removed, for on the popular level these religious alternatives to "pure" Yahwism were never completely shut out of the realm of possible adherence.

Official and Popular Religion

Throughout history, there has often been a disconnect between the official religion, or dominant theology, and what nontheologically trained laity practice. This is also true of ancient Israel. For example, even though the OT, at least in the final forms of its several books, is thoroughly monotheistic, archaeological investigation has located many different statues of deities in clearly Israelite sites. Though none of these statues—so far—have represented male deities (and thus confirming, with proper hesitation, the strictures against representing Yahweh in a statue), they do exist and were used, perhaps particularly in situations related to procreation and child-rearing. Perhaps something of this is going on in the four (aborted?) attempts to reform the religious practice of Judah during the reigns of Asa, Jehoshaphat, Hezekiah, and Josiah. Though Josiah seems to be the most successful of the four, moreover, the nation is destroyed less than a generation following his reform. Theologically, this is explained through Yahweh's anger being too great even for Josiah's faithfulness to overcome, but sociologically it could perhaps be explained through human willingness to try "whatever it takes" to achieve one's desired end, especially considering divine assistance (see Johnston 2007, vii).

■ **7-9** These verses give the name of several officials sent out **to teach in the towns of Judah** (v 7). This action is in support of the religious reforms. A similar activity can be seen in Neh 8:8, in which thirteen Levites read from the book of the law and explained it "so that the people understood what was being read." In the book of Acts, Philip ran up to a chariot and asked the Ethiopian eunuch inside if he understood what he was reading, then climbed up to explain after the other man said he did not (Acts 8:30-31). King Jehoshaphat sends out sixteen people—five **officials** (v 7) and eleven **Levites** (v 8). Klein notes: "Here was a further example of Jehoshaphat's high ideals, instructing the people in divine revelation so that it might govern their lives" (1999, 547). He further suggests that the royal officials were in attendance to "lend authority to the enterprise," which is a curious statement. It seems to indicate that the religious establishment needed the "secular" establishment to give it credence. In actuality, at least in the records left behind in the OT, the priests and Levites generally got along just fine without the authorization (or imposition) of the monarchy. Some may view this as a dark side to Jehoshaphat's lofty ideals.

■ **10-11** These verses describe some of the benefits heaped on Jehoshaphat from surrounding nations. In v 5, the Chroniclers reported that gifts began to flow toward the king from people in Judah. Here, one reads that **some Philistines brought Jehoshaphat gifts and silver as tribute, and the Arabs brought him flocks** (v 11). Two comments are in order. First, that **tribute** is being brought to a Judean king is evidence of some kind of expansion or, at least, fear on the part of the other nations that Jehoshaphat might try to expand his territory at their expense. Second, this is one of the few times **Arabs** are mentioned in the OT. The first time these tribes are mentioned in Chronicles has to do with tribute being sent to Solomon, so this, therefore, provides a key for understanding the passage. Jehoshaphat's influence is extending far and wide, much like that of his ancestor Solomon. Sadly, however, the reign of Jehoshaphat will not end as happily as Solomon's did, even though the internal discomfort in Solomon's Israel made the picture far less rosy than it at first appeared.

■ **12-19** The final eight verses describe tremendous numbers of soldiers stationed in Jerusalem and various other places by Jehoshaphat. The immediate impression is that these numbers are stylized figures, not intended to represent a genuine count. It may be that these large numbers function in the same way as victory stela in the ANE, on which it was common to proclaim that an enemy had been entirely destroyed, even if in reality the casualty figures were much smaller. It would certainly be within what was expected in such documents to give numbers modern and postmodern readers see as amazingly inflated. In the same way, going through and recording an actual count, expected particularly by moderns and their search for verifiability of facts, would have sounded very odd indeed to the ancients. In sum, the numbers reported here would extend into a wildly improbable total population for Judah at the time described. The careful reader should always keep the Chroniclers' historical context in mind, therefore, when seeking the meaning of a text that sounds particularly strange.

2. Alliance with Ahab (18:1—19:3)

BEHIND THE TEXT

Once the commentary reaches the end of the material on King Jehoshaphat, it will be said that Jehoshaphat's reign concluded with a mixture of positive and negative results (→ 2 Chr 20:33-36). The present text is perhaps one of the principal negative events in Jehoshapat's reign, at least according to the evaluation of the Chroniclers. It is also one of the few times that the great (and terrible) King Ahab of Israel appears in the Chroniclers' History. As noted above, the Chroniclers pay little attention to the kings of northern Israel—even ones like Ahab and his father, Omri, who figure quite prominently in extrabiblical texts from Assyria and Moab—because, for them, they are not important. By the time the Chroniclers wrote, northern Israel was a distant memory, so far back in the mists of time that it may as well never have existed. Yet, they knew that it did, so they did include it in their history when they had to, and the reign of Jehoshaphat was one of those times, because the king of Judah had made an alliance with Ahab—which the Chroniclers surely believed was a grievous mistake.

IN THE TEXT

■ **1-4** Verse 1 reports that **Jehoshaphat had great wealth and honor**. At the outset, then, things are so far, so good with this king, one of those who will in the course of time effect a great religious revival in Judah. Yet things fall apart quickly for Jehoshaphat, because **he allied himself with Ahab by marriage**. The Hebrew verb *ḥathen* ("make oneself a daughter's son"; so BDB 369) is somewhat rare, related to the nouns "father-in-law" and "son-in-law," both of which are spelled with the same Hebrew consonants. This word only occurs in the *hitpaʿel* verb stem, which usually indicates a reflexive action ("I submitted myself to God"). The *hitpaʿel* imperfect of this verb, at first glance, looks like the word *thaḥat* ("under, below"), giving the appearance of submission to a higher authority. In fact, this is what happens in the case of Jehoshaphat and Ahab, as v 3 makes clear: **I am as you are, and my people as your people**. Culturally, a man's father-in-law is an important influence on his life. In terms of royal life, however, Jehoshaphat is by this action and speech declaring himself to be subservient to Ahab. While this is probably a recognition of the "facts on the ground," it is still a radical statement on the lips of a king of Judah. In other words, it is well known from the external history that the kingdom of Israel under Omri and especially under Omri's son Ahab was a significant power on the world scene of the time. Indeed, certain inscriptions from Assyria and Moab refer to Israel as the "House of Omri," indicating the importance of this dynasty (see Kelle 2002). So, even though, according to what was apparently the dominant mode of thinking in Judah at the time, Yahweh continued to reside in the south and had abandoned the north, the southern king voluntarily submitted himself to his northern counterpart. Jehoshaphat did not give his daughter to be married to Ahab's son in order to cement a relationship. Instead, he submitted himself to Ahab, clearly indicating that he was the subordinate in the relationship.

■ **5-8** Along with dedicating his allegiance to the king of Israel, Jehoshaphat demands that Yahweh be consulted prior to the two kings going to war against the Arameans (whose capital was Ramoth Gilead; vv 3-4). Ahab first summons **the prophets—four hundred men** (v 5), who give the "go signal." The answer they give is striking: **Go . . . for God will give it into the king's hand**. In this subtle move, the Chroniclers indicate the unorthodoxy of what Ahab—and, ultimately, Jehoshaphat—is doing. Orthodoxy and unorthodoxy, of course, are terms only discerned in context. In other words, a Buddhist is generally unable fully to determine whether a Christian or a Muslim is acting within the bounds of Christian or Islamic orthodoxy, which are, in turn, radically different from one another. However, the slight against Ahab's attempt is made clearer in v 6, with Jehoshaphat's question, **Is there no longer a prophet of the Lord here whom we can inquire of?** Within the bounds of the story, it is clear to Jehoshaphat that the prophets who previously spoke did not represent Yahweh. Though the Chroniclers are clearly intentionally hesitant in identifying the god(!) to whom Ahab has recourse here, using the generic term in v 5 equally clearly indicates their belief that it is not Yahweh! Intertextually, the notion that **four hundred men** prophesied victory for Ahab reminds the reader of the four hundred prophets of Baal involved in the theomachy (battle between the gods) on Mount Carmel (1 Kgs 18). One cannot say for sure if these are the same people. They may not be, however, since those four hundred prophets have already been slaughtered at Elijah's orders by the time this episode occurs in 1 Kgs 22. Nevertheless, the confluence of the numbers is interesting.

In any event, Jehoshaphat retains at least something of his piety when he asks for **a prophet of the LORD** (2 Chr 18:6) to come. Ahab is at first reluctant to call **Micaiah son of Imlah** (v 7). The Chroniclers match the Deuteronomists' overall portrayal of Ahab as a sniveling wimp when they record his words to the effect that he hates Micaiah **because he never prophesies anything good about me, but always bad**. Jehoshaphat keeps dignity as well, chiding Ahab with the reminder that such a response to one of Yahweh's prophets—or, for that matter, to anyone—is beneath the dignity of the king. As an aside, one perhaps wishes that modern politicians and other leaders would follow Jehoshaphat's advice on this point much more often than they do!

■ **9-17** The summons for Micaiah, and the event of the prophecy regarding the proposed war, is accompanied with much pomp and circumstance. This is, after all, a state visit. In this scene, one name, apparently out of the four hundred mentioned above, is **Zedekiah son of Kenaanah** (v 10). This prophet performs a sign act such as will be seen later in prophets such as Jeremiah and Ezekiel. In vv 10-11, the prophets are all speaking in unison, this time clearly saying that Yahweh will give Ramoth Gilead to King Ahab's power. In light of the unanimous approval, the messenger sent to fetch Micaiah tells him, **Let your word agree with theirs, and speak favorably** (v 12). Micaiah responds simply that he can only say what Yahweh tells him to say. This calm, though derisive statement recalls the similar words of Balaam son of Beor in Num 22:18. There, Balaam refused to curse the Israelites as King Balak of Moab wanted, unless that was also what Yahweh wanted. The form of these two passages is thus consistent: the reader expects three things from such stories. First, there will be a command from an official to prophesy in a certain manner. Second, the prophet so commanded will declare his (usually, though sometimes her) allegiance instead to what Yahweh (or another god) says. Third, the result will always turn out against the one who originally conscripted the prophet. Thus Balaam, hired to curse the Israelites, instead blesses them at the command of Yahweh (Num 23—24). Here, the commandment to prophesy in a manner favorable to King Ahab again turns against Ahab, with Micaiah proclaiming,

I saw all Israel scattered on the hills like sheep without a shepherd (2 Chr 18:16). The metaphor of sheep to describe God's people is well known in both the OT and the NT. Ahab's reaction to Micaiah's prophecy, moreover, is what one has come to expect: **Didn't I tell you that he never prophesies anything good about me, but only bad?** (v 17). One can hear the whine in the king's voice, which again is not behavior befitting one of such a stature, especially when dressed in royal robes and sitting at court. Thus it always is with tyrants.

■ **18-27** Yet **Micaiah** has not yet finished his diatribe against Ahab. Jehoshaphat is included in the critique, surely, though this is only implicit. Micaiah tells a story of Yahweh's intentional misleading of Ahab by asking for someone to **entice Ahab king of Israel into attacking Ramoth Gilead and going to his death there** (v 19). This is the only time in the Bible—along with the counterpart text in 1 Kgs 22—that Yahweh is involved in deliberate deceit of someone who seeks an oracle from him. **A spirit came forward** (v 20) and offered to accomplish the deception, a plan that Yahweh approves. Yahweh is removed two steps from the deception of Ahab, however. The plan is suggested by the spirit, and Yahweh sends this ingenious spirit to deceive the prophets, not the king directly. That the prophets are said to have been deceived draws a predictably sharp reaction from **Zedekiah**, the prophet who just a few verses earlier had been dancing around with an iron horn, predicting Ahab's goring of the Arameans. The word translated **slapped** by the NIV can be used for any number of violent physical actions with one's hand: strike, punch, slap, wound, etc., but also simply "touch." One of the violent options is called for in context.

Micaiah does not respond equally violently, but nevertheless puts Zedekiah in his place. Similarly, when Ahab orders Micaiah to be put in prison **(give him nothing but bread and water until I return safely**, v 26), Micaiah shows himself deft with words and retorts, **If you ever return safely, the LORD has not spoken through me**. This speech recalls the famous test for prophets in Deut 18, with its modification in Jer 28. According to the latter text (Jer 28:8-9), the prophecy is sure without need of verification. Only the prophets who prophesied peace and prosperity should be checked according to whether their words are fulfilled. In Jeremiah's argument with Hananiah, therefore, the anomalous prophet is the one who promises peace when all others promise destruction. In the present text, this is balanced by a prophet (**Micaiah**) who prophesies doom when **Zedekiah** and the other 399 are prophesying victory. The reader aware of this intertextual connection will expect, then, that the word of the true prophet will be confirmed. Said fulfillment is the subject of the next portion of the story.

■ **28-34** Following the advice of the majority over against the lone naysayer—even though the naysayer has suggested Yahweh sent a deceitful spirit into the majority—**the king of Israel and Jehoshaphat king of Judah went up to Ramoth Gilead** (v 28). That the Chroniclers decline to mention Ahab's name here is interesting. The interpreter should not make too much of it, but the explanation that this is a stylistic variation seems unsatisfactory, mainly because of the contrasting use of Jehoshaphat's name. As, according to Micaiah's sermon, Yahweh engaged in a bit of deception, so Ahab tries to similarly deceive the Arameans. Along the way, he puts Jehoshaphat at risk of being assassinated. That Ahab would plan and carry out such a stratagem testifies to his nefarious character much more colorfully than would any narrative comment along the lines of "Ahab was so nefarious that . . ." Unfortunately for Ahab, the game he is playing does not turn out the way he would have liked. Whereas Jehoshaphat is saved by Yahweh (v 31), testifying to his being favored by Israel's God, Ahab is mortally wounded by a lucky shot from an Aramean bow. This event testifies to Yahweh's ultimate displeasure with Ahab. In very dramatic fashion, Ahab is allowed to live long enough to see his army get routed, and, as the Chroniclers' laconically report, **Then at sunset he died** (v 34).

■ **19:1-3** When Jehoshaphat returns home from seeing his father-in-law and erstwhile superior killed, **Jehu the seer, the son of Hanani** (v 2) greets him with a rebuke tempered by praise. It is unclear if the father of **Jehu** is the prophet **Hanani** who rebuked Jehoshaphat's father Asa near the end of the latter's life, though this possibility cannot be excluded either. It was perhaps not a welcome word, even though Jehu said, **There is, however, some good in you** (v 3). In fact, this speech by Yahweh's prophet will exemplify how Jehoshaphat is ultimately evaluated by the Chroniclers, with a mixture of positive and negative. He comes out, at the end of it all, perhaps with more positive than negative, but he still failed to completely eliminate negative.

FROM THE TEXT

The story of Yahweh sending the deceitful spirit into the prophets in order to entice King Ahab into his death has, perhaps rightly, troubled many readers. However, if one looks behind and beyond the apparent involvement of the True God in a matter of bald-faced deceit, there is a greater lesson to be had. Leaders often face difficult decisions, and the ability to make more right choices than wrong ones is what separates good, effective leaders apart from their weak, feckless counterparts. Usually, effective leaders surround themselves with competent advisers, and beyond making right decisions leaders are tasked with trusting their advisers. Not only does this help the reputation of the leader, but it also gives the advisers a sense of self-worth and dignity that they would not otherwise have. So, then, one of the major decisions leaders must make, aside from what to do in a given situation representing a crisis for the organization, is which adviser to trust. The decisions made by Ahab and Jehoshaphat in this story, and their outcomes, may teach both leaders and subordinates something very important, if only they are willing to listen.

Ahab, for his part, failed the test concerning which advice he should take. On the one hand, he had an excessively negative view of Micaiah, who, according to him, "always prophesied bad." He only summoned the prophet because Jehoshaphat insisted on it. In spite of what Micaiah said, he believed the majority, certainly because the majority agreed with his preconceived idea of what should be done. In the American idiom, then, the four hundred prophets were yes-men, and by following their advice, rather than the advice of the prophet whom he hated, Ahab effectively signed his own death warrant. Leaders should take away from this text the warning that they should not refuse to listen to someone's advice because they "hate" that person or because that person's advice has always run counter to their perceived notions of the right.

By contrast, Jehoshaphat correctly sought all sides of the debate before acting. This is so even though he at first followed incorrect advice, as did Ahab. He agreed to go with his father-in-law to Ramoth Gilead, but first he insisted that prophets of Yahweh be consulted alongside prophets of whatever god whose favor Ahab had been seeking. When it became clear to him that things were not going to go well for his Judean/Israelite alliance, and indeed when his life was in danger, he again turned to the correct God, the True God Yahweh, and was spared. After the climax of the story, he was criticized for having initially made the wrong decision but was extolled for doing some things right. Leaders can learn from his experience that, even if the advice they initially follow turns out to be incorrect, they can and should correct their course when this becomes apparent. This is, at base, a matter of humility in leadership as well as a matter of a leader being confident in his or her ability.

3. Jehoshaphat's Reform (19:4-11)

IN THE TEXT

■ **4-11** As has already been noted, the positive judgment of Jehu son of Hanani is part of the overall ambiguous evaluation of Jehoshaphat's reign. The present story of Jehoshaphat's religious reform demonstrates, in part, the positive part of the evaluation. Verse 4 notes that Jehoshaphat remained in Jerusalem for a while before beginning the reform movement. Perhaps he needed some time to recover from the setback he suffered at Ramoth Gilead. At any rate, the reform efforts apparently enjoy tremendous success. This particular reform takes the nature of legal reorganization, in contrast to the other reforms discussed by the Chroniclers. By doing this, Jehoshaphat lives up to his name, which means "Yahweh is judge." Klein connects the social and religious aspects of this reform when he writes:

> To effect justice for the people was the king's divinely sanctioned duty . . . Earlier, Jehoshaphat had taken seriously the responsibility to affirm his faith as a member of a new generation (17:4). Now he encourages the people to respond to the challenge of social ethics. (1999, 555)

In addition, although the Torah probably reached its final form a century or so later than Jehoshaphat, a specific mandate in Deuteronomy may lie behind his action in reforming the judicial administration: *You shall appoint judges and officials for yourself in all the settlements which Yahweh your God is giving you, and they shall govern the people with justice and righteousness* (Deut 16:18). Maimonides, the great medieval Jewish philosopher and theologian, numbers this among the "positive commandments of the Torah" (quoted in Septimus 2007, 308). The Chroniclers do not indicate directly that Jehoshaphat was following "a command of Moses" in this passage, though the intertextual connection is undeniable.

The main part of the passage consists of Jehoshaphat's instructions to the judges. Principal among these instructions, in turn, is the admonition that the judges should judge fairly. This seems in perfect accord with the idea that would ultimately become Deut 16:18. The text seems to fall into two different parts, establishing judges and officials first for the provincial areas (2 Chr 19:5-7) and second for the capital city of Jerusalem (vv 8-11). The instructions given to both sets of judges are basically identical, though with moderate variation. One key variation comes in v 10: Jehoshaphat tells the judges to help the people keep from sinning. The final injunction is **Do this, and you will not sin**. A simplified form of this instruction comes to the provincial magistrates in v 6, which indicates simply that Yahweh **is with you whenever you give a verdict**. If Yahweh is present with the judges, then they should judge with equity.

Finally, an interesting point of administration comes in v 11. Jehoshaphat here indicates that **Amariah the chief priest will be over you in any matter concerning the Lord, and Zebadiah son of Ishmael . . . in any matter concerning the king**. A couple of comments are in order. First, on the face of it this seems to separate the judges' responsibilities into what might be called, for lack of better terms, "religious" and "secular" law. An extreme form of such division in later history is the so-called separation of church and state in the Constitution of the United States, along with other countries that do not have an established religion. Second, it is unclear whether the setting up of these two persons as those who would hear appeals applies to the provincial judges as well as those in the capital. One might justifiably suppose this to be the case, but this is not made explicit. This is yet another place where modern and postmodern readers are left by the Chroniclers wanting more than they, in their context, were willing to give.

4. War Against the Ammonites and Moabites (20:1-30)

BEHIND THE TEXT

The Israelites—whether in the united kingdom, the northern kingdom of Israel, or the southern kingdom of Judah—have always "enjoyed" a problematic relationship with their neighbors to the east and southeast. Ammon bordered Israel on the east. It was located roughly where the Hashemite Kingdom of Jordan is today. Interestingly, the name "Ammonites" is reflected in the name for the modern capital of Jordan, the city of Amman. Moab, on the other hand, lay to Israel's southeast and also often was an enemy, going at least as far back as King Balak's attempt to curse the Israelites through Balaam (Num 22). Moab was also the home of the harried heroine of the wonderful short story of Ruth, which proclaimed Yahweh's faithfulness even to foreign widows, those traditionally thought to lie outside of the favor of the God of Israel.

This animosity that the Ammonites and the Moabites had for Israel, moreover, is not particularly surprising when one considers a key fact. Israel had a tradition regarding questionable circumstances for the origins of both the Ammonites and the Moabites. According to Gen 19:30-38, the Ammonites and the Moabites were the descendants of the incestuous sex of Lot's daughters with their father. The children born of this union are named, in the first case, Moab (which means "from the father"); and, in the second case, Ben-Ammi (which means "son of my people"). As far as we know, the Ammonites and Moabites did not have similar disgusting traditions about their own origins. If they knew about Gen 19—and it stands to reason that they did—then it should come as no surprise that they had a deep-seated hatred for all things Israelite.

IN THE TEXT

■ **1-4** The story of Jehoshaphat's victory over an alliance involving, directly or indirectly, at least four different enemies may be divided into four scenes. In this first scene, the king is told of the attack and a general alarm is raised. The Chroniclers first indicate that the invading force is composed of **the Moabites and Ammonites**, the well-known historical enemies of the Israelites. They are accompanied, however, by **some of the Meunites**, which group is far less well-known. The first point to notice is that the NIV here cites the Septuagint, correcting an apparent transmission error. The Hebrew reads "some of the Ammonites," which clearly makes no sense in context. This emendation requires a further one in v 2. Multiple Hebrew manuscripts, in addition to the Septuagint and Vulgate, read **Aram** instead of the NIV's **Edom**. In favor of "Edom" is the geographical proximity of Edom to Moab and Ammon (all three were on the opposite side of the Dead Sea), not to mention the historical enmity between Edom and Judah—perhaps every bit as potent as that described above, seeing as how Jacob, the ancient ancestor of Judah/Israel, had stolen something of great value from Esau, who fulfilled the same role for Edom. Jarick, for his part, is not convinced that the emendation from Aram to Edom should be made, however. He writes that the Arameans might well have joined up with their neighbors to the south in seeking revenge upon Jehoshaphat,

> since Jehoshaphat has not long returned from fighting against the Arameans at Ramoth-Gilead (19.1) and it may be that the Annalists have in mind that the real instigator behind this incursion into Judahite territory is the kingdom against which the king of Judah had so recently and foolishly dared to strike. (2007b, 127)

Jarick's theory is attractive, and it is commended by the majority of the manuscript tradition, even in spite of the fact that majority witness is not always a reliable indicator in textual criticism. Nevertheless, whoever the enemy was, the king and people seek the counsel of Yahweh. They apparently know—or, at any rate, the Chroniclers know—that this is the best thing to do in such a situation. Even a general as great as Joshua, during the conquest of Canaan, at least once failed to seek Yahweh's advice and lost the first battle of Ai as a result (see Josh 7).

■ **5-12** Jehoshaphat's prayer **at the temple of the** LORD **in the front of the new courtyard** (v 5) recalls many similar prayers throughout the OT. The thought behind this prayer is that, since Yahweh is **the God who is in heaven** (v 6), and since he has delivered the people in the past, he should be able to remove the present threat of the Ammonites, Moabites, and Edomites/Arameans. Though the prayer is couched in the language of piety, there is an implicit challenge to Yahweh's integrity here. A similar strategy, taken to an extreme, typifies the complaints of the book of Job. Verses 10-12 recall a bit of Israelite history, suggesting that the **men from Ammon, Moab, and Mount Seir** were not killed, precisely because Yahweh turned the Israelites away from their territory during the wilderness wanderings. Instead of being grateful for having been spared, **they are repaying us by coming to drive us out of the possession you gave us as an inheritance**. That Yahweh gave them the land as an inheritance means that they can rely on Yahweh to save them from the present threat.

■ **13-19** The fervent prayer of the king on behalf of the people is answered through an oracle given to **Jahaziel son of Zechariah, the son of Benaiah** (v

14). Perhaps uncharacteristically, the genealogy of the prophet is given back to four generations. The identification of the prophet as **a Levite** is perhaps the most significant part of the genealogy. As a Levite, he is connected to the religious establishment at least in a way. Whether he himself served in the temple is not stated in the text, though it is certainly a possibility. Yahweh, through this priest-prophet (shades of Jeremiah and Ezekiel can be heard here as well), informs Jehoshaphat and the people that they will have victory without even fighting. **Do not be afraid; do not be discouraged** (v 17), in addition, recalls similar injunctions to people throughout biblical history. One may consider the encouragement given to Joshua, appointed to succeed Moses, in Josh 1:9. Upon hearing this word, Jehoshaphat and all the people spend time in worship of Yahweh, who has answered the implicit challenge given in the prayer of Jehoshaphat in 2 Chr 20:5-12.

■ **20-30** The final eleven verses of the narrative describe how the victory came about without, as it were, a shot being fired. The couplet cited in v 21 recalls that given in 1 Chr 16:14. Rather than Judah having to engage the enemy, they are able to watch as the enemies set upon each other. The note that the third group of soldiers attempting to attack Judah were **men from Mount Seir** (v 23) perhaps helps to decide the text-critical question noted above. After the invading armies are finished killing each other off, Jehoshaphat and the Judeans swoop in and carry off the spoil, **and they found among them a great amount of equipment and clothing and also articles of value—more than they could take away** (v 25). This last statement is perhaps recalled in the NT, when the resurrected Jesus causes the disciples to catch so many fish that "they were unable to haul the net in because of the large number of fish" (John 21:6). The last two verses give a familiar statement from the conquest narratives, namely that the fear of Yahweh fell upon all the surrounding peoples **when they heard how the** L**ORD** **had fought against the enemies of Israel** (2 Chr 20:29). This sounds again a key note of the Chroniclers' theology: even though Yahweh had now—that is, in their time—ascended to being considered the only God over all the kingdoms of the earth, Yahweh had had a special relationship with Judah and Israel for all of its existence. Such was this relationship that the Israelites often did not even have to fight against their enemies. According to this line of reasoning, if God was for them, who could be against them (Josh 1:5; Rom 8:31).

FROM THE TEXT

The careful interpreter should avoid, in this context, the temptation to see contemporary circumstances in the biblical text. Specifically, a naive reading of a text like this may tend to justify oppressive, treacherous, or even violent acts taken in defense of some perceived "divine" promise. It is long past time for the world and human society to move beyond violence undertaken in the name and under the blessing of religion. In fact, such violence has led many deep thinkers to become atheists, eschewing religion as the apparent source, or at least apparently a principal source, of war, oppression, deprivation, and terrorism. In other words, reading about a miracle in the past should inspire faith in God—this is true without doubt. It should not, however, inspire an expectation that such things will or should continue to happen in order for God to be God. It should also not inspire confusion of the ancient Davidic kingdom with the modern State of Israel. Most importantly, support for (or, for that matter, resistance against) the foreign policy of the State of Israel—particularly in its dealing with the Palestinians—should not be made a litmus test of the authenticity of another's faith in God or belief in the divine inspiration of the Bible.

5. Conclusion of Jehoshaphat's Reign: Positive and Negative (20:31—21:1)

IN THE TEXT

■ **31-34** At the end of the reign of Jehoshaphat, as noted above, the final evaluation that the Chroniclers give him is a mixture of positive and negative evaluation. The careful reading will recall the diametric opposition between the Chroniclers' and Deuteronomistic Histories with regard to the removal of the high places. One sees here (v 33) that external consistency is restored, unfortunately at the price of internal consistency. However, the present commentary proposes that the same solution offered above should be applied here. For the same reason as it was necessary for the religion of Judah to be "reformed" several times, it can be said both that Jehoshaphat was successful at removing the high places and commend him for it and that Jehoshaphat was not successful at removing the high places and reprove him for it. In other words, the matter of the high places is an example of the mixture of positive and negative comments in the final evaluation of Jehoshaphat. Essentially, however, he comes off good in the eyes of both the Chroniclers and the Deuteronomists. Verse 34 gives an interesting variation on the theme of citing older, no-longer-extant materials. The Chroniclers suggest that **the annals of Jehu son of Hanani** are included **in the book of the kings of Israel**. This phrase indicates that the otherwise unknown royal official (who may or may not be a prophet, given some of the other citations of prophets) contributed to the official palace archives. Royal scribes like this were well-known, highly skilled and, comparatively speaking at least, highly paid individuals in various ANE societies.

■**35-37** Breaking the usual pattern, the Chroniclers add mention of one more event from Jehoshaphat's life. The Chroniclers recount an alliance between Jehoshaphat and **Ahaziah king of Israel** (v 35), which includes the building of the first substantial Israelite/Judean navy since the days of King Solomon (see 2 Chr 8:18). The venture fails, however, because the ***ships were not able to sail to Tarshish***. The NIV reads **sail to trade** (v 37), which is why, of course, the ships would want to sail to such a faraway port as Tarshish. The intertextual connection this brings to the book of Jonah should not be ignored. One wonders how the story of the reluctant prophet to Nineveh might have gone had the ship sailing to Tarshish not been able to leave port, like these here. The words of the prophet **Eliezer son of Dodavahu of Mareshah**, who is otherwise unknown, prove true. Yahweh destroyed the ships because of the wicked alliance with the wicked King Ahaziah. Thus the mixed evaluation of Jehoshaphat's reign continues all the way up to the end of his life.

■**21:1** The king's life ends, appropriately described, in the first verse of ch 21. **Jehoshaphat** gives way to **Jehoram**, one of the most interesting kings in Judah's history, mainly because of his connection to the house of Omri in the northern kingdom of Israel, established by his father marrying his mother, who was the daughter of Omri's son Ahab.

E. The Reign of Jehoram (21:2-20)

BEHIND THE TEXT

King Jehoram is yet another of those kings who are called in for censure by the Judean historians. Both the Deuteronomists and the Chroniclers are agreed that he was wicked. His wickedness is confirmed, according to the dominant theology, by the fact that he died a disgraceful death, not worthy of a king in the line of David. Yet, there is at least a possibility that with Jehoram the historians are in fact dealing with a non-Davidide. Jehoram's reign is established in the usual way; yet, as has already been seen, things fall apart quickly for this king who does not live in the way that Yahweh requires.

An intriguing possibility presents itself regarding Jehoram. Jehoram's reign takes place during the reign of King Joram of Israel. The Deuteronomists report in 2 Kgs 8:16 that Jehoram became king in the fifth year of Joram. The similarity of the two names, coupled with the historical proximity of their reigns, led historians such as Miller and Hayes to conclude they were the same person! They write "that Ahaziah of Israel who died without any sons was succeeded on the throne in Samaria by his brother-in-law (married to Athaliah, Ahaziah's sister), who was already king of Judah" (Miller and Hayes 2006, 320-21). They follow here the programmatic suggestion of John

Strange (1975, 191-201) and are themselves followed by Davies and Rogerson (2006, 78). Earlier the phenomenon of two people having the same name was discussed with regard to the genealogy of Saul in 1 Chr 9:36. There the Chroniclers were clearly dealing with different generations, so the comparison is not quite exact. If the suggestion is correct, it would be the first time that the kingdoms had been united, if only briefly, since the beginning of the reign of Rehoboam. Definitive evidence, unfortunately, is lacking for a conclusive answer to this question.

IN THE TEXT

■ **2-4** These verses are a preliminary note or introduction to the reign of Jehoram. This is the only place in the Chroniclers' History where such a list is given. Further, this seems to be a genuine *novum* or unique idea, for no mention is made of this fratricide in 2 Kgs 8. In dramatic terms, it sets up the violent scene that is to follow in the next few verses. **Jehoram's brothers, the sons of Jehoshaphat** are introduced into the story only to be killed almost as quickly as their names are read. Jarick points out that this kind of "reprehensible actions have not been seen in the Annals before this event" (2007b, 133).

This correct assertion requires a nuanced response. On the one hand, although Solomon had many brothers, there was not this kind of violence associated with his rise to power. On the other hand, however, as was noted above, the Chroniclers present a far less violent account of Solomon's succession to David—in marked contrast to 1 Kgs 1—3. It seems certain that the Chroniclers admit the violence associated with Jehoram but exclude that associated with Solomon because they judge Jehoram to be wicked and Solomon to be righteous, in spite of a few missteps he made along the way. It was also noted above that even in the Deuteronomistic account, Solomon himself never "gets his hands dirty"; in other words, he has people to do his killing for him. Surely that is also the case with Jehoram in this text, though the Chroniclers do not make this explicit, surely to make their indictment of this wicked king all the more serious.

As for the names of the brothers listed, two in particular stand out. The second son—the first of Jehoram's younger brothers—is **Azariah**. The fourth brother and fifth son is **Azariahu**. In the text as it stands, the two names are simple variant spellings of each other. Several possibilities to explain this present themselves. It could either be an error on the part of the Chroniclers or perhaps "the earlier Azariah had died before the younger one was born" (Jarick 2007b, 132). Alternatively, it seems that the suggestion of two people of the same generation could not have the same name is gratuitous. Though it would certainly be unusual, this possibility is not necessarily excluded. A third possibility is suggested by the editors of *BHS* in a footnote to this verse. The proposed emendation is to *'uzziyyahu* ("Uzziah"). A king by this name will rule around seventy-five years after Jehoram (→ 2 Chr 26). As will be noted below, Uzziah is called Azariah by the Deuteronomists in 2 Kgs 15. This establishes that Uzziah and Azariah were variant spellings of one another, and thus this note has much to commend it. Whatever option is chosen, however, the interpreter must be careful not to allow one's own biases—which are based in the several contexts that make up one's life—to unduly influence how one understands the text. As has been repeatedly shown, the Chroniclers are not to be held to the same standards as contemporary writers—and not even all contemporary writers should be held to the same standard.

■ **5-7** Jehoram's murder of all his brothers, as tragic and shocking as it is, turns out to be only the prelude to the very wicked reign of a very wicked king. From a religious standpoint, it is unfortunate that such degeneration from the standard could take place practically on the heels of Jehoshaphat's great reform, the story of which was recounted in the previous chapter (→ 2 Chr 19). The key phrase in this regard comes in 21:6: **He followed the ways of the kings of Israel, as the house of Ahab had done, for he married a daughter of Ahab**. One might be tempted to think that this verse suggests the very act of marrying the daughter of Ahab was the grievous sin Jehoram committed. The OT has plenty of examples of kings who, having married foreign women, get sidetracked away from following the true God Yahweh into following the gods of the foreign wife. The most notable example of this, from the Deuteronomistic standpoint at least, is none less than King Solomon. However, this is a mistaken reading. Jehoram's having married Athaliah, the daughter of Ahab who will eventually become the only queen regnant in Judah's history, is merely a contributing factor to his sin. The actual sin is that he **conducted himself after the manner of kings of Israel**. He certainly could have done this without having married Athaliah. The Hebrew verb "walk" is often used to describe not so much physical activity as an orientation of one's life or the lifestyle one chooses for oneself. A prominent example is Yahweh's instruction given to Abraham: "walk before me faithfully and be blameless" (Gen 17:1). Yet, even though Jehoram was wicked, Yahweh did not cut Judah off completely. The expression **He [Yahweh] had promised to maintain a lamp for him [David] and his descendants forever** (2 Chr 21:7) is a theologically significant phrase. Regardless of the sin of individual successors to David, Yahweh promised never to make a full end of Israel. The phrase "not make a full end of you" is repeated often through Jeremiah as a functional equivalent to the phrase here. Though the word may sound somewhat hollow given the experience of exile, it could also serve as a powerful symbol of hope.

■ **8-11** These verses describe some of the negative events associated with Jehoram's reign. The dominant view, of course, is that these events are evidence of divine wrath against the king for his wicked behavior. This is made explicit in vv 10*b*-11. Klein puts the matter rather vividly when he writes: "In 2 Chronicles, the Lord keeps short accounts in claiming moral debts, if a new generation disdains the spiritual baton passed down from its predecessors" (1999, 569). This had certainly been the case with Jehoram, having brought the nation all the way back from the positive track upon which Asa and Jehoshaphat had set it and back into the negative legacy of impudent men like Rehoboam and his father-in-law, King Ahab. Along the way, the Chroniclers use the term **Judah** to refer to the southern kingdom (v 10*a*), though as has been noted they typically refer to the southern kingdom with the name "Israel," though according to the Deuteronomists that term should be reserved for the northern kingdom.

■ **12-15** The identity of the actual source of the **letter from Elijah the prophet** (v 12) is difficult to determine. This is so because, according to the Deuteronomists, Elijah was already dead by the time Jehoram became king, or at the very least he died early in his reign (2 Kgs 1:17; 3:11). Jeremiah's letter to the exiled community (see Jer 29) is another example of a prophetic message delivered by letter. Alternatively, this could have come from a different Elijah, since no further information is given for him, like the name of his father or his city of origin. The prophetic source predicts that Jehoram will be inflicted with some kind of gastrointestinal disease, which is certainly not an easy way to transition out of mortal life. What is most important to note is that the theology remains consistent: this judgment is to be executed on Jehoram—and Jehoram, in a manner of speaking, is to be executed—because of the things he did: causing Judah (note **Judah** again in v 13) to sin and murdering all of his brothers. One should also take note, in light of what was said above, that Jehoram's having married Athaliah *is not mentioned* among the sins he has committed!

■ **16-17** Accompanying the prediction of personal difficulties to be visited on Jehoram is a prediction of disaster for the nation. Whereas Edom and Libnah revolted from Judean rule as a judgment upon Jehoram, here the territory of Judah itself is threatened. The threat comes from Israel and Judah's ancient and virulent enemy **the Philistines**, along with **Arabs who lived near the Cushites** (v 16). Though Jerusalem itself is not attacked, some of the royal properties are confiscated by what was surely a border raid, along with Jehoram's **sons and wives** (v 17). The only one left was **Ahaziah**, who is called *Jehoahaz* in v 17. **Ahaziah** and *Jehoahaz* are variants of one another, formed by reversing the two elements of the name. Both of them mean something like "Yahweh has grasped," and indeed this prince, **the youngest** of Jehoram's sons, has been grasped out of a very dangerous situation.

■ **18-20** The final three verses discuss the painful punishment inflicted on the king's own person. It is quite beside the point to speculate on what precisely this disease was. The Chroniclers likely would not have had at their disposal such sophisticated medical terminology anyway. Therefore, they described it in the awfully vivid terms that they did, in order to demonstrate by negative example that Yahweh's word should be followed. Because Jehoram did not follow Yahweh's word, the punishment even continued after his death, since his body was not given a proper burial. A comparison with Jeremiah is again helpful, for King Jehoiakim's body was similarly abused, not buried on the plots of land reserved for the bodies of the kings (see Jer 36:30). Thus ends the ignoble reign of King Jehoram, who is certainly the wickedest king in Judah so far, by far. His wickedness will be exceeded by Jehoiakim, perhaps, but as for now the Chroniclers mince no words in describing how poorly they feel about the son of Jehoshaphat.

F. The Reign of Ahaziah (22:1-9)

IN THE TEXT

■ **1** The Chroniclers report that *the residents of Jerusalem* (NIV: the people of Jerusalem) made a king out of **Ahaziah**, his **youngest son**. The phrase *residents of Jerusalem* is unusual. On the one hand, this may be an equivalent term to the oft-repeated "people of the land," who seem to have quite a large role in determining who the king will be, or at least confirming the choice of a king made by someone else (usually the reigning monarch). On the other hand, this phrase could mean that the Jerusalemites were taking a bit more authority than belonged to them, over against the provincial areas. The former option seems best, since the burden of proof for the second is rather high. Postmodern criticism enjoys reading "between the lines," though in some cases this leads to fanciful and strained conclusions that support one's preconceived notions. As in most situations, the solution that seems "simpler" might turn out to be more accurate.

This being said, however, it remains interesting that the **youngest son** of Jehoram was chosen by the people. Earlier, it was noted that Rehoboam had chosen Abijah—certainly not the oldest of his surviving sons—to be king after him because he loved his mother Maakah compared to all his wives and concubines. No such motivation is given here as to why Ahaziah is chosen, so in this case free speculation may be warranted. No reasonable option may be excluded. In other words, the raising of Ahaziah (whose name means "Yahweh is my strength") presents at least two interesting problems, to the first of which a simple solution seems at hand, while to the second of which there is not such an easy answer.

■ **2** There is a slight difference in the manuscript evidence concerning the age of Ahaziah. The MT says he was *forty-two years old*, while the NIV, following some LXX manuscripts and the Syriac translation, reads **twenty-two years old**. The latter seems to commend itself, especially given that the reader already knows Ahaziah is the youngest son of Jehoram (v 1). In the latter part of the verse, the reader is introduced to a character who will prove significant very soon. In fact, **Athaliah, a granddaughter of Omri** will take the throne for herself in a move of which the Chroniclers and the Deuteronomists disapprove, after the **one year** of Ahaziah's reign.

■ **3-9** Indeed, Athaliah's influence is already to be felt during the reign of Ahaziah, for the Chroniclers report that **He too followed the ways of the house of Ahab, for his mother encouraged him to act wickedly** (v 3). One should not use this text in a way that contributes to the negative view of women promulgated by Augustine in particular, making females and femininity responsible seemingly for all sin, and especially the first one in the garden of Eden. In other words, just because Athaliah is evil does not make all women evil! In any event, such a judgment is ridden with perspectival bias, so this is another reason why too much should not be made of this.

That this is so is demonstrated by the further summary of Ahaziah's reign. Specifically, **the house of Ahab . . . became his advisers, to his undoing** (v 4). Thus Athaliah is but one influence on the young king. The Chroniclers do not indicate any specifically religious sins that Ahaziah committed, though they do suggest that, like many of the other Judean kings before him, he entered into improper and costly alliances with the Israelite kings, going into wars that he shouldn't have gotten into. In this instance, the Israelite king **Joram son of Ahab** brings Ahaziah with him against **Hazael king of Aram** (v 5). Joram is wounded and seeks treatment at Jezreel. According to the Chroniclers, one of the worse things Ahaziah did was go down to visit Joram at Jezreel, for this is how **God brought about Ahaziah's downfall** (v 7). The two of them together meet **Jehu son of Nimshi, whom the** LORD **had anointed to destroy the house of Ahab.**

The Dan Stela

In 1993, an archaeological find in the ancient city of Dan threw tremendous light on the biblical record, while at the same time casting doubt on the present text. The so-called Dan Stela was a text written in Aramaic, apparently a victory monument of King Hazael of Aram. The relevant section of the stela comes in lines 7-9: "[And I killed . . .]ram son of [. . .] the king of Israel, and I killed [. . .]yahu son of [. . . the ki]ng of the House of David." On the one hand, this is apparently independent evidence for the existence of the Davidic dynasty. On the other hand, however, this text ascribes to Hazael what the Chroniclers ascribe to Jehu. Some modern scholars may claim that it is a fallacy to believe the biblical text in the face of this "contradictory" evidence. However, it is perhaps equally fallacious to disbelieve the biblical text because of this external evidence. This may be an example of kings taking credit for something that someone else did. The deaths of Joram and Ahaziah were surely advantageous to Hazael, even though an Aramean takeover of Israel and Judah was not immediately in the works. Thus, in the typical bluster of ANE kings, Hazael could claim that he had killed his rivals, even if in "actual history" he may not have done so.

Jehu, after killing all those associated with the house of Ahab, also kills Ahaziah. Second Kings 9:14-29 has a much more dramatic version of the deaths of Joram and Ahaziah, including Jehu's arrow shot into Joram's back, which emerges through his chest! Ahaziah is killed, and **there was no one in the house of Ahaziah powerful enough to retain the kingdom** (v 9). This note sets up the reign of Athaliah in the next section.

G. The Reign of Athaliah, Judah's Only Queen Regnant (22:10—23:21)

BEHIND THE TEXT

22:10—
23:21

Queen Athaliah is interesting because she is unique. While all of the kings of Judah had queens who ruled alongside them, only Queen Athaliah ruled in her own right. Alice Laffey writes:

> Feminist interpreters see the narrative about Athaliah as a realistic portrayal of the lengths to which a woman, in the patriarchal culture of ancient Israel, would have to go in order to attain independence and the opportunity of significant decision making. (1998b, 138)

Athaliah was not herself a descendant of David, so that her six-year reign represents a break in the Davidic dynasty. Her descent is ultimately unclear, however; the Chroniclers are uninterested in the genealogy of her father Ahab. Though there is an "Omri" listed in 1 Chr 9:4 as a Benjamite, none of his sons are listed, so one is unsure whether this is the same Omri who founded the Israelite capital at Samaria and a dynasty that ruled Israel for some four decades. The Davidic dynasty is only picked up again through Joash—though Athaliah just narrowly misses killing him and effecting a complete usurpation. Laffey continues:

> Had Joash died, the history of Kings Joash, Amaziah, Uzziah, Jotham, Ahaz, Hezekiah, Manasseh, Amon, Josiah, Jehoahaz, Jehoiakim, Jehoia-

kin, and Zedekiah would never have been written. The Davidic dynasty would have lasted a mere 150 years instead of the 400 years with which it is credited. (1998b, 139)

The statement is in reference to a woman named Jehosheba, who was instrumental in protecting baby Joash (→ 2 Chr 22:11).

IN THE TEXT

■ **10** Interestingly, the Chroniclers specify which royal family Athaliah set out to kill. This is significant because only rarely, as has been shown, do the Chroniclers deal with the royal house of Israel. The specificity seems unnecessary, especially since 2 Kgs 11:1 leaves it out.

Laffey, writing from the standpoint of the presentation of women in the text, suggests that the Chroniclers have some ulterior motives:

Although Athaliah is identified in the Deuteronomistic History as the mother of Ahaziah, the Chronicler makes plain that at least one reason for the evil Ahaziah perpetrated was that "his mother was his counselor in doing wickedly" (22:3). (1998a, 122)

Laffey misses, however, the fact that not only Athaliah but also all "the house of Ahab" was giving Ahaziah bad advice (22:4). This may have been a stronger argument in her favor. Therefore, as has already been seen, the women are presented in relationship to their men, either giving them more prestige, or, as in this case, making their wickedness all the more wicked. Further, Athaliah's evil counsel surely enhances *her own* wickedness as the queen. However, the caution against extending this to all women should not be forgotten.

■ **11-12** The endurance of the Davidic monarchy is, in this text, both threatened with and saved from extinction by the actions of two different women. While this may at first shock the reader used to the strong patriarchal flavor of the OT and ancient Israelite society in general, significant men have required salvation brought about by significant women all the way through the text. To take just one example, in the book of Exodus, the baby boy who will grow into a great leader is saved from death by five women. First, the Hebrew midwives Shiphrah and Puah defy the pharaoh's order to kill the boy Hebrew babies. Second, his mother, Jochebed, following the letter if not the spirit of the law, casts the baby into the Nile (but enclosed in a basket). Third, the daughter of the pharaoh realizes that the baby belongs to the Hebrews but does not kill him because of that fact. Finally, fourth, Moses's sister, Miriam, following along just out of sight, appears just at the right time to offer the services of a Hebrew woman to nurse the child. The nursemaid, of course, just happens to be the child's mother, thus making her the first, third, and sixth brave woman looking out for him.

In this text, as noted above, the Davidic line is threatened through the actions of Athaliah, who, in the logic of the narrative, should perhaps be expected to be evil since she herself came of such an evil line. Athaliah's murder of the royal household, while gruesome, was not completely out of line in the historical context. It has already been shown how, in the Deuteronomistic version of the history at least, the rise of the great King Solomon to power was accompanied with tremendous bloodshed. In other words, having killed rivals to the throne is not what makes Athaliah wicked in the eyes of the Judahite historians. Rather what makes her evil is her lack of a Davidic heritage. One wonders then, in that respect, if Athaliah had been a daughter of the Davidides instead of the Omrides, whether she would have on that basis been accepted as a ruler of Judah. This is a question that cannot be answered, but it is nevertheless interesting to raise.

However, things are set right again by **Jehosheba, daughter of King Jehoram** (v 11). Her name in the Hebrew text is ***Jehoshab'at*** (or sometimes "Jehoshebeath"; see 2 Kgs 11:2). The difference is probably due, as in most of the cases so far considered, simply to different traditions regarding the name. Whatever her actual name, however, **Jehosheba** saves **Joash** from the murderous Athaliah and thus accomplishes the first step in continuing the royal line. Laffey notes: "Only eight Davidic kings, including David, preceded Athaliah, while thirteen followed. Jehosheba's courage made the continuation of the dynasty possible, yet virtually no one knows her name" (1998b, 139)! Jehosheba's name (in this form) means something like "Yahweh has sworn on oath," which lends great insight into the significance of her action. The careful reader will recall that Yahweh had sworn on oath to David that he would always have a descendant on the throne of Israel. Thus through the actions of a woman named "Yahweh has sworn," Yahweh keeps that which he had sworn! Other people, and in particular men, will be involved later, but it was a woman who, as the old saying goes, "got the ball rolling." To sum up: without the women, the men of Israel wouldn't have gotten very far at all.

■ **23:1-10** Although Athaliah reigned for six years—during which time the "legitimate" heir was in hiding, thanks to his aunt—she was not memorialized in the typical way for Judean monarchs. That is, there is no "regnal formula" for Athaliah. This omission is surely due to both the Deuteronomists and the Chroniclers having considered her not a legitimate ruler, and hence they tried to erase her from the history, even though they could not be ultimately successful in this undertaking.

These two active women—Athaliah in "breaking things" and Jehosheba in "restoring things"—quickly fade into the background, however. Replacing them on center stage is **Jehoiada** (v 1), who is called a priest and the husband of Jehosheba in 22:11. His status as a priest—and more than that, a man—is probably what made him a likely candidate to "take the reins" in this situation. Verse 1 says, **In the seventh year Jehoiada showed his strength**. On the one hand, a reader could wonder why it took him so long. On the other hand, however, he might have waited a while in order to allow the baby Joash to become old enough to sit on the throne.

It seems strange, on first reading, how such a large group of people as is reported in v 2 (**the Levites and the heads of the Israelite families from all the towns**) was able to assemble without the queen having gotten information about the demonstration. In the contemporary situation, one would expect press and various onlookers to be in attendance, but this is not the case in the present story. Perhaps this is a subtle attempt on the Chroniclers' part to comment on Athaliah's ineffectiveness as a ruler. Although she was *mostly* successful at eliminating her rivals, mostly successful is slightly unsuccessful, and it was this one lack of success that would cost her in the end. **Jehoiada** makes a covenant with all the important assembled persons and initiates a conspiracy to take down the ruler deemed illegitimate, and more importantly to protect the legitimate heir to the throne.

■ **11-15** Queen Athaliah finally becomes aware of the conspiracy—and, apparently, of her failure to remove all of the royal line—when it is too late to do anything else. When **Athaliah tore her robes and shouted, "Treason! Treason!"** (v 13). She was, technically, in the right. Just as, in the Deuteronomistic History, when Samuel anoints David while Saul is still alive and reigning, has committed treason against his king, so also have Jehoiada and all the leading officials done so. Nevertheless, they make quick work of the queen, threatening to kill anyone who follows her. In a show of piety, Jehoiada instructs his soldiers, **Do not put her to death at the temple of the LORD** (v 14). Instead, they execute the former queen as she was trying to escape.

■ **16-21** After having taken care of the usurper, **Jehoiada then made a covenant that he, the people, and the king would be the LORD's people** (v 16). He and his supporters then go and restore the religious situation as they had restored the political situation. Removing items connected with the worship of alien gods (chiefly Baal), they also restored the purity of the people, with **gatekeepers at the gates of the LORD's temple so that no one who was in any way unclean might enter** (v 19). Finally, Athaliah, like Jehoram before her, died "to no one's regret" (21:20). In fact, **All the people of the land rejoiced, and the city was calm, because Athaliah had been slain with the sword** (23:21). In the ideology of the Chroniclers, and among most of the elites, the members of the Davidic dynasty were the only legitimate rulers in Jerusalem. Not even a brief six- or seven-year interregnum could, in their estimation, undo what Yahweh had promised so long ago to David.

H. The Reign of Joash (24:1-27)

IN THE TEXT

■ **1-3** The story of the boy-king **Joash** falls into three parts. In these first three verses the Chroniclers introduce the king to their readers. At **seven years old** (v 1) he was the youngest ever to assume the throne, beating perhaps the greatest king of all, Josiah, by one year (→ ch 34). Though a king so young would naturally be vulnerable, and indeed only escaped elimination by the slimmest of margins (see 22:10-12), Yahweh's blessings were certainly upon him since **he reigned in Jerusalem forty years** (24:1). In the theology of both the Deuteronomists and the Chroniclers, a lengthy reign spelled Yahweh's blessing; thus, the rapid succession of kings near Judah's downfall were wicked of a piece (→ ch 36). In spite of all this, however, 24:2 foreshadows ill things to come, saying that **Joash did what was right in the eyes of the LORD all the years of Jehoiada the priest**. Jehoiada was the one who took over from his wife Jehosheba in protecting baby Joash from the usurper Athaliah, as the previous chapter detailed. Verse 2 hints at, then, some kind of regency status for the priest. Jehoiada is called the "chief priest" in v 6 below, though this phrase is not the same as other instances translated "high priest." The importance of the priest for the king's life is demonstrated in that **Jehoiada chose two wives for him** (v 3), thus working to restore the Davidic monarchy to strength through increasing the chance of producing a strong and competent heir.

■ **4-16** The second part of King Joash's story details positive things that he accomplished during his reign, most notably restoring a particular aspect of temple worship, namely the collection of required offerings from the population. The king is initially dismayed when **the priests and Levites** did not immediately carry out his instructions to collect the taxes **due annually from all Israel** (v 5). The law being referred to in the Torah is found at Exod 30:12, as Radak explains: "This refers to the money from the shekels—the half-shekels that all the Israelites would give once a year" (Kimchi 2008, 247). It is possible to take this in a cynical way, equating piety with supporting the work of the priests who refuse to support themselves otherwise. But this is an overreading, for religious institutions, buildings, and personnel have ultimately always been supported by the faithful. It is, rather, a matter of deep responsibility for faithfulness on the part of those in leadership for that which has been entrusted to their care.

The king upbraids **Jehoiada the chief priest** for failing in the responsibility of requiring **the Levites to bring in from Judah and Jerusalem the tax imposed by Moses the servant of the** LORD (v 6). Thus, the priest who took on himself the duties of royal protector and, especially, dynastic protector, later finds his own work being taken over by the very king he had thus protected! This surely demonstrates that leaders of all sorts must constantly be on guard not to fail in their basic responsibilities, especially when they point out such failings in others (see Matt 7:3). After a parenthetical comment summarizing the religious aspects of Athaliah's wickedness (2 Chr 24:7; her "political" wickedness had already been described), the solution devised by the king to make up for the Levites' failure is detailed in vv 8-12. **A chest was made and placed outside, at the gate of the temple of the** LORD (v 8). Intertextually, this note reminds of the episode recounted in Mark 12:41-44. The collection box in the Markan story may not have been for the collection of the half-shekel tax. At least, it may not have been exclusively for that purpose, as indicated by the large sums of money being brought by the wealthy and by the fact that a woman was bringing an offering there. The half-shekel tax, moreover, was reserved for Israelite men (see Exod 38:26). As has been noted, intertextual traces like this are worth chasing, even if they ultimately turn out not to carry as strong a connection as they at first appeared to do. The interpreter does not know where a trace will lead unless he or she has the fortitude to pursue it. In any event, in the present story the strategy works amazingly well: **a great amount of money** was collected by people giving into this chest (v 11). Further, **the rest of the money**, that is, the funds not used for the repair of the temple, was used to make **articles for the** LORD**'s temple: articles for the service and for the burnt offerings, and also dishes and other objects of gold and silver** (v 14). The segment ends with a note on Jehoiada's righteous death and, perhaps unusually, burial **with the kings in the City of David**. This honor was afforded him **because of the good he had done in Israel for God and his temple** (v 16).

■ **17-27** Unfortunately, however, the death of the good high priest has negative implications for the nation and its king. The foreshadowing back in v 2 (→) made the reader expect such a devolution, and King Joash does not disappoint the readers at the same time as he disappoints his God. As has been seen throughout the history of Israel's and Judah's kings, things turn sour for King Joash. Thus the third part of his story in the Chroniclers' History details some of the ways in which Joash turned away from the piety that had served him so well throughout the earlier part of his reign. Like Jehoshaphat, at the end of his life he earns from the Chroniclers a mixed review.

In direct contrast to King Manasseh later (→ ch 33), who turns near the end of his life from wickedness to righteousness, Joash turns from righteousness to wickedness. That this could happen exemplifies the lesson suggested above with Jehoiada not being able to secure the Levites' obedience. Leaders must constantly and consistently be on their guard not to let complacency lead them into error. **Zechariah son of Jehoiada the priest** (a prophet with priestly connections, like Jeremiah and Ezekiel later) warns the king to the effect that **Because you have forsaken the LORD, he has forsaken you** (v 20). Yahweh's forsaking of Joash takes two forms: defeat at the hands of an external enemy and assassination at the hands of an internal conspiracy. The old enemy **Aram** (v 23) enjoyed victory over Joash's army. Verse 24 gives an arresting comment, namely that **the LORD delivered into their hands a much larger army**. This is a typical phrase, to be sure, but while usually the antecedent of "their" in such usage is Israel or Judah, here it is the enemy! This unusual phrase is not as unusual as at first appears, however. The book of Jeremiah, for example, has many examples of similar ideas, calling the Babylonian king Nebuchadnezzar Yahweh's chosen servant (see Jer 27:6). As for the internal conspiracy, two ministers, **Zabad, son of Shimeath an Ammonite woman, and Jehozabad, son of Shimrith a Moabite woman** assassinated the king in his bed (2 Chr 24:25-26). The detail that the assassins were, respectively, of Ammonite and Moabite descent recalls Jehoshaphat's war against the Ammonites (→ 20:1-30, esp. Behind the Text). The final comment about Joash is a dismissive one. Though it is a familiar practice of the Chroniclers to point the readers to other (lost) texts, here the reference is to the **annotations on the book of the kings** (24:27). The NIV phrase seems to indicate that Joash's deeds only belong in footnotes or marginal corrections. The Hebrew word, however, is *midraš*, which typically refers to study notes or commentary on a written document. It is used most extensively in postbiblical Jewish writings. The NIV translation is not far off the mark, however. Either way, Joash is relegated to the arena of secondary literature. Thus the Chroniclers dismiss him as one who, though he started out with much potential and with the providential protection of Yahweh resting upon him—and indeed accomplished much that was good—could not ultimately sustain his favored position and fell into gross error, arrogance, and sinfulness.

FROM THE TEXT

Those who enjoy the benefit of grace have a definite responsibility to remain faithful to the work of God's grace in their lives. Especially, as noted above, those in leadership must live up to their responsibility to be faithful to God. Wesleyans may read texts like this as a warning against resting upon grace received without recognizing that God demands obedience as a response. Instead of bashing Reformed theology, we should focus on how Wesleyans would read this text. Moreover, much can be said about grace and the tragic turn of events brought about by one's decision to say no to grace.

I. The Reign of Amaziah (25:1-28)

IN THE TEXT

■ **1-4** Like the story of King Joash, that of his son **Amaziah** (v 1) may be told in three parts. Amaziah's turn to wickedness might not have been so pronounced as his father's, but it is still presaged, in the summary of his reign, with the phrase **He did what was right in the eyes of the Lord, but not wholeheartedly** (v 2). In other words, Joash's fall may have been more precipitous, since according to the Chroniclers there was no hint of it in his earlier career. By contrast, **Amaziah** had apparently always been holding something back. On the other hand, one could read these notes relating to Joash and Amaziah as mere stylistic variations, but this alternative seems trite. Given the insistence of this commentary on seeing the Chroniclers as thoughtful creative writers, attributing differences like this simply to stylistic concerns is extremely unsatisfying. By contrast, one should rather see the changes that the Chroniclers employ as key narrative clues to what is about to take place in the historical record. The Chroniclers, of course, intuitively knew everything that had happened; or, at least, they had sources that told them everything that had happened. This material they carefully arranged for maximum rhetorical effect, and the result is blindingly brilliant.

The Chroniclers report that Amaziah's **mother's name was Jehoaddan; she was from Jerusalem** (v 1). That the new king was of pure Judahite descent was doubtlessly important in order to reestablish and solidify the once-again-fledgling Davidic monarchy, which had almost been wiped out when Amaziah's father was an infant. Thus, in fact, the true significance of the high priest Jehoiada having chosen wives for King Joash is finally revealed (v 3). No information is given regarding Joash's second wife, for her offspring do not seem to advance the story being told. In the course of time, the care taken by Jehoiada to preserve the line threatened to be of little account, as Joash showed himself unable to maintain the promise demonstrated through how he came to the throne. In spite of this, the line did continue. Furthermore, in spite of the fact that Amaziah did not follow after Yahweh with his whole heart (v 2), the lamp held out for David was not—yet, at least—extinguished (see 1 Kgs 15:4). Things do not start off poorly for Amaziah, however. For although he did exact revenge on the conspirators who murdered his father, **he did not put their children to death, but acted in accordance with what is written in the Law, in the Book of Moses** (2 Chr 25:4). The law being referenced is found in Deut 24:16: "Parents are not to be put to death for their children, nor children put to death for their parents; each will die for their own sin." The reverse of this principle had become something of a proverb by the time of the exilic prophets Jeremiah and Ezekiel, the former proclaiming: "In those days people will no longer say, 'The parents have eaten sour grapes, and the children's teeth are set on edge.' Instead, everyone will die for their own sin" (Jer 31:29-30*a*; see Ezek 18:1-3).

■ **5-16** After having secured his reign and eliminated those responsible for the death of his father, Amaziah **found that there were three hundred thousand men fit for military service, able to handle the spear and shield** (2 Chr 25:5). This number should be treated like other similar figures throughout the history. The interesting addition in this text is the employment of mercenary troops from **Israel**, for whose services the king of Judah paid **a hundred talents of silver** (v 6). This detail comes back again when Amaziah, having been warned by the unnamed **man of God** (v 7) not to attack anyone, essentially demands a refund from Yahweh! He is reassured, however, that **the LORD can give you much more than that** (v 9). So his investment would not go for naught, even though he could not retract the pay he had already given to these mercenary soldiers.

Yet darkness lies just beyond the horizon, for the mercenaries **were furious with Judah and left for home in a great rage** (v 10). While Amaziah and the regular troops are off enjoying a great, if excessively violent, victory over **men of Seir** (v 11), the Ephraimite/Israelite mercenaries are busy raiding **towns belonging to Judah from Samaria to Beth Horon** (v 13). Things continue to devolve for Amaziah, because of what he does in celebration of his victory. First, **he brought back the gods of the people of Seir** (v 14*a*). This is not an unusual tactic; in fact, it was rather common. The Babylonians and the Philistines in particular were masters of it. Imprisoning the defeated enemy's divine cult images in the temple of one's own god was a way of adding insult to injury. But, Amaziah goes a step further. He **set them up as his own gods, bowed down to them and burned sacrifices to them** (v 14*b*). This activity is so out of character with respect to typical ANE behavior that one wonders if the Chroniclers are engaging in a bit of propaganda, making Amaziah appear much worse than he might actually have been. Even if this is the case, that Amaziah committed some kind of religious offense is probably beyond question, even if its specific nature escapes postmodern readers. A final point to note is another intertextual trace: The critique leveled against the king in v 15 recalls the taunt given by the Rabshakeh, an official of the Assyrian king Sennacherib, in 2 Kgs 18:34-35.

■ **17-28** Perhaps in response to the erstwhile Israelite mercenaries in the employ of the Judahite king, **Amaziah** (v 17) sent a challenge to the king of Israel. **Jehoash . . . king of Israel** responded very dismissively to this challenge, referring to his southern neighbor as a **thistle in Lebanon** (v 18). Whatever the nature of his religious sins might have been, Amaziah makes a catastrophic blunder. The Chroniclers ascribe this mistake to the workings of Yahweh to punish Amaziah and Judah **because they sought the gods of Edom** (v 20). The statement recalls the deceitful spirit sent by Yahweh to lure Ahab into his death (→ ch 18). **Judah was routed by Israel** (v 22), perhaps predictably. At any rate, the reader has come to expect a great defeat when the king of Judah (or Israel, as is infrequently the case in Chronicles) fails to listen to Yahweh. Thus one of the dominant motifs of the OT is demonstrated again: follow Yahweh and do what Yahweh requires and you will have success; ignore Yahweh and fail to do what Yahweh requires and you will have failure (see Jer 21:8). The Chroniclers finish their account of the life of Amaziah in their typical way, appealing to the source **the book of the kings of Judah and Israel** (2 Chr 25:26). Amaziah ends his life like his father did, at the wrong end of unnamed assassins' swords. Both the Deuteronomists and the Chroniclers are silent on their identity, or even whether they should be viewed as religious loyalists, political enemies, or both. In contrast to his father, Amaziah, he is given the proper burial fit for a king in the line of David. The old saying, "Like father, like son," is thus demonstrated clearly in the sinful lives and violent deaths of Joash and Amaziah, who did not follow Yahweh with their whole heart (against Deut 6:5).

J. The Reign of Uzziah (26:1-23)

BEHIND THE TEXT

King Uzziah had significance for more than just the Deuteronomistic and Chroniclers' Histories. That is, his time saw the launch of the career of one of Israel's greatest prophets, Isaiah of Jerusalem (the so-called First Isaiah). More specifically, Isaiah volunteered for service *in the year of the death of King Uzziah* (Isa 6:1). According to Isa 1:1, the prophet's career continued on also through the reigns of Jotham, Ahaz, and Hezekiah. Isaiah does not seem to have direct communication with Uzziah and Jotham—at least such is not mentioned explicitly in Isaiah's book or in either of the two histories. Isaiah's connections with Ahaz and Hezekiah are made more explicit, as will be seen at the appropriate time.

IN THE TEXT

■ **1-5** **Uzziah** was made **king in place of his father Amaziah** (v 1). He is called Azariah by the Deuteronomists (see 2 Kgs 15), likely reflecting a variant spelling tradition. As with his father, the Chroniclers are careful to note that **his mother's name was Jekoliah; she was from Jerusalem** (2 Chr 26:3). Though, in contrast with Amaziah, the influence of the old high priest Jehoiada is no longer to be felt here, the other point that the Davidic dynasty may still have been on unsure footing probably holds good even to this late date. Finally, in the introduction, the Chroniclers include—as they did with Joash and Amaziah before Uzziah—a significant tinge of darkness in their portrayal. It would be helpful to restate the dark twinges relating to each of these three kings. First, Joash was good as long as Jehoiada was still alive. Second, Amaziah followed after Yahweh, but not wholeheartedly. Finally, third, with regard to Uzziah, the Chroniclers write: **As long as he sought the LORD, God gave him success** (v 5). The negative side of that casts, of course, a dreary foreshadow. Once again, these cannot be mere stylistic variations. Instead, they demonstrate, as was noted earlier, the unbridled skillfulness of the Chroniclers' writing. Though in two of the three cases the wording is the same as the Deuteronomists, to suggest that the Chroniclers merely copied from their sources seems as unsatisfactory as the simplistic appeal to stylistic variations.

■ **6-15** First, the good parts about Uzziah. Uzziah enjoyed some military successes against **Philistines**, **Arabs**, and **Meunites** (vv 6-7). The Meunites have been seen before during the reign of Jehoshaphat. **Arabs** were also previously seen during Jehoshaphat's time, but in the earlier era they brought tribute to the king rather than going to war against him, as they do with Uzziah. This probably means that Jehoshaphat had already subdued them, whereas Uzziah had to do so again—assuming for the moment that the same people are being referred to (a tricky proposition indeed when dealing with a designation like "Arabs," which may refer to any number of different tribal and geographic identifiers). Verses 9-10 continue the good report of Uzziah's reign by detailing the improvements made to Jerusalem. Finally, vv 11-15 indicate the strength of Uzziah's army, which should make any king proud. The last line of v 15 again shows the Chroniclers' creativity (and this time they certainly do not quote the Deuteronomists), with darkness creeping in again: **he was greatly helped until he became powerful.**

■ **16-20** The Chroniclers do not wait long at all to pay off on the dark line they dropped at the end of v 15: **But after Uzziah became powerful, his pride led to his downfall** (v 16). The intertextual link to Prov 16:18 ("Pride goes before destruction, a haughty spirit before a fall") should not be missed. Whereas the Deuteronomists excoriate Azariah/Uzziah for not removing the high places (2 Kgs 15:4), a familiar refrain with them, the Chroniclers describe Uzziah's sin as having **entered the temple of the LORD to burn incense on the altar of incense** (2 Chr 26:16). Of course, the king was forbidden to do so, a fact that **Azariah the priest** (v 17) points out to him. It is interesting that the name of the priest is equivalent to the name given the king in the Deuteronomistic tradition. Uzziah is struck with **leprosy** because of his unwillingness to step back and let **the priests, the descendants of Aaron** (v 18) do the job for which only they are qualified by the Torah.

■ **21-23** Uzziah lived apart from everyone **until the day he died . . . in a separate house** (v 21). Thus, once again, one who had so much promise at the beginning of his life became a severe disappointment by the end of his life. Three generations of kings have wound up this way, and one wonders if the trend will continue. Furthermore, the "additional source" cited by the Chroniclers in this case is one that might be known to us: **The other events of Uzziah's reign, from beginning to end, are recorded by the prophet Isaiah son of Amoz** (v 22). This citation will occur again during Hezekiah's time (→ 2 Chr 32:32). This writing was probably not the same as the biblical book of Isaiah, since it only mentions Uzziah once (twice if one counts the superscription), and then only as a temporal reference (Isa 6:1). Therefore, this reference is to a lost document written by Isaiah, probably having something to do with court records or archives. Isaiah is well known to have been one who dealt with the centers of power in Judah, thus giving the lie to the notion that the prophets were always madmen crying in the wilderness, speaking truth to power even when power refuses to listen.

K. The Reign of Jotham (27:1-9)

IN THE TEXT

■ **1-9** On the one hand, the **sixteen years** of the reign of **Jotham** (v 1) receive very scant attention from the Chroniclers. As has been seen, when the Deuteronomists applied this technique it generally signaled a negative view of the king in question. On the other hand, in the case of Jotham the Chroniclers do not mean by their relative slighting of this king to indicate that he is not worthy of their comment—only being included for the sake of completeness. For with Jotham the somewhat disturbing trend that had exhibited itself during the previous three generations of Davidic kings (Joash, Amaziah, and Uzziah), or in other words every king since the restoration of the monarchy after Athaliah's usurpation, is finally reversed. This tendency was to start out with tremendous promise, but then fail after a certain point. Yet the Chroniclers write concerning Jotham that **he did what was right in the eyes of the LORD, just as his father Uzziah had done** (v 2). Only thus far does the comparison go, however, for **unlike him he did not enter the temple of the LORD**. Jotham did not infringe on the sanctity of the holy place, an action that caused divine judgment to break out on his father in the form of leprosy. However, to paraphrase Shakespeare, something is still rotten in the state of Judah. The Chroniclers indicate this through the phrase **The people, however, continued their corrupt practices**. On the one hand, this statement "bursts the bubble" of good feelings engendered by the arrival, at long last, of a king who is not divided in heart, as were his father, grandfather, and great-grandfather. On the other hand, it continues the downward spiral of the conditions in Judah until such point as the situation can be prepared for the arrival of Jotham's grandson Hezekiah and the third of the four great religious reforms the Chroniclers discuss in detail.

The chief accomplishment of Jotham's reign that enters into the history is his subduing of Judah's old nemesis **the Ammonites** (v 5). Jotham's success against the unnamed Ammonite king results in a three-year vassal relationship, during which the subjected Ammonites send **a hundred talents of silver, ten thousand cors of wheat and ten thousand cors of barley** once a year into the Judahite coffers. This kind of relationship is standard throughout the entire history of the ANE. Multiple attestations of this kind of thing exist, including the Black Obelisk of the Assyrian king Shalmaneser V, which depicts the Israelite king Jehu bringing such tribute to his imperial overlord. After having described this success, the Chroniclers close out the books on Jotham in the familiar way, making reference once again to **the book of the kings of Israel and Judah** (v 7). Jotham is buried with the kings and succeeded by his son Ahaz.

L. The Reign of Ahaz (28:1-27)

IN THE TEXT

■ **1-4** The good mood, and hopeful impression, created by the piety of King Jotham precipitously falls away and is quickly forgotten during the reign of his son **Ahaz** (v 1). Whereas the summary of Jotham's reign indicated that he was faithful to Yahweh as was "his father Uzziah," here the Chroniclers write, **Unlike David his father, he did not do what was right in the eyes of the LORD**. Citing David as the head of the dynasty here serves two functions. First, it brings to full circle the events put in motion generations ago by Jehoiada the priest: the Davidic monarchy is saved and finally firmly established. Second, it demonstrates conclusively the well-known practice of calling a royal a "son" or "daughter" of his or her predecessor, regardless of direct biological descent.

The main point of the section, of course, is the sinfulness of King Ahaz. Among the abominable things he is said to have done is that **he burned sacrifices in the Valley of Ben Hinnom and sacrificed his children in the fire** (v 3). Naturally not all of his children were so sacrificed, or else the line would have once again been threatened with destruction. **The Valley of Ben Hinnom**, in Hebrew, is *ge ben-ḥinnom*, which, in a slightly altered form (i.e., without *ben*), will become the name for hell as the place of eternal punishment for the wicked in the apocalyptic literature, particularly that of the intertestamental period. In the Greek of the NT, it is called Geenna, or in English Gehenna.

■ **5-8** The punishment for Ahaz's religious offenses is swift, taking the form of two military defeats, the first to **the king of Aram** (v 5*a*) and the second to **the king of Israel** (v 5*b*). With respect to Ahaz's defeat by Israel, the Chroniclers' wording highlights their tendency to use the terms "Israel" and "Judah" interchangeably. Thus v 8 reads: **The men of Israel took captive from their fellow Israelites who were from Judah two hundred thousand wives, sons and daughters**. Though it would have been simpler perhaps to say, "The men of Israel took captive Judeans . . . ," this would not fit well with the Chroniclers' usual program. Consistency of usage thus triumphs over the confusion generated in later readers.

■ **9-15** The Judahite captives taken by the Israelites become the subject of the prophecies of one **Oded** (v 9), who, like many of the prophets named by the Chroniclers, shows up on the scene only for this single, brief encounter. Oded tells the Israelites that they have gone too far. Though Yahweh had given Judah into your hand, he says, **you have slaughtered them in a rage that reaches to heaven**. This speech convinces the Israelites—who, despite the impression given through an examination of what the Deuteronomists have to say about them, are generally speaking not completely wicked—and they **gave up the prisoners and plunder in the presence of the officials and all the assembly** (v 14). They **took them back to their fellow Israelites at Jericho, the City of Palms** (v 15), indicating again that the Chroniclers believed there to still be a close connection between Israel and Judah.

■ **16-21** Ahaz, meanwhile, continues to act wickedly, even as his enemies and fellow Israelites make a turn for the better. He seeks help from **the kings of Assyria** (v 16). The plural is odd here, and at least one item in the manuscript tradition tries to correct it to singular. In any event, appeal to what at that time was the big, wicked superpower in the ANE was tantamount to political disaster for Ahaz. His son Hezekiah will pay the price for this poor decision later on, but for now **Tiglath-Pileser king of Assyria came to him, but he gave him trouble instead of help** (v 20). The king referred to is Tiglath-Pileser III (744-727 B.C.), also called Pul, his Babylonian throne name, in 2 Kgs 15:19.

■ **22-27** The last episode of Ahaz's life represents a kind of theological "grasping at straws." **He offered sacrifices to the gods of Damascus** (2 Chr 28:23), trying to cast his lot with the winning side. This was indeed one of the options that could be taken in his henotheistic context, where the gods of victorious nations were thought to have conquered the gods of defeated nations. Ahaz grows more and more desperate, and less and less successful, up to the point of his death. Unlike the previous four kings who, in spite of their failures, were given proper burial, **Ahaz . . . was buried in the city of Jerusalem, but he was not placed in the tombs of the kings of Israel** (v 27). This is just one step removed from the ultimate indignity suffered by King Jehoiakim later, whose body was left out to rot in the elements and be consumed by wild beasts (see Jer 36:30). After such a dark time—especially coming as it did after an excessively bright time—the reader is left hoping, perhaps begging, for the story to turn right again. The Chroniclers promise such a happy turn with the note that **Hezekiah his son succeeded him as king** (2 Chr 28:27). Even though Ahaz was altogether wicked, Yahweh had not yet made a full end of his people (see Jer 5:18 and many other references in the book).

M. The Reign of Hezekiah (29:1—32:33)

▶ Overview

Hezekiah is the third of four Judean kings after the division who receive extended treatment from the Chroniclers. The principal distinguishing mark for all of them, as noted, is that all of them—Asa, Jehoshaphat, Hezekiah, and Josiah—reform the religion of Judah during their reigns. In the Deuteronomistic History, Asa (1 Kgs 15:14) and Jehoshaphat (1 Kgs 22:43) are criticized for not removing some unauthorized shrines. By contrast, Hezekiah and Josiah are the only two kings who are judged in unqualifiedly positive terms. The Chroniclers also criticize Asa and Jehoshaphat, but only the latter specifically for the issue of failing to remove the high places. As stated in the introduction, these differences between the Deuteronomists and the Chroniclers are interesting to note, so long as the implication is not drawn from them that one or the other was deceptive or unnecessarily altered the history. Both groups of historians told the story the way they did in order to support certain interests, and therefore to accuse either of deliberate falsification misses the point entirely.

29:1-36

Like that of Jehoshaphat, the account of Hezekiah's reign is given in five sections. In addition, like the reign of Josiah around a century later, one of the principal events of Hezekiah's reign is a grand Passover celebration. This indicates the importance of the Passover as a covenant-renewal ritual in the theology of the Chroniclers. Hezekiah will also be demonstrably under Yahweh's favor, since a miraculous deliverance from the power of an invading army will be accomplished while he is on the throne.

1. Hezekiah's Reform (29:1-36)

BEHIND THE TEXT

Hezekiah's religious reform is the third of the four great reformations described by the Chroniclers. In addition, along with Josiah he is the only one who is described in completely positive terms. Although they both will make some errors in judgment along the way—and in Josiah's case his error will cost him his life (→ 2 Chr 35:22-34)—neither one has specifically religious errors laid to his account. Nevertheless, even the nearly perfect righteousness of Kings Hezekiah and Josiah is not enough to stave off the ultimate punishment of Judah that Yahweh is threatening. In other words, though the sun is still shining, the darkened clouds are beginning to thicken on the horizon of the narrative, and soon enough they will choke the light out completely—if only for a season.

IN THE TEXT

■ 1-11 The note that Hezekiah **did what was right in the eyes of the LORD, just as his father David had done** (v 2) recalls the summary of the reign his father, Ahaz, to whom a negative form of this formula was applied in 2 Chr 28:1. Indeed, the contrast between father and son seems to be a central point of the passage. This is demonstrated in that the first thing Hezekiah does is the reverse of one of the last actions of Ahaz. Hezekiah **opened the doors of the temple of the LORD and repaired them** (v 3). This was done **in the first month of the first year of his reign**, and reversing the action taken by Ahaz in 28:24. Hezekiah thus did not take long at all to turn around the wickedness of his father into positive action. In 29:4-11 he gives a rousing speech to **the priests and the Levites**, telling them what **our parents** (v 6) did and what he himself intends to do to change it. (Incidentally, the gender inclusive language in the NIV of v 6 seems unnecessary, since the things that Hezekiah intended to reverse were things done directly by, or at least at the orders of, his father. In other words, regardless of the involvement of his mother, it was his father who set these things in motion. Verse 9 may be a reflection of the Chroniclers' own time period in the mouth of Hezekiah, as it makes reference to the exile. In any event, there is a definite connection between Hezekiah's time and the Chroniclers' time. In both, the condemnation of Yahweh has come upon the people; thus, in both, there is the opportunity to make things better and turn away Yahweh's wrath.

■ **12-24** Having thus charged the Levites with their work, King Hezekiah steps back and allows them to do it. This section describes the work accomplished in several steps. Verses 12-14 give the names of the Levites so employed. Following this, vv 15-17 describe the work they did. The Levites report back to Hezekiah in vv 18-19 what they have done, emphasizing throughout that their work is intended to reverse the things King Ahaz has done, thus continuing the developing theme of the passage. Finally, the temple is rededicated beginning with v 20. Unlike Uzziah, who entered into the temple grounds to himself offer a sacrifice, Hezekiah maintains the established limits. True enough, **the king had ordered the burnt offering and the sin offering for all Israel** (v 24), but he did not do it himself, thus avoiding calling condemnation down on himself. At least in this respect, then, Hezekiah not only reversed what his father had done but also learned from the mistakes of the past.

■ **25-36** The final section of the chapter details the "opening ceremonies" for the restored temple. The note that the **cymbals, harps and lyres** were established in accordance with the instructions of **David** (v 25) recalls the statement in the beginning of the chapter that Hezekiah always followed the example of "David his father" in doing what was right in the eyes of Yahweh. Near the end of the section, the Chroniclers note that **the Levites had been more conscientious in consecrating themselves than the priests had been** (v 34). Radak indicates that the Levites helping the priests do their work was in response to an "emergency" situation (Kimchi 2008, 260). Normally, of course, only priests would be allowed to participate in altar work of this kind. Indeed, the whole situation was a response to the emergency situation that had been brought about by the sin of King Ahaz. Nevertheless, the king and all the people had occasion to rejoice at the completion of the work of restoration, **because it was done so quickly** (v 36).

2. Passover Celebration (30:1—31:1)

BEHIND THE TEXT

The distinguishing feature of the religious reforms conducted by Kings Hezekiah and Josiah, when compared to those conducted by Kings Asa and Jehoshaphat, is the emphasis on celebrating the Passover. The reason or reasons why the Chroniclers thought it necessary to emphasize the restoration of the Passover festival in their recounting of these two reforms and not the others is a matter shrouded in mystery. Perhaps it is ultimately of little importance why they did this. What is, instead, more important is that they did do so. Stated more plainly, the final form of the book of Chronicles includes references to the Passover at these points and not at the others. The text, and not any reconstruction of the intent of the author—an uncertain business anyway—is the primary datum with which the interpreter has to work.

IN THE TEXT

■ **1-12** The chapter can be divided into two sections. This first section details how **Hezekiah sent word to all Israel and Judah and also wrote letters to Ephraim and Manasseh, inviting them to come to the temple of the LORD in Jerusalem and celebrate the Passover to the LORD, the God of Israel** (v 1). It is unclear why **Ephraim and Manasseh**, two of the northern tribes, are singled out for special mention. The historical problem here concerns precisely when this summons was sent out. The Deuteronomists report that Samaria, the capital of northern Israel since the days of King Omri, fell in "Hezekiah's sixth year, which was the ninth year of Hoshea king of Israel" (2 Kgs 18:10). Eight years after Samaria's fall, in the fourteenth year of Hezekiah, Judah experienced a mighty deliverance from Assyria, which had destroyed Samaria (→ ch 32).

So, then, either the Passover celebration described in this chapter took place before the fall of Israel, or a significant portion of the population remained behind in the northern kingdom. The latter idea is suggested by the content of Hezekiah's letter, specifically 30:6: **People of Israel, return to the LORD, the God of Abraham, Isaac and Israel, that he may return to you who are left, who have escaped from the hand of the kings of Assyria**. Moreover, this idea seems to be corroborated by certain bits of external evidence. The destruction of Israel gave rise, of course, to the "mystery of the ten lost tribes of Israel." On this "mystery," Eric H. Cline notes the external evidence in favor of a relatively insignificant exile. He writes: "So although perhaps 20 percent of the inhabitants were carried off into exile, the vast majority of the so-called Ten Lost Tribes went either nowhere or south to Judah. In brief, the Ten Lost Tribes were never lost; we know exactly where they went" (2007, 172). Perhaps some of those who went from Israel to Judah answered the call of Hezekiah's letter; but this speculation can never be more than that.

A further word can be said about Hezekiah's letter. He calls Yahweh **the God of Abraham, Isaac and Israel**, using the name to which Jacob's name was changed after his "wrestling match" with "a man" in Gen 32:22-32. The interpreter may recall the suggestion earlier, regarding the division of the kingdoms and Jeroboam's establishment of alternate worship sites. Jeroboam may well have intended these places to be places where Yahweh could be worshiped, so that the citizens of the new kingdom of Israel should not have to go to Judah and give their offerings and, ultimately, allegiance, back to the temple in Jerusalem. In other words, that the Israelites should have to **return to the LORD** is a matter of perspective; perhaps, from their perspective, they had never left. One is always on shaky ground when, in the context of religious disputes like this, saying this or that group has left the proper path. By contrast, the one making such a judgment may well be the one that has left! That, in this case, matters of perspective are important finds a kind of confirmation in the response that Hezekiah's messengers receive: **The couriers went from town to town in Ephraim and Manasseh, as far as Zebulun, but people scorned and ridiculed them** (v 10). On the surface of the text, the reader is certainly "supposed to" have scorn for those who had scorn for the "true" messengers, especially in light of the fact that **some from Asher, Manasseh and Zebulun humbled themselves and went to Jerusalem** (v 11). It should be admitted in this connection that the historical endurance of the southern perspective does speak rather persuasively for the correctness of the official position. Nevertheless, it should also be recognized that, at the time in question, the people responding to the message either scornfully or humbly were, in every case, acting on the basis of limited information. Those who are on the "other end" of things, which is to say, modern and postmodern readers, should perhaps not be so quick to criticize people who made what eventually turned out to be the "wrong" decision.

■ **13-27** If the first part of the chapter discussed the summons to Jerusalem to celebrate the Passover, then the second part, which runs to the end of the chapter, describes the event to which they were summoned. The festival begins with a clearing away of **altars** that were likely dedicated to some foreign gods, though this is not made explicit. That the people **threw them into the Kidron Valley** (v 14) gives a strong hint in this direction, for the altars were not given the respect due to articles associated with deities. One would expect such behavior in the setting of "revolutionary monotheism," and a helpful analogy may be drawn between the behavior described here and the iconoclasm of the Protestant Reformation in Europe, smashing religious images and other artifacts popularly associated with the Roman Catholic faith that had been, in the minds of some, superseded.

30:1-27

The **Passover Lamb** was slaughtered **on the fourteenth day of the second month** (v 15), which was in accordance with the instructions of the Torah (Lev 23:5). The first and seventh days of the festival were to be nonworking holidays. The statement at the end of 2 Chr 30:15 is interesting: **The priests and the Levites were ashamed and consecrated themselves**. As in the previous situation during Uzziah's time, according to Radak, "not enough priests had sanctified themselves for there to be enough (*day*) of them to bring the offerings" (Kimchi 2008, 262). Once this situation is corrected, however, the sacrifices continue. The priests and Levites, having consecrated themselves, **had to kill the Passover lambs for all those who were not ceremonially clean and could not consecrate** their lambs to the LORD (v 17). This unfortunate situation included **most of the many people** who had come from the now-destroyed northern kingdom to join in the Passover celebration. They did so, however, **contrary to what was written** (v 18*a*). Just as the priests and Levites made up for the people's deficiency, however, so also did Hezekiah, praying, **May the LORD, who is good, pardon everyone who sets their heart on seeking God—the LORD, the God of their ancestors—even if they are not clean according to the rules of the sanctuary** (vv 18*b*-19). This is an important statement, for it seems to free those responsible for leadership in religious matters from the need to bar from "the table" those who might not be "ready" to receive the grace of God. Perhaps it is best to leave such things up to God, as Hezekiah did!

Rather than settling for only one week of festivities as required by the Torah, Hezekiah and all the people opt for a double festival, **so for another seven days they celebrated joyfully** (v 23). The celebration is like nothing that had been seen in Jerusalem **since the days of Solomon son of David king of Israel** (v 26). The impression left by this statement is that the temple is being rededicated, at least after a fashion. In the context of the Chroniclers' primary audience, this may well have been the case, since the document most likely was completed somewhere around the time of the completion of the second temple, which had the potential to be even more magnificent than the first (see Hag 2:9).

■ **31:1** Finally, after the end of the super-size Passover, the Judahites, along with the Israelite refugees, **went out to the towns of Judah, smashed the sacred stones and cut down the Asherah poles** (v 1). The people were so energized in their faith in Yahweh that they could not help but to continue the reformation that their king had set in motion. For his part, Hezekiah had to have been pleased for, in a manner of speaking, his investment of piety had begun to pay dividends even greater than the original investment he had made in calling all of the people back to renew the central festival of the Passover.

FROM THE TEXT

The Christian equivalent of the Passover meal is, of course, the Eucharist. Some Christian groups take great concern to make sure those who receive the meal are properly prepared, usually through knowledge or through adherence to a particular version of Christianity. The determination of such preparation often depends on certain theological views of church membership, particularly whether one's denomination practices an "open" or "closed" table. Many Wesleyan denominations, at least on the official level, allow all Christians to receive, regardless of their denominational affiliation. Theologically, this is in large measure based on the Wesleyan theology of universal atonement. A difficulty arises when a pastor or other person responsible for administering the Eucharist does not know whether particular persons are Christians. Hezekiah's example in this text may provide relief for those concerned with this issue. While observing proper safeguards for the sanctity of the ritual, pastors and leaders need only to trust that God will allow those to come whom he determines are properly prepared. The determination is thus left up to God, not to the human leaders.

3. Restoring Temple Personnel (31:2-21)

IN THE TEXT

■ **2-21** After the grand reinstitution of the Passover and something of an iconoclastic revolution—the former of which, as noted, is unique at this point in the Chroniclers' presentation of Judah's kings, with the second being familiar—**Hezekiah** (v 2) turns to the matter of organizing collections for the worship and upkeep of the temple. It is important to note that religious purification took place before financial considerations. Money, as the saying goes, follows ministry, and never the other way around.

The contributions come from several sources. First, **The king contributed from his own possessions** (v 3), indicating that even the state establishment, in ancient Israel, was subservient to the religious establishment. Second, **He ordered the people living in Jerusalem to give the portion due the priests and Levites so they could devote themselves to the Law of the LORD** (v 4). This statement seems to indicate some sort of tax system on the Jerusalemites, not unlike the taxes levied on residents of certain European countries for the upkeep of largely empty Christian churches. The Israelites, apparently, do not resent this levy as much as non-Christian Europeans, for they **generously gave the firstfruits of their grain, new wine, olive oil and honey and all that the fields produced** (v 5). In fact, the people were so faithful in their giving that those who were responsible for collecting the offerings **piled them in heaps** (v 6).

Hezekiah asked the priests and Levites about the heaps (v 9), and he was told that an overabundance had come into the temple treasury. **Hezekiah gave orders to prepare storerooms in the temple of the LORD, and this was done** (v 11). An intertextual trace takes the reader to the story of the "rich fool" in Luke 12:16-21. The line at the end of the parable about those being imperiled who are not rich in the things of God satisfies one's wonder at the surplus gained by the temple establishment during the time of Hezekiah. Certainly wealth carries a temptation toward sinful excess, and it would perhaps not cause quite so much consternation if the temple had what it needed to function and not an excess. This is so because religious institutions—regardless of the particular religion of which they are a part—should never grow wealthy, for that is a sure sign of having stepped away from the things of God. The temple establishment seems to be the only group, in this text, to be in danger of falling into the temptations associated with wealth, for Hezekiah and the people had been contributing to the work of the temple rather than hoarding the wealth with which they had been blessed. Hezekiah, moreover, continually **prospered** because, **In everything that he undertook in the service of God's temple and in obedience to the law and the commands, he sought his God and worked wholeheartedly** (v 21). For Hezekiah, his prosperity was an occasion for greater service, rather than amassing his wealth into bigger and better barns. Such is, or should be, the lesson for all those who would tout material blessing and monetary prosperity as the mark of one's faithfulness before God. In other words, it is quite a far departure from the truth to say that God desires to make faithful people wealthy. This is so because it is more often wealthy people who have great difficulty being faithful.

4. Deliverance from Assyria (32:1-31)

IN THE TEXT

■ **1-8** The fourteenth year of Hezekiah's reign (see 2 Kgs 18:13) was an eventful one. The crisis that came up in this year—701 B.C. according to modern calendars—is perhaps surprising in terms of the dominant Hebrew theology of blessings and curses. In other words, someone as faithful as Hezekiah should normally have expected a stream of uninterrupted blessing from Yahweh. However, the Chroniclers set up the story by confounding the king's (and the readers') expectations. Instead of Judah and its king enjoying the blessing "due" to someone so "faithful," the Chroniclers report, **After all that Hezekiah had so faithfully done, Sennacherib king of Assyria came and invaded Judah** (2 Chr 32:1). Usually, invasions by foreign leaders happen because the Judean king has been *un*faithful, and Yahweh has appointed the foreigners—be they Edomites, Egyptians, Arameans, or whoever—to punish Israel and/or Judah for their unfaithfulness. Though this theological claim is somewhat shocking, suggesting that God would allow or even direct punishment and death, at the same time it is a powerful statement against the rhetoric and self-aggrandizement of imperial authority. This aspect will be brought out more fully in the remainder of this passage. A contrasting expectation—on the part of the readers if not on the part of the king—therefore, is that Yahweh will effect a miraculous deliverance from the otherwise undeserved threat.

The Deuteronomists use the story of the Assyrian threat as an occasion to bring down Hezekiah a notch or two. That is, in the 2 Kgs 18 version of this story, Hezekiah, instead of relying on Yahweh as he should have done, instead offers to buy the Assyrians off as a matter of first resort (2 Kgs 18:14). By contrast, the Chroniclers suggest a vastly different immediate response to the threat posed by the Assyrians, Hezekiah **consulted with his officials and military staff about blocking off the water from the springs outside the city** (2 Chr 32:3). This action, touted in 2 Kgs 20:20 and later on in this chapter (2 Chr 32:30), is one of the signature accomplishments of Hezekiah's reign and was happily confirmed by the discovery of the Siloam Tunnel by archaeologists in the late nineteenth century (Finkelstein and Silberman 2001, 256).

The Siloam Tunnel Inscription

The tunnel commissioned by Hezekiah, which was intended not only to prevent the Assyrians from getting fresh water as indicated in this passage (2 Chr 32:4), but also to attempt to make the city of Jerusalem siege-resistant if not siege-proof, providing fresh water to the city from the nearby Gihon spring. The tunnel was securely dated by an eighth-century Hebrew inscription on the wall, detailing the final steps of the tunnel's construction. The portion of the inscription that remains legible reads as follows:

When the tunnel was driven through. And this was the way in which it was cut through. While [. . .] were still [. . .] axe[s], each man toward his fellow, and while there were still three cubits to be cut through, [there was heard] the voice of a man calling to his fellow, for there was an overlap in the rock on the right [and on the left]. And when the tunnel was driven through, the quarrymen hewed [the rock], each man toward his fellow, axe against axe; and the water flowed from the spring toward the reservoir for 1,200 cubits, and the height of the rock above the head[s] of the quarrymen was 100 cubits. (Quoted in Finkelstein and Silberman 2001, 256-57)

Finkelstein and Silberman can barely contain their excitement when they write: "How they managed to meet despite the fact that the tunnel is curved is a matter of debate. It was probably a combination of technical skills and intimate knowledge of the geology of the hill" (257).

Along with the various fortifications of the city Hezekiah had done, he also sought to encourage the people. Having organized them under the direction of **military officers**, he gives them what by now is a familiar, if not legendary/traditional speech for Israelite and Judean military operations: **Be strong and courageous. Do not be afraid or discouraged because of the king of Assyria and the vast army with him, for there is a greater power with us than with him** (v 7). The first part of the phrase is the legendary speech going back at least as far to Yahweh's calling of Joshua son of Nun (Josh 1:9), with only a slight difference in vocabulary (the words translated **afraid** here and in Joshua are synonymous but not identical).

■ **9-19** Sennacherib has some traditional and legendary words of his own, sending by the hand of an aide a theologically laced taunt meant precisely to tear down the resolve of the people on the wall. A monument discovered by archaeologists in Assyrian territory depicts the siege of **Lachish**, from which the letter described here was sent. The speech is reminiscent of a harangue in modern politics, in which a speaker deliberately misrepresents the statements and/or actions of an opponent for maximum rhetorical effect. The resulting statements are not necessarily "untrue." However, by selective rearrangement of the facts one can generate within the hearers a vastly different impression.

Sennacherib's political/theological speech takes three avenues of attack. First, he sarcastically asks why Yahweh would save Judah when Hezekiah removed **this god's high places and altars, saying to Judah and Jerusalem, "You must worship before one altar and burn sacrifices on it"** (v 12). Later on, during the reign of King Manasseh (→ 33:17), the Chroniclers will maintain that the high places remained in existence, but that the people sacrificed only to Yahweh there and no other gods. In the same speech, Sennacherib ratchets up the rhetoric, asking the people again, **Were the gods of those nations ever able to deliver them from my hand? Who of all the gods of these nations that my predecessors destroyed has been able to save his people from me?** (32:13b-14). Implicit in this statement is Sennacherib's having granted the argument that Yahweh commanded the tearing down of the shrines alluded to in v 12. The Assyrian ruler recognizes—in the tradition and common theological formulations of the day—that a god/goddess who commanded something would not then punish the people for carrying out his or her commands (→ 1 Chr 21:1 for 1 Chr 21's "updating" of 2 Sam 24).

The third part of Sennacherib's speech takes on a more personal tone. That is, the envoy sent from Lachish and other **officers** (v 16) departed from the script their leader had sent with them when **they called out in Hebrew to the people of Jerusalem who were on the wall, to terrify them and make them afraid in order to capture the city** (v 18). The word translated **Hebrew** is *yehudit*, literally ***Judean***. The word "Hebrew" is never used, in the Hebrew Bible, to denote the language spoken in Israel and Judah within the OT. It is, however, used as an ethnic designation when others refer to Abraham (Gen 14:13); Joseph (Gen 39:14 and several others); to the nation as a whole (mostly in Exodus, with scattered references in 1 Samuel and Jeremiah). Jonah also uses the term to refer to himself (Jonah 1:9). In the Deuteronomistic version of this story, envoys from Hezekiah come out and beg the Assyrian official—who is there given the title "Rabshakeh," an obscure term—to speak to them in Aramaic, the official language of diplomacy, rather than in the "Judean" the people understand (1 Kgs 19:26; Isa 36:11). The Chroniclers thus tell a truncated version of the story, but the effect is to heighten rather than ease the tension.

■ **20-23** **King Hezekiah and the prophet Isaiah son of Amoz cried out in prayer to heaven about this** (v 20). This note serves a double function. First, it shows something of the OT's understanding of the power of prayer. Particularly, OT prayer is often a matter of corporate pleading for deliverance rather than individual pleading. This is so even though many examples of individual prayers are exhibited in the OT. Second, it gives the lie to the notion that the OT prophets (the true ones, at any rate) were always on the outside of power structures. Here, Isaiah is a direct counselor and, as the duplication of this story in 2 Kgs 18—19 and Isa 36—37 attests, something of a close, personal adviser to King Hezekiah. Yahweh sends a miraculous intervention to save his people from the threat. This is the second time that Isaiah son of Amoz was involved in an Assyrian crisis—the other is reported in Isa 7, involving King Ahaz, and includes a famous prediction of a miraculous birth so familiar to Christians because of Matthew the Evangelist's application/interpretation of it to refer to Jesus.

■ **24-31** As has been noted, the Deuteronomists take note of Hezekiah's seeming unwillingness to make appropriate prayers to Yahweh, saving such for the last resort. In fact, 2 Kgs 20:12-15 reports that after Hezekiah **became ill** (2 Chr 32:24*a*) with an unspecified malady, he showed off the palace and the temple to the Babylonians. This action calls Hezekiah in for the scorn of the prophet Isaiah, for "the time will surely come when everything in your palace . . . will be carried off to Babylon" (2 Kgs 20:17). This is in fact what happens, though not during Hezekiah's time. In their version of the episode, the Chroniclers report merely that **he prayed to the LORD, who answered him and gave him a miraculous sign** (2 Chr 32:24*b*). They do not elaborate further on this. The different treatment Hezekiah receives in the two histories is probably due to the slightly better opinion the Chroniclers have of him than the Deuteronomists. The Deuteronomists' great hero was Josiah, and they had, as a result, to emphasize poor decisions on the part of the other kings, even those who otherwise could do no wrong—David and Hezekiah. The Chroniclers, however, were not so biased toward Josiah and therefore were not obligated to make sure they took Hezekiah and David down a notch. Thus they ignored in David's life "the matter of Uriah the Hittite" (1 Kgs 15:5, KJV) and the infelicitous action of Hezekiah in showing off his wealth to those who would ultimately take it from them. The ultimate difference, finally, between the Assyrians and the Babylonians is the fact that, while the Assyrian Sennacherib claimed, essentially, that Yahweh had ordered him to sack Jerusalem, in the case of the Babylonian Nebuchadnezzar, Yahweh had in fact commanded him to do so. In other words, Judah would be delivered from Assyria during the time of Hezekiah, but they would be delivered to Babylonia during the time of Jehoiachin and Zedekiah.

5. The Death of Hezekiah (32:32-33)

IN THE TEXT

▪ **32-33** With these verses the Chroniclers bring the story of the good king Hezekiah to a close. As with the death reports of some of the other kings, the variations on the familiar pattern are interesting with regard to Hezekiah. While the pattern of citing additional information that readers may consult—unfortunately lost to modern readers—is well established, once again here the document cited is otherwise unknown. As with the death notice of King Uzziah (26:23), the Chroniclers cite **the vision of the prophet Isaiah son of Amoz** (32:32). Isaiah 1:1, incidentally, uses these same words. With Uzziah, the note was only that the events had been written down by Isaiah. In addition, the inclusion of Isaiah's work in the royal archives (**in the book of the kings of Judah and Israel**) has been seen before with reference to King Jehoshaphat (20:34). Of all the writing prophets, Isaiah is the one most often linked with so-called state prophets, or counselors to the king (→ 2 Chr 18:18-22 for a story of Yahweh sending a deceitful spirit into such court prophets). By way of comparison, Jeremiah had many conversations with the kings (Jehoiakim and Zedekiah in particular), but he was certainly not an adviser at court in the same way Isaiah was. The Chroniclers finish the story by stating that Hezekiah was buried with the rest of the kings, using another phrase with interesting variation on the pattern: Hezekiah **was buried on the hill where the tombs of David's descendants are** (32:33). This is a variation on the idea of kings being buried together, and again shows the literary genius of the Chroniclers. The Deuteronomists, by contrast, are not nearly so inventive in 2 Kgs 20:21, saying only that "Hezekiah rested with his ancestors," a traditional phrase in its own right.

FROM THE TEXT

Hezekiah's life represents one of the few high points in the final years of Judah's independent existence. His religious reform moved the nation in significant ways. However, his own pride and arrogance spelled an unfortunate end for him. Leaders often live ambiguous lives, and particularly those who have great success face the temptation to become prideful. Many once-great leaders end their careers or their lives in disgrace. This fate can be avoided, but only with great care to remain faithful to what God has required.

N. The Reign of Manasseh (33:1-20)

BEHIND THE TEXT

King Manasseh is an enigmatic figure in the history of Judah. On the one hand, his experience seems to give the lie to the dominant theology—expressed by the so-called Deuteronomistic school. This theology suggests that one is rewarded for righteous behavior before Yahweh (particularly by a long life and peaceful death) and one is punished for wicked behavior before Yahweh (particularly by a short life and violent or otherwise uneasy death). Elsewhere in the Writings section of the OT, the book of Job masterfully calls such a simplistic view of the world into question. Yet Manasseh's story does so as well, because his reign lasting fifty-five years is the longest of all the reigns of the kings of Judah, besting Uzziah/Azariah by three years (→ 2 Chr 26).

On the other hand, King Manasseh is the only king in Judah's history to start out poorly (in terms of religious orthodoxy) then finish strongly. In other words, the Chroniclers perhaps recognized that his lengthy reign should not have been if he were in fact as wicked as the sources (mainly 2 Kings) claimed. So they included something that the Deuteronomists left out, namely a story of Manasseh's repentance and restoration into God's favor. This experience, so the Chroniclers maintain, is what explains Manasseh's lengthy rule.

One further issue needs clarification before the discussion of the Chroniclers' account of Manasseh. Other kings' dalliances with other gods have been considered (for example, Amaziah and the gods of the Edomites, 2 Chr 25:14-15). Manasseh delves into the worship of other gods at the beginning of his reign, which sets up the Deuteronomists' judgment on him as irredeemably evil. Historically, the ANE had been filled with polytheistic societies, which believed in many gods, the principal among which often being considered the patron god (or goddess) of a particular city or nation. Israel's theology was in marked contrast to this. In a 2007 essay, Jan Assmann helpfully described the key difference between polytheism and a particular form of monotheism he termed "revolutionary," as opposed to "evolutionary." Assmann writes:

> Revolutionary monotheism is based on the distinction between true and false, between one true god and the rest of forbidden, false, or nonexistent gods. The introduction of this distinction into the realm of religion constitutes a radical break. (2007, 28)

Because the dominant Israelite theology was in fact monotheistic, various "returns" to polytheism had, therefore, to be treated as gross aberrations from the norm, whereas in the history of religion it was actually the other way around.

IN THE TEXT

■ **1-9** Manasseh's story can be told in two parts. Manasseh's life was lived in contrast to the lives of Joash, Amaziah, and Uzziah. These three kings started off faithful, but then soon veered into unfaithfulness. By contrast, from the beginning of his reign Manasseh **did evil in the sight of the LORD, following the detestable practices of the nations the LORD had driven out before the Israelites** (v 2). In the Torah, Moses warned the people not to emulate such practices, among which are specifically listed child sacrifice, divination, sorcery, the interpretation of omens, and witchcraft (Deut 18:9-10). The Chroniclers report Manasseh as guilty of all these things and more, including that the king **consulted mediums and spiritists.** The conclusion is telling: **He did much evil in the eyes of the LORD** (v 6).

Continuing the critique of Manasseh's practices, the Chroniclers do not specify what **image he had made** (v 7). In other words, this is the first reference in the chapter to Manasseh having made any sort of image, which then might be, in a double affront, installed in the Jerusalem temple. The Deuteronomists report in 2 Kgs 21:7 (the equivalent of 2 Chr 33:7) more specifically reports that this was a "carved Asherah pole," much like the ones King Asa is said to have destroyed long ago (see 2 Chr 14:3). In any event, the image is set up in the very place of which Yahweh had warned David and Solomon that it should be kept pure of all the practices of the other nations. **But Manasseh led Judah and the people of Jerusalem astray, so that they did more evil than the nations the LORD had destroyed before the Israelites** (33:9). Thus not only did the wicked king emulate the practices of the former inhabitants of the promised land, but in fact he did worse than they did. In such a situation, coming from the standpoint of the dominant theology, one can only expect great suffering to be inflicted upon Judah for the sins of its king and people.

■ **10-20** The expectation just described is not to be disappointed. Once again, the Chroniclers employ the familiar motif of an external enemy being used to punish Yahweh's people. The enemy thus appointed in this instance is **the army commanders of the king of Assyria** (v 11). The Assyrians **took Manasseh prisoner, put a hook in his nose** and, as can be seen on some iconography from the Assyrian Empire, likely attached the other end of the chain to the buttocks of the prisoner in front of the humiliated Judean king.

Then, something remarkable happens. In the Deuteronomistic version of the history, there is no mention of Manasseh's repentance and personal transformation. However, the Chroniclers do not leave King Manasseh in his defeated position, but instead note that the dreadful experience was enough to turn Manasseh from his wicked ways. After all, throughout the OT Yahweh is never depicted as a deity who takes delight in punishing his people or in allowing them to be punished (see Lam 3:33). The purpose of punishment is never destruction, but always reformation (see Modine 2009a). The Chroniclers demonstrate that this is so in their report that **the LORD was moved by his entreaty and listened to his plea; so he brought him back to Jerusalem and to his kingdom. Then Manasseh knew that the LORD is God** (v 13). Upon returning to Jerusalem, Manasseh reverses all his previous efforts, for the true measure of "intellectual" repentance is "actualized" repentance, or repentance with reparations. In other words, orthodoxy (right belief) is nothing without orthopraxy (right action); between the two of them, the latter is far more important than the former. After all of his practices aimed at purging the temple of the things he in his former state had introduced, the Chroniclers admit that things are not quite completely as they ought to be: **The people, however, continued to sacrifice at the high places, but only to the LORD their God** (v 17). Negatively, such a statement may be plaintive wishing on the part of the Chroniclers. Positively, however, it *does* reflect historical reality: the Jerusalem temple was really the only accredited place for the worship of Yahweh from the time of the great religious reformation of Manasseh's grandson, Josiah. Even then, it was only in operation as the exclusive proper place for about forty years before its destruction by the Babylonians. Then, after the exile was completed and the temple rebuilt, it never again enjoyed that exclusive status, as Jews were by that time scattered throughout the world, at the beginnings of the so-called Diaspora.

Finally, the end of Manasseh's story is given in the familiar way, but with a twist. The citation of **the annals of the kings of Israel** (v 18) is familiar enough. However, an additional feature of this instance of the formula stands out. Two of the events just described in the lengthy part of the story are mentioned again, namely that Manasseh prayed to Yahweh in his distress and that God moved in his favor because of that prayer. The Chroniclers suggest that an expanded version of the story, including such information as the content of **his prayer to his God and the words the seers spoke to him** (v 18) may be found in the sources.

The Prayer of Manasseh

An apocryphal document called the Prayer of Manasseh was included with the Latin Vulgate and in some editions of the Septuagint, but it is not considered a genuine part of the text of Chronicles by either Jews or Western Christians. Some Eastern Orthodox communities do accept it, however. In the King James Bible, it is printed among the apocryphal writings. The text of the prayer runs as follows:

O Lord Almighty, God of our fathers, of Abraham and Isaac and Jacob and of their righteous posterity: thou who hast made heaven and earth with all their order; who hast shackled the sea by thy word of command, who hast confined the deep and sealed it with thy terrible and glorious name; at whom all things shudder, and tremble before thy power, for thy glorious splendor cannot be borne, and the wrath of thy threat to sinners is irresistible; yet immeasurable and unsearchable is thy promised mercy, for thou art the Lord Most High, of great compassion, long-suffering, and very merciful, and repentest over the evils of men. Thou, O Lord, according to thy great goodness hast promised repentance and forgiveness to those who have sinned against thee; and in the multitude of thy mercies thou hast appointed repentance for sinners, that they may be saved. Therefore thou, O Lord, God of the righteous, hast not appointed repentance for the righteous, for Abraham and Isaac and Jacob, who did not sin against thee, but thou hast appointed repentance for me, who am a sinner. For the sins I have committed are more in number than the sand of the sea; my transgressions are multiplied, O Lord, they are multiplied! I am unworthy to look up and see the height of heaven because of the multitude of my iniquities. I am weighted down with many an iron fetter, so that I am rejected because of my sins, and I have no relief; for I have provoked thy wrath and have done what is evil in thy sight, setting up abominations and multiplying offenses. And now I bend the knee of my heart, beseeching thee for thy kindness. I have sinned, O Lord, I have sinned, and I know my transgressions. I earnestly beseech thee, forgive me, O Lord, forgive me! Do not destroy me with my transgressions! Do not be angry with me for ever or lay up evil for me; do not condemn me to the depths of the earth. For thou, O Lord, art the God of those who repent, and in me thou wilt manifest thy goodness; for, unworthy as I am, thou wilt save me in thy great mercy, and I will praise thee continually all the days of my life. For all the host of heaven sings thy praise, and thine is the glory for ever. Amen. (RSV 1957, 189)

FROM THE TEXT

Even if the Prayer of Manasseh is not authentic—as it seems not to be, using language and thought forms more characteristic of Hellenistic Judaism than of First Temple Judaism—nevertheless the thought lying behind it, as well as the lessons taught by the life of King Manasseh, are undeniably genuine and powerful. A cardinal tenet of Wesleyan theology is that the grace of the atonement is available for all, regardless of how wicked their acts had been prior to awakening to the gospel of Jesus Christ. Indeed, says Wesley, no one is able to do anything worthy of good consideration prior to the Holy Spirit working in his or her life, but this does not change the fact that there are varying degrees of sinfulness in which people engage before coming to faith. King Manasseh is an example of one of the most wicked people imaginable nevertheless coming to faith and being restored to a right relation with God. If it can happen for King Manasseh, then surely it can happen for those who, though sinful, are not *as* sinful as was this king of Judah. Moreover, the reverse must also be true: if the grace of God can atone for the sinfulness of someone who commits "ordinary sins," then it must also cover the "extraordinary" sins of someone like Manasseh. If either is not covered, then it is the same as if neither are covered. And if neither are covered, then the promise of the grace of God is a lie. Since we know that the grace of God is true, then we can be confident that all sins will be forgiven if we but confess them to God (see 1 John 1:9).

O. The Reign of Amon (33:21-25)

IN THE TEXT

■ **21-25** In the Chroniclers' history, **Amon**—like Ahaziah, Athaliah, and Joash—has his reign end in assassination. This is perhaps a fitting end for him, since he was a wicked king like his father, Manasseh. However, as noted with Manasseh, there is always a chance for someone who is wicked to repent (see 2 Chr 7 for Yahweh's promise to heal the land after Israel's collective repentance). In further contrast to Manasseh, Amon **did not humble himself before the** LORD (v 23). In other words, Manasseh increased his humility before Yahweh, whereas **Amon increased his guilt**. No more specific information is given as to the nature of Amon's sinfulness other than that he **worshiped and offered sacrifices to all the idols Manasseh had made** (v 22). This was enough, however, for Amon to be found under Yahweh's wrath. Though it is not explicitly stated in this way, Yahweh allowed the king to be killed, but then turned around and punished the attackers, much in the same way that, as the prophet Habakkuk complained, Yahweh punished a wicked Assyria with an even more wicked Babylon. Then, as Jeremiah preached, Yahweh would eventually punish the king of Babylon and restore Israel. Thus the conspirators who murdered King Amon were themselves punished through "street justice" administered by **the people of the land** (v 25; → Behind the Text for 2 Chr 36:9-10).

P. The Reign of Josiah (34:1—35:27)

▶ Overview

King Josiah is the last of the four kings who receive extended treatment from the Chroniclers. According to the Deuteronomists, moreover, he is the only king who does not come in for any critique. In other words, there is no statement for Josiah along the lines, "He did everything well in the sight of Yahweh, except . . ." This kind of exception even pertains to David in 1 Kgs 15:5—though the Chroniclers eliminate it in service of their own theological agenda. The reign of Josiah, in both historical epics, represents the final high point in a Judean national history that can only be characterized as having been on a downward spiral for many centuries. The roots of the Judean downfall are obscure, for both the Deuteronomists and the Chroniclers. As will be seen below, ultimately the Chroniclers are unable to provide a convincing explanation for the downfall of the nation, and so the only recourse they have is to somewhat nebulous religious concepts. Their solution to this ultimate question is an ingenious one, to be sure, and as outsiders later readers are not in a position to evaluate the comprehensiveness of the view they—as insiders—take regarding the fate of their nation. Before the Chroniclers get to their rapid-fire discussion of the last four kings, however, they tell the story of Josiah in four episodes. The first three episodes have to do with the action for which Josiah is most famous, the last of the four great religious reforms to have been discussed in the Chroniclers' History. The final episode tells of Josiah's heroic, if tragic, death on the battlefield, which might have served to dash the hopes of the people that had been generated by the height of religious fervor attending the reform movement.

1. Josiah's Reform (34:1-13)

BEHIND THE TEXT

The religious reform led by King Josiah is the fourth of the great reformations described by the Chroniclers. Although the results of this last reform are not long enduring—like the other three in this regard—it nevertheless seems to be the culmination of all other efforts at correcting the religious behavior of Judah. In the version of the Deuteronomists, Josiah is the only king who is never called in for any sort of critique. It has been noted that the Chroniclers are not as concerned to present Josiah as the perfect king.

With the exception of Jehoshaphat, each of the kings who reformed Judah's religion followed a king who was wicked. Josiah, in turn, was followed by a succession of wicked kings down to the end of the kingdom of Judah's independence. As will be seen, even before these wicked kings step up on the stage, the end of Josiah's life will come about in a most unexpected way.

IN THE TEXT

■ **1-7** The first thing the careful reader notices is that in the Chroniclers' version, the main part of the reform takes place before the discovery of the book of the law. Thus this entire episode is missing from the Deuteronomistic version of Josiah's story. It was important that the Deuteronomists arrange the material different from the Chroniclers, for they had a different story to tell. For them, the reign of Josiah really was the golden age, if not in terms of world prestige like the time of Solomon, then certainly of religious piety, for finally with Josiah the exclusivity of the Jerusalem temple was established, if only briefly. Moreover, the discovery of the book of the law in the temple was that which, according to the Deuteronomists, set everything in motion. A fairly firm scholarly consensus maintains that the law book found (or possibly created) during the reign of Josiah was, for the most part, coextensive with the Deuteronomic law code now found in Deut 12—26. An alternative view holds that this book was either the whole Pentateuch or parts of it. If this is the case, the material has been rearranged before the final form of Deuteronomy was produced. The Deuteronomistic History, furthermore, took its name from the fact that Deuteronomy formed the background of its general theological outlook. To restate, then, Josiah was the most important king for the Deuteronomists, because it was during his reign that the all-important Deuteronomic law code was promulgated, if not created. This means that Deuteronomy was of primary importance. If this is so, then Josiah could not have engaged in his reform work prior to the discovery (or creation) of the Deuteronomic law code.

By contrast, the Chroniclers had no particular need, as noted, to paint Josiah a brighter shade than the other kings, leaving all of the dark colors to one side. In addition, they were not particularly concerned about the importance of Deuteronomy and especially the Deuteronomic law code. This is why, as seen above in the Hezekiah material, they left out Isaiah's scolding of the king after the incident with the Babylonians, which the Deuteronomists were so keen to include. Also, this is surely why they included the present episode, with Josiah going through and destroying all of the pagan elements of Judah's popular religion. Not only this, but also in none of the other religious reforms detailed by the Chroniclers (Asa, Jehoshaphat, and Hezekiah) did the king in question wait around for a long period of time before beginning the work. Josiah began this in **the eighth year of his reign, while he was still young** (v 3). Hezekiah began the work immediately upon ascending the throne (see 29:3). Although the Chroniclers do not specify when Asa and Jehoshaphat began their reforms, it is reasonable to suppose that they began early in their reigns, for there is, as the saying goes, no time like the present when something as important as reforming the religion of ancient Israel needs to be done.

34:1-13

■ **8-13** If the reforms of Asa, Jehoshaphat, and Hezekiah did not "stick," then neither did the "first reform" of Josiah, accomplished in the eighth year of his reign. Thus, Josiah ordered a further cleansing of **the land and the temple** in **the eighteenth year of** his **reign** (v 8). This is one way to read the seemingly doubled stories of religious reformation. A simpler alternative, however, immediately presents itself, namely that the repair work on the temple was not for the purpose of purifying it of foreign elements, but instead for simple maintenance purposes. In support of this alternative, the Chroniclers give no indication that, in the intervening decade between the reform and the start of the temple renovation, any sort of falling back into discredited practices had taken place.

The Chroniclers give no direct information regarding the source of **the money that had been brought into the temple of God** (v 9). It was indeed collected by **the Levites . . . from the people of Manasseh, Ephraim and the entire remnant of Israel and from the people of Judah and Benjamin**. This statement recalls, in intertextual fashion, the collection that Hezekiah reinstituted as a function of his own reform in the previous century (→ 2 Chr 31). In the Deuteronomistic version of the story, the high priest **Hilkiah** is told that the persons doing the work are so trustworthy that no accounting of the funds need be given (see 2 Kgs 22:7). No such detail is given here by the Chroniclers, though in the modern situation the need for transparency in financial disclosure is an item for the trustworthiness of an organization much more than the trustworthiness of particular individuals. This **Hilkiah** may or may not be the father of Jeremiah the prophet (see Jer 1:1); in neither case is the patronym (the name of his father) known, which would settle the issue.

2. The Book of the Torah (34:14-33)

BEHIND THE TEXT

As has been noted, in the Deuteronomistic History, the finding of the book of the Torah during the reign of Josiah is a striking climax. Indeed, this event sets in motion Josiah's great reform, which is the best thing that ever happened since it finally resulted in, among other things, the centralization of worship in the Jerusalem temple. This centralization necessarily entailed a closing of the various alternative shrines, such as the temple of Yahweh at the city of Arad near the Negev desert in the extreme south of the land of Judah. This temple is the only temple dedicated to the true God ever found in the Holy Land. Solomon's temple remains shrouded in mystery and legend, for reasons already detailed above. Nevertheless, that Solomon's temple did in fact exist is beyond reasonable doubt. Furthermore, that the finding of the book of the Torah is the central event for the Deuteronomists—but not so for the Chroniclers—becomes clear even from a surface-level reading of the text. This is not to say that this event is unimportant for the Chroniclers. Rather, it is to once again recognize that the two versions of Israel and Judah's history are written at different times, by different people, for different reasons, with different emphases. Theologically, it is important for Wesleyans to maintain that both the Deuteronomists *and* the Chroniclers are inspired by God. Thus the very real differences between them are not of such a character that the reader must decide between one or the other, as if one must be "true" and the other, therefore, "false." To think so is to attach modern categories of truth and falsehood to ancient documents and ancient writers who did not think in such terms. The more excellent way, by contrast, is to recognize that God's inspiration of the biblical writers was for the purpose of communicating a particular message at a particular time. Later readers can discern new significance—indeed, create new meaning—out of these old texts, and they too can be inspired by God in the process and its results.

IN THE TEXT

■ **14-21** The story of the finding of the book of the Torah falls into three sections. The intent of the first eight verses is twofold: the scene is established in vv 14-15, then the book is read to the king, with an expected reaction, in vv 16-21. As was noted above, the repair work done to the temple comes after the greater share of the Josianic reform has already taken place. Thus, when **Hilkiah answered and said to Shaphan the scribe, "I have found a Torah scroll in the House of Yahweh"** (v 15), this great find comes in the middle of the story rather that at its beginning.

The Meaning of the Hebrew Word *Torah*

The Hebrew word *Torah* is traditionally translated "Law," particularly in the phrase, "Law, Prophets, and Writings," describing the three divisions of the Hebrew Bible. The order of the books in the Hebrew Bible is quite different from English Bibles, which generally follow the Latin Vulgate, which itself followed the Greek Septuagint. Comment has already been made on this matter, relating to where the books of Chronicles fit in the canon (→ Introduction). Recent translations, however, have rendered this word more appropriately with "Teaching," "Instruction," and other similar words. The Torah refers, in one sense, to the "five books of Moses," or the Pentateuch (Genesis—Deuteronomy). These books contain a large number of laws. The most commonly attested number is 613, but at any rate there are many laws, a certain amount of which are positive (i.e., "Remember the Sabbath day . . ." [Exod 19:8]) and a certain amount negative (**Do not take the name of the LORD in vain**). In another sense, however, "Torah" can refer to all of Scripture from Genesis at the beginning to Malachi (English order) or 2 Chronicles (*BHS* order) at the end. In yet a third sense, "Torah" can refer to all of Jewish legal tradition, both inside and outside the Bible, encompassing things like the Mishnah (around A.D. 300), the two versions of the Talmud (Jerusalemite, around A.D. 350; Babylonian, A.D. seventh century), or the voluminous output of medieval Jewish scholars like Radak (1160-1235) and Maimonides (1135-1204). Thus, though "Torah" does mean "Law," it is also much more than that. Recognizing that it has this deeper significance will go far toward finally putting to rest the misunderstanding that the OT is exclusively a book of law. This is usually said in order to disparage it in comparison to the NT, thought to be exclusively a book of grace.

King Josiah's reaction to the reading of the Torah scroll is a typical sign of distress or mourning: **he tore his robes** (v 19). In spite of the clear cultural value of this gesture, only one other person is described as doing so in the entire Chroniclers' History: the usurping queen Athaliah (23:13). Later on in this chapter, Josiah will receive commendation from Yahweh for having torn his robes in response to the contents of the Torah scroll, but as was seen Athaliah's gesture was not greeted with such approval, since she had already committed an offense against the great Davidic monarchy. As for the content of the scroll, scholarship has generally assumed that it contained at least a substantial portion of the law code now found in Deut 12—26, the so-called Deuteronomic law code. An ongoing debate has to do with whether the book had been created at some time in the past and hidden in the temple, only to be found by Hilkiah, or if the book was created at the time of the "finding." The choice one takes in this matter seems unimportant. What is more important is that both the Deuteronomists and the Chroniclers look with favor upon the response of the king to the content of the scroll. Thus, it would seem, the response of the modern and postmodern reader to the content of the scroll should be similar. Of course, one simply does not know *precisely* what was in the scroll, but just as one must have an expanded notion of precisely what the Torah is (see the sidebar "The Meaning of the Hebrew Word *Torah*" above), so one must have an expanded notion of what "scroll" or "book" demands a response of humility before God. Josiah, surely, provides an effective role model, and even though seeking role models in the characters of the OT is a risky proposition (so Bright 1967/1975, 105), certain responses to the words of God are always proper. Josiah, after tearing his robes in the traditional way, sends **Hilkiah, Ahikam son of Shaphan, Abdon son of Micah, Shaphan the secretary and Asaiah the king's attendant** (2 Chr 34:20) to seek the meaning of the scroll through prophetic counsel. The word they receive back is the principal subject of the next section.

■ **22-28** The five officials sent by King Josiah take their request **to the prophet Huldah, who was the wife of Shallum son of Tokhath, the son of Hasrah, keeper of the wardrobe** (v 22). Three interesting things are worth comment. First, the 2011 NIV's **prophet** is far superior to "prophetess," as Huldah's title is often translated. True enough, the Hebrew word is of a feminine form (because, in this case, it describes a female), but English "prophetess" implies a diminutive ("little prophet"). Male and female prophets are prophets; male and female lawyers are lawyers; and male and female pastors are pastors. Second, a female prophet was consulted (only a few are mentioned in the OT at all; two others are Miriam and Deborah). Two male prophets active at this same time period, both of whom have books named after them, were passed over in favor of Huldah. These prophets were Jeremiah and Zephaniah. Jeremiah may have been the son of the high priest who led the delegation to Huldah (see Jer 1:1). The third point is related to the second and has to do with the note that Huldah lived in the **Second District** or **Area Two** (either of which is a more accurate translation of *mišneh* than the NIV's **New Quarter**). Zephaniah, the second "writing" prophet contemporary with Huldah, has a prophecy of doom that specifically mentions this "Second District" or "Area Two." Zephaniah 1:10 reads as follows: ***It will be on that day, says Yahweh, that a sound of outcry will come from the Fish Gate, and a howling from the Second District/Area Two***. Robert Bennett, commenting on Zeph 1:10, mentions in passing that Huldah lived in the Second Quarter but does not make anything of it (1996, 679). As the Fish Gate and the Second District were both located in the northern part of the city, Zephaniah's prophecy may just be a reference to the enemy Babylonians coming from the north (like the enemy from the north in Jer 1:14; 4:5-6; 6:22, and various other references). On the other hand, it is at least plausible that Zephaniah could be aiming a subtle critique at Huldah, his contemporary. If this is the case, two motivations present themselves: either Zephaniah was angry that Huldah was consulted and not himself—in addition to or instead of Huldah—or the ambiguous results of Huldah's prophecy threw her into a bit of disrepute.

Huldah's prophecy has two parts. First, in 2 Chr 34:24-25, she gives something of a standard line of judgment: **I am going to bring disaster on this place and its people—all the curses written in the book that has been read in the presence of the king of Judah** (v 24). Some of these curses undoubtedly made it into the final form of Deut 28. The second part of Huldah's prophecy specifically relates to the fate of the king. Although, Yahweh says through his prophet, Jerusalem will be destroyed through its wickedness, Josiah himself will be spared **because your heart was responsive and you humbled yourself before God when you heard what he spoke against this place and its people** (2 Chr 34:27). The prophet goes on to tell the king that Yahweh **will gather you to your ancestors, and you will be buried in peace** (v 28). Huldah's prophecy will become sadly ironic later on in 35:20-27. This is so because Josiah, in fact, does not die in peace, but instead violently, killed like Ahab by a million-to-one shot from an enemy bow. Perhaps, if the theory suggested above concerning Zephaniah is correct, this is why Huldah is attacked vicariously through the mention of her home area as a source of wailing—remembering that the suggestion, though not wholly without merit, cannot be conclusively demonstrated.

■ **29-33** After receiving this double-edged prophecy from Huldah, Josiah **called together all the elders of Judah and Jerusalem** (34:29). One wonders if Jeremiah and Zephaniah, two prophets whose advice was not sought when the

Torah scroll was found, were included among those so summoned. Josiah **read in their hearing all the words of the Book of the Covenant** (v 30). There is no reason to suggest that this document was different from the one found in the temple. After the reading, **he had everyone in Jerusalem and Benjamin pledge themselves to it** (v 32). This was done even though, according to the prophecy of Huldah, things were so far gone that the destruction of Jerusalem could no longer be avoided. A similar tension is evident in the book of Jeremiah, with the tide eventually turning toward the inevitability of punishment (see Modine 2009a, 120-34). The last verse of the chapter sounds an ominous note, even on the heels of such a grand display of piety: **As long as he lived, they did not fail to follow the** Lord, **the God of their ancestors** (v 33). Other statements like this have been noted, such as Joash's piety during "all the years of Jehoiada the high priest," which tragically disappeared after the death of the latter, his sponsor and spiritual father (2 Chr 24:2).

3. Passover Celebration (35:1-19)

BEHIND THE TEXT

Among the four great religious reforms that the Chroniclers discuss (conducted by Kings Asa, Jehoshaphat, Hezekiah, and Josiah), the latter two are distinguished in that the story as told includes a Passover celebration. This is perhaps equivalent to the way in which these two reform movements are presented by the Deuteronomists. Neither Hezekiah nor Josiah is accused by 2 Kings of a specific sin, although the Deuteronomists hint that Hezekiah failed when he paid tribute in the form of temple implements to the Babylonians. They make no similar claim, implicit or explicit, regarding Josiah, thus contributing to the thesis that, for their understanding, the reign of Josiah and the things that took place during it—specifically the finding of the Torah scroll and the final centralization of Yahweh worship in the Jerusalem temple—as the high point of Judean history. The Chroniclers, not needing to support such a claim, thus reported the events of Hezekiah's and Josiah's reigns in a more "straightforward" manner. The difference has to do with the intent of each document. Neither is to be understood as manipulating the truth; all they did was tell a story in a particular way for particular purposes, which come to light through careful reading of the texts. Neither, moreover, tried to obscure or hide their real intent. Given that this is the case, later readers should have no reason to suggest or believe that the biblical writers cannot be trusted. In a theological view, as has already been affirmed, both are inspired by God to serve their own constituencies and historical situations, and readers can learn much about those constituencies and situations by reading the document that was intended to address them.

IN THE TEXT

■ **1-7** As with the Passover celebrated by King Hezekiah in the previous century, **the Passover lamb was slaughtered on the fourteenth day of the first month** (v 1). Though the Jewish calendar altered somewhat—particularly in terms of when the year began, whether spring or fall—the Passover was instituted in Exod 12 as the beginning of the year. Josiah institutes something of an innovation when he tells the Levites, **Put the sacred ark in the temple that Solomon son of David king of Israel built. It is not to be carried about on your shoulders** (2 Chr 35:3). This naturally makes one wonder where the ark had been, and why it, therefore, needed to be put back into the temple. One possibility is that it was removed for the reconstruction efforts described in the previous chapter. Alas, however, the Chroniclers did not see the information as necessary.

In any event, having freed the Levites of the ark-bearing duties, Josiah orders the Levites to **prepare yourselves by families in your divisions, according to the instructions written by David king of Israel and by his son Solomon. Stand in the holy place with a group of Levites for each subdivision of the families of your fellow Israelites** (vv 4-5). These verses will seem a little ironic at the end of the chapter. Verse 6, moreover, has the Levites **prepare the lambs for your fellow Israelites, doing what the L**ORD **commanded through Moses.** Earlier (30:17), the priests and Levites were sacrificing the Passover lambs for those who, for unstated reasons, were unable to do so for themselves. No such detail is given here, though one suspects that the size and importance of this particular Passover celebration would require the religious functionaries to complete the required actions as representatives of the people. This may be due to the fact that Amon, Josiah's father, was so wicked, or perhaps it is to be connected to the refurbishing of the temple and the final centralization of worship in it. The Chroniclers again leave the reader wanting more details, which they did not consider important enough to mention. In favor of the suggestion that the size of this particular Passover celebration was the most significant factor is the note that **Josiah provided for all the lay people who were there a total of thirty thousand lambs and goats for the Passover offerings, and also three thousand cattle—all from the king's own possessions** (v 7). This slaughter of thirty-three thousand livestock surely took a great deal of time, particularly since it all had to be done at a centralized location. The Chroniclers are not interested in such logistical details, but nevertheless it is an important question to ask. The more important point, however, is that **all of the animals slaughtered came from the king's own possessions**. This note

35:1-15

serves two purposes. First, it ascribes great generosity to King Josiah. By this action, the king made unnecessary the provision afforded the poor in Exod 12:4 (*If the household is too poor to afford a lamb, it shall join with the nearest neighbor, considering the number of persons; you shall pay for the lamb according to what each household will eat*). Second, however, it indicates that the royal household had access to tremendous wealth, which others, naturally, did not. Thus there is a light side and a dark side to this note. The light side is that the poor were provided for; the dark side is that there were poor people who needed to be provided for.

■ **8-15** Following the king's example, **officials also contributed voluntarily to the people and the priests and Levites** (v 8). However voluntary this giving might have been, it was certainly motivated in part by a desire not to be seen as stingy when the king had been so generous. Through the officials, **five thousand Passover offerings and five hundred head of cattle** were given **for the Levites** (v 9). This brings the total number of animals sacrificed at this gathering to a staggering 38,500! Whether these numbers can be taken at face value is a matter of considerable debate. However, it is sufficient to note that this Passover celebration was an undoubtedly significant event. Verses 10-14 describe, in summary fashion, the operation of the sacrificial ritual, which the Chroniclers are careful to note was accomplished **as it is written in the Book of Moses** (v 12). Verse 14 makes clear what was supposed above, namely that the sacrifice of nearly forty thousand livestock took a great deal of time: **After this, they made preparations for themselves and for the priests, because the priests, the descendants of Aaron, were sacrificing the burnt offerings and the fat portions until nightfall.** The logistical elements of this operation continue to stagger the imagination, and thus form part of an answer to the question raised above. One may safely conclude that the sheer size of the event was the deciding factor in the requirement that only priests and Levites participated, and not ordinary laypersons as suggested in Exod 12:6. That text stipulated that "all the assembled congregation of the Israelites shall slaughter it [the Passover sacrifice] at twilight" (NJPS). The final note of the operation of the Passover is that various other persons—**musicians** and **gatekeepers**, specifically—**did not need to leave their posts, because their fellow Levites made the preparations for them** (2 Chr 35:15). It is a risky proposition, as noted above, to seek models for contemporary practice in an ancient text, but this note about division of labor among the religious establishment is nonetheless interesting.

■ **16-19** The final four verses present a summary of the event, emphasizing that everything that took place was **as King Josiah had ordered** (v 16). The Chroniclers claim that **the Passover had not been observed like this in Israel since the days of the prophet Samuel** (v 18). This is perhaps a way in which the Chroniclers reflect the treatment of Josiah's reign by the Deuteronomists. This is so because, although the Chroniclers detail a similarly large Passover celebration by Hezekiah that the Deuteronomists omit, v 18 logically includes the Hezekian Passover as well. Moreover, the statement here is even stronger than the earlier one, reaching back to the days of Samuel, the last judge, whereas the Hezekian Passover was the best since Solomon (30:26). This assessment of the Chroniclers is similar to the Deuteronomists' evaluation of King Josiah: "Neither before nor after Josiah was there a king like him who turned to the LORD as he did—with all his heart and with all his soul and with all his strength, in accordance with all the Law of Moses" (2 Kgs 23:25). The Chroniclers are not far from the Deuteronomists in presenting Josiah as the greatest king there ever was, perhaps even greater than David and Solomon, in his commitment to the law of Moses.

4. The Death of Josiah (35:20-27)

IN THE TEXT

■ **20-27** The lengthy story of Josiah's life here comes to an abrupt end. Indeed, Josiah's death is a tragedy, particularly because it comes as a shocking end to an otherwise blessed life. One could in fact say that Josiah is the greatest of Judah's kings, because there is no sin attributed to him in either the Deuteronomistic or the Chroniclers' Histories. That he nevertheless dies violently is troublesome for the dominant theology, to say the least.

35:16-27

The Chroniclers tell the story of Josiah's death in a way that decidedly departs from how the Deuteronomists do so. Therefore, in case the reader is not quite convinced that the Chroniclers are creative writers in their own right, one may look here and perhaps be finally convinced. The first point to consider is how the Chroniclers deliberately structure the story of Josiah's death to sound like that of Ahab in 2 Chr 18 (vv 33-34). Christine Mitchell devoted a 2006 article to comparing Josiah's death not only to Ahab's but also to Saul's in 1 Chr 10, Ahaziah's in 2 Chr 22, and Amaziah's in 2 Chr 25. As noted above, the prophecy of Huldah (34:23-28) sounds tragically ironic. The prophet had said the king would die peacefully, and perhaps he would have done so had he not been **opposing God** (v 21). This phrase, in the mouth of Pharaoh Necho, is a warning to Josiah to keep away from the armies of Egypt. This prophetic-like judgment upon Josiah is interesting in that it comes from a non-Israelite ruler. Necho wants to know: **What quarrel is there, king of Judah, between you and me?** Though Josiah naturally has an interest in protecting his own territory, staying out of the Egyptians' way would have been the wiser course of action.

In a way, then, one might say that the life story of Josiah, with its abrupt and tragic end, is like the stories of the succession of kings following the reestablishment of the Davidic dynasty after the Athaliah incident. Joash started out as a baby skillfully rescued by Jehosheba and then turned away from Yahweh after his mentor Jehoiada—high priest and husband of his initial savior—died. Amaziah followed Yahweh, but not wholeheartedly. Uzziah had success and blessing from Yahweh while he was becoming strong, but after he became strong he left Yahweh behind, to disastrous ends. So Josiah, another boy king—only one year older than Joash at accession, as noted already—started out with such great promise, reforming the worship of Israel in a way not seen, only to make a poor decision, against the will of God, that cost him his life.

A final point to note in this text concerns the phrase **Jeremiah composed laments for Josiah, and to this day all the male and female singers commemorate Josiah in the laments** (v 25). One such lament may be recorded in Jer 22:10: *Do not weep for him who has died, and do not lament for him. Instead, weep for the one who has been driven way, for he will never return again and see the land of his birth*. The second part of this line probably refers to Jehoahaz, the king who reigns briefly after Josiah before being replaced by the Egyptians (so Modine 2009a, 188). It is this fact, then, that carries the ultimate irony of Josiah's death: Even though Pharaoh Necho recognized that there was no quarrel between Egypt and Judah at the present time, nevertheless after killing Judah's king the Egyptian monarch still took it upon himself to set upon Judah's throne a king according to his own liking.

FROM THE TEXT

Josiah died as a result of a tragic miscalculation. Leaders are especially susceptible, especially when they have achieved a certain amount of success, to thinking they can do no wrong. Nevertheless, even if Josiah had survived the battle of Megiddo, history might still have judged his actions to be in the wrong. This is so because, in the light of history, decisions made by leaders are judged by their implications. In other words, though leaders cannot know at the time of the decision what will happen, if their decisions lead themselves or their nation into disaster, then they are judged negatively, as though they should have known what was the best course of action yet failed to take it. Josiah, in his case, had been warned not to engage Pharaoh Necho, and so he probably should be judged as an accomplice in his own death.

Q. The Reign of Jehoahaz (36:1-4)

IN THE TEXT

■ **1-4** The very short reign of Jehoahaz, just three months, illustrates a principle that has never really gone out of fashion. Both in ancient and modern society, when the army of one nation conquered the army of another nation, the victorious nation was often entitled, among other things, to choose a new ruler for the defeated nation. Thus when the United States military defeated the military of Saddam Hussein's Iraq, the United States exercised a large share of control over the establishment of a new Iraqi government, at least for a period of time. So it was also when the Egyptian armies of Pharaoh Necho defeated Judah at the battle of Megiddo in 609 B.C.

The **people of the land** (on which phrase, → 36:9-10 regarding Jehoiachin) attempted to assert their rights and choose their own ruler. So they **took Jehoahaz son of Josiah and made him king in Jerusalem in place of his father** (v 1). However, the king of Egypt had somewhat greater rights in this particular situation, and soon deposed this second-to-last popularly elected king **and carried him off to Egypt** (v 4). **Eliakim**, whose name is changed to **Jehoiakim**, is **a brother of Jehoahaz**. Though this was an imposition, to be sure, at the very least the Egyptians did not end the Davidic dynasty with the appointment of Jehoiakim. The Davidic dynasty would in fact end with the coming of the Babylonians, but perhaps at this point there was still some hope left that Yahweh would not fully abandon the people to their sins. That hope was soon to be dashed, however, as Jehoiakim was to prove "evil in the eyes of" Yahweh (36:5). As for Jehoahaz, the Deuteronomists report that he, too, "did evil in the eyes of the LORD, just as his predecessors had done" (2 Kgs 23:32). The Chroniclers omit this detail, perhaps owing to their general tendency to abbreviate matters relating to the kings who are judged unworthy or evil. This tendency was first discussed in relation to Saul all the way back in 1 Chr 10. Further evidence of this may be seen in a close reading of the Jehoahaz material in 2 Kgs 23, which, although it is only five verses (vv 31-35), contains significantly more material about the reign of the (assumedly) elder son of Josiah than does 2 Chr 36. In reality, the Chroniclers only deal with Jehoahaz directly in vv 1-2 of the present text.

R. The Reign of Jehoiakim (36:5-8)

IN THE TEXT

■ **5-8** Perhaps a little surprisingly, the eleven years of King Jehoiakim's reign receive as many verses' worth of attention from the Chroniclers as the three months allotted to Jehoahaz. By contrast, Zedekiah, who also reigns for eleven years, receives eleven verses (an average of one per year). However, this statement is in need of immediate qualification, for as was seen above, Jehoahaz disappeared from the scene almost as quickly as he appeared. His selection as king got one verse, and his deposition from the throne got one verse. As for **Jehoiakim**, once again he merits far much more attention from the Deuteronomists than the Chroniclers. In addition, he is a significant player in the book of Jeremiah. In Jeremiah, King Jehoiakim is most directly involved in the episode of the two scrolls containing Jeremiah's prophecies against Judah (see Jer 36). As the scroll is read in the king's presence, he takes a scribe's knife and cuts off columns as the reader finishes them, throwing them into the fire. This action, naturally, calls him in for even greater punishment than that to which he was already entitled, according to the word of Yahweh spoken through Jeremiah.

It is perhaps unexpected that the Chroniclers would make no mention of this episode, since they are so often interested in the prophecies of Jeremiah (see 2 Chr 35:25; 36:12, 21, 22). In fact, though Jeremiah had significant dealings with all five of the last kings of Judah—Jehoahaz somewhat less so, due to the brevity of his reign—the Chroniclers only mention that Zedekiah failed to "humble himself before Jeremiah the prophet, who spoke the word of the LORD" (→ 36:12). Though the judgment perhaps sounds repetitive, this is more than likely due to the accelerating pace of the narrative more generally. The sense of impending doom hangs heavy over the narrative of the final chapter of the Chroniclers' History, just as it did over 2 Kgs 25. Both of them, however, contain a note of hope—unfulfilled, to be sure—of a future beyond the ominous events described in the last chapter, having in the main to do with the ultimate fall of Jerusalem. As will be seen, the details of the hope—that is, the event that takes place as the emblem of hope not-quite-lost, is different in 2 Kgs 25 than in 2 Chr 36. Nevertheless, it is a note of hope, even in the midst of great national tragedy and disaster for Yahweh's chosen city, Jerusalem.

S. The Reign of Jehoiachin (36:9-10)

BEHIND THE TEXT

Throughout the history of Israel and Judah, the people seem to have a large role to play in the selection of the monarch. The changing perceptions of the role of the people in affairs of state can be seen through the different understandings and uses of the term "people of the land." In both of the historical epics dealing with the preexilic period, "the people of the land" are viewed rather positively. The situation is markedly different in Ezra-Nehemiah, however. There, the "people of the land" are the ignorant, unwashed masses who are excluded from participation in the events accompanying the rebuilding of

Jerusalem's walls and the temple and the rededication of the latter. Incidentally, as has been noted in the introduction, this is one of the key differences between Chronicles and Ezra-Nehemiah, which renders doubtful the supposition of common authorship.

The importance of this for the reign of Jehoiachin is that he seems to be the last "popularly elected king." In other words, he is the last king whose reign over Judah is confirmed by the people of the land. However, he does not remain long on the throne, since he is soon replaced by the Babylonians. The prophet Jeremiah makes a sardonically mournful statement, perhaps with Jehoiachin in mind: *Do not weep for the one who has died . . . Weep rather, for the one who is going away, because he shall never come back to see the land of his birth* (Jer 22:10). It is not, of course, certain that this text refers to Josiah as the recently dead greatest king of recent memory, nor to Jehoiachin as the one who has gone into exile never to return. Nevertheless, Josiah and Jehoiachin certainly fit the parameters of the statement.

IN THE TEXT

■**9-10** Like many of his fellow kings in the last few years of Judean independence, **Jehoiachin** (v 9) enters and exits the stage in the matter of just a few breaths. He gets a few more verses in the Deuteronomistic History, appearing in 2 Kgs 24:8 and being carried into exile in v 15 of the same chapter. Jehoiachin's exile, and in particular a dispute over how long it should last, forms the center of the famous debate between the prophets Hananiah and Jeremiah (Jer 28). In the much briefer version of the Chroniclers, they say only that *Jehoiachin did what was evil in the sight of Yahweh*, without comparing him to his father, Jehoiakim. A further difference between the Deuteronomists and the Chroniclers comes in the relationship between Jehoiachin and Zedekiah. Second Kings 24:17 (and the NIV here) calls Zedekiah **Jehoiachin's uncle**, whereas the Hebrew texts say the two kings are brothers. It is likely that this discrepancy is due to the accidents of history, the fading of memory, and the lack of complete records. It is surely not grounds for doubting the authenticity of either 2 Chr 36 or 2 Kgs 24; taking refuge in such action is the recourse of the impatient mind. At the end of the day, the standard of the ancients regarding historical details of this type is surely different from the standards of modern historiography. Furthermore, it is likely that non-Western societies would be much less uncomfortable with this discrepancy.

36:11-21

T. The Reign of Zedekiah (36:11-21)

BEHIND THE TEXT

The reign of Zedekiah, even though he is judged to be wicked (see 2 Kgs 24:19), is given far more attention in the Deuteronomistic History than it is here. Moreover, King Zedekiah figures prominently in the book of Jeremiah as well, holding some clandestine meetings with the prophet while the latter was confined to prison in Jerusalem (see Jer 37:1—38:28a; three episodes with interludes are discussed in Varughese and Modine 2010, 213-24). Throughout all of that material, and especially in Jeremiah, King Zedekiah is presented as an indecisive and ineffectual ruler, often giving far too much license (see Jer 38:5).

The question of whether Zedekiah would be deposed, replaced by Jehoiachin—himself deposed by the Babylonians in favor of Zedekiah—formed the nucleus of the debate between Jeremiah and Hananiah, the famous "dueling banjos" scene of Jer 28. This episode, and in particular the viewpoint assuredly lying behind Hananiah's position, leads Daniel Smith-Christopher to an interesting, if somewhat curious conclusion regarding the relationship of Zedekiah to his predecessor. He writes: "Jehoiachin himself, recognized by the Deuteronomistic Historian *and by Zedekiah* as the true ruler, was deported to Babylon" (2002, 58 [emphasis added]). Though on the face of it, it is more likely that Zedekiah did not think of himself as illegitimately on the throne, this statement does raise some intriguing possibilities. Given that Jehoiachin was a "popularly elected king," it is at least possible that the Babylonian puppet Zedekiah was patriotic enough to want to resist the rule of the Babylonians, even though it would have cost him the throne.

IN THE TEXT

■ **11-14** The story of Zedekiah needs to be told in two stages. The first stage runs from his being placed on the throne by the Babylonians until his ill-advised revolt against his imperial benefactors. Verse 12 gives the by-now-familiar judgment that Zedekiah **did evil in the eyes of the Lord his God**. This is similar to the judgment the Deuteronomists pass on him in 2 Kgs 24:19-20, laying the ultimate blame for what happened to Jerusalem on him. Of course, from a theological standpoint one should say that it was the cumulative effect of Judah's sinfulness that ultimately led Yahweh to turn away from Judah and Jerusalem. Such a statement is well within the parameters of ANE thought (→ sidebar at 1 Chr 8:8-12, "The Moabite Stone"). However, Zedekiah was the one under whose watch these disastrous events took place, and indeed it was his rash act that set the final scene in motion. For Zedekiah also rebelled against King Nebuchadnezzar, who had made him take an oath in God's name (2 Chr 36:13). The latter part of this phrase—not mentioned by either the Deuteronomists or the editors of Jeremiah, both of whom comment simply: "Now Zedekiah rebelled against the king of Babylon" (2 Kgs 24:20b; Jer 52:3b)—is interesting, and perhaps caution against assenting to Smith-Christopher's assertion (→ 2 Chr 36:11-21 Behind the Text) that Zedekiah did not consider himself the proper ruler. If he had sworn on oath to be loyal to the Babylonians, then to step down—even in favor of the one who he perhaps considered to be the true king—would be a violation of an oath against God. This is something that the sage known as the Preacher (Hebrew: *qoheleth*) warned so strongly against: "It is better not to make a vow than to make one and not fulfill it" (Eccl 5:5).

Both the Chroniclers and the Deuteronomists have the idea that Babylonian hegemony over Judah is Yahweh's will. This idea has clear implications: to rebel against Babylon is to rebel against Yahweh. This idea surely serves to argue against and trivialize the power-claims of the empire, but it also renders problematic, if not downright blasphemous, the theology of the land. In other words, certain persons certainly believed that because Yahweh had given the land to the people in accordance with the oath sworn so many centuries ago to Abraham, then nothing would allow it to be taken away, not even the armies of mighty Babylon. However, for people such as the Deuteronomists, the Chroniclers, and the prophets Isaiah, Jeremiah, and Ezekiel, everything that happened in world history and especially everything that happened to Judah was the will of Yahweh. Yahweh had turned against the chosen nation of Judah in anger, because **all the leaders of the priests and the people became more and more unfaithful, following all the detestable practices of the nations and defiling the temple of the** LORD (2 Chr 36:14). Far from keeping Jerusalem from harm because it was his holy city, Yahweh allowed Jerusalem to be destroyed because the holy city had already been profaned by the unholiness of the people living in it.

■ **15-21** In the end, of course, Zedekiah did rebel against the king of Babylon, with the results one would expect. The description of the fall of Jerusalem here is shorter and not quite as graphic as the version found in 2 Kgs 25 (with parallel in Jer 52); however, it is nonetheless shocking. The felt pain is unmistakable. Furthermore, the later time of writing for Chronicles is indicated by the note that the exile lasted **until the kingdom of Persia came to power** (2 Chr 36:20). Also striking is the note that **God gave them all into the hands of Nebuchadnezzar** (v 17). This makes clear that what happened to Jerusalem is Yahweh's doing—but it is certainly not "marvelous in our eyes" (contrast Ps 118:23)!

Three other notes deserve mention for their radical distinction from the Deuteronomistic and Jeremianic accounts. First, the Chroniclers do not include the note found in 2 Kgs 24:14 and Jer 52:16 that the poorest residents of the land were left behind to tend the fields for the benefit of the empire. Such a practice was common: exploitation of the land, people, and resources of the outlying colonies for the benefit of the central imperial administration. The Chroniclers' omission of this probably has to do with the theological point they are advancing, namely that the land had to be completely emptied of its inhabitants in order to satisfy Yahweh's anger.

The second point is related to the first. For the Chroniclers suggest that the **land enjoyed its sabbath rests; all the time of its desolation it rested** (2 Chr 36:21). This idea hearkens back to the laws regarding the Sabbath year found in Exod 23 and Lev 25. More specifically, through telling the story in this way the Chroniclers apparently intend to suggest the fall of Jerusalem and the emptying of the land happened in order to fulfill the "prophecy" of Lev 26:33-35, which also accuses the people of failing to keep the Sabbath rest for the land. Archaeological investigation has conclusively shown that the land was not emptied of its inhabitants. Rather, the number of exiles relative to the total population of Judah was quite small, something like 5 to 10 percent of the population, working off the numbers given in Jer 52:28-30. Nevertheless, in spite of the small numbers, the psychological toll was breathtakingly large, as it is with all such dislocations both ancient and modern.

This allusion to the book of Jeremiah brings the reader to the third interesting aspect of the Chroniclers' version of the fall of Jerusalem. For in 2 Chr 36:21 there is a direct allusion to the prophecy of Jeremiah that the land lay desolate **until the seventy years were completed in fulfillment of the word of the LORD spoken by Jeremiah**. This prophecy is found in two places in the book of Jeremiah: 25:11-12 and 29:10. A close reading of those two passages, however, reveals that the prophecy of seventy years—inexact in any case—referred to the nation serving the king of Babylon, not to the desolation of the land. Though the quote is not precise, the reader should recall what was said in the introduction, namely that interpreters of Scripture are not to be considered bound to the original intent of the authors, even so far as this can be determined with certainty. The prophecy of seventy years, in other words, is put to different use by the Chroniclers than by Jeremiah. At the end of the day, both writings are inspired by God. If the details differ in certain respects, that should not bother the reader in the least. It must not be forgotten that modern standards of logic and consistency are not shared by ancient writers, and least of all by God.

FROM THE TEXT

Drawing a lesson from the story of the fall of Jerusalem seems rather easy from the standpoint of Wesleyan theology. It seems this text could be marshaled as evidence against the Reformed idea of perseverance of the saints, popularly known as eternal security. Put in the simplest terms possible, believers are eternally secure so long as they continue to believe. In his 1767 sermon titled "The Repentance of Believers," John Wesley wrote the following:

> Continue to believe in him "that loved thee, and gave himself for thee," that "bore all thy sins in his body on the tree"; and he saveth thee from all condemnation, by his blood continually applied. *Thus it is that we continue in a justified state.* (Wesley 1767/1991, 414 [emphasis added])

With respect to this text, the holiness of Jerusalem was not of a character such that God would refuse to let anything happen to Jerusalem. Instead, Jerusalem's holiness had been profaned among the nations, and so God scattered the chosen people among the nations (see Ezek 36:22). If God would allow this to Jerusalem, then the idea that God will preserve the elect in salvation regardless of what they do may be found wanting. Such an idea seems to be the logical implication of a doctrine of assurance understood as eternal security (Dunning 1988, 446-47). Nevertheless, that God allows punishment for sin, including final separation (however that is to be understood), should not be cause for fear or alarm. Rather, it should be a cause for joyous hope. For God is always and ever willing to redeem even those who willingly turn away (cf. Heb 6:4-6). Though such redemption may seem impossible from a human standpoint, "with God all things are possible" (Matt 19:26).

U. The Ending That Does Not End (36:22-23)

BEHIND THE TEXT

A perennially fascinating issue in OT study is that major sections of the literature end outside the promised land. On the one hand, this may cause the uncareful reader to wonder why the promised land is in fact so important, since the people never seem to be there very long at all. On the other hand, however, that the people never seem to make it to the promised land, except relatively briefly in their long existence as a people, makes the longing all the more significant, and the hope in God all the more trenchant.

For some examples of this phenomenon, one may consider the following three examples. First, Genesis ends with the death, embalming, and burial of Joseph at the age of 110, having grown old and died in Egypt (Gen 50:26).

Second, Deuteronomy, and hence the Torah, ends with a note that never again did there arise a prophet with the great significance of Moses, who had seen God face-to-face (Deut 34:10-12). Finally, 2 Kings ends with the release of King Jehoiachin from prison, though he remains in exile (2 Kgs 25:27-30). A near-exact replication of this may be found in Jer 52:31-34—though it is uncertain which replicates which, if either. The apparently unsatisfying ending led the present writer to apply the same title to the commentary on Jer 52:31-34 as is given here, "The Ending That Does Not End" (Varughese and Modine 2010, 314).

IN THE TEXT

■ **22-23** Second Kings and 2 Chronicles end rather abruptly, in ways that are decidedly unsatisfying from a literary point of view. Like a blockbuster movie perennially leaving un-tied-off narrative threads, promising a sequel in the next year, both of Israel's great historical epics leave the reader wanting more. That Ezra 1:1-8 picks up where 2 Chr 36:23 leaves off naturally made many readers suspect that the two documents were related. Peter Craigie's work is a good example. He makes a striking claim when he writes:

> The narrative of Chronicles is consciously resumed in Ezra-Nehemiah; indeed the closing verses of Chronicles . . . are repeated in the opening verses of Ezra, suggesting either an artificial division between the books (the last chapter of Chronicles ends in the middle of a sentence!) or a conscious editorial attempt to link them together. (1986, 251)

Unfortunately, the lack of evidence in favor of this evocative statement causes it to lose its punch. However, as demonstrated in the introduction, the repetition of the Edict of Cyrus in the two places can bear other explanations. First, the edict is repeated again in Ezra 6:3-5, this time in Aramaic, which was the official language of the empire. This means that the repetition being discussed should not be made to bear more weight than it is able. Second and more importantly, independent authors of Ezra-Nehemiah could certainly have begun their work in the same way that Chronicles ended. In other words, it does not follow from the duplication that the same authors created it.

The two historical works (Chronicles and Ezra-Nehemiah) *are indeed* linked with one another, based on the irrefutable fact that the former continues the story of the latter. This does not mean, however, that the same hands created them. For a more contemporary example, one may consider the two volumes of *Called unto Holiness* (Smith 1962; Purkiser 1983). These together served as the official history of the Church of the Nazarene until their replacement by *Our Watchword and Song* (Cunningham 2009). The two volumes were written by different people, yet Purkiser told the same story as Smith, just in a different time frame. Surely some repetitions could be found, but this would not be evidence for common authorship of the two volumes of *Called unto Holiness*!

Cyrus king of Persia (2 Chr 36:23) is a key figure for OT history. The so-called Second Isaiah even goes so far as to call him Yahweh's messiah (Isa 45:1)! The Chroniclers suggest that Cyrus pronounced his famous edict **in order to fulfill the word of the LORD spoken by Jeremiah** (2 Chr 36:22). For whatever reason, the Chroniclers have ascribed to Jeremiah words that came from the mouth of—or flowed from the pen of—the anonymous prophet of the exile. This is likely not a deliberate deception, for the Chroniclers would have no need for such a thing. Neither is it a careless slip of the pen, for the Chroniclers have been nothing but careful in their reporting all the way through the lengthy narrative. The reason behind this finally eludes understanding or explanation. Most likely, it is unimportant for the proper interpretation of the Chroniclers' History. Radak seems to think so, for he simply ignores it and returns to a citation of Second Isaiah in his commentary on the passage (Kimchi 2008, 282). Jarick also, though he typically passes up no opportunity to disparage those whom he calls the Annalists, passes over this in silence (2007b, 195-96).

FROM THE TEXT

The hope at the end of the book is a delayed hope, a hope on the way to completion. In an introduction to Ezra-Nehemiah, the present author suggested the following:

> The completed hope—or, at least, hope on the way to completion—expressed in the Books of Ezra and Nehemiah . . . was that the sin that caused God to drive the previous generation out of the land could be purged from the community . . . This kind of hope neither ignores challenges nor withers before them. (Modine 2009b, 5)

Ezra-Nehemiah picks up where Chronicles leaves off, and thus represents, in part, a further step along the road toward the hope being completed. This is probably the case because of Chronicles' dangling ending. Moreover, just like Jeremiah, which ends with a similar cliffhanger, the Chroniclers were no doubt convinced that God would come through on his promises after all. Though the hope was still unfulfilled by the time the Chroniclers got to the end of their historical epic, they had no doubt that it would be fulfilled—someday, and probably someday soon.